A Develyshe Pastime

A Develyshe Pastime

Graham Hughes

SPORTS
BOOKS

Published in Great Britain by
SportsBooks Limited
PO Box 422
Cheltenham
GL50 2YN
United Kingdom

Tel: 01242 256755
Fax: 0560 3108126
email: info@sportsbooks.ltd.uk
www.sportsbooks.ltd.uk

© Graham Hughes 2009

Cover design by Alan Hunns

A catalogue record for this book is available from the British Library.

ISBN 978 1899807 79 6

Printed and bound in England by
Cromwell Press Group

For Gwenyth Mary Hughes
1941–1997

Contents

Acknowledgements

Thank you:

    To Mike Morrogh at Shrewsbury School.

    To Simon Berry at Harrow School, and Dominic Davis, captain of the Harrow football School XI at the time of my visit.

    To Fergal McGill of the Gaelic Athletic Association.

    To Heather Cooke at the Writers Bureau, for her valuable advice.

    To my relatives and friends who have shown so much interest in this book, and given me so much encouragement.

Introduction

The 'F' Word

'Each country seems to have a foot-ball spirit of its own, and that spirit can be satisfied only with a characteristic game.'
– Walter Camp, pioneer of American football, 1910

Towards the end of 2004, a linguistic storm was brewing down under. The Australian Soccer Association was rebranding itself as 'Football Federation Australia'. It was a 'symbolic move', said chairman Frank Lowy, in order 'to bring the "World Game" in Australia into line with the rest of the football world'. Followers of rugby league, rugby union and Australian Rules football were aghast at this brazen use of a word they considered their own.

Around the same time, in the United States, the Dallas Burn soccer team became FC Dallas, as part of a process of eradicating 'Americanisms' from Major League Soccer. Among the attendant publicity was a report explaining that the 'FC' stood for 'Football Club' – perhaps a bit perplexing to the average Texan, to whom the word 'football' means something quite different. There was more to come: in 2006, New Zealand Soccer announced that it would be rechristened as 'Football NZ'.

Few words in the English language have been the subject of so much confusion, misunderstanding and dispute over their meanings as 'football'. This has all been exacerbated by the increase in global communications, with the rise of the internet and satellite television.

So, what is football? Some people, mainly the British, claim the word means only one thing – association football, or soccer – to the whole English-speaking world except for Americans. This isn't true. It has different meanings in a number of countries. In some countries, it even has different meanings in different regions, or different sections of society. To North Americans, it means various forms of the gridiron game. In Australia, depending on which part of the country you're in, 'football' can mean rugby league, rugby union, or Australian Rules 'footy'. To many Irish people, it means Gaelic football. Even in some

1

corners of Britain, where rugby is king, it is sometimes referred to as 'football'.

Let's turn to a dictionary for some help. In the United States, the Merriam-Webster online dictionary gives us a generic definition of this tricky word:

> *any of several games played between two teams on a usually rectangular field having goalposts or goals at each end and whose object is to get the ball over a goal line, into a goal, or between goalposts by running, passing, or kicking.*

This is pretty comprehensive – and, probably with Australian Rules in mind, was recently amended to point out that the field is *usually* rectangular, and might have more than two goalposts at each end. The dictionary goes on to give alternative explanations, suited to different countries. If we agree with the broad scope of this definition, it shows us that football is not a specific sport with a single set of rules. Instead, it is a *family* of sports, and the 'F' word can mean any one of them, or all of them at once.

In everyday speech, 'football' generally means whichever form of football is the most familiar to the speaker. This habit leads many people to think that 'their' game is the only one that *anybody*, anywhere in the world, should refer to as 'football', and this is where the problems begin. The main exception is rugby (union and league), which is usually referred to as such – most likely because it has a short, snappy name of its own. As I mention in chapter 1, even the original meaning of the word 'football' isn't entirely clear.

Whichever way we look at it, football – as a whole – has made a huge impact on the modern world. Almost everywhere, *some* form of football is a major sport, inspiring fanatical devotion, extensive media coverage, patriotic fervour, and even violence. Millions of people get much of their regular entertainment from watching two teams chasing a ball around a field, and millions play these games themselves.

In most countries, of course, the most popular form of football is soccer. Some would claim that this proves its superiority; others might argue that popularity is no proof of quality. There is, of course, one especially prominent nation that has largely resisted the allure of soccer: the United States. All kinds of theories have been put forward to explain this, most of which are almost certainly wrong (more on this later). In any case, contrary to a widespread myth, the US is not the *only* country where soccer has failed to become the leading sport. The likes of basketball, ice hockey and cycling are hugely popular in many parts of Europe, as is baseball in parts of Central America, the Caribbean and the Far East.

Also, there are other nations, such as Canada, New Zealand and Pakistan (and, at least until very recently, Australia), where soccer has not made a great impact. It is interesting to note that these countries (along with the US) are former British colonies, which have inherited many aspects of British culture, and yet have not taken a great liking to Britain's biggest sporting export. However, other football codes with British roots have found success in most of these countries, as has cricket. Soccer was also a relatively minor sport in the Republic of Ireland, until the national team became a force in the late 1980s.

In all of these countries, soccer's relative failure, and the successes of other sports, can be explained mostly by historical events, rather than by making simplistic, stereotypical assumptions about the supposed 'character' of each nation (at the risk of contradicting the venerable Walter Camp, quoted at the start of this introduction). Likewise, the reasons why other forms of football have become popular in some regions, while remaining largely unknown in others, are more complex than many people seem to think.

National and class identities have, however, been factors in the various splits within the football world, and in the development of distinct forms of football with their own unique cultures. Rugby broke up into two independent sports, basically along class lines. Gaelic football is closely linked with Irish culture and nationalism. The birth of American football could be seen as part of a young nation's attempt to create its own traditions (as with its earlier rejection of cricket in favour of baseball). Canadian football, despite its strong similarities with the American game, is at least *presented* as something distinctly Canadian.

Sports history, in this writer's humble opinion, is a neglected subject, although there has seen something of a boom in recent years. Sports coverage in the media is almost entirely focussed on the here-and-now: the latest controversy, the rumour mill, the reasons why you must watch the big game this weekend. I am not suggesting we should live in the past, but surely there is a place for reflection on the stories, roots and traditions behind the sports we love. Sports history is not merely about statistics and record books. It is also about the tales of how and where these sports began, how they became popular, how the rules, tactics and playing styles evolved, and the people who helped to make all this happen.

Football's roots are in a range of local games – often loosely regulated and roughly contested – which were played in various parts of the world, hundreds or even thousands of years ago. The story of how it evolved from these beginnings into a range of modern, well-organised, mass-audience sports, is a story worth telling. It deserves to be told in a global context, without bias or prejudice. This is what I have attempted to do in these pages.

Readers will inevitably have their own preferences for one or two forms of football, and may have negative perceptions about one or two others. But I hope this book will at least go some way towards fostering an appreciation for the bigger picture. You might find yourself getting the urge to learn about, and watch, a type of football that has never interested you before. You might even enjoy it.

A few notes about the terminology used in this book. As referred to already, words such as 'football' and 'soccer' can create confusion and irritation in many people, depending on where those people are from, and how the words are used. I have tried to tackle this problem as effectively as possible without appearing pedantic, although it would be impossible to please everyone.

In some parts of the book, 'football' means one specific sport, but only where the context makes it clear which one is meant. For example, in the *Gridiron Glory* chapter, which is entirely about American football, it would have been cumbersome to use the 'American' prefix repeatedly, so 'football' is mostly used instead. Meanwhile, although the word 'soccer' makes many Brits come out in a rash, there are times when it *has* to be used (unless we are to persist with 'association football'); and, in any case, there is nothing actually wrong with it.

Imperial measures are used in some parts of the book, and metric units in others, depending on which are more appropriate in the context. So, for instance, an American or Canadian football team must gain 10 *yards* to keep possession, whereas an Australian Rules player may only carry the ball for up to 15 *metres* without bouncing it.

I've also tried to avoid using words and expressions which might not be understood by readers in all parts of the English-speaking, football-watching world. So, for example, 'field' is generally used instead of 'pitch', and 'stadium' in preference to 'ground', with a few exceptions where appropriate. British spellings are used throughout, even though they may occasionally look incongruous to some readers, such as 'offence' or 'defence' in an American football context. If anyone still manages to be confused or irritated, I apologise (rather than *apologize*), but, please believe me, I have tried.

Graham Hughes
Chester
September 2009

Chapter 1

Chasing the Sun

*'Come, do thou too, father and stranger, try thy
skill in the sports ... for there is no greater glory
for a man so long as he lives than that which he
achieves by his own hands and his feet.'*
– Laodamas to Odysseus, in Homer's *Odyssey*

A question has cropped up on a number of those all-purpose, free-for-all 'answers' websites: 'Who invented football?' It is a question that could be answered in a thousand different ways. Where should we begin?

This is a story that goes back a long way. The great civilisations of the ancient world, having just about mastered the art of survival, found a place in life for recreation and exercise, often in the form of organised sports and games. Some of them resembled today's football games, and similar modern sports such as handball and basketball. Some had religious or spiritual overtones, and were taken extremely seriously.

Much of the early history of football, and its forerunners, is pretty vague. We can't always trace a line of descent from one football-like game to another. Until the 19th century, few writers thought football deserved any more than a passing mention in their chronicles of contemporary life. Except, that is, when it came to condemning the game for the mayhem that came in its wake, or its perceived evils. As a result, this part of the story can only be pieced together from fragments of information, glued together by a lot of speculation, with qualifiers such as 'probably' and 'possibly' cropping up more often than they ideally would.

The earliest known football-related game was most likely *tsu chu* (meaning 'kick ball', and sometimes spelt as *cuju*), played in China at least from around 2000 BC, but perhaps as early as 5000 BC. Tsu chu began as a ceremonial activity to celebrate the emperor's birthday. During the Qin Dynasty of 255 BC to 206 BC, it was also adapted into a physical training exercise for soldiers.

Tsu chu was played with a ball made of animal fur or hair, stuffed inside stitched leather panels. The rules varied, but it appears that the players could not handle the ball, and had to keep it off the ground. Their target was a small net, just 30 to 40 centimetres in diameter, and raised nine metres from the ground on bamboo poles in the middle of the playing field. This was clearly a game that needed a great deal of skill, and the leading players were suitably revered.

Its heyday came during the Han dynasty, between 206 BC and 220 AD, when it was played extensively. Liu Bang, the first Han emperor, set up a playing area outside the Imperial Palace, and invited some of the best-known players to perform there for the benefit of his football-mad father as well as himself. A later emperor, Wu, also known as Han Wudi, who reigned from 141 BC to 87 BC, was another fan of the game, and was even known to play it. Tsu chu thrived until as late as the Qing Dynasty of 1644 to 1912. Soon after that, it was displaced by soccer, although the old game did undergo something of a revival in the 21st century.

Some time between 300 BC and 600 AD, tsu chu found its way across the East China Sea (possibly via Korea) to Japan, where it is thought to have inspired the similar game of *kemari*, which was played at the imperial court in Kyoto. Unlike tsu chu, kemari was not competitive. There was no target to aim for, no scoring system, and no reason for players to challenge each other for possession of the ball. Instead, each player would keep the ball in the air by kicking it repeatedly, and then pass it to another. It was, more or less, what we know today as 'keepy-uppy'.

Kemari was played by between two and twelve players, in a rectangular area known as a *kikitsubo*, marked out by four trees, typically a cherry tree, a maple, a willow and a pine. The ball was around 25 centimetres in diameter, with a deerskin cover stuffed with barley grains or sawdust. The player in possession, the *mariashi*, would shout 'aryiaa!' ('here we go!') each time he kicked the ball, and 'ari!' ('here!') when passing it.

The game peaked in popularity between the 10th and 16th centuries, when it was widely played by people of all classes across Japan. It inspired poetry, plays and story writing. Players wore elaborate costumes with huge, billowing sleeves, and high-peaked *eboshi* hats, reflecting the game's ceremonial nature. Legend has it that one emperor, with the help of his co-players, once kept the ball up for more than a thousand kicks, and commemorated the feat by retiring the ball and giving it a high court rank.

The explorer Marco Polo (1254–1324) is believed to have come across kemari on his travels and brought it back to Europe, although it is unlikely that this had any lasting influence. It went into decline in the Edo period of 1603 to 1867, but is still played as part of spring festivities at various shrines.

In 1519, a group of Spanish conquistadors in Mexico came across some Aztecs playing a ball game known as *tlachtli*. It is not clear whether the Spaniards took much interest in the game itself, but they were certainly fascinated by the ball, which was made of a durable and bounceable substance unfamiliar to European eyes: rubber.

Tlachtli was a descendant of *pok-a-tok*, a game played by the Maya people, perhaps as far back as 3000 BC. A playing court at Paso de la Amada, on the Pacific coast, dating from around 1600 BC, can still be seen today. Similar games were played as far south as Nicaragua, perhaps as far north as Arizona, and on some Caribbean islands. Tlachtli, pok-a-tok and other variants are known generically as the *Mesoamerican ball game*.

A typical Mesoamerican court was H-shaped, and sunken into the ground. There were stone walls at its sides, topped by rows of seats for spectators. At each end of the court was either a disc-shaped marker inset into a sloping wall, between three and nine metres above the playing surface, or, in later versions of the game, a stone ring with a hole less than 30 centimetres wide. Players could only touch the ball with their knees, elbows and hips, and had to prevent it touching the ground, which would lose points for their team.

A team could win the game, regardless of the score, by hitting a marker with the ball, or by passing it through a ring. The game could be seen as a forerunner of basketball and volleyball, as well as football. It was a dangerous pursuit, largely because of the hard, heavy ball, perhaps sometimes weighing nearly three kilograms, and there is evidence that players wore helmets and other protective gear.

The game had great significance in the Mesoamericans' religious and spiritual lives. The ball symbolised the sun, with its movement around the court representing the sun's movement across the Earth. A game of pok-a-tok is recounted in the *Popol Vuh*, the holy book of the Quiché Maya, as an analogy for a struggle between good and evil.

While some encounters were probably of a recreational nature, others were taken much more seriously. At the extreme end of the scale, the players might well have been slaves or prisoners of war, watched by members of the ruling elite. On these occasions, the ball's arrival at one of the markers or rings represented the arrival of dawn. The losers – or possibly the winners, depending on which account we believe – would then be sacrificed to the gods (let's hope the rules were a little clearer at the time). Sometimes the winners were allowed to confiscate spectators' belongings, while the losers had to fight to keep theirs.

The Mesoamerican ball game, denounced as a heathen activity by Spanish priests, faded into obscurity in most areas during the colonial era; but some versions still survive in western parts of Mexico, such as *ulama* in the coastal state of Sinaloa.

Ball games were also played in other parts of the Americas. If we are to believe Eduardo Galeano's *Football in Sun and Shadow* (an entertaining read, but with a certain whiff of fantasy about some of its anecdotes), Indians in the Bolivian Amazon region claim to have been playing a kicking game with a rubber ball and goalposts since time immemorial; and a Spanish Jesuit priest found something similar going on in Paraguay in the 18th century. At some undetermined time in the past, Inuits in modern-day Alaska and north-western Canada are thought to have played *aqsaqtuk*, a football-style game on ice, with a ball made from animal hide and whale bones, stuffed with moss, hair, wood shavings and feathers.

In ancient Egypt, as in Mexico, sport had great social and cultural importance. Engravings and drawings in pharaohs' temples depict a wide range of games and activities: running, swimming, rowing, boxing, wrestling, gymnastics, hunting, archery, javelin throwing; and games resembling football, handball, baseball and hockey. The Egyptians are thought to have pioneered concepts in sport with which we are familiar today: rules, refereeing, team uniforms, sportsmanship, and awarding prizes to winners.

At the tombs in Saqqara, dating back to around 3000 BC, there are drawings of various ball games, including a kicking game. The tombs at Beni Hassan, in Minia, feature a picture of girls kicking a ball to each other. Balls have been found in other tombs dating from about 2500 BC, made from linen, palm, papyrus fibre, straw or wound-up catgut, and encased in deerskin or leather for added bounce. Details are a little scarce, but it is believed that large groups of people played ball-kicking games during fertility rites, as a way of tilling the soil; sometimes with the two teams representing opposite entities such as winter and summer.

Egyptian ball games spread to Assyria, Babylonia, Mesopotamia, Phoenicia and Greece. A number of ball games were played in ancient Greece, although it might come as a surprise to learn that they never featured in the ancient Olympics. Their rules, and the distinctions between them, are not entirely clear today. While athletics and chariot racing were highly organised, and their results diligently recorded, nothing of the sort seems to have happened with ball games. The scant evidence suggests that they were informal, few people watched them, and few particularly cared about who won.

However, it is known that one ball game, *episkyros*, devised some time around 800 BC, had similarities with modern rugby and handball. The playing area had three parallel lines, each known as a *skyros*, drawn out using stone chips. Each team would start in its own half, and would throw the ball above opponents' heads, trying to force them over their back line. *Phaininda* had much in common with episkyros, but involved deceptive tricks, such as fake passes. Its name may have come from this feinting technique, or from one of the game's pioneers, whose name is given variously as Phainestios and Phainindos.

Harpaston, named after a verb meaning to 'seize' or 'snatch', was a later variation of phaininda, while *passé-boule* was closer to basketball. The balls used in earlier times were made from linen and hair, wrapped in string and sewn up. Later balls, such as the *follis*, generally larger, were made by inflating a pig's bladder, which was sometimes wrapped in deerskin or pigskin to prevent it bursting.

It is unlikely that any of these games involved kicking. A marble relief at the National Museum of Archaeology in Athens shows a man balancing a ball on his thigh, watched by a boy; but this probably had more to do with juggling than with anything we would regard as a sport. In *Sport in Greece and Rome*, H.A. Harris suggested that kicking would have been out of the question: the games were played barefoot, and the modern soccer technique of using the instep of the foot, rather than the toes, most likely had not been thought of. The playwright Antiphanes (388–311 BC) wrote of a game, probably phaininda:

> *He seized the ball and passed it to a teammate while dodging*
> *another and laughing. He pushed it out of the way of another.*
> *Another fellow player he raised to his feet. All the while the*
> *crowd resounded with shouts of 'Out of bounds', 'Too far', 'Right*
> *beside him', 'Over his head', 'On the ground', 'Up in the air',*
> *'Too short', 'Pass it back in the scrum'.*

After the Romans had conquered Greece in the second century BC, they discovered harpaston, and liked what they saw. They developed it into *harpastum* – a faster, more physical game than its precursor, and probably closer to rugby. Pushing was allowed, and players could tackle a ball-carrier by dragging him to the ground. The ball, about 20 centimetres in diameter, was harder than the type used in Greece, and made from stitched leather, stuffed with animal fur or chopped sponges. Teams usually had between five and 12 players, but some accounts suggest that they were sometimes much larger.

A team would either try to keep possession of the ball in its own half for as long as possible, or to carry it over the opposition's line. Another variation appears to have involved throwing the ball into a goal, handball-style. As the game became more sophisticated, teams began devising complex strategies, with players having specialised roles. Although harpastum was played mainly (perhaps solely) with the hands, we can be sure that some kind of ball-kicking was going on in Rome, judging by the writer Cicero's account of how a man was killed when a ball was kicked into a barber's shop, hitting the barber who was shaving him.

Just as Chinese emperors had done with tsu chu, Julius Caesar and his generals used harpastum as a basis for military training exercises. The Roman legions took the game to other parts of the empire, and it became popular with the natives in some places, perhaps most importantly in Britain and France. As late as the fifth century AD, Sidonius Apollinaris, the Bishop of Clermont in Gaul, wrote of a visit to a friend's house in Nîmes, where 'teams of ball-players facing one another were exchanging catches, with swift turns and agile ducking.'

So, should the British file football under 'what the Romans did for us'? Not necessarily – it has been suggested that pre-Roman Britons played ball games of some sort – although, even if this is true, harpastum was probably a more advanced game, and closer to today's football sports, than these indigenous games.

In 217 AD, the people of Derby are said to have divided themselves into two teams representing the two halves of the town, and played football in the streets to celebrate a victory over the local Roman troops, using the head of a defeated soldier as a ball (a practice that they apparently copied from the Romans themselves)[1].

It is unclear whether any kind of football survived the upheaval and population shifts that followed the Romans' departure from Britain in the fifth century AD. There's no reference to the game in Anglo-Saxon literature; the closest thing we have to written evidence of football in Britain in the Dark Ages comes from the ninth-century Welsh chronicler Nennius, who wrote vaguely of boys 'playing at ball' in present-day Monmouthshire.

One plausible explanation is that the Celts who migrated westwards from England to Wales in Anglo-Saxon times had adopted harpastum; that it then evolved in their hands (literally) into the Welsh game of *cnapan*, and that cnapan eventually influenced football in England. On the other hand, some have suggested that cnapan began in pre-Roman Celtic times.

Whether it evolved organically or from harpastum – or from another game imported from the continent – a custom of *folk football*, sometimes less flatteringly known as *mob football*, had taken root in the British Isles by the late 11th century (it might have begun to flourish as early as the 8th century). Folk football involved huge teams, perhaps as many as a thousand people on each side, playing across vast areas in towns, villages or the countryside. The rules, if they could be called that, were loosely defined.

Folk football games often formed part of the celebrations of religious festivals, typically Shrove Tuesday and Easter. Some early games might well have been pagan rituals celebrating the vernal equinox, with the ball representing the sun, and its movement around the field supposedly ensuring a successful harvest – a custom remarkably similar to those attributed to ancient ball games in Mexico and Egypt. Another theory is that the game was a contest to seize an object that represented (or possibly was) a prized possession – an animal's head, for example – and take it to a safe haven, often a church porch. On an even grislier note, there are further tales, from both Kingston upon Thames and Chester, of football being played with the severed head of a defeated Danish prince, some time around 1000 AD.

More than a thousand years after the Romans landed, the growth of football in Britain probably got its next boost from another foreign invasion: the Norman Conquest in 1066. By this time, the Roman game of harpastum had spread to northern parts of what is now France, particularly Brittany, Normandy and Picardy.

Here, the unruly game of *la soule* (known in some places as *la choule*, and sometimes played with sticks) could well have been inspired by harpastum. But it might also have been rooted in *seault*, a game played in the region by Celtic druids in pre-Roman times; or in *chugan*, played by the Arab people of the Iberian peninsula.

La soule is regarded as a Celtic tradition, associated with pagan sun-worshipping rituals and dances. Its name is thought to have been derived from the Gaulish word for 'sun'; then again, another theory is that it meant 'sandals', although it is not clear why. There was a Flemish and Dutch variation, known as *sollen*. The earliest accounts of la soule come from the 12th century; but some form of football was already popular in Normandy at the time of Duke William's conquest of England, where it might have rubbed off on the natives.

Eleventh-century folk football in the British Isles was mostly a rural affair. Teams from neighbouring villages would play against each other, chasing an inflated pig's bladder over streets, fields and even rivers. The 'rules' and customs varied wildly from one place to another. Local landmarks such as churches, bridges and wells were typically used as goals.

Football was being played all over the islands. It was especially popular in Scotland; and, as mentioned earlier, a boisterous form of football known as *cnapan* (or sometimes *criapan*) was often played in Wales, quite likely an influence on the Welsh love of rugby in modern times. Various types of football were played in Ireland – the beginning of a largely distinct football culture which will be looked at later. The game found its way into London in the 12th century, causing quite a stir. The chronicler William FitzStephen wrote excitedly of a game in 1175:

> *After dinner the youth of the city goes out into the fields for the*
> *very popular game of the ball … The elders, the fathers, and the*
> *men of wealth come on horseback to view the contests of their*
> *juniors … There seems to be aroused in these elders a stirring of*
> *natural heat by viewing so much activity and by participation in*
> *the joys of unrestrained youth.*

FitzStephen's account is thought to be the first clear written reference to football in Britain. At this time, though, the word 'football' had probably not yet been coined. Instead, the game was referred to as 'ball play', 'the game of ball', and so on. The first known appearance of the 'F' word came in 1314, when Nicholas Farndon, Mayor of London, made a 'Preservation of the Peace' proclamation, referring to 'certain tumults arising from great footballs in the fields … from which many evils may perchance arise.'

It has been claimed that the origin of the word 'football' had nothing to do with kicking: instead, it meant that the game was played on foot, rather than on horseback. Another theory, put forward by Wojciech Lipoński in his *World Sports Encyclopedia*, is that the name came about because the ball was 'foot-sized', in contrast with the smaller balls used in other sports. Also, as with the Roman and French games that preceded it, folk football was mainly played with the hands; and, in many cases, the ball was too hard and heavy to kick.

Oblivious to all this, some more blinkered and/or lazy sports historians tend to regard folk football as simply an early form of soccer, ignoring its resemblance to rugby. Some North American accounts of football history laughably refer to folk football, and even the Roman ball-handling game of harpastum, as 'soccer'.

In most accounts of medieval football, the focus is on the violence and mayhem associated with it. The game was notorious for causing damage, injuries, and even deaths. It was usually an anarchic affair, with no defined playing area, no restrictions on who could join in the fray, and few (if any) limits on what they could do to each other, or to anyone or anything that got in their way.

Games would usually start in the morning and carry on until sunset, if not later. The biggest problems came about when football was played in towns, with players rampaging through cramped streets, wreaking havoc and wrecking property. The recorded history of football in this period is little more than a litany of deaths and horrific injuries. An account from 1280 tells of how:

*Henry, son of William de Ellington, while playing at ball at
Ulkham on Trinity Sunday with David le Ken and many others,
ran against David and received a wound from David's knife from
which he died the following Friday.*

In 1321, a similar mishap brought about the demise of a man whose
name was only given as William; this time the knife was being carried by
a canon, William de Spalding, who was granted a dispensation by Pope
John XXII for his role in the man's death. Another gruesome tale, from
1320, was related in 1879 in the *Chester Courant*. John Boddeworth (or
Budworth, or perhaps Bodiworth), a servant of the Abbot of Vale Royal in
Cheshire, was murdered by locals who objected to the amounts of money
he had extracted from them on his master's behalf. They celebrated by
decapitating his corpse and using his head as a ball, 'which they kicked
about with great fury and agility'.

Observers often denounced all this apparent chaos and butchery,
and it soon drew the attention of the ruling classes. A long series of
attempts at banning football, locally and nationally, would follow in the
coming centuries. As well as the Mayor of London's banning order in
1314, others were issued by Edward III in 1331 and 1365, and by Richard
II in 1389. Both claimed that football was weakening the military, by
diverting men from their archery practice. It was a similar story in
France: Philip V banned the game in 1319, as did Charles V fifty years
later. In Brittany in 1440, the Bishop of Tréguier threatened soule players
with excommunication from the church.

It is clear that these bans were hardly successful; otherwise, there
would have been no need to keep on repeating them. This was a time
of social unrest and class conflict, with the working class rising up in
protest over all kinds of grievances. Without an adequate policing system,
the aristocrats and landowners had trouble keeping things under control.
Folk football – noisy, exuberant and riotous – was one kind of disturbance
that gave them an almighty headache. The failure of all those bans shows
us how popular the game was; it was an outlet for youthful energy, and
a part of local tradition and social life.

The royal banning orders in England kept coming thick and fast:
from Henry IV in 1410 (imposing a 20-shilling fine and six-day prison
sentence), Henry V in 1415, Edward IV in 1477, and Henry VII in 1496. In
Scotland, James I outlawed football in 1424, followed by James II in 1457,
and James IV issued a royal decree in 1491: 'It is statute and ordained
that in na place of the Realme there be used Fute-ball, Golfe, or other sik
unproffitable sportes.'

There were local bans as well: Halifax in 1450, Leicester in 1467,
Liverpool in 1555, London in 1572, and Manchester (where the local

authority even appointed 'football officers' to deal with the problem) in 1608, 1655, 1656 and 1657. The Mayor and Common Council of Chester abolished the city's annual Shrove Tuesday game in 1533, later replacing it with a foot race on what is now the Roodee racecourse. In 1660, magistrates in Bristol prohibited a range of Shrovetide pursuits including football, cock-throwing and, of course, dog-tossing. On the other hand, Henry VIII, at some time in his reign from 1509 to 1547, is believed to have owned a special pair of shoes which he used for playing football.

Some recent historians, such as Adrian Harvey in *Football: The First Hundred Years – The Untold Story*, and Hugh Hornby in *Uppies and Downies: The Extraordinary Football Games of Britain*, have challenged the conventional view that folk football was overly violent and anarchic. Hornby contends that the main motive behind the bans was the authorities' fear of disorder, rather than concerns about deaths (which were rare), injuries and damaged property.

As well as the wilder forms of the game, mostly played on festival dates, there were 'smaller', more orderly types of football, which were played more frequently. In Cornwall, *hurling* (not a close relation of the Irish stick-and-ball game) came in two varieties. *Hurling over country* was a typical folk football game, played over a distance of three or four miles; but *hurling to goales*, as described in 1602 by the chronicler Richard Carew, seems to have been strikingly modern.

In hurling to goales, the two goals consisted of pairs of bushes, eight to 10 feet apart, and were '10 or 12 score paces' from each other. The first team to carry the small, hard, silver-coated ball through their opponents' goal would win the game. Teams were relatively small, with up to around 30 players, each of whom was paired with an opponent. A player carrying the ball could be tackled, but only by his opposite number. *Hurling to goales* also featured scrum-like formations, an element of one-on-one wrestling, and such advanced concepts as goalkeepers and *off side*. Throwing the ball forward was not allowed, but rugby-style lateral passing was a part of the game.

At least as early as 1450, the East Anglian game of *camp-ball* (from the Middle English *campen*, meaning to fight or contend), which had much in common with hurling to goales, was sometimes played in fields (*camping closes*) that had been marked out specifically for it. Some of the closes were fenced off; and one at Boxford, Suffolk, even had a stand erected by around 1750.

Camp-ball came in various forms: non-violent *civil camp*; the self-explanatory *savage*, *rough*, *boxing* or *fighting camp*; *kicking* (as opposed to ball-carrying) *camp*; and an occasional cross-country version with large teams. One 300-a-side match between Norfolk and Suffolk was said to have lasted 14 hours and caused nine fatalities. In Wales, *cnapan* had similarities with Cornish hurling and *camp-ball*, but was undeniably a pretty rough game, sometimes featuring players on horseback who attacked each other with cudgels.

From the 16th century onwards, Shrove Tuesday was the biggest date on the football calendar. It was the last day of indulgence before the hardships of Lent, and, in many towns and villages, football became a central part of the festivities. One of the best-known annual fixtures took place in Ashbourne, Derbyshire, where almost the entire town would turn out to play, and the goals were three miles apart. Ashbourne's Shrovetide game is still played in the 21st century, as is the one in Atherstone, Warwickshire, which is believed to date back to around 1200. Folk football also survives as an annual event in other places around Britain, from St Ives in Cornwall to Kirkwall in the Orkney Islands.

In *The People's Game*, James Walvin suggests that the authorities were relatively lenient towards the Shrovetide games, on the understanding that order would be restored the next day. It was thought that working people should be given a limited chance to let off some steam, otherwise their pent-up anger and energy might boil over into something even more destructive. In the 16th century and beyond, the game was popular with apprentices – mostly a radical bunch of young men who loved to stir things up, while governments, employers and landowners faced a constant battle to restrain them.

As if the tales of death, injury and broken windows were not enough, football's detractors had another stick with which to beat it: religion. For most workers, Sunday was the only day of the week that offered any substantial time for recreation. Inevitably, as the game became too popular to be reserved for annual feast days, Sunday football became a regular sight in many towns and villages. In the eyes of many devout Christians, though, any strenuous activity on a Sunday was a violation of the Sabbath.

In 1531, Sir Thomas Eliot published *The Boke of the Governour*, a blueprint for what he considered to be a respectable way of life. Football clearly had no place in it. It was a game 'wherein is nothinge but beastly furie and extreme violence whereof proceedeth hurte and consequently rancour and malice do remaine with them that be wounded'. More condemnation came from the Bishop of Rochester in 1572, demanding that the 'evil game' be banned. In the 16th and 17th centuries, there were numerous cases of people being prosecuted for playing (or even watching) football on Sundays and other Christian holy days, particularly while church services were in progress.

The emergence of the Puritans had much to do with all this. With their strict interpretation of the Bible, and insistence on a 'godly', austere lifestyle, they frowned upon recreation in general, and especially on such riotous games as football. Many Puritans, such as the pamphleteer Philip Stubbes, saw it as a route towards sin. In his *Anatomy of Abuses in the Realme of England*, in 1583, Stubbes was exceptionally scathing, counting the game among the 'develyshe pastimes' that were corrupting the nation:

> *For as concerning football playing, I protest unto you that it*
> *may be rather called a friendlie kinde of fight than a play or*
> *recreation, a bloody and murthering practice than a felowly*
> *sporte or pastime. For dooth not everyone lye in waight for his*
> *adversarie, seeking to overthrowe him and picke him on his nose,*
> *though it be upon hard stones?*

Stubbes went on to catalogue the injuries he associated with the game: broken legs, arms, backs and necks, noses gushing with blood, and so forth. Religious objections to football were nothing new, but it seems that they became more frequent and vehement as the Puritan movement gained momentum in the late 16th and 17th centuries, with prosecutions becoming increasingly common.

The Puritans' stance on football even gave them a shared cause with their adversaries in the monarchy and aristocracy, who still saw it as a threat to property and social stability. James I (1603–25), for example, disapproved of his son Henry playing football, and forbade it from the royal court. But, in a show of defiance to the Puritans, he encouraged Sunday sporting activity in his 1618 *Declaration of Sports*, albeit with no explicit mention of football.

Throughout the Middle Ages, and the rest of the pre-industrial era in Britain, opinions on football were polarised. The political and religious authorities denounced it as harmful or sinful, while many working people played it avidly, despite the numerous attempts to stamp it out. There is little evidence of anyone taking a more balanced approach. A rare exception was Richard Mulcaster, headmaster of Merchant Taylors' School (1561–86) and high master at St Paul's School (1596–1608), both in London.

Although he did not approve of folk football, Mulcaster believed that a more disciplined, regulated form of the game could have social and physical benefits. He suggested it would do 'much good to the body, by the chiefe use of the armes', and that it would 'strengtheneth and brawneth the body ... it is good for the bowells, and driveth down the stone and gravell from both the bladder and kidneies.' Mulcaster also advocated employing 'trayning maisters' at schools. His views were based on his studies of humanist writing, much of it coming from Italy, where these beliefs were associated with a different kind of football: *calcio*.

Calcio (the Italian word for 'kick') had its roots in the Roman game of harpastum, but had emerged as a distinct game in Florence by the early 16th century. One famous encounter took place in Piazza Santa Croce, during the Siege of Florence at the hands of the Medici in 1530, symbolising the unity and defiance of the city's people.

Although it was a violent game, with elements of boxing and wrestling, calcio was well regulated. It had a fixed playing area, a specified number of players per team (usually given as 27, but some accounts suggest 20 or even 10), and an established set of rules – first formalised in 1580 by Florentine noble Giovanni de Bardi, possibly the first written rules of any form of football.

Calcio had much in common with modern rugby. The ball could be played with the hands and feet, and a ball-carrier could be tackled by wrestling him to the ground. For a goal (*caccia*) to be scored, the ball had to be thrown over a designated spot at the opposing team's end of the court. The teams were arranged into formations, similar to those that would be used in the British football codes of the late 19th century: goalkeepers (*datori indietro*), full-backs (*datori innanzo*), half-backs (*sconciatori*), and forwards (*innanzi* or *corridori*). The word 'scrummage' might have originated from the calcio term *scaramuccia*.

Games of calcio were played in front of large crowds, sometimes in covered stands, every night from Epiphany to Lent – usually in city squares, but sometimes on the frozen waters of the River Arno. Popes Clemente VII, Leo XI and Urbano VIII all played the game in their pre-papal days. It has been claimed that Machiavelli took part, and that Leonardo da Vinci was a keen spectator. Calcio was popular with the upper classes and merchants of Florence, and consequently came to the attention of foreign visitors, Richard Mulcaster included.

The game went into decline, though, and was abandoned in 1739. It was revived in 1930, to celebrate the 400th anniversary of the game played during the siege of Florence. It is still played at the Piazza Santa Croce, three times a year in late June and early July, with players dressed in authentic period costume. Today, though, the word 'calcio' is better known to Italians as their word for soccer (and, probably less relevantly, for calcium). The older game is known as *calcio storico*, meaning 'historical football'.

Some Italians – notably those with an interest in luring tourists to Florence – suggest that calcio was the ancestor of soccer and rugby. Calcio was clearly ahead of its time, and it is conceivable (but unlikely) that Mulcaster's knowledge of the game eventually had some influence on the evolution of modern football in Britain in the 19th century.

His views on organised sport were similar to ideas that would emerge nearly 300 years later at English public schools. But, although he was a respected educationalist, not even the prospect of healthier bowels and bladders was enough to entice his British contemporaries to take up his ideas.

The Puritans' influence began to wane after the Restoration in 1660, and many draconian laws about leisure activities were relaxed. For a hundred years or so, football flourished again. Charles II even gave it a royal blessing, attending a match in 1681. But the ruling classes still saw the game as a threat to the established order – an excuse for workers to gather in large numbers and create a racket. And they did have something to worry about: in the 17th and 18th centuries, football's rabble-rousing potential was often used for political ends.

In Northamptonshire and Lincolnshire in the 1760s, for example, games were organised by activists protesting against *enclosures* – the fencing off of open space which many poor people had relied on for their livelihoods. Gatherings were arranged on the pretext of playing football, but their real purpose was to destroy the fences. The authorities sent troops of dragoons to quell the unrest, with little success.

In the late 18th and early 19th centuries, folk football faced new challenges. Britain was becoming urbanised and industrialised. The search for work was forcing many people to move from small towns and villages to the expanding cities. Their everyday lives were turned upside down. With long working hours and cramped living conditions, and with countless fields being replaced by streets and buildings, they had little time or space for recreation.

By now, there was a powerful law enforcement system, helping the authorities to suppress football more effectively than before, particularly in cities. Employers wanted to keep tight control over their workers, and collaborated with law officials in clamping down on their leisure activities – especially football, with its ability to disrupt a whole town for a day or more. Also, Shrove Tuesday, the focal point of the folk football calendar, was no longer a holiday in all areas.

Football's decline was noted in a survey of British sport carried out by Joseph Strutt in 1801: 'It was formerly much in vogue among the common people of England, though of late it seems to have fallen into disrepute, and is but little practised.' Perhaps Strutt was exaggerating the game's demise: it was still played often in some rural areas, which had been largely untouched by the Industrial Revolution. An article in the *Oswestry Observer* in 1887 suggests that *cnapan* had still been hugely popular in parts of Cardiganshire early in that century:

... it seems that about eighty years ago the population, rich and poor, male and female, of opposing parishes, turned out on Christmas Day and indulged in the game of football with such vigour that it became little short of a serious fight. The parishioners of Gelland and Pencarreg were particularly bitter in their conflicts; men threw off their coats and waistcoats, and women their gowns, and sometimes their petticoats.

Towards the middle of the century, though, the noose had really been tightened around folk football's neck. The 1835 Highways Act banned it from public highways, imposing a fine of up to 40 shillings. Soon afterwards, the Derby authorities banned the town's Shrovetide game, prompting a protest in 1846 that led to the deployment of troops and a reading of the Riot Act. As if that weren't enough, along came another wave of religious condemnation, led by members of nonconformist denominations, who, like the Puritans before them, viewed the game as sinful and intolerably violent.

In some places, football began to adapt to the new restrictions on time and space, with games being played by predetermined numbers of players, on fields with fixed boundaries. Joseph Strutt's 1801 survey makes the game seem surprisingly uniform and regulated, giving the length of the playing area as '80 or 100 yards', and saying that the goals were marked by sticks 'two or three feet apart'. As with camp-ball and Cornish hurling, the game that Strutt described bore some resemblance to modern forms of football; although we should note that it also had much in common with games that had been played elsewhere in Europe, hundreds, even thousands of years earlier.

Although it survived in some towns, where it even enjoyed something of a revival between around 1830 and 1860, folk football in Britain was in terminal decline. There's also little evidence of any kind of football being played in mainland Europe during this period (except that *la soule* seems to have kept going until well into the 20th century in Brittany). The story of football, though, was about to take a curious twist. Its next chapter would be played out by the British upper and middle classes – the very sections of society that had been trying to stamp it out for centuries.

Chapter 2

Growing Pains

'I love football so, and have played it all my life.
Won't Brooke let me play?'
– Tom Brown, in *Tom Brown's Schooldays* by
Thomas Hughes, 1857

While football in pre-industrial Britain was mainly a working-class pastime, it was not exclusively so. University students at Oxford and Cambridge, for example, played it in the 16th and 17th centuries. Their game was just as rough and chaotic as that of the working class, and was banned at Oxford as early as 1555, albeit without much success. Football was played at Cambridge from the 1570s onwards – a young Oliver Cromwell is believed to have taken part – but inter-college games were banned in the 1580s.

The earliest mention of any ball game at a public school appears to be in the 1519 Latin textbook *Vulgaria*, written by Robert Horman, a former Winchester student and headmaster who also had Eton connections. One sentence was translated as 'We wyll playe with a ball full of wynde'. Robert Matthew, a Winchester scholar in the 1640s, referred to football in a poem. Eton College bought its playing fields in 1443, just three years after it was founded, and there's a document referring to 'football fields' from 1766, the year when the school claims that its first recorded Wall Game took place.

Early in the 19th century, although some public school officials doubted whether football was suitable for the aspiring young gentlemen in their care, it developed into a more organised, disciplined game at these schools, giving it a new air of respectability in the eyes of the upper and middle classes.

It is likely that some public school pupils played in (or at least watched) folk football games in their home towns, or near their schools. Most of these schools were originally located in town centres, allowing the boys to join in with community activities. The beginnings of football at Rugby

School might well have been inspired by a game that the locals played each New Year's Eve in the 18th century, before the school was moved to a new site, complete with playing fields, on the town's outskirts.

But, while many working-class children lived in cramped squalor, and worked long hours in factories or mines, public school pupils were leading healthier lives, with more leisure time. With most of the boys living on-site, and with plenty of open space available, conditions were ideal for team sports.

Life at the public schools, though, was hardly a bed of roses. The living was spartan, and ruled by hierarchical brutality. The late 18th and early 19th centuries saw a catalogue of rebellions by pupils, including riots at Rugby School in 1797 and 1822. Discipline was left mostly in the hands of senior pupils, who often took great pleasure in dishing it out. Football, a competitive game with plenty of physical conflict, was a perfect way of releasing pent-up energy; and for the older boys to remind their juniors that they were in charge.

British society was changing rapidly, and industrial progress was breeding a new middle class of businessmen. These were self-made entrepreneurs, whose wealth depended on the success of their businesses, in contrast with the inherited riches the upper class enjoyed. Many of the new industrialists hoped the public schools would give their sons an education that would prepare them for the worlds of business, science, politics and law.

But they wanted their sons to learn in an orderly, controlled environment, and were uneasy about the schoolmasters' hands-off approach to discipline, which gave the senior boys free rein to do whatever they liked to whomever they did not like, with little guidance from above. Reform was on the way, and no-one would play a bigger part in it than Dr Thomas Arnold, headmaster of Rugby School from 1828.

Dr Arnold was a deeply religious man – a theologian with a strong belief in Christian morality. After taking over at Rugby, he set out to instil his values of 'godliness and good learning' in his pupils, hoping to mould them into well-educated, Christian 'gentlemen' with a sense of social responsibility. The old *laissez-faire* attitude to discipline was too anarchic for Arnold's liking. Although he did not break up the old disciplinary structure, he tightened the system by making the prefects directly responsible to him, and making sure they understood the standards he expected them to enforce.

Under Arnold's leadership, Rugby School built a strong reputation, and influenced many new public schools that were founded in this period. His methods were popular with upper-middle-class parents, whose sons were enrolling at the school in growing numbers. While Arnold was not wildly enthusiastic about sport, he did tolerate it (except for field sports, which he banned), and it seems that he quietly approved of it, as a way for the senior boys to exert their authority.

Thomas Arnold left Rugby in 1841, just a year before his death, to take a post at Oxford University. His ideas about religion, morality and education helped to give birth to an influential movement, of which he might not have entirely approved: *muscular Christianity*. This was an ethos based on the idea that physical strength and courage were important in the development of young Christian men, helping to prepare them for facing the challenges of the 'real world' in later life. Sports, especially tough ones such as football, were seen as useful for cultivating such qualities. Arnold believed that schools had a character-forming role; the same role was now being ascribed to sports, especially those which involved teamwork, hard running, physical struggle, and the odd bit of violence.

Some major figures in the literary world were advocates of muscular Christianity. One of them was Thomas Hughes, a former pupil of Arnold's, whose *Tom Brown's Schooldays* depicted life at Rugby in the 1830s, and underlined football's role as a part of life at the school. Hughes believed that the physical training of men was vital 'for the protection of the weak, and the advancement of good causes'.

Charles Kingsley, a colleague of Hughes's in the Christian Socialist movement in the middle of the century, wrote novels such as *Alton Locke*, and *Hereward, The Last of the English,* which featured heroic warriors, using their strength and bravery to do good deeds. The expression 'muscular Christianity' has often been attributed to Kingsley. He denied responsibility for it (as did Hughes, despite penning such works as 1879's *The Manliness of Christ*); but the characters he created, along with his robustly athletic approach to life and his strong religious and moral beliefs, typified what the movement was about.

Muscular Christianity also had its disciples across the Atlantic, especially in the wake of the American Civil War, with the Young Men's Christian Association (YMCA) helping to spread the word. It would influence the growth of North American college sport in the late 19th and early 20th centuries. Former theological student James Naismith invented basketball in 1891 at a YMCA in Springfield, Massachusetts, with similar ideas in mind. He told a conference of the National Collegiate Athletic Association in 1914 that basketball should be run 'on such a basis that it will be a factor in the moulding of character, as well as to encourage it as a recreative and competitive sport'. Sport in Australia, New Zealand and (white) South Africa would also be heavily influenced by muscular Christianity.

It was even suggested, by Kingsley among others, that its influence on public school sport helped in Britain's military successes during this period. The Duke of Wellington is believed to have said (although it has been hotly disputed) that the Battle of Waterloo in 1815 'was won on the playing fields of Eton'.

Eventually, some people – even Thomas Hughes – would question these grand claims about the importance of sport, wondering whether the whole thing had gone a little too far. At some public schools in the mid and late 19th century, classroom work had taken a back seat while huge chunks of time were dedicated to sport. Muscular Christianity was especially prevalent at Edinburgh-area schools such as Loretto and Merchiston Castle, where boys were put through gruelling fitness and training regimes, which might well have contributed to Scotland's strength on the rugby field towards the end of the century. Alec Waugh, in his 1917 novel *The Loom of Youth*, wrote scathingly of the 'blind worship at the shrine of the god of Athleticism'.

Although the movement had lost some credibility by that time, it had already made its mark on sporting culture in Britain, North America and beyond. Had it not been for the earnestness of the disciples of muscular Christianity, sport might not have become the serious pursuit that it is today. Baron Pierre de Coubertin, the French founder of the modern Olympic movement, admired the British approach to sport, and used its emphasis on morality and 'gentlemanly' honour as a model for the principles behind the Olympic Games.

Back at the public schools, schoolmasters gradually started warming to the idea of sport in the first half of the 19th century. They saw it as a relatively harmless way of keeping potentially disruptive boys busy, as well as helping to instil discipline and build character. Team sports fitted in with the public school ethos of being part of an exclusive, almost homogeneous group, with everyone expected to follow certain rules and conventions.

Cricket was already well established, and was something of a role model for emerging sports such as football and hockey. A game of manners and etiquette, cricket's spirit of 'gentlemanly' competition and fair play was thought to be ideal for public schools. But it was not suited to the cool, damp climate that Britain endures for most of the school year, and it did not provide the physical conflict demanded by the muscular Christianity brigade. While cricket would still be the main summer sport, football took centre stage for the rest of the year. At most of the schools, football was a leisure activity, rather than a part of the curriculum. The schoolmasters played no part in organising it, but generally encouraged the boys to play.

Sports historians tend to gloss over the public school football games of the 19th century, as if they were mere historical curiosities, overshadowed

23

by later events. But, as these games laid the foundations for the better-known forms of football that emerged in Britain, North America and Australasia soon afterwards, they surely deserve a close look.

At first, these games were little more than horseplay; but they gradually developed clear objectives and rules, which were passed on verbally from one generation of pupils to the next. By the 1840s, things were getting serious. Rules were written down, and were typically agreed and regularly revised by committees of senior pupils, such as the annual *levée* meetings at Rugby. There were various reasons for tinkering with the rules: to reduce violence and injuries, to keep the game in line with each school's ethos, and simply to make it more enjoyable.

Although each school had its own rules and style of play, some elements of the game were common to a number of them. Unlike folk football, public school football mainly involved kicking, rather than carrying, a ball. Handling was usually allowed, but only in limited ways, such as catching the ball 'on the full' after a kick, earning an opportunity to drop-kick or punt it with some degree of freedom (the *mark* or *fair catch* rule).

Ball-carrying, of course, eventually became acceptable at Rugby, and at some newer schools where Rugby's code was adopted. But some of modern rugby union's other features can be likened to elements of the games played at Eton, Harrow and Winchester, as well as the Rugby School game itself.

Most aspects of the game varied wildly from school to school: the playing areas, goal structures, methods of scoring, restarts, offside rules, ways of passing and advancing the ball, and acceptable ways of tackling. The rules and playing styles were largely dictated by the sizes, shapes, ground conditions and surroundings of the playing fields or courts.

As with other aspects of public school life, each school developed its own customs, quirks and terminology in football, some of which can seem downright bizarre to the uninitiated. At Eton, Harrow and Winchester, the local versions of football that evolved in the 19th century are still played today, mainly in the spring term; the pupils also play soccer or rugby, or both, in the autumn.

Eton College, near Windsor, Berkshire, has two football codes of its own. The *Field Game* is recognisable as a forerunner of soccer and rugby, unlike the odd-looking *Wall Game*. It is not clear which existed first, but it seems that they used to be closer to each other than they became. The Wall Game is played on a much narrower strip of grass than it used to be, making the wall a more dominant feature.

The earliest known rules of the Field Game were drawn up in 1847, although it had probably already been played in a similar form for decades, after evolving from casual kickabouts which might have started centuries earlier. Today, almost every Eton pupil plays the game, for at least three years. Knockout competitions and practice matches are played throughout the Lent Half (spring term), with teams representing the various houses at senior and junior levels. Old Etonians return regularly to play against the best of the current crop. In the early days, some of the ways of forming teams were a little more eccentric, such as Tall v Short, Boats v No Boats, and even Step-and-fetch-its v Puff-wheeze-and-gasps.

The size of the playing area was not specified in those early rules, and still is not officially defined, but by the 1930s it was established at 130 by 90 yards. The goalposts are seven feet high and 12 feet apart; a crossbar, at the top, was introduced in the mid 19th century. *Tram lines* are drawn, parallel with the sidelines, a third of the distance between each sideline and the goals. Lines are also marked across the width of the pitch, three yards and 15 yards from each goal-line. A full-sized team has 11 members: seven *bully-players* (forwards), a *fly*, and three *behinds*, one of whom is nominated as the *goals*. Some competitions feature smaller teams.

Play is started, and restarted after various types of stoppage, by means of a *bully*, much like a rugby scrum. At a *set* or *open* bully, three players from each team face each other (the other four bully-players form a second row behind them), with their hands or forearms touching each other. One team is awarded *heads*, allowing its players to bind lower down than their opponents, which improves their chances of driving the bully forwards. A player from the opposing team rolls the ball into the gap between the two rows. Somebody then has to kick it forwards, bringing it into open play.

Back-heeling the ball out of a set bully is an offence known as *furking*. Sometimes a *tightly-formed* or *close* bully is formed, bringing the two rows into closer contact, with both sides allowed to bind low. Anyone who loiters alongside the bully can be penalised for *cornering*. Charging and holding are forbidden. Today, no handling is allowed inside the playing area, although the 1847 rules permitted players to use their hands to stop the ball on the ground.

There are no fewer than five ways of being offside (known as *sneaking* in Eton parlance), too numerous and complex to explain here. The main effect of today's sneaking rules is to restrict movement in front of the ball, which means that forward passing is mostly ruled out. Backward passing is also against the rules, so open play is essentially a mixture of dribbling and a kick-and-chase approach.

A goal, worth three points, is scored by kicking the ball between the goalposts and under the crossbar. Another method of scoring is the *rouge*[2]. For a rouge to be scored, the ball must first become *rougeable*, meaning it has crossed the goal-line after being touched by a defender, or after rebounding off an attacker from a defender's kick.

If an attacker gets the first touch on a rougeable ball, he scores a rouge – earning five points, and the chance to add two more by converting it. A conversion attempt begins with the ball on the junction of the three-yard line and one of the tram lines, and all the defenders standing at least three yards away. An attacker kicks the ball forwards, trying to achieve either another rougeable ball or a goal, either of which would complete the conversion.

On the other hand, if a defender makes the first contact with a rougeable ball, the attacking team can either claim a point (after which the defending team can kick the ball away), or have a bully on the three-yard line. Although the Field Game is sometimes seen as a precursor of soccer, the rouge has similarities with the try in rugby, and the touchdown in its North American descendants.

The Eton Wall Game is a more exclusive affair than the Field Game. It only has one major match each year: the St Andrew's Day clash in November, between teams representing the Collegers (pupils with scholarships) and Oppidans (fee-payers). Both teams practise in the autumn, against teams made up of Old Etonians, schoolmasters and current pupils. More practices and matches follow in the Lent Half, giving younger boys a chance to play. The game might have originated at any time from 1717, when the wall was built, to 1766, the year of the first clear reference to the game. Its rules, first written in 1849, have much in common with those of the Field Game, but it has developed its own very distinct character.

The main reasons for the Wall Game's quirks are the playing area and its surroundings: it is played on a strip of grass 118 yards long, but only six yards wide, with the 11-foot high (and not entirely straight) brick wall on one side. At each end is a small area known as *calx* (the Latin word for chalk), marked by a chalk line on the wall, a few yards away from its end. The goal at one end, *good calx*, is a door in another wall, at a right angle to the main wall. At the other end (*bad calx*, in case you hadn't guessed) is a small tree – a recent replacement for a much taller and thicker tree, now dead, which used to have the rectangular goal marked on it in chalk. The current tree just has one horizontal line, marking the top of the goal. Some spectators sit on top of the wall, peering down at the action below.

Each team has 10 players, divided into *bully-players* and *behinds*. Play is restarted with a *bully*, as in the Field Game, but with the players on their hands and knees, and with this mass of bodies pressing against the brick wall. The ball is rolled into the bully, and must touch the wall before anyone can try to move it forwards. *Furking* (kicking the ball backwards from a bully) is only allowed if the bully takes place in one of the calx areas. *Sneaking* (offside) in the Wall Game is similar to one of its definitions in the Field Game, where a player is ahead of a teammate who plays the ball (except in a bully in calx), or goes beyond all of the opposing bully-players.

When the ball comes loose from the bully – which isn't very often – it can be kicked upfield. If a behind catches the ball *full pitch* (that is, without it bouncing) from an opponent's kick, he is entitled to a drop-kick. Apart from this or when attempting a *shy*, no handling is allowed. If the ball crosses the sideline, play is restarted with a bully opposite the position where it was first touched after going out of play.

The most realistic way of scoring is the *shy*, worth a single point. This is achieved when an attacker uses his foot to prop the ball up against the wall in the opposing team's calx, touching it with his hand and shouting 'Got it!' If the umpire agrees, he calls 'Shy!'; the player can then try to convert the single point into 10 points with a *thrown goal*, by throwing the ball onto the goal at an acute angle, from the *furrow* (the boundary opposite the wall), within calx. A goal can also be scored by kicking the ball onto the goal from open play, earning five points. Kicked and thrown goals are not easy to come by, as the goals are easily defended. At the time of writing, no-one has managed either of these feats in the St Andrew's Day fixture since 1909.

The Eton Wall Game, it must be said, is hardly renowned as a spectator sport. The narrow playing surface allows little room for open play. The action progresses slowly, with bullies moving inch-by-inch along the wall, and with the ball usually invisible to spectators. The game is characterised by the huge effort made by the mud-soaked players, as they heave and strain to push their opponents (and the ball) in the right direction. It is believed to have inspired the fictional game of quidditch in the *Harry Potter* stories.

At Winchester College in Hampshire, a local version of football began to take shape around 1790, when the simple game of *Hills Football*, played on St Catherine's Hill, gave way to the more complex one that evolved in the Meads area. The first known printed rules were not published until 1863, but documents from 1842 give us some idea of how the game was played then.

Today, it is played in the spring term, with matches at senior level involving three teams representing the main groups of pupils: College, Commoners and Old Tutors' Houses. In earlier times, as with the Eton Field Game, teams were devised in various other ways, from alphabetical splits and Prefects v Inferiors, to less obvious arrangements such as World v the Rifle Corps.

Winchester football is played on a narrow strip of grass, now measuring

73 by 24½ metres, alongside the River Itchen. The sidelines were once marked by hurdles, then later by ropes supported on posts set out at 10-yard intervals, an arrangement still in place. For senior games in the first half of the 19th century, in tune with the hierarchical nature of public school life at the time, around 40 junior boys were used as *kickers-in*, to fetch the ball and put it back into play when it crossed the sidelines (a tradition dating back to Hills Football, when the ball often had to be retrieved after rolling down the hillside); the ropes were there to keep these boys off the playing area.

They were mostly relieved of these duties in 1844, when eight-foot-high canvas sheets, also supported by posts, were erected to prevent stray kicks travelling too far. The canvas sheets were replaced by netting in 1866, to allow spectators to watch. Despite this, the playing area is still known as the *canvas*. But the juniors were not completely off the hook. Thanks to a rule introduced in 1860, all junior boys who were exempted from playing at junior or middle level had to stand outside the canvas sheets, and fetch the ball if it flew over them. Now just two *watchers-out* stand outside the netting.

Even more unfortunate, perhaps, was the player on each side who was nominated to be the *goal*, and who also had to act as an umpire. This boy would have to stand on the goal-line, with rolled-up gowns on his feet, waiting for opponents to kick the ball in his direction. This was still a part of the game in 1842, the date of the earliest clear documentation of the game, but had been scrapped by 1863 when the full rules were first printed. It is possible that goalposts were used for a short time during the interim period, but today there is no goal structure at all, human or otherwise.

Winchester College football, also known as *Wincoll Football*, *WinCoFo* or even *Winkies*, rivals the Eton games for peculiar lingo. For instance, since the 1870s, the area behind each goal-line has been known as *worms*. The number of players per team varies between six and 22. About half of them are *ups* or *hot-men* (forwards); the others are the *behinds*, including *hot watches*, similar to scrum-halves in rugby; and, behind them, *kicks*. When the ball goes out of play, or a foul is committed, play is restarted with a *hot*, a scrum-like procedure.

The offside rule is known as *behind your side*. If a player is in front of the ball when a teammate kicks it forwards, he must go back as far as the position where it was kicked before getting involved in the play. If a forward kick is touched by a player from the same team, they will be penalised for *tagging*. Dribbling is also forbidden. Tripping was explicitly allowed in the 1863 rules, but was outlawed by 1876.

A player can catch a kicked ball 'on the full', and may then take up to three steps backwards before punting it. If an opponent is chasing him, he can run with the ball in his hands. *Kicks* are allowed to handle the ball in order to stop or steady it. Any other use of the hands, known as *handiwork*, is against the rules.

The scoring system has changed quite a bit since the days when a player (the goal) stood at each end of the field. Back then, a *pass*, worth one point, was achieved by simply kicking the ball over the goal-line. A *gowner* (two points) involved kicking it over the gowns at the goal's feet. Three points could be scored by kicking a *goaler*, where the ball passed over his head. It might come as a relief to learn that nothing was to be gained from blasting the ball directly at him, except, perhaps, for some sadistic pleasure. Today, a direct kick over the goal-line scores three points (a *goal*), but only one is scored if the ball hits another player, a rope, a post, or the netting before it gets there (a *behind*).

The main features of the Winchester game are the hots, and a lot of hard forward kicking, which is often countered with determined blocking, known as *raising a plant*. The pattern of play depends largely on the conditions, the team sizes, and the quality of the long kicking. On a dry pitch, with some expert kickers on show, an open, high-scoring game can be expected. In muddy conditions, though, the play often becomes bogged down in the hots, making for a gruelling, physical struggle to gain territory. In the 19th century in particular, the emphasis was more on bravery and hard work than on skill and ingenuity.

Harrow School, on the north-western outskirts of London, was founded in 1572. The school bought a playing field, next to the School Yard, in 1680, and acquired more fields in 1750. Most of the pupils came from the surrounding area, and local folk football almost certainly had an influence on the ball games they played at the school. Informal *fug football* was played on the School Yard, and, later, on nearby Roxeth Common. The rules had evolved into something like their modern form by the mid 19th century, and schoolmaster Edward Bowen formalised them on a printed sheet some time around 1860.

Football, along with cricket, was compulsory for Harrow pupils at this time. Senior boys, in their role as *slave-drivers*, organised the games, and rounded up any juniors who tried to avoid playing. Matches were, and still are, played on an inter-house basis, and between current pupils and Old Harrovians.

The goals, known as *bases*, each consist of two posts, 18 feet apart and 12 feet high, with no crossbar. For a replay after a drawn match, the width of the bases is doubled. There are usually 11 players on each side. In the early days, junior boys would stay back to defend their bases, while the seniors performed the attacking roles, known as *following up*.

The game has been largely shaped by the boggy conditions at Harrow, thanks to the poor drainage (the playing fields are at the foot of a hill), and to the notorious swamp-like qualities of the local clay, which is thought to be hundreds of feet deep, and has a great capacity for retaining rainwater. The sticky surface encourages players to keep moving: unlike the games that developed at Eton, Winchester and Rugby, Harrow football doesn't feature scrummages, or anything similar.

The muddy field is also thought to be one of the reasons for the curious nature of the ball: a foot in diameter, and with two flattish surfaces on opposite sides, giving it a pumpkin-like shape. Although its shape helps it to roll along the soggy ground, its size, together with the leather casing's tendency to gather mud, makes it heavy (twice the weight of a soccer ball, even when it is not caked in mud) and a little unwieldy. Boys have reportedly knocked themselves unconscious by heading it.

While the ball may look strange to outsiders, the open play of the Harrow game makes it bear quite a resemblance to modern soccer, perhaps more so than the Eton and Winchester games. The scoring system is simple: a *base* is scored by kicking the ball between the opposing team's goalposts, at any height. Play is restarted with a one-handed throw-in if it crosses a sideline, or with a kick-in if it goes over a goal-line without a base being scored.

When a player makes a *fair catch* after a kick (in other words, he catches the ball without letting it bounce), he can call 'yards'; if he doesn't, he's liable to be tackled. He can then advance three yards and punt the ball, without being impeded. If the player chooses, he can ask the umpire to place a stick in the ground at the point where he took the catch, and can then take three long strides to establish how far he can advance before kicking the ball. It has been suggested that, in earlier times, a player could throw the ball at the goal after claiming 'yards' – similar to the throw-at-goal in the Eton Wall Game.

After making a fair catch near the opponents' base, a player can try to score by carrying the ball into the base in three strides. If he fails, he can go back to the point where he made the catch, and take a kick at the base; two defenders can form a 'wall' at the position he reached with his third stride. Other than this, and using a hand to block the ball, no handling is allowed. A common move is for a player to dribble the ball, then turn around and chip it into the hands of a teammate, who then calls for 'yards'. Most bases are scored by punting the ball from a 'yards' situation, rather than by kicking a 'live' ball from open play.

A player who takes 'yards' must be behind the one who has kicked the ball to him, to avoid being offside. Offside also applies to forward kicks along the ground: if a teammate of the kicker is in front of him when the ball is kicked, he must wait until an opponent has touched it before having any involvement in the play. This rules out forward passing, except where the receiver runs onto the ball from an onside position *after* the kick. Any means of tackling is allowed, provided it is not done from behind, and that the tackler's shoulder makes contact with his opponent. A player can be tackled not only if he has possession of the ball, but even if he only *intends* to get it.

Edward Bowen, author of Harrow's first written football rules, celebrated the game in his words to the song *Forty Years On*, now the school's anthem. The perceived link between bravery on the football field and prowess on the battlefield is unmistakable:

> *Routs and discomfitures, rushes and rallies,*
> *Bases attempted, and rescued, and won,*
> *Strife without anger and art without malice –*
> *How will it seem to you, forty years on?*
> *Then, you will say, not a feverish minute*
> *Strained the weak heart and the wavering knee,*
> *Never the battle raged hottest, but in it*
> *Neither the last nor the faintest, were we.*

As if this were not clear enough, another verse was added in 1954 in honour of Harrow old boy Sir Winston Churchill:

> *Sixty years on – though in time growing older,*
> *Younger at heart you return to the Hill:*
> *You, who in days of defeat ever bolder,*
> *Led us to Victory, serve Britain still.*
> *Still there are bases to guard or beleaguer,*
> *Still must the battle for Freedom be won:*
> *Long may you fight, Sir, who fearless and eager*
> *Look back to-day more than sixty years on.*

Boys at the Charterhouse, Westminster and Shrewsbury public schools also had their own forms of football in the 19th century, but eventually abandoned them in favour of the standard soccer and rugby codes.

Today, Charterhouse School is located in leafy Surrey suburbia. Until 1872, though, it was based in the more cramped confines of Smithfield, east London, on the grounds of the Charterhouse monastery. Football was sometimes played on a grassy area known as The Green; but, on wet days, a stony, covered passageway known as the Cloisters was used instead.

Kicking the ball high into the air was forbidden, to protect the windows of the surrounding buildings. Instead, dribbling was the order of the day, along with violent scrummages involving perhaps 50 or

60 boys. When the ball eventually came out of a scrummage and was collected by a *dribbler*, he was likely to be knocked over and trampled by a phalanx of onrushing *fags* (junior boys). Bruises and shredded clothing were a matter of routine.

Football began at Westminster School some time around 1710, to the alarm of clergymen at nearby Westminster Abbey, who complained about the noise and commotion that came with it. Facing the same kind of space restrictions as the boys at Charterhouse, the Westminster pupils played in a similar style. Charterhouse and Westminster met in England's first inter-school football match, in 1863.

Goals were scored by kicking the ball between two trees at the opponents' end, making it either hit or pass above some railings, vaguely similar to the Rugby School method. Dribbling was the main feature of the Westminster game, but, as at Charterhouse, a player with the ball at his feet might be stopped by almost any means. The fags' main role was to defend their goal en masse: as one old boy recalled in 1903, 'the small boys, the duffers and the funk-sticks were the goalkeepers, twelve or fifteen at each end'. In common with some other public schools, there seems to have been a strong element of bullying in the way the game was played.

At Shrewsbury, where playing fields were available, the game appears to have resembled the more expansive style of football played at Harrow. Some matches were played between teams from within the same house, others between representative house teams. Sometimes, as at other schools, the basis for organising the boys into teams was something a little more idiosyncratic, such as Aquatics v Landlubbers, or Patriarchs v Babies.

Football was compulsory at Shrewsbury, and was consequently known as *douling* or *dowling*, based on the Greek word for 'slave'. The usual punishment for missing a game was, suitably enough, a 'kicking' from the team captain. The game began to blossom after the Rev. B.H. Kennedy became headmaster in 1836. Kennedy encouraged football, unlike his predecessor, the Rev. Samuel Butler, who had dismissed it as 'only fit for butchers' boys'.

Games at Shrewsbury often featured unlimited and unequal numbers of players, and were loosely regulated; although a set of rules, quite similar to the Harrow code, was drawn up in 1866. Forward passing was practically eliminated by the rugby-style offside law, making the game largely a test of dribbling ability.

If a player caught the ball full-on after it was kicked, he was allowed to take a *fair kick*, which could be either a *hoist* (punt) or a drop-kick. No other handling was permitted. Goals were scored by kicking the ball between the goalposts at any height, until a crossbar was introduced in the 1870s. In one significant difference from the Harrow rules, play was sometimes restarted by means of a type of scrum known as a *squash*. Shrewsbury boys continued playing internal games by their local rules until around 1903; but, from 1876–77 onwards, they followed standard soccer laws when playing against other schools.

Football became popular at Rugby School in the early 19th century, as an informal game with simple rules. Games were played on half-holidays, on a field known as the Close. By the 1820s, although still unwritten, the rules had become more disciplined and complex. The whole school – around 300 boys – would take part, initially on a 'scratch' basis, with captains picking the teams on the day; but later using other arrangements such as Sixth Form versus the rest of the school (the *VIth Match*), or the Headmaster's House against a team from all the other houses (the *School-House Match*). Matches often stretched out over five days.

Each team was fronted by around 20 large senior boys – the *players-up*, sometimes known as the *fighting brigade* or *die-hards*. Behind them were the *quarters*, and finally a large throng of *goalkeepers*, usually junior boys, whose main job was to defend their goal-line. The quarters and goalkeepers were expected to collect the ball, and kick it upfield, whenever it came their way.

The ball, made from a pig's bladder encased in leather, had an oval-like shape. Apparently this was simply because of the shape of a pig's bladder, rather than any perceived benefits of using an oval ball. The large playing field was bounded by a gravel walk on one side, and a line of elm trees on the other.

Each goal consisted of two posts, 18 feet high and 14 feet apart, joined by a crossbar at a height of around 10 feet. In contrast with most other public school football codes, goals were scored by kicking the ball *over* the crossbar. A goal could be scored from a drop-kick (kicking the ball as it touched the ground), but not from a punt. Results were decided on goals alone, with victory going to the first team to score twice.

Until at least the 1820s, it was understood that players could not carry the ball forwards. Play was often restarted by means of a *scrummage*, described in *Tom Brown's Schooldays* as 'a swaying crowd of boys, at one point violently agitated' – seemingly more like the rucks and mauls in modern rugby union, rather than organised scrums.

If a player caught the ball on the fly, the 'mark' or 'fair catch' rule came into effect. He could either take a few steps backwards and punt or drop-kick the ball, or place it on the ground for a teammate to kick. Any teammate who was in front of the ball when it was kicked would be offside, and could not touch the ball until someone else had done so.

When the ball went out of play on either side of the field, it was thrown back in at a right angle, between two lines of opposing players, as with the line-out in modern rugby union. If it crossed a goal-line (without a goal being scored), the first team to touch it on the ground would then kick it back into play from the goal-line. If the defending team touched the ball down, they would simply kick it downfield; but if the attacking team got the first touch, the restart gave them a good opportunity to score a goal.

This process of converting a *try* or *touchdown* (both terms were used in Britain at various times in the 19th century) was more elaborate than the simple place-kick in today's rugby codes. An attacker would make a short kick back from the goal-line into the hands of a teammate, who would try to catch the ball before being charged down by opponents advancing from behind their goal-line.

If he managed this, the catcher would then make a mark on the ground with his heel, where the ball was caught, following the 'mark' or 'fair catch' rule. The defenders would then have to stay behind this spot, for as long as he was holding the ball. The catcher would retreat a few yards, and hold the ball in place for a teammate to kick for goal. This would eventually evolve into today's methods of converting tries in rugby, or touchdowns in American and Canadian football[3].

Some well-known modern football terms are thought to have been coined at Rugby School: *drop-kick*, *punt* and *place-kick* (or just *place*). The game also featured *offside* (originally *off your side*), although, as mentioned earlier, this has also been attributed to Cornish hurling. As the game became more sophisticated in the 1830s and 1840s, specialised roles emerged. Good kickers and fast runners would position themselves behind the scrum, waiting for the ball to come their way.

Much of the historical debate over Rugby School football has centred on the practice of carrying the ball. This provided a new way of earning a try (which, until then, could only be achieved by touching the ball down after *chasing* it over the line, following a kick), and was known at the time as *running-in*. It is often said to have been invented by William Webb Ellis during a game in 1823, as commemorated by a statue of Webb Ellis outside the school, and the naming of rugby union's World Cup trophy in his honour.

The Webb Ellis story, though, might well be a myth. He certainly did exist, and attended the school from 1816 to 1825. But the earliest known reference to him carrying the ball did not appear until 1876 (although we should bear in mind that nobody kept records of football at Rugby in those early days). That year, Matthew Bloxam, whose time as a Rugby pupil overlapped with that of Webb Ellis, credited him with the act in a letter to the school newspaper *The Meteor*.

Bloxam repeated the claim in another letter four years later, with a little more detail. In both cases, though, Bloxam said he had heard about Webb Ellis's exploit from someone else, without naming this third party (possibly his brother John, who most likely played football with Webb Ellis at Rugby). By the time the Old Rugbeian Society followed the matter up in 1895, Bloxam had passed away; the story's original source was never tracked down.

In his book *Rugby's Great Split*, Tony Collins smells a conspiracy, suggesting that the Webb Ellis story was fabricated by the public school old-boy network. The game was in the midst of a class conflict in the late 19th century. Collins suspects that Old Rugbeians invented the tale as a way of emphasising the game's upper- and middle-class background, and obscuring the fact that ball-carrying had been commonplace in working-class folk football for centuries. In another twist to the tale, three boys from Ashbourne, Derbyshire, a hotbed of folk football, are thought to have attended Rugby at the same time as Webb Ellis, and may have played a part in the story.

The Rev. Frank Marshall, an imposing figure in late 19th-century Yorkshire rugby, claimed that the game was the 'legitimate refinement' of folk football. But the London-based rugby authorities ignored this view (even though Marshall was on their side in the dispute over payments to players), as did the Old Rugbeians. There are certainly grounds for scepticism, given the obvious motives of the Rugby old boys, and the inconsistencies in their findings. A booklet published by the Old Rugbeian Society in 1897, *The Origin of Rugby Football*, merely claims that running-in was introduced 'at some date between 1820 and 1830 ... in all probability done in the latter half of 1823 by Mr W. Webb Ellis'.

Another part-contemporary of Webb Ellis's at Rugby, T. Harris, suggested that Webb Ellis had been considered untrustworthy, and 'inclined to take unfair advantages at football'. Harris also said that running with the ball, other than when taking a few steps before kicking it, had been forbidden throughout his time at the school. The committee did not take kindly to Harris's evidence, asking him to 'mitigate his strictures upon Ellis', which hardly suggests that they were open-minded about the results of their research.

On the other hand, several other Rugby old boys supported the claim made by Bloxam, who was considered to be a meticulous historian. Just three years after these exchanges, and apparently with no new evidence, the committee put up a stone tablet at the school that left no room for doubt:

This stone commemorates the exploit of William Webb Ellis,
who with a fine disregard for the rules of football as played in

his time, first took the ball in his arms and ran with it, thus
originating the distinctive feature of the Rugby game, A.D. 1823.

Even if Webb Ellis *was* the first boy at Rugby to run with the ball, it cannot be said with any certainty that he was breaking the rules. The laws of the game at that time were generally understood, but not formally defined. The first published rules would not appear until 1845, and even then they would be rather vague.

Thomas Hughes's account of a match in *Tom Brown's Schooldays* (a fictional match, admittedly, but based on his memories from around 1834) makes no clear mention of players carrying the ball, and he told the committee in 1895 that he thought the practice had been introduced during his time at the school, from 1834 to 1842. If Webb Ellis did carry the ball in 1823, it might well have been regarded as an embarrassing gaffe, rather than the great innovation it was later hailed as by the Old Rugbeians; and, to this day, by rugby union authorities and historians.

Perhaps no-one can say for sure who first carried the ball at Rugby, but it is believed that the first outstanding exponent of the ploy was the quick and powerful Jem Mackie in the late 1830s, a claim that Hughes backed. Mackie's success as a ball-carrier encouraged other boys to follow suit.

Running-in was finally acknowledged as an accepted part of the game at a meeting of the Bigside Levée rules committee in 1842. There were tight restrictions, which would eventually be lifted: the ball could not be carried after being picked up off the ground or caught on the bounce, and a ball-carrier could not pass the ball to a teammate by hand. It was not openly legalised in the written rules until 1846. Even then, ball-carrying would only be a minor part of the game until the 1870s – a point overlooked by those making grandiose claims about Webb Ellis's supposed place in rugby history.

When *running-in* first crept into the game, it was regarded as an unfair, though not necessarily unlawful, practice, which invited a hostile reaction from opponents. After all, they had to find *some* way of tackling a ball-carrier, and there were no rules specifying how they could do so. Thomas Hughes once half-joked that if someone had been killed while running with the ball, a jury of Rugby boys would have brought a verdict of 'justifiable homicide'.

Opponents often tackled ball-carriers by wrestling them to the ground, and were allowed to hamper their progress by means of *hacking* – that is, kicking their shins. Some boys enhanced their hacking power by wearing boots with metal toecaps attached. Clearly, it was a rough game, and injuries were frequent. During one School-House match, when the butler of the School House was asked to help an injured boy from another house, his response was hardly sympathetic: 'Let them bury their own dead'.

For a match in 1839, the School House team wore red velvet caps – the first time a team at Rugby had worn any kind of uniform (seven years later, the teams in inter-house matches would begin wearing different-coloured jerseys). Queen Adelaide, consort of King William IV, attended this match at her own request, which gives us some idea of the recognition that Rugby-style football had gained since it began as an informal pastime a few decades earlier. The school would stick with its own rules until 1890, when it joined the Rugby Football Union and adopted its code, which itself had evolved from the Rugby School game.

Around the middle of the 19th century, a number of new public schools, such as Cheltenham, Clifton, Loretto, Marlborough and Uppingham, adopted football. Most of them chose to follow the Rugby rules, probably reflecting not just the strong reputation the school had built during and since Thomas Arnold's tenure as headmaster, but also the appeal of the physical nature of Rugby football. Some of these schools took up the game with a fanatical zeal, taking the muscular Christianity ethos to new extremes. *Mens sana in corpore sano* – a healthy mind in a healthy body – was the mantra of muscular Christianity's advocates.

As these schools emerged, and the older ones expanded, overall attendance at public schools was far higher than it had been earlier in the century. A rapidly growing number of boys were playing football. When the Clarendon Commission reported on public schools in 1864, it found that football and cricket were now regarded as integral parts of the pupils' education, and of social life at the schools. The belief that sport helped to build character, instilling values of manliness and honour, had become a powerful force.

By this time, the public schoolboys' love of football, fuelled by a potent mixture of muscular Christianity and youthful energy, had become so great that many of them wanted to carry on playing in their adulthood. Some played football at their universities, especially at Cambridge, where it became popular in the 1840s. As early as 1838, it tickled the fancy of Dr G.E. Corrie, Master of Jesus College:

> *In walking with Willis we passed by Parker's Piece, and there*
> *saw some forty Gownsmen playing at football. The novelty and*
> *liveliness of the scene were amusing!*

Other sports were becoming established at the universities, particularly cricket and rowing, which had seen regular Oxford-Cambridge encounters since 1827 and 1829 respectively (with Oxford's 1827 cricket team featuring a certain W. Webb Ellis, perhaps his *real* claim to fame). Cricket was also flourishing at county level, and a regular North v South match had been introduced in 1836. It had had a *de facto* governing body of sorts, the Marylebone Cricket Club, since the late 18th century. Hockey and athletics were also on the rise. The arrival of the railways helped things along, encouraging school and university teams from different towns and cities to play against each other.

The public schools had breathed new life into football (mostly through the efforts of pupils rather than teachers) at a time when its traditional folk form had nearly died out. But it was a fragmented, localised game, without standard rules. If it was going to find a place in Britain's blossoming sports scene, it needed to find some cohesion.

In 1846, two Shrewsbury School old boys, H. De Winton and J.C. Thring, helped by Old Etonians, made a short-lived attempt at forming a football club at Cambridge University. They revived the idea two years later, this time with more success, but there was a problem: nobody could agree on the rules. The students' loyalties to their old schools remained strong, and they wanted to stay true to the rules of their former schools. There are accounts of Old Etonians 'howling' at Old Rugbeians for carrying the ball, while the latter regarded Eton-style football as cowardly.

Attempting to sort out this mess, Thring and De Winton arranged a meeting involving 14 students – two from each of six public schools, and two others without public school affiliations – to thrash out a set of common rules. They gathered at 4.30pm, and took nearly seven hours to produce a result. Sadly, there is no known surviving copy of these original *Cambridge Rules*; but we do know that they were simple, fitting comfortably onto one sheet of paper, and would form a crude basis for what later emerged as association football.

Their game had much in common with those played at Harrow and Shrewsbury. Handling was allowed, but only in certain situations, and carrying the ball was forbidden.

The rules were pinned up around Parker's Piece, a public park in central Cambridge. A copy of a revised set of rules, issued some time around 1856, was found many years later, and is now in the library at Shrewsbury School. These *Laws of the University Foot Ball Club* were certified by two old boys each from Eton, Harrow, Rugby and Shrewsbury, and two other students.

Among them was an offside rule which could be seen as a hybrid of the earlier rugby-style law and the one that would eventually be adopted in soccer. If a player kicked the ball forwards, a teammate who was in front of him was not allowed to touch it until an opponent had done so – *unless* there were at least three opponents between himself and their goal-line. On the other hand, players were not permitted to 'loiter' between the ball and their opponents' goal.

Cambridge-style football – which we might loosely call 'soccer'[4] – soon spread beyond the schools and universities. Public school old boys and Cambridge graduates took it back to their home towns, where they helped to form clubs. Sheffield was a vital hub of activity. In 1855, Sheffield Cricket Club began using a field on Bramall Lane (now Sheffield United's home), where some of the members soon started playing football, under rules similar to those used at Cambridge University.

Two years later, club members William Prest and Nathaniel Creswick were looking to arrange some regular sporting activity for the winter. They formed Sheffield Football Club, now generally thought to be the world's first 'soccer' club, other than those formed at schools and universities (although it has been claimed that Surrey Football Club, with membership restricted to members of Surrey County Cricket Club and various social clubs, had been formed as early as 1849, possibly playing under similar rules[5]).

The Sheffield club drew up its own rules, mixing elements of various public school and college codes, including a fair catch rule, with aspects of working-class football. The most notable feature, in relation to the Cambridge Rules, was the absence of any offside law. Players known as *kick-throughs* took advantage of this by lingering near their opponents' goal throughout the game.

A slightly later version of the rules also provided a secondary way of scoring: by kicking the ball between one of the main goalposts and an outer post, similar to the *behind* in modern Australian Rules football. Complicating the story further; this was known as a *rouge* – quite different from its namesakes in the Eton Field Game and present-day Canadian football. Matches were decided primarily on goals, but rouges were used as tie-breakers in drawn games.

At first, Sheffield FC played among themselves, with teams organised in various ways such as married v unmarried, or A–M v N–Z. Soon, though, they had other local clubs to play against. Hallam FC was formed in Sandygate, in the west of the city, in 1860. Just two years later, there were 15 clubs in the area.

Many players at these clubs came from humble backgrounds, and the public school and grammar school old boys found it difficult to teach and enforce the rules – especially with regard to carrying the ball, a practice that might still have been familiar to some of the working-class players from folk football. Legend has it that the Sheffield FC players once provided each opposing player with a pair of white gloves, and two silver florin coins which they were expected to hold throughout the game, preventing them from holding the ball. Another version of the story suggests that the idea was to prevent players pushing opponents with open hands.

The game also grew in nearby counties, and clubs were soon formed in Lincolnshire and Nottinghamshire. Among them was Notts County, the oldest club surviving today in professional English soccer, which began informally in November 1862, before being officially founded as Nottingham FC two years later.

A number of clubs also sprang up in the London area. A group of Harrow old boys formed Forest FC in Epping Forest, Essex, in 1859 (the club would be renamed as Wanderers after moving to Battersea Park in 1864). Two more clubs with Harrow connections were founded around this time: Old Harrovians, and the enigmatically named (or unnamed?) No Names, usually known as 'N.N.', in Kilburn.

Barnes FC set up home in the Mortlake area, alongside the River Thames, in 1862. Forest's secretary placed an advertisement in *Bell's Life* magazine in October of that year, looking for teams willing to play against them 'on the rules of the University of Cambridge'. Barnes FC soon answered the call.

Also in 1862, one of the prime movers from Cambridge, J.C. Thring, drew up a set of rules for Uppingham, the public school in Rutland where he was now an assistant master. Billed as *The Simplest Game*, Thring's football code consisted of just ten rules. Unsurprisingly, they closely resembled the Cambridge Rules which he had helped to develop, with a similarly restrictive offside law.

Rugby-style hacking was prohibited by a rule stating that 'kicks must be aimed only at the ball'. Tripping and 'heel kicking' were also forbidden. Interestingly, there was no provision for the fair catch or mark: players could only use their hands to stop the ball and place it on the ground for a kick.

While the Cambridge-style game was spreading around the country in the middle of the 19th century, Rugby School's version of football was also catching on. Its profile was boosted by the success of *Tom Brown's Schooldays*, published in 1857, with its detailed account of a School-House match.

Even at Cambridge University, not everyone preferred the Harrow-style game that led to the Cambridge Rules. Rugby old boy Albert Pell tried to form a rugby club there in 1839, without much success. The medical students' club at Guy's Hospital in London is believed to have been formed as early as 1843 (although there's no surviving documentary evidence from that year, a fixture card from 1883–84 refers to this being the club's 40th anniversary season, and there is other supporting evidence from the 1860s).

Guy's, still with us (under the unwieldy name of 'Guy's, Kings and St Thomas' Hospitals RFC', following two mergers), thus claims to be the world's oldest rugby club. But, as its membership was only open to students at the hospital, the claim is sometimes qualified by stressing that it was a *closed* club.

In their early days, the Guy's team played on Blackheath Common, which they later shared with a new club, Blackheath FC, formed by former pupils of Blackheath Proprietary School. As with Guy's, Blackheath FC's birth date is disputed, but it is usually given as 1858. Richmond FC arrived on the scene in 1861, playing by Harrow rules at first, but switching to rugby a year later when Old Rugbeians became the dominant force at the club.

As public school old boys returned home, rugby found its way northwards, initially making a bigger impact than the Cambridge-style game in most areas. Even in Liverpool and Manchester, two cities now inextricably linked with soccer, rugby was the dominant code at this stage, and would remain so for a quarter of a century.

Rugby football made its first appearance outside the student world in 1857, when Frank Mather, a local Old Rugbeian, organised a game on the grounds of Liverpool Cricket Club in the Edge Hill district. Relatives of Liverpool-born future prime minister William Gladstone are thought to have suggested the idea, as an alternative Saturday afternoon pastime for the local gentry whenever they fancied a change from hare-coursing. Richard Sykes, captain of the Rugby School team, was invited to play (the game was to take place during the Christmas holidays, when Sykes would be at home in Manchester), and was asked to bring a ball, of the type used at the school.

Around 50 players turned up, about half of them with Rugby School connections, and were divided into two teams, 'Rugby' and 'The World'. The match drew plenty of attention among the city's upper-middle class (or 'the best families of the Liverpool district', as U.A. Titley and Ross McWhirter put it in their *Centenary History of the Rugby Football Union*[6]), and led to the formation of Liverpool Football Club – no relation to today's soccer club of that name.

Richard Sykes also helped to bring the game to the Manchester area. He played in its first rugby match, at the Western Cricket Ground in Salford in 1860, and became captain of Manchester FC when it was founded that year. Most of the club's players were old boys from Rugby School and Cheltenham College. Other clubs, including Sale FC, sprang up nearby over the next few years.

While a soccer-style game was catching on in Sheffield, most other parts of Yorkshire turned to rugby. It was played at Leeds Grammar School from 1851 onwards, and at St Peter's School in York from 1856. Ex-pupils of these schools would go on to form rugby clubs in these cities in the 1860s.

The game also found its way to other parts of the British Isles. Dublin University Football Club, organised by members of Trinity College, was set up in 1854, thanks partly to former Rugby and Cheltenham students. It claims to be the oldest rugby club in continuous existence, as the Guy's Hospital club was suspended for some time in the 19th century. Many of the players had learned the game at public schools in England, but there is evidence that some form of football had been played on the college fields as far back as the 1780s. In 1870, the Dublin students found some opposition in the shape of a team known as Wanderers, founded by former members of the university club itself.

A middle-class football club of some sort existed in Edinburgh as early as 1824, lasting for a decade. Rugby was being played at the Edinburgh Academy by 1851, and a team of its alumni formed the Edinburgh Academicals Football Club in 1857. The following year, a team from nearby Merchiston Castle School played against them, and also faced another Edinburgh school, Royal High, in Britain's first inter-school football match (five years before Charterhouse and Westminster followed suit in England).

Other Scottish clubs, such as West of Scotland and Glasgow Academicals, were formed in the 1860s. Unlike in England, former pupils of the elite Scottish schools often stayed in the same cities into their adulthood, making for a vibrant 'old boy' network that provided a fertile breeding ground for sporting clubs – which, along with the teams of the schools that spawned them, would play an important role in shaping Scottish rugby. The game also gained a foothold in south and west Wales in the same period, largely thanks to the influence of the Rev. Rowland Williams, a rugby-loving Cambridge graduate who became vice-principal at St David's College, Lampeter, around 1850.

As with Cambridge-style football, the rules of rugby had not yet been universally agreed, even though, unlike the hybrid Cambridge game, it had originated from a single source. The first written laws had been drawn up at Rugby School in 1845 (by a committee including W.D. Arnold, son of former headmaster Thomas Arnold), after the school had expanded to such a degree that word-of-mouth was no longer an adequate way of ensuring the rules were understood.

These 37 rules defined such important elements of the game as the *try at goal* (where the ball was punted back from the goal-line after being touched down, and was then place-kicked towards the goal), *running-in*, and *off side*. Hacking was openly allowed, with some restrictions. But the rule book was vague about such basic points as team sizes, field dimensions, game duration and scrummaging. For anyone who had not seen a match at Rugby School, it would hardly have been a helpful guide to how the game was played.

Some Old Rugbeians, struggling to teach the game to the uninitiated, were not satisfied with this state of affairs. A revised set of rules was finally published at the school in 1862. This time there was a lengthy introduction, which filled many of the gaps, explained much of the jargon, and described some tactical aspects of the game, including the roles of backs and half-backs.

By this time, although games at Rugby School still involved huge teams, club matches were usually only 20-a-side. Hacking was still allowed – in fact, it was positively encouraged – but the rules did have some provisions for keeping violence under control. A player could only be hacked if he was carrying the ball or in a scrum, and it could not be done above the knee, or from behind.

Hacking was a thorny issue, though. Some clubs considered it essential for rugby's 'manliness', while others, mainly in northern England, argued that it was against the spirit of the game. It is also comforting to know that 'throttling' and 'strangling' in the scrummage (and, hopefully, elsewhere) were expressly forbidden. Also in 1862, Blackheath FC produced its own set of written rules, along the same lines as the latest Rugby School laws. It claims to have made a significant innovation at the time, introducing the idea of passing the ball backwards or sideways by hand – until this time, players had only moved the ball by kicking or carrying it.

Football was evolving quickly in the early 1860s, but with a certain degree of chaos. Although it was generally diverging into two branches – the dribbling game favoured at Cambridge, and the Rugby-style version with its scrummaging, ball-carrying and (usually) hacking – there was no formal distinction between them. They still had much in common, and some optimists hoped that the differences could be ironed out, producing a single, uniform football code.

Some clubs had yet to decide which set of rules to follow. The time when soccer and rugby would be regarded as two separate sports was a long way off, and it would be even longer before most Britons began to see the word 'football' as synonymous with soccer. New clubs routinely included the 'Football Club' suffix in their names, whichever code they adopted.

Many provincial clubs were happy to stick with their own rules, as members mostly played amongst themselves, rather than against other clubs. But those in the London area, being close together, were playing regularly against one another. There were often tiresome pre-match arguments over the rules that would be followed, and the need for a standard code became increasingly urgent. With this in mind, the captain of Barnes FC, a man with the wonderfully Victorian name of Ebenezer Cobb Morley, wrote a letter to *Bell's Life* in the autumn of 1863, suggesting that a group of club representatives should agree on a set of rules.

At the same time, there was also some interest in standardising the laws among schools and universities. In October 1863, a year after Cambridge graduate J.C. Thring had drawn up his rules for *The Simplest Game* at Uppingham School, a nine-man committee gathered at his old university to work out a common code, hoping it would also be adopted at other institutions. Led by the Rev. R. Burn of Shrewsbury School, and featuring two old boys each from Eton, Harrow and Rugby, along with one each from Marlborough and Westminster, they came up with a new set of Cambridge Rules, published the following month.

At a time when the press generally took little notice of football, a notable exception was *The Field* ('The Country Gentlemen's Newspaper'), where John Cartwright – arguably the world's first football writer – showed a particular interest in the game, and campaigned for uniform rules. Thinking along the same lines as Morley, Cartwright proposed a 'headquarters for football', similar to the Marylebone Cricket Club, in an article published on October 31, 1863. He was probably unaware of a report in the same issue, headlined 'Formation of a Football Association'.

Morley's letter in *Bell's Life* had led to a meeting at the Freemason's Tavern on Great Queen Street in London, on October 26. As well as his Barnes club, there were representatives from Blackheath FC, Blackheath School, Crusaders, Crystal Palace (not the present-day club of that name), Forest, Kensington School, No Names, Perceval House School, Surbiton, and the War Office Club.

Despite the public schools' vital role in football's evolution, none of them sent delegates, although there was an observer from Charterhouse. Richmond, perhaps preferring to keep up their flexible approach to the rules because of their frequently changing membership, also stayed away, but said they would be interested in the outcome. Morley proposed a motion, seconded by A.W. McKenzie of Forest FC:

> *That it is advisable that a football association should be formed*
> *for the purpose of settling a code of rules for the regulation of the*
> *game of football.*

Everyone agreed, except for the Charterhouse observer, who was reluctant to get involved in such an association without knowing whether his peers at the other public schools supported it. The motion was carried, and the Football Association was up and running. At a second meeting, it was agreed that membership would be open to any club of at least a year's standing, for an annual subscription fee of one guinea. The public schools all declined the invitation, preferring to continue with their own rules.

Morley was elected as Honorary Secretary, and, at the third meeting, was charged with the tricky task of drafting the rules. Many of the delegates were old boys from schools such as Harrow and Shrewsbury, and preferred the dribbling style of football played at those schools, with handling only playing a minor role. But there was a spirit of compromise in the air, and it was hoped that the rules could include what were considered to be the best elements of both the dribbling game and rugby.

At the fourth meeting, on November 24, Morley presented his draft rules. They made sizeable concessions to rugby: a player catching the ball on the full, or after a single bounce, would be allowed to run with the ball or throw it to a teammate; and a ball-carrier could be charged, held, tripped, and even hacked.

But, crucially, at the same meeting, Morley also presented a copy of the Cambridge Rules, and said he preferred them to the laws he had drafted himself. He admired their simplicity, and believed they were truer to the spirit of the game. They prohibited carrying and throwing the ball; and hacking, a practice that Morley feared would discourage potential newcomers to the game. If the FA adopted these rules, no compromise would be offered to the rugby contingent at all.

The FA hoped to bring Cambridge University into the fold. At first, the delegates who were to meet with the university's football club were told to insist on allowing ball-carrying and hacking – despite Morley's preference, which some other members shared, for Cambridge's existing rules.

Whether the Cambridge footballers would have been willing to play by these compromise rules is unclear, but the matter became academic as the story took another twist at the fifth meeting on December 1. A membership application had arrived from Sheffield FC, the second provincial club, after Lincoln FC, to show an interest. In their letter, the Sheffield players stated their opposition to ball-carrying and hacking, believing they were more suited to wrestling than to football.

The tide was turning in favour of the Cambridge Rules. The only dissenting voice was that of the FA's treasurer, Francis Campbell, captain of rugby-playing Blackheath FC. Campbell proposed that the meeting be adjourned until the Christmas period, when some school representatives would be back in London and available to vote; but his motion was defeated by 13 votes to four.

As the meeting continued, the FA redrafted the laws, bringing them into line with the Cambridge Rules in their entirety. Trying to forge some unity, Morley suggested to Campbell that he could propose rule changes at the next annual general meeting a year later. Campbell, though, was mightily disgruntled, and in no mood to face the prospect of a whole season of Cambridge-style football, which he said would 'do away with all the courage and pluck from the game', disdainfully adding that he would 'be bound to bring over a lot of Frenchmen who would beat you with a week's practice'.

At the sixth meeting, on December 8, Campbell again protested vehemently at the exclusion of ball-carrying and hacking, warning that a wholesale adoption of the Cambridge Rules would destroy football. He announced Blackheath's withdrawal from the FA, and, with the mood turning ugly, the meeting was adjourned. When it reconvened a week later, without Campbell, the remaining delegates agreed to adopt the draft laws.

From a modern perspective, the original FA rules were strikingly simple. In time, they would prove to be *too* simple. They did not specify the shape or size of the ball, the length of a game, or the number of players (although 11-a-side was generally agreed as the norm, possibly influenced by cricket). There was no mention of referees, or of what would happen if anyone was so ungentlemanly as to break a rule.

Some aspects of the code were very different from present-day soccer laws. The fair catch was still allowed, and offside was rugby-style. There was even a procedure similar to the try and conversion in rugby (and to the rouge in the Eton Field Game): if the ball crossed the goal-line outside the goalposts, and was then touched by an attacking player, the attacking team could take a free kick at goal, 15 yards from the goal-line, and in line with the position where the ball was touched. These 'touchdowns' were sometimes recorded in the scoring.

Eager to put the rules into action, Ebenezer Cobb Morley arranged a match for his Barnes club against Richmond at Mortlake on December 19; even though the latter club had not joined the FA, and sometimes played rugby. The match was well received, despite finishing goalless. An exhibition match was played in Battersea Park in early January, between teams selected by the FA's secretary and president. As the new year began, the association already had 22 member clubs.

Although Blackheath's captain had been hopelessly outnumbered at those early FA meetings, the club was far from alone in wanting to play rugby, and soon found some opponents in the shape of none other than Richmond. After the first encounter between the two clubs in 1864, the latter finally settled on rugby, and Blackheath v Richmond has been a regular fixture ever since.

Any lingering hopes of a compromise had been dashed. A chasm had opened up between the two factions, who had failed to agree on a form of football that would represent the 'true spirit' of the game. Left out in the cold, the rugby clubs began to forge their own way forward, and would eventually form their own union to organise and regulate their game.

Could things have turned out differently? We could speculate endlessly about the various twists and turns that those early FA meetings might have taken, depending on who had been there, and how the discussions might have turned out. Some historians have claimed that hacking, rather than ball-carrying, was the main bone of contention between Blackheath and the other clubs. But the two issues were tied together: even the most wild-eyed proponents of hacking thought it should only be allowed when a player was carrying the ball, or in a scrummage. In any case, hacking would soon be eliminated from rugby, and its removal would do little, if anything, to bring the two codes closer together.

Perhaps the gulf between the two schools of thought was too great for there to be any chance of a reconciliation. It could be argued that a game based on kicking and dribbling skills would be ruined if players were allowed to carry the ball in any circumstances at all; and that the rugby players enjoyed the ball-carrying part of their game so much that they were not prepared to restrict it for the sake of compromise. There were also other important elements of rugby that never featured in the FA's game, or in the earlier Cambridge Rules, such as the oval-shaped ball, the H-shaped goals, and scrummaging.

Football had come of age. No longer just a game for schoolboys, it was starting to become a part of middle- and upper-class British adult life, and was ready to spread further.

Chapter 3

Ball of Confusion

*'Any club challenging this club, plays the club rules, but if this club
sends a challenge we play the rules of the club challenged.'*
– Law 11 of Southend FC's constitution, 1870

After the Football Association was launched in 1863, soccer and rugby
went their separate ways. Soccer became the favourite sport of the British
working classes, and its popularity spread around the globe. Meanwhile,
rugby split into the union and league codes in 1895, which continued as
popular sports in Britain and parts of the Commonwealth.

At least, that is how the conventional wisdom goes. As with much of
this story, though, the truth is much murkier. Far from being a clean break,
the 1863 split was initially just one milestone among decades of bickering
and confusion, although it would become significant in the longer term.
For much of the second half of the 19th century, many football clubs
were undecided about which set of rules to follow. Some switched from
one code to another at least once, some alternated frequently between
the two main codes, while others used their own rules. Some were still
trying to make their minds up well into the next century.

Sports historians usually airbrush this messiness out of the picture,
focusing on one particular code, as if the split had been perfectly clear-
cut. In particular, soccer history writers tend to dismiss rugby as a minor
irritant that the FA successfully shrugged off at its formative meetings.
But the history of soccer and rugby in this period, even after 1863, should
be treated as one history, not two.

As the FA set out to establish its code (known formally as *association
football*) as the national standard, Wanderers FC, the London club earlier
known as Forest FC, acted as the game's roving ambassadors. Among the
club's players were Edward Bowen, once a prime mover in Harrow School
football; a burly young forward named Charles Alcock, who would play
a vital role in the game's growth over the coming decades; and even a
future president of the Rugby Football Union, Arthur Guillemard.

Wanderers had started as a group of Harrow old boys, but by now their membership was open to men from other backgrounds (Guillemard, unsurprisingly, was an Old Rugbeian) and included some army officers. They played against public school teams, including Charterhouse, Westminster and Harrow itself; and against the likes of Reigate, Crystal Palace (not the current club of the same name, as mentioned earlier) and Civil Service.

Despite the efforts of Wanderers and the FA, the new organisation's rules made little impression in these first few years. Clubs in cities such as Sheffield and Nottingham had an independent spirit, and, although most of them did not openly oppose the FA, they felt no great urge to adopt its laws. Lincoln FC rapidly lost interest in the association, and resigned from it in 1866.

Sheffield FC, though, played an important role in promoting soccer-style football in south Yorkshire and the northern Midlands. They played twice against Lincoln, and once against Nottingham FC (later to become Notts County), in the 1864–65 season. The latter club found some local rivals the following season, as Nottingham Forest Bandy[7] Club began playing football on free weekends.

Despite playing by their own rules, Sheffield had some influence on the FA. Their idea of fixing a tape to the goalposts, eight feet above the ground, was adopted by the FA in February 1866. A month later, the club travelled to London for a challenge match against a combined FA team. The London side won by two goals and four touchdowns to nil, the first goal coming from Ebenezer Cobb Morley, whose letter in *Bell's Life* had led to the FA's formation.

There were still disagreements over the rules. The FA rejected three changes that Sheffield proposed in 1867: the inclusion of rouges in scoring, the awarding of a free kick for illegal handling, and a change in the offside rule. Thanks to all this wrangling, a proposed rematch in Sheffield never materialised, and a group of clubs formed the Sheffield Football Association in the autumn of that year.

Around this time, Sheffield FC stopped playing against local opponents, setting their sights on the national stage. But, by the modest standards of the time, the area's football scene was thriving in the late 1860s. In some ways, it was ahead of its time. In February and March of 1867, twelve local clubs took part in a knockout tournament, with a silver cup awarded to the winners. That September, the Wednesday Cricket Club, named after the day of the week when they played, became Sheffield Wednesday Cricket and Football Club, following a path trodden by Sheffield Cricket Club a decade earlier.

Later that season, the club's footballers won a four-team knockout competition arranged by theatre manager Thomas Youdan[8], beating

Garrick in the final at Bramall Lane in front of 400 spectators. Meanwhile, the Sheffield rules carried on evolving: rouges were abolished, and throw-ins and corner kicks were introduced.

The London-based FA, determined to improve its game, continued to review its rules. Significant changes were made in the period from 1866 to 1870, remoulding the game into something much closer to the one we know. Handling was gradually wiped out, with the *fair catch* being eliminated in 1866. By 1871, only one player on each side – the goalkeeper (a role first specified in the laws in 1865) – was allowed to handle the ball in open play. Initially, there was no rule requiring the goalkeeper to wear a different-coloured jersey from the outfield players. He also could handle the ball anywhere in his team's half of the pitch – after all, there was no penalty area.

Offside was a tricky subject, with two distinct schools of thought. The tradition at Eton, Harrow, Rugby and Shrewsbury had influenced the FA's original law: a player would be offside if he was in front of the ball when it was kicked forwards, and then had to stay away from the play until the ball had been touched by an opponent, or until he retreated to an onside position.

At Charterhouse and Westminster, however, the offside law was based on the attacker's position in relation to the last two opposing defenders, rather than the ball. In 1866, the FA adopted a similar law: to remain onside when the ball was played forwards, an attacker needed to have at least three opponents (one of whom could have been the goalkeeper) between himself and the goal-line. Eventually, this would pave the way for a more open passing game. Old habits died hard, though, and most teams would stick with their dribbling style for some time to come.

In September 1867, the FA felt bullish enough to declare its confidence in these revamped rules. The first representative match at county level was staged two months later, perhaps following the example of county cricket, between Middlesex and a combined Surrey/Kent team in Battersea Park.

While the FA's game was making its early, unsteady progress, rugby also continued its growth from public-school curiosity to adult pastime. By the mid 1860s, there were around 20 rugby clubs in the London area alone, with Blackheath and Richmond leading the way. Most games in and around the capital were played on public parks, and were often disrupted by spectators wandering onto the playing area. Eventually, clubs began using enclosed playing fields, with barriers to keep onlookers at bay.

Rugby was also continuing to catch on in parts of northern England. After a few years of informal rucking, a group of young men in Bradford, mostly former students at Brabham College, founded Bradford FC in 1866, adopting the Rugby School rules. A rugby club was formed in Rochdale in November 1867; a few years later, its junior sections would merge to create Rochdale Hornets. Near Manchester, clubs were set up in Swinton in 1866, and in Broughton in 1869.

Ex-pupils of St Peter's School formed the York Amateurs club in 1868, and clubs following some sort of rugby code were established in Huddersfield, Hull, Leeds and Preston during this period. Darlington Cricket Club began playing rugby in 1863, with some rules that would later become standard: hacking was banned, and the teams were 15-a-side, five fewer than the usual number.

When a Blackheath v Richmond match in November 1866 was cancelled because of fog, the two teams held a meeting to talk about potential rule changes. Both clubs had been badly hit by injuries, many of them blamed on hacking. They agreed that *unnecessary* hacking should be eliminated, a decision that was also reached at Rugby School soon afterwards.

Rugby was starting to resemble its modern forms, but still had no standard rules. Blackheath and Richmond were seen as the game's standard-bearers in the London area, and Rugby School still had some clout. Some northern clubs, though, paid little attention to anyone else's ideas about how the game should be played. Many of their members had not played it at school, and either did not know, or chose to ignore, the intricacies of its traditional rules and customs. Local rules sprang up all over the place; Hull FC even had a law against standing on the crossbar to block an attempt on goal.

The confusion over rules went beyond the squabbles between the London and Sheffield associations, and the disputes over how rugby should be played. For many years after the FA's formation, there was no widely accepted distinction between the two varieties of football in the British Isles. If we take a look at the goings-on at some clubs, it soon becomes clear just how muddled the situation was.

The Wasps club was founded in London in the 1867–68 season, intending to play rugby; but they struggled to find suitable opponents that season, and often resorted to playing soccer instead. In Northamptonshire, Wellingborough Town also began as a rugby club in 1867, but soon discovered the FA's rules, and took a liking to them; they started playing their home games under those laws, but most of their away games were under rugby rules. Clapham Rovers switched between soccer and rugby on alternate weekends in the first half of their debut 1869–70 season, and then decided to field separate teams for the two codes. Sale FC also alternated weekly between FA and rugby rules at one stage, before settling on rugby.

Henry Almond[9], a Charterhouse old boy working for the North Staffordshire Railway, formed a club known as Stoke Ramblers, the forerunners of Stoke City, perhaps in 1863, but certainly by 1868, mostly made up of railway workers. They adopted the Sheffield FA's rules, but also sometimes played rugby. Another Staffordshire club, Burton FC, founded in 1870, played their away games by whichever rules their hosts preferred, until they adopted rugby full-time in 1876.

A railway clerk, Henry Jenkinson, placed an advertisement in the *Leeds Mercury* in March 1864, appealing for 'a number of persons' to form a football club. Even though he was proposing to play between 7am and 8am on weekdays, the response was enormous, and his new Leeds Athletic Club soon had 500 members. Their rules were roughly based on the rugby code, but with a notable exception: ball-carrying was not allowed. The original rules of Hull FC, founded in 1865, only allowed players to carry the ball after catching it from a kick, whereas by now the London-area clubs were allowing this to be done after picking it up from the ground.

All this flip-flopping between soccer and rugby might seem strange today; but it becomes more understandable if we consider how football was generally being played in the 1860s and early 1870s. Tactics and techniques were, by present standards, a little crude. Whichever code was being followed – soccer, rugby, or a local hybrid – football was basically a game of kick-and-chase.

Each team would have a large forward line, marauding closely together as a pack. Behind them would be a small number of backs and half-backs, whose main roles were to kick the ball downfield and to act as the last line of defence. Typically, a forward would dribble the ball towards the opposing goal, with the rest of the forward line backing him up in case he lost possession (or sometimes running in front of him, forming a protective screen). Opposing forwards would try to stop his progress, perhaps by tripping or hacking him if the rules still allowed it.

Even in rugby, ball-carrying had not yet become the game's dominant feature. Passing the ball by hand was even rarer: it was usually seen as a cowardly act, only performed by players who were afraid of being tackled. Scrums – perhaps the most distinctive feature of rugby until ball-carrying and passing by hand became prevalent – often continued for minutes on end, sometimes with around 30 players involved. Half-backs waited behind the scrum, with three-quarter-backs or full-backs in deeper positions, but did not expect to receive the ball from their teammates in the scrum. Rather than heeling it backwards, the pack would try to kick it forwards.

Players in the middle of a scrum usually stood upright, and could rarely see the ball. Advocates of hacking claimed that it was the only realistic way for a team to make progress in a scrum: it allowed them to clear opponents out of the way, giving them some room to find the ball and drive it forwards. Backs were expected to tackle ball-carriers, and to field any kicks from the opposition that went beyond their forward pack. If they got possession of the ball, they would either carry it until they were tackled or scored a try; or kick it, in order to gain ground or try to score a goal.

Soccer was similarly basic, perhaps even more so. In the public school tradition, its main features were dribbling, charging and 'following-up' (backing up a teammate as he dribbled the ball). Even after the drastic 1866 change in the offside law, which made forward passing possible, few teams grasped the opportunities it presented. Some took a long time to adopt the art of dribbling: at first, their main tactic, for want of a better word, was to kick the ball straight ahead and 'follow up' after it. Defence was of little concern, and a 1-1-8 formation was the norm. Goalkeepers were fair game when it came to charging: it was considered acceptable to bundle them over the goal-line, whether they had the ball or not.

Throw-ins had to be directed at a right angle to the touchline, as with a rugby line-out, until 1880, and were thrown one-handed until 1882. The rule that provided for a free shot at goal, after a 'touchdown' behind the opponents' goal-line, had disappeared by this time. Heading the ball was unheard of: if a player found the ball flying towards his head, he would duck out of the way, or (while the rules still allowed it) catch it or knock it down with his hands. The roles of half-backs and full-backs began to develop towards the end of the 1860s, but they were still roughly similar to those of their counterparts in rugby: they were generally expected to back up the forwards, and kick the ball into their opponents' half.

The first representative rugby match came in March 1870, when a Lancashire select team beat their Yorkshire opponents by a goal and two touchdowns to nil, in a 20-a-side encounter in Leeds. The Yorkshire line-up featured four players from Sheffield FC, who were unfamiliar with the rules of rugby, and struggled to cope with its rough tackling. One of them became so confused that he grabbed hold of the ball and hammered it against a Lancastrian's head, apparently thinking this might be an accepted part of the game.

It was the first and, unsurprisingly, the last, time that Sheffield's soccer[10] players had anything to do with the rival code. Perhaps it was naïve to invite them to play in a rugby match, and the farcical results could be seen as a sign that the two football codes were growing further apart. Ball-carrying and passing by hand were becoming more commonplace in rugby, whereas handling in open play (except by goalkeepers) had disappeared from both the Sheffield game and the London FA's version.

Football, in its various forms, was becoming a well-known and respectable pastime for adults as well as for schoolboys. It was still almost exclusively an upper-middle-class activity, and purely amateur: after all, these well-heeled gentlemen barely needed any extra income, and in any case, the game had yet to grow into a money-spinning business. Attendances for the biggest matches were in the hundreds, rather than thousands.

In some areas, though, particularly in northern England, football was becoming popular among the lower middle class: railway clerks, accountants, bank workers, and the like. Many clubs were based around social, family and business ties, limiting their membership to certain sections of society. Others had open membership policies, but, perhaps intentionally, charged subscription fees that deterred the less well-off from joining.

Compared with cricket, football was still somewhat lacking in organisation and cohesion, with small pockets of activity going on in various areas. There were some representative matches between county or regional sides, but fixtures at all levels were arranged on an ad hoc basis, with little at stake. Games were often cancelled at the last moment, or started later than advertised, as teams failed to turn up on time. Playing conditions were frequently atrocious, with the grass too long to allow even the most basic skills to be displayed.

Results were considered unimportant, and the rules of play were more of a gentlemen's agreement than a fixed code; although this did not stop lengthy arguments from breaking out during games. But the FA was about to take the first crucial steps towards soccer's well-organised modern framework, with its cups, leagues and international matches, led by a busy young man named Charles Alcock.

Charles W. Alcock was born in Sunderland in 1842, into a family that typified the new middle-class breed of self-made industrialists and entrepreneurs. His father, also Charles, was a broker and owner of ships, in a town with a thriving shipbuilding industry. Despite their own comfortable circumstances, the family lived near the town centre, not far from the humbler areas where shipbuilders and other workers lived.

The family moved to London in 1855, and the younger Charles enrolled at Harrow School along with his elder brother, John. Sport, especially football (Harrow-style) and cricket, played an important part in life at the school, under the influence of headmaster Dr Charles Vaughan. Vaughan was a former Rugby pupil, and a disciple of the Thomas Arnold school of Christian, gentlemanly ethics. He believed that sport was valuable in developing character and teaching valuable lessons for future life, and sanctioned the launch of the Philathletic Club in 1852–53, allowing boys to run sporting activities. Vaughan's influence helped bring about a revival in Harrow football, at a time when it had almost died out.

On leaving Harrow in 1859, Alcock emerged as a confident, articulate man, with good social skills and a flair for organisation. He joined his father and elder brother in the family business, while spending his spare time moving in Old Harrovian social and sporting circles. He was a founding member of Forest FC in 1859, along with his brother John, the team captain, who would soon become one of the founders of the FA.

By around 1866, Charles Alcock had become honorary secretary and captain of his club (now known as Wanderers FC), had joined the FA committee, and was showing a strong aptitude for the organisational side of sport – arranging matches, ensuring they went ahead as planned, and communicating information to other players and administrators. In 1867, he called for a renewed effort to establish the FA rules as a common code.

A year later, in his other guise as a writer and editor (he had left the family business by now), Alcock launched the *Football Annual*, initially covering both soccer and rugby – a publication that reflected the game's growth, and promoted debate about the rules and other matters of interest. He became the FA's honorary secretary in 1870, and would remain at its helm for 25 years, a period in which its game would be transformed beyond recognition.

It did not take long for the FA's new leader to make his mark. Alcock published a notice in *The Sportsman,* of which he was now the sub-editor for football, cricket and athletics, in early 1870:

> *A match between the leading representatives of the Scotch [sic]
> and English sections will be played at The Oval on Saturday, 19
> February, under the auspices of the Football Association.*

Interested players were invited to contact the organisers. After a postponement caused by frost, the match was played on March 5, with Alcock himself captaining England. The result was a 1-1 draw. Although it could be regarded as the first international football match in either code, few historians recognise it as such. Some see it as the first *unofficial* international, or *pseudo-international*, while others ignore it completely.

The main sticking point is the way that the Scottish team, if we can call it that, was selected. Soccer players, unlike rugby players, were thin on the ground in Scotland at the time. The 'Scotch' side consisted entirely of London-based players, some of whom had pretty tenuous connections with Scotland: a taste for Scotch whisky, for example, or a habit of going north of the border for a spot of grouse shooting. Just as importantly, they were selected by the FA, with nobody in Scotland having any say in the matter.

Another match was arranged the following autumn, again at the Oval, but this time with a more serious attempt to involve some genuine Scots. Alcock posted an advertisement in the *Glasgow Herald*, appealing for players. The only response came from the Queen's Park club in Glasgow, nominating just one of its members, Robert Smith, who was living in London. England won this time, 1-0.

Unlike the earlier game, this one prompted a reaction in Scotland, but the general feeling among Scots was that a rugby match would be a fairer test of the two nations' footballing strengths. A letter duly appeared in *The Scotsman*, suggesting that ten Scottish-based rugby players should travel to London to team up with ten English-based compatriots, for a match against an English select 'twenty'.

The idea came to nothing at first, but a group of Scottish rugby players came up with another proposal in December 1870: a Scotland v England rugby match, in Glasgow or Edinburgh, featuring the best players from each side of the border. With rugby having no governing body, the challenge was directed to the FA. The Scots suggested that the game could be regarded as a return fixture to the recent soccer match at the Oval. Alcock showed some interest in the idea, but insisted on the teams being eleven-a-side, which the Scots would not accept.

Instead, the challenge was taken up by Blackheath FC, whose secretary, Benjamin Burns, organised a committee to select the England team. A match was arranged for March 27, 1871, at Raeburn Place in Edinburgh. As well as being the first rugby international, it has been referred to as the first *official* international football match of any kind, as both teams were selected by committees based in their respective nations.

In front of a 'large and fashionable assemblage' of somewhere between 2,000 and 4,000 spectators, Scotland triumphed, scoring the only goal of the game, with each side managing a try. The try that led to the goal was hotly disputed by the Englishmen, prompting a comment by the umpire, Loretto School headmaster Hely Hutchinson Almond, which might still find favour in some quarters:

> *When an umpire is in doubt, I think he is justified in deciding*
> *against the side which makes the most noise. They are probably*
> *in the wrong.*

A return match was played at the Oval in February 1872, with England coming out on top. Apart from a few interruptions, the two national rugby (union) teams have met every year since then, with the venue alternating between the two countries. Since 1879, the Calcutta Cup has been awarded to the winners. With the addition of Wales and Ireland, and eventually France and Italy, these encounters evolved into today's Six Nations championship.

The challenge from the Scots had another effect on English rugby. With the FA's influence increasing around the country, and with no real hope for a reconciliation between the two codes, the need for rugby to have its own governing body was becoming more apparent.

Violence and injuries were causing some concern, especially after a Richmond player died in October 1870 from internal injuries sustained in a match. The game had a dangerous, unruly image in many people's eyes, and its followers struggled to portray it as a respectable, gentlemanly pastime. A nationwide authority for rugby, which could clarify the rules, and dish out discipline when necessary, would help to dispel people's fears.

Charles Alcock, foreseeing a future where soccer and rugby would 'live and flourish' in parallel, had a letter published in *The Field* in September 1869, suggesting that an organisation should be set up to establish standard rules for rugby. His idea found some support, and the arrival of international rugby stirred the major London-area clubs into action. Blackheath secretary Benjamin Burns, and his Richmond counterpart Edwin Ash, wrote to the *Times* in December 1870 with a proposal:

> *An opinion has for some time prevailed among the supporters*
> *of Rugby football that some code should be adopted by all clubs*
> *who profess to play the Rugby game, as at present the majority*
> *have altered in some slight manner the game as played at Rugby*
> *School by introducing new rules of their own.*

Secretaries of interested clubs were asked to contact Burns and Ash. A meeting was arranged for January 26, 1871, at the Pall Mall restaurant in London, to be chaired by Richmond captain E.C. Holmes. Representatives of 21 clubs from in and around the capital turned up[11], and agreed to form the Rugby Football Union.

Another Richmond member, Algernon Rutter, was appointed as the RFU's president, with Ash becoming its honorary secretary and treasurer. Rutter, Holmes and L.J. Maton of Wimbledon Hornets – all Old Rugbeians – were asked to draft a set of rules. As well as being familiar with the Rugby School code, all three were aware of the variations that London clubs had adopted.

In contrast with the simple list of 13 rules agreed by the FA in 1863, rugby's rule book was always going to be a complicated affair. Rugby School's code had 37 rules, preceded by a long introduction and six definitions. The game relied on a long-standing tradition of accepted practice, which was understood by Old Rugbeians and many others, but might well have been difficult to put into words.

Progress was slow at first, until Maton suffered a broken leg in a rugby match, and found himself with an unexpected stretch of spare time. Rutter and Holmes offered to give him a generous stash of tobacco if he could finish the task before returning to action. Sure enough, Maton presented a draft set of 59 laws, approved by Rutter and Holmes, to the RFU committee on June 22, ready for a special general meeting two days later. He later claimed to have drawn them up single-handedly. Among the differences from those used at Rugby School were the prohibition of hacking and tripping, a simpler method of converting tries, and a clearer offside law.

Three more 'unofficial' England–Scotland soccer internationals were played in 1871 and 1872, all at the Oval – an indication of how one-sided the arrangements were. From April 1872 onwards, Charles Alcock had little difficulty in securing the use of the Oval. Not content with being the FA secretary, a journalist, a writer and editor of books, and a footballer for Wanderers and England, he became the first paid secretary of Surrey County Cricket Club, the primary users of the Oval.

Alcock was even known to write letters to himself; when C.W. Alcock of the FA wrote to C.W. Alcock of Surrey CCC, requesting the use of their ground for a football match, he must have been pretty confident of getting a positive reply. He would keep his post with Surrey until his death in 1907, and helped to organise England's first home cricket Test match, against Australia in 1880.

In Scotland, soccer was starting to gather momentum. Queen's Park, the first Scottish club, had been formed in July 1867, probably evolving from a group of YMCA members who played informally at the Queen's Park Recreation Grounds on the south side of Glasgow. They dominated the game in Scotland until well into the 1870s, playing for some years without even conceding a goal, and had to travel south of the border to find any serious opposition.

In the autumn of 1872, Alcock contacted the Queen's Park committee, who arranged a Scotland–England match at the West of Scotland Cricket Club in Partick on November 30. It was the first *official* soccer international, as the Scottish side was selected by the Queen's Park committee, the closest thing to a governing body Scotland had at the time. All the chosen players were either members or associates of the club.

A crowd of around 4,000 saw the game, which ended scoreless. English observers were impressed by the Scots' style of play: a 'combination' game with an emphasis on passing and teamwork, in contrast to England's individualistic dribbling approach. A return match was played the following February at the Oval, with England running out 4-2 winners. As in rugby, the meeting became an annual fixture, with Wales and Ireland later joining in, giving birth to the Home International Championship.

Encouraged by the success of the international matches, Queen's Park wanted to take things a step further, by helping to set up a Scottish equivalent of the FA. They invited representatives of other emerging clubs – Clydesdale, Dumbreck, Eastern, Granville, Rovers, Third Lanark Rifle Volunteer Reserves and Vale of Leven – to a meeting in early 1873, where they formed the Scottish Football Association.

Around the same time, the leading lights of Scottish rugby founded the Scottish Football Union. Its six member clubs were all resolutely middle-class institutions, based in Edinburgh and Glasgow. (Half a century later, the distinction between the two Scottish governing bodies finally became a bit clearer, as the rugby organisation changed its name to the Scottish *Rugby* Union.)

The chance to represent their country gave English soccer players a new incentive to improve their skills, and to get themselves noticed by the FA. The clubs, however, still had nothing tangible to play for. In July 1871, Charles Alcock (who else?) put a proposal to his fellow FA committee members that would change all this. Eventually, it would change the face of the game. The proposal was accepted, and minuted as a resolution:

> *That it is desirable that a Challenge Cup should be established*
> *in connection with the Association for which all clubs belonging*
> *to the Association should be invited to compete.*

Alcock's idea was almost certainly inspired by his memories of the annual Cock House knockout tournament at Harrow School, although the competition that the Sheffield FA began staging in 1867 might also have had some influence. It has been suggested that budding cricket legend W.G. Grace, a friend of Alcock's (and arguably one of the pioneers of modern, competitive sport), was involved in thinking up the scheme.

The FA still had a limited influence on football around the country, and hoped the new competition would give wavering clubs a new reason to join and adopt its rules. With the RFU having been founded just a month earlier, the move was also probably intended to establish the FA's supremacy in the wider football scene.

Invitations were sent to member clubs. Another meeting was held in October, to finalise the list of entrants and decide the competition's rules. The committee expected – accurately, as it turned out – that the cup ties would be more competitive than the ad hoc 'friendlies' that had made up the clubs' fixture lists up to then. They were concerned that this might lead to more arguments over decisions, which had previously been left in the hands of team captains. To try to maintain order, they decided that each cup tie would have two neutral umpires to settle disputes between captains, with a referee on hand in case the umpires disagreed on anything.

The clubs rustled up £20 to commission a trophy for the winners, an 18-inch-high silver cup provided by Martin, Hall and Company: the original Football Association Challenge Cup. The tournament, though, got off to an uncertain start. Around 50 clubs had joined the FA by then, but only 15 chose to enter. Many already had full fixture lists for the season, and were reluctant to cancel matches to make way for cup ties. Some also feared that the competitive element of the Cup might spoil the 'gentlemanly' spirit of the game.

Of the 15 clubs that had agreed to enter the competition, three dropped out before it started. Queen's Park (the only club outside the London area to take part, after Donington Grammar School, of Lincolnshire, had withdrawn) were given a bye to the semi-finals, because of the costs and difficulties of travelling between Glasgow and south-east England.

The semi-finals, like the final, were staged at the Oval. After drawing with Wanderers, Queen's Park declined to return to London for a replay, letting their opponents into the final by default. A crowd of 2,000 saw the first FA Cup final on March 16, 1872. In what the *Sporting Life* described as 'a most pleasant contest', Wanderers beat the Royal Engineers by a goal to nil, and their captain – suitably enough, Charles W. Alcock – was the first to raise the trophy.

After this slow start, the FA Cup started to have its intended effects over the next few years. New clubs sprang up around the country at a rapid rate, playing by the FA's rules. Many of them, along with a host of older clubs, joined the FA, which became widely accepted as the authority on how football, of the round-ball variety, should be played and organised. County and district associations were set up, many staging their own cup tournaments. The FA Cup, though, was dominated by familiar names for quite some time. The first seven finals involved just four clubs: Old Etonians, Oxford University, Royal Engineers and Wanderers. It would take a decade before a club from northern or central England reached the final.

In February 1876, a group of businessmen from the Wrexham area discussed putting together a Wales soccer team, hoping to challenge the Scots to a match. They were led by Llewelyn Kenrick, a young solicitor who played for the Druids club in Ruabon. His idea had been prompted by suggestions that a Welsh national *rugby* team should be formed, an idea that would lay dormant for some years.

Kenrick and co. soon founded the Football Association of Wales at a meeting in Ruabon, and arranged a game against Scotland in Glasgow, in March of that year. Druids FC entered the FA Cup the following season, and the Welsh Cup was launched a year later. For the next decade or so, Welsh soccer was dominated by northern clubs, with rugby more prominent in the south.

The Scottish FA set up its own cup competition in 1873–74, as interest in the game continued to grow there. Unsurprisingly, Queen's Park won the tournament the first three times it was held. Within a decade of being formed, the association had 133 members.

Queen's Park helped take soccer to Ireland in 1878, when they and another Scottish club, Caledonians, played an exhibition match at the Ulster Cricket Ground in south Belfast. The game had been arranged by a Belfast businessman, John McAlery, who had come across the sport while on honeymoon in Edinburgh.

A year later, McAlery founded Ireland's first club, Cliftonville FC, in north Belfast. Cliftonville arranged a meeting for representatives of seven Belfast-area clubs at the Queens Hotel in November 1880, and the Irish Football Association was born. Ireland's first international came in 1882, a 13-0 drubbing by England in Belfast. As in Wales, soccer in Ireland would be a mostly northern affair for some time. The Irish FA went on to take control of the game throughout the island, until the partitioning in 1922 led to nearly three decades of bickering between it and the Dublin-based FA of Ireland over jurisdiction.

Soccer's expansion beyond the British Isles took a while to get going, with little of any great significance happening until around the turn of the century. When it did happen, of course, it happened on a phenomenal scale – but that is a story for later.

Although soccer was beginning to flourish in the 1870s, it was far from being the dominant code. The Rugby Football Union had 113 member clubs by late 1874, less than four years after its inception. Twenty-one of them were in northern England, where rugby was growing quickly, with county unions being formed in Yorkshire, Lancashire and Cheshire in the middle of the decade.

The game was getting more coverage in local newspapers, which helped to boost interest. Attendances, although still drawn mainly from the middle classes, were on the rise, especially when clubs from neighbouring towns met. By January 1874, northern rugby had gained enough stature for a North v South match to be held, a fixture that became an annual event, helping to attract even more players to the game.

As covered in chapter 2, rugby reached Ireland when students at Trinity College, Dublin, formed a club in 1854. The North of Ireland

Football Club was founded in 1868, by members of the Belfast-based North of Ireland Cricket Club. Others followed in quick succession by the mid 1870s: Queen's University in Belfast, Lansdowne in the Dublin area (joining Dublin University and Wanderers), University College of Cork, Dungannon in County Tyrone, and Ballinasloe in County Galway.

In December 1874, seven clubs joined forces to form the Dublin-based Irish Football Union (IFU). Just a month later, though, a similar body was set up in Belfast – the Northern Football Union of Ireland, which governed the game in the Belfast area, while the IFU oversaw events in Leinster, Munster and parts of Ulster.

Ireland's first representative inter-provincial rugby match was staged in 1875, pitting Leinster against Ulster, as was its first international, a defeat by England at the Oval. The two unions co-operated to select the team for that game, and merged in 1880 to create the Irish Rugby Football Union. Throughout the island, the game's popularity was mainly confined to the unionist community, while nationalists were generally less receptive to English sports.

In south Wales, rugby clubs were formed in all the major towns in the 1870s. The game's growth in south-western England, centred around clubs such as Gloucester and Clifton, helped to stimulate events across the border. Neath, founded in 1871, is the oldest existing club, and was possibly the first to be formed in the region, although Chepstow and Blaenau Gwent might well have been founded earlier. Newport and Swansea joined them in 1874 (the latter having started as a soccer club two years earlier, then switched to rugby after struggling to find opponents), followed by Cardiff in 1876.

Llanelli's official birth date is 1872, but there is doubt about this, and their first recorded game did not take place until four years later. Old Rugbeians helped to form the club, and Cheltenham College old boys were involved in the clubs that merged to form Cardiff RFC. Although the leading members of the Welsh rugby clubs were from the more affluent parts of society, working-class men – mainly dockers, miners and steelworkers – became increasingly involved in the game, and intense inter-club rivalries began to take shape. It was a trend that would soon be followed, in both rugby and soccer, in other parts of Britain.

In March 1880, delegates from nine rugby clubs in south Wales, led by Newport's Richard Mullock, met in Swansea to discuss forming a Welsh union and national team. Wales's first international came the following February, a heavy defeat by England at Blackheath. There was some criticism of the team selection, with players from west Wales allegedly being unfairly overlooked, prompting another meeting in Neath the following month. Eleven clubs were represented this time, giving birth to the Welsh Rugby Football Union.

The clubs in Glasgow and Edinburgh that had formed Scotland's national union in 1873 were soon joined by an affiliated group of clubs in the Borders region: Gala, Hawick, Kelso, Langholm and Melrose. The rugby boom in these towns might well have been sparked by Queen's Park's decision to cancel a tour of the area in 1872, so that they could travel to London for their FA Cup semi-final. As in south Wales, these clubs featured players from all social classes; the elitist leaders of the Scottish Football Union generally regarded them with a mixture of suspicion and outright disdain.

Although soccer would eventually conquer the world, it was rugby that became the more widespread code outside the British Isles in these early years. Much of this can be attributed to the British army and navy, who mostly preferred the oval-ball game. Members of the armed forces played rugby in Britain's colonies, introducing it to locals. Another factor was the tendency for upper- and middle-class colonial families to send their sons to schools and universities in Britain. Some of these young men would return as keen rugby players, and teach the game to friends and colleagues back home.

It has been said that Australia's first rugby matches were played in Sydney in the 1820s, between soldiers and crews of visiting ships – a claim that perhaps should be taken with a pinch of salt, as the game was in its infancy at that time, and had probably never been played outside the grounds of Rugby School. The first formal matches in Australia under conventional rugby rules probably took place in and around that city in about 1865, with the founding of the short-lived Sydney FC and the more influential Sydney University FC.

The game caught on slowly at first, but was boosted by two matches between the university side and the crew of the visiting HMS *Rosario* in 1869. Nine local clubs, most of whose members were of middle-class stock, came together in 1874 to form the Southern Rugby Union (renamed as the New South Wales Rugby Union in 1892). They were soon joined by others from outside Sydney, a city that would be home to 79 clubs by the turn of the century.

Rugby also became popular, gradually, in Queensland. The Brisbane club was formed in 1867, initially playing Victorian Rules (later known as Australian Rules). An English migrant, Fred Lea, has been credited with converting the city to rugby, shortly after arriving there in 1878. Around this time, Brisbane finally found some local opposition, in the shape of Excelsior and Wallaroo. By 1882, there were several other clubs in the colony, and there was talk of setting up a Queensland union and representative team. The first New South Wales v Queensland match was played in Sydney in August of that year, the start of a great rivalry that still lives on in both rugby union and rugby league.

The Northern Rugby Union was founded in Queensland in 1883. It was renamed as the Queensland Rugby Union ten years later, by which time it had more than 70 clubs. New South Wales and Queensland remained as separate rugby entities for quite some time; there would be no combined Australian team until the turn of the century, and no national governing body for rugby union until 1949. In the late 1880s, rugby began developing in state-run schools, helping to widen its appeal.

New Zealand's proud rugby tradition can be traced back to Charles Monro, son of Sir David Monro, speaker in the House of Representatives. The younger Monro was sent to London to complete his education at Christ's College, Finchley, where he learned the game. In 1870 he returned home to Nelson, at the northern end of the South Island. Nelson Football Club had been using a mixture of soccer and Victorian Rules for some years; the latter would soon briefly pose a threat to rugby in New Zealand. Monro persuaded the club to switch to rugby, which they played against a team from Nelson College in May of that year. Monro also introduced the game to Wellington's football club soon afterwards.

A month after that first match in Nelson, the sailors from the *Rosario*, having helped keep the game alive in Sydney, played a rugby-like game against locals in Auckland. A club was soon formed there, initially using a variation on the Westminster School rules, but soon switching to rugby. Over the next few years, more clubs were set up in the Auckland area, and in other North Island towns such as Hamilton and Wanganui.

Two arrivals from England, A.StG. Hamersley and W.F. Neilson, helped establish rugby in the Canterbury province of the South Island in the mid 1870s. It soon had a presence in all of New Zealand's major towns, quickly becoming well-organised and, in contrast with Australia at this stage, popular with all sections of society. Different rugby styles developed in different regions, such as the passing-based game that emerged in Canterbury in the mid 1870s.

Provincial unions were formed in Canterbury, Wellington, Otago and Auckland in the late 1870s and 1880s, and inter-provincial matches became regular fixtures. The New South Wales team toured both islands in 1882, and an unofficial New Zealand side paid a return visit two years later. A mostly Maori team, known as the New Zealand Natives, went on a troubled, gruelling 14-month tour in 1888–89. They won 78 of their 107 rugby matches in Australia, the British Isles and their homeland (also playing eight games under Victorian Rules, and two soccer matches), displaying an impressive, innovative playing style, and introducing their startled hosts to the *haka*, the Maori war dance.

The New Zealand Rugby Football Union (NZRFU) was formed in 1892. At a time when there was little sense of New Zealand as a nation, the idea came up against resistance from the Canterbury and Otago unions, which were affiliated to the RFU and considered forming a South Island union before joining the NZRFU in 1895. The NZRFU's first official team toured Australia in 1893, wearing all black, as suggested by Thomas Ellison, one of the 1888–89 Maori tourists who had worn that colour. Ellison would go on to write an influential coaching manual, *The Art of Rugby Football*, in 1902.

In South Africa, a form of football found its way to Cape Town in 1861, partly based on the Winchester College game, which allowed players to carry the ball if they were being chased. Winchester old boy Canon George Ogilvie became headmaster at the Diocesan College, often known as the Bishop's School, and introduced the game to his students. Ogilvie was nicknamed 'Gog', based on the only part of his signature that anyone could decipher, and the game known as *Gog football* or *Gog's game* became popular all over the locality.

A Civilians v Military match was played in Cape Town in 1862. The Hamilton club was formed there in 1875, possibly the oldest football club in South Africa (although Swellendam might have been founded as early as 1865), initially using a mixture of rugby and Winchester rules, and played against Villagers the following year. Gog football was the prominent game until around 1878, when Hamilton adopted full rugby rules – a decision that might have been prompted by the arrival of England international William Milton at the club, although it has also been attributed to British troops stationed nearby.

Other local clubs such as Villagers and Gardens soon followed suit, as rugby became Cape Town's dominant code. Six clubs in the area created the Western Province Rugby Union in May 1883, and a tournament was held in the province later that year, won by Hamilton. In a sign of things to come, the first mainly Afrikaans-speaking club was formed that year at Stellenbosch, in farming territory to the east of the city.

In 1884, a combined Cape Town team played against a side from the central mining town of Kimberley, which would become the base of the Griqualand West union, formed in 1886. Other provincial unions were soon set up in Eastern Province and Transvaal, and the South African Rugby Board (SARB) was founded in 1889. An RFU-approved British Isles touring team visited two years later, winning all 20 matches, which included the first three appearances by a South African national side.

South Africa's racial divisions were reflected in its sporting institutions. Although several non-white clubs were formed in Cape Town in the

1880s, the provincial union and the SARB were exclusively white. The Western Province Coloured Rugby Union was set up in 1886, followed by the South African Coloured Rugby Football Board in 1896, and, later, by other unions catering for specific ethnic groups.

Rugby arrived in eastern Canada in the 1860s, introduced by British soldiers. Clubs were soon formed in Toronto, Montreal, Ottawa, Hamilton and Halifax, Nova Scotia. The team from McGill University in Montreal took the game south of the border, teaching it to Harvard students. One of the English pioneers of New Zealand rugby, A.StG. Hamersley, helped to establish the game in British Columbia in the 1880s.

Later, the story started to take a different twist in North America. Towards the end of the 19th century, the game in Canada started picking up elements of the new form of football that was evolving in the United States, rather than sticking to the RFU's laws. Perhaps largely because of this, Canada (and the US) had little involvement in the international rugby scene that was starting to take shape.

The game also cropped up in some countries outside the British Empire. Closest to home, it reached France in 1872, when British students formed a club in Le Havre. Casual games were being played in Paris by 1877, involving Frenchmen as well as British expats, and various colleges in and around the capital took up the game over the next few years. Two multi-sport clubs with rugby sections, Racing Club de France and Stade Français, were formed in Paris in 1882 and 1883 respectively. They began competing for the title of national champions in 1892; the first title match was refereed by future Olympic Games founder Baron Pierre de Coubertin.

Rugby soon spread to the south and south-west, which eventually became its French heartland, in the 1890s. There was no national team until 1906, and no union set up specifically for rugby until 1919; but when France's governing body for sport, the Union des Societés Françaises des Sports Athletiques, was created in 1887, it took responsibility for the game.

Other early outposts of rugby included Argentina, Uruguay, Fiji, Sri Lanka (then known as Ceylon), Tonga and Japan – all places where Britain had either colonial or economic interests.

Soccer's boom in the 1870s, largely driven by the FA Cup, made life tricky for many English rugby clubs. They were finding it harder to attract players and spectators, and feared that their game could become marginalised. Before long, some rugby institutions were looking to follow the FA's lead by running their own knockout tournaments.

William Collins, a rugby player and Cheltenham College old boy, joined the Committee of the United Hospitals in London in 1872, and began pushing for it to launch a rugby cup competition. He finally got his way two years later, as teams from London's ten teaching hospitals began competing for the United Hospitals Challenge Cup, a tournament that still survives.

In 1876, rugby-playing officer cadets at the Royal Military Academy in Woolwich came up with a bigger idea: a cup competition for all members of the RFU. They offered a trophy worth £150 for the winners. The RFU agreed to the idea at first, and began making plans for the competition. But when the Academy's governor heard of the plan, he took exception to it, and the tournament never got off the ground. If it had done, just four years after the launch of the FA Cup, rugby's future might well have turned out very differently.

Yorkshire County Football Club, the county's newly-formed rugby organisation, began staging the Yorkshire Cup in 1877. Even in the early rounds, some ties attracted crowds the organisers could barely have imagined, such as the 8,000 spectators who crammed into Halifax's ground for their first-round match against Wakefield. Halifax won the trophy in December, beating York at Holbeck's ground in Leeds. The competition went from strength to strength in the next few years, reflecting dramatic changes that were starting to take place in football culture.

The South Wales Football Club launched a similar tournament, the South Wales Cup, around the same time. Its competitive nature soon led to concerns about rough play, crowd trouble and poaching of players. The Cheshire County Rugby Union also began running a Challenge Cup in 1877–78, but it attracted little interest, and was scrapped after four seasons, on the grounds that it was 'detrimental' to the game in the county and 'tending to promote bad feeling between clubs'.

In the Scottish Borders, the Melrose club devised the sevens version of the game in 1883, and began staging a tournament in this format. Soon afterwards, some neighbouring clubs launched their own sevens competitions. The Scottish (Rugby) Football Union, zealously opposed to anything that even hinted at professionalism, swiftly stepped in to ban the awarding of prizes to the winners.

Other regional and county cup competitions were launched between 1880 and 1884, in Cumberland, Durham, Northumberland, west Lancashire and the Midlands. But opinion was divided over the idea of tournaments, particularly one that was nationwide. Some rugby followers feared that the old emphasis on 'gentlemanly' endeavour and fair play was in danger of giving way to a must-win mentality, described by RFU honorary secretary G. Rowland Hill as an 'evil spirit'.

Also, in such a physical sport, many thought it essential for players to restrain themselves from no-holds-barred, reckless aggression, and were concerned that the game would become unacceptably dangerous if stakes were raised too high. Another proposal for an RFU challenge cup was put forward in 1881, but was rejected. Largely because of its conservative stance, rugby was losing ground in the battle of the football codes.

Both forms of football evolved rapidly in the 1870s, as teams began taking things more seriously. They were putting more thought into formations and strategies, in contrast with the rough-and-tumble, kick-and-chase approach of earlier years. As mentioned earlier, the Scotland soccer team's performance in their first official international, against England at Glasgow in 1872, made quite an impression on their visitors.

Rather than showing off their individual dribbling skills, as the English were inclined to do, the Scots adopted a more thoughtful, joined-up style of play. They used a 2-2-6 formation – a bit reckless by today's standards, but slightly more cautious than the 1-1-8 and 1-2-7 line-ups that were favoured south of the border. Their defence was well organised, and the forwards worked in pairs. Short passes, and plenty of movement off the ball, were important parts of their game.

Although the Scots won most of the early internationals, English clubs were generally slow to adopt their 'combination' playing style. There were exceptions, though. The Royal Engineers, arguably England's best team for most of the 1870s, were moving in a similar direction, possibly even before 1872. Their formation evolved first from 1-1-8 to 1-2-7, with the forwards organised into set positions, and later into a Scottish-style 2-2-6, and they combined short passing with old-school dribbling. Unlike many of their rivals, the Royal Engineers spent much of their spare time practising.

Sheffield FC had a similarly progressive approach, and might well have pioneered the idea of heading the ball, a practice copied by the Royal Engineers. Teams in the Sheffield area started using the 2-3-5 or 'W' formation in the early 1880s, an idea soon adopted by Cambridge University, and which would later become the norm throughout England until the 1930s (the 3-2-5 variation would then survive until the 1960s).

As the game became more competitive, and teams worked harder at finding ways to win, the FA's simple laws started to look inadequate, especially when it came to enforcing the rules about foul play. In earlier, more casual times, the idea that anyone might deliberately trip an opponent, handle the ball illegally, or break the code in any other way, was not even considered. If a player violated a rule (accidentally, of course), he would simply be expected to step aside and let someone else take possession of the ball. This custom probably had its roots in Harrow football, where a note in the rulebook advised: 'If you inadvertently break a rule ... stand away at once.' (The Harrow rules still state this, although, in these more cynical times, they now make provision for the umpire to punish *deliberate* transgressions.)

The FA Cup, and the early international matches, soon showed up the weaknesses in the laws. In 1873, the FA adopted a Sheffield rule that provided for free kicks to be awarded for handball, an idea that was soon extended to other offences. A year later, the FA decided that every match played under its auspices – not just FA Cup ties – must be officiated by two umpires, and also empowered umpires in FA Cup ties to send players off the field for persistent fouling.

From 1880 onwards, a referee was also required, and was allowed to caution or dismiss players for violent or unsporting conduct. Other features of the modern game were also introduced around this time, all pioneered by the Sheffield association: goal kicks and corner kicks in the early 1870s, and a crossbar, instead of a tape, in 1875.

To some extent, rugby's tactical revolution in this period was led by the university teams of Oxford and Cambridge, where clubs had been formed in 1869 and 1872 respectively. When they met in the first Varsity Match in 1872, they lined up in the usual way: 20-a-side, each with three full-backs, three half-backs and 14 forwards. Three years later, though, the match was played by teams of 15: two full-backs, a three-quarter, two half-backs, and ten forwards.

It was hoped that the smaller numbers – originally a Scottish suggestion – would help to create a more open, attractive and intelligent style of play. Many people began to agree; and, on a more practical level, clubs found it easier to put a team together when only 15 players were needed. Fifteen-a-side had become the norm by 1877, although it would not be written into the laws of the game until 1892.

In the 1881–82 season, Cambridge started using the *wheeling* technique at scrums, which Blackheath had pioneered a few years earlier. Rather than pushing blindly, and trying to kick the ball forwards, they began trying to rotate the scrum to their advantage, and to direct the ball towards their own backs. The reduction in team sizes also helped in this respect: with fewer players in the scrum, the ball could be seen more often, making it easier to manipulate the scrum.

Other changes can be attributed, at least partly, to Oxford University. Like the more progressive soccer teams in the 1870s, they developed a systematic 'combination' style of play, based on teamwork and passing. This was the beginning of a new, scientific approach to rugby, with an emphasis on linking players into an effective unit. It featured short passing by forwards, and long passing by backs. Forwards and backs also passed to each other, creating a new approach to attacking play, and good kickers and tacklers were important to the system. The practice of heeling the ball backwards out of a scrum (rather than kicking it forwards) emerged in Edinburgh school rugby, and was copied by the Oxford students; although not universally approved at first, it was within the rules, and was gradually accepted.

Much of the credit for these improvements has been given to Henry 'Harry' Vassall, Oxford's captain from 1879 to 1881, who was known as a renowned tactician; along with his outside-half Alan Rotherham, who played a key role in their passing game. Cambridge, in turn, were influenced by Oxford's 'combination' approach to open play. Together with the scrum strategy that Blackheath and Cambridge University used, it revolutionised the way the game was played. These ideas were developed further in south Wales in the late 1880s, as an intricate short-passing style began to emerge.

More innovations came in the mid 1880s. Until then, most teams had employed a full-back, three three-quarters, two half-backs and nine forwards. Cardiff, though, sacrificed a forward to make way for another three-quarter. The system worked well, and would start to catch on in the 1890s. Some positions became more specialised than before. Half-backs, for example, were divided into scrum-halves and outside-halves (or stand-off halves). As early as 1882, the forwards at Thornes, a small-town Yorkshire club, were taking up set positions in the scrum. Their wing-forwards stood outside the scrum, waiting to tackle the opposing scrum-halves, or to protect their own.

Along with its tactics, rugby's laws were evolving. Umpires were formally introduced in 1874, but control was still left mainly in the hands of captains. Referees, whose role was to settle disputes between the two umpires, were first used in international matches in 1881, and later began appearing in club matches. Their powers gradually increased, eventually leaving the umpires with a secondary role as touch judges. In 1888–89, as concern about injuries grew, referees were given the power to send players off the field for rough play.

A significant rule was introduced in 1877, requiring a player to put the ball down immediately after being tackled. Until now, tackles had usually been followed by scrums or mauls, which sometimes lasted several minutes. This change, along with the progress in tactics, helped to speed the game up; in Scotland, it encouraged a dribbling style of play. The set scrum, as opposed to the earlier ad hoc scrums (which were more like present-day rucks and mauls), appeared in the rule book in 1879.

Under the Rugby Football Union's original laws, any infringement was followed by a scrum (although the offender could probably expect some kind of retribution, most likely a hack on the shin in the scrum). As with soccer, the rules were initially drawn up on an assumption that players would adhere to the traditionally accepted way of playing the game. In 1882, though, the RFU decided that a tougher approach was needed, and introduced the penalty kick; although it was not possible to score a goal from such a kick until six years later.

As teams developed systematic ways of moving the ball downfield, the simple scoring system, based purely on goals scored, began to look inadequate. A team could execute a well-planned move to take the ball over their opponents' goal-line, only to miss the conversion attempt and come away with nothing.

Two alternatives were suggested to the RFU in 1875. One was a points system, with ten for a goal, five for a try, and one for a 'touch in goal' by the defending team. Under the other scheme, three tries would be equivalent to a goal. The RFU rejected both ideas, but by the end of the year they, along with their Scottish counterparts, had agreed that tries should count as a tie-breaker if a game finished level on goals. The rule was amended two years later: only *unconverted* tries were to count as tie-breakers. A points system was adopted in New Zealand as early as 1875, but the governing bodies in the British Isles were more hesitant. Although various systems were tried out by different unions over the coming years, no consensus was reached.

By this time, the RFU's control over rugby's laws was being challenged. The trouble began in March 1884, when England beat Scotland with the help of a disputed try. The Scottish union wanted the result to be decided by a neutral adjudicator, but the English insisted on the referee's decision being final. Neither side backed down in a hurry, and the stand-off led to the 1885 match between the two being cancelled.

The Irish union proposed forming a committee to settle international disputes. The Irish, Scots and Welsh – without the English – duly created the International Rugby Football Board in 1886 for this purpose. (It was renamed as the International Rugby Board in 1997, and is variously referred to historically as the IB, IRB and IRFB; 'IRB' will be used from here onwards.)

At first, the RFU refused to have anything to do with such a body – mainly because it had far more member clubs than any of the other unions, and was unwilling to share power equally with them. Tensions rose further when the RFU tried to impose its preferred scoring system, and the penalty kick rule, on the other nations for international matches.

The Irish, Scottish and Welsh unions soon wanted the IRB to govern the rules of the game, as well as arbitrating over disputed incidents. The row was finally settled in 1890: the RFU joined the board, on the condition that it would be represented by six delegates, with the other unions having two each. From here onwards, the rules of the game at international level, and increasingly at club level, would be governed by the IRB.

The RFU had finally adopted a points scheme in 1889, based on one used at Cheltenham College. Just one point was awarded for a try, with two more added if it was converted. A drop goal was worth three points, and a successful penalty kick was worth two. A joint IRB decision in November 1891 standardised the system, with two points for a try, three for a conversion or penalty, and four for a drop goal. In March 1893, the English and Welsh unions increased the value of a try to three points, with only two points for the conversion; the IRB followed suit the next year. It was a significant change: a try was now more valuable than a conversion.

In the 1870s and early 1880s, although soccer and rugby were beginning to drift further apart as their rules and styles of play evolved, many clubs around the British Isles still had trouble choosing between the codes. In the West Midlands, where football was being boosted by a boom in trade, it was still common practice for a match to be played according to the home team's preferred code; or on a half-and-half basis, with the two halves of the match being played under different sets of rules (it has been claimed that this was how the idea of half-time came about). It was not unusual for players to spend much of the interval adjusting the goalposts to prepare for the second half.

Villa Cross Wesleyan Chapel Cricket Club, in Birmingham, held a half-and-half trial match against a local rugby club in 1874. After their 1-0 win, with the goal coming in the soccer half of the match, Villa Cross decided that they preferred those rules, and Aston Villa FC was soon up and running. In Coventry, however, a half-and-half match in 1873–74 had a different result, with the players going on to form the rugby-playing Coventry FC. Coventry *City* FC, the soccer club, would start up in 1883 as Singers FC, a team of cycle factory workers.

A group of Rugby School old boys formed a rugby club, Wolverhampton FC (now Wolverhampton Rugby Club), in 1875. Two years later, though, ex-pupils of St Luke's school, in the Blakenhall area of the town, formed a soccer club, St Luke's FC. They became the football section of Wolverhampton Wanderers Cricket and Football Club soon afterwards, and would go on to eclipse their rugby-playing neighbours.

Things were much the same in Yorkshire, but with rugby winning the battle in most areas. Hull White Star FC (later to be involved in a merger that created the present-day Hull FC rugby league club), having trouble finding local opposition in either code, played soccer against Lincolnshire clubs, but usually played rugby against Yorkshire opponents.

Experiments with rugby in Sheffield had little effect, and soccer continued to dominate. The powerful Sheffield FA tried to convert rugby clubs in the west of the county to their own game, with some success in the Leeds area, and they also had a strong influence in Derbyshire.

Rugby clubs sprang up in the north-east in the 1870s, in Newcastle, Tynemouth and South Shields. Meanwhile, the Tyne Association Football Club was formed in Newcastle in 1877, mostly by public school old boys. Other soccer clubs would follow, including Newcastle East End, which would evolve into Newcastle United. The Sunderland and District Teachers Association Football Club was set up in October 1879. A year later, membership was opened up to non-teachers, and the club became Sunderland AFC.

Harrow old boys had quite an impact on the Lancashire football scene, helping soccer to become the preferred code in many areas. Turton FC, near Bolton, was founded in 1872, partly by the Harrow-educated John Charles Kay. Turton even played by the Harrow rules for two seasons, before adopting the FA laws, which they helped to popularise in towns such as Bolton and Blackburn. Ex-Harrow pupils were also involved in the birth of Darwen FC in 1870; however, they played rugby initially, before switching to soccer in 1875.

By around 1880, despite all this uncertainty, the footballing map of Britain was gradually taking shape. Overall, soccer was becoming the more popular game, among both players and spectators – largely because of the competitive stimulus generated by the FA Cup, and the framework provided by the local and district associations.

The rugby scene was more fragmented, and, crucially, was starting to become divided along class lines. Soccer also had other advantages over rugby: it was easier to learn, and was considered safer to play. Rugby still had its strongholds, though – most of Yorkshire, parts of Lancashire, the west country, the southern midlands, south Wales and the Scottish Borders – and it had the upper hand in Britain's 'white settler' colonies. Meanwhile, both codes were beginning to come of age in terms of tactics and skills: at this point we can finally start to regard them as two different sports.

Chapter 4

Pigskin Pioneers

'You men will come to no Christian end!'
– A passing professor at the first intercollegiate football
game in the United States, Rutgers v Princeton, 1869

When the Pilgrim Fathers arrived on the Massachusetts coast in 1620, facing the rigours of a New England winter and wondering what kind of reception to expect from the locals, perhaps football was not uppermost in their minds. Still, although some of their fellow Puritans back in England had been busy denouncing folk football in recent years, it is thought that the Pilgrims took it with them to the New World. They might well have foreshadowed an American tradition, by playing football on their first Thanksgiving Day the following year.

Legend has it that they came across some Native Americans playing a football-like game known as *pasuckquakkohowog*, roughly meaning 'they gather to play a ball with the foot'. As with most early forms of football, this game was played over a vast area (sometimes a mile long and half a mile wide), with very large teams, and was pretty violent.

By this time, though, other British settlers in the American colonies had already brought folk football with them. The first game is believed to have been played in Virginia in 1609. As in Britain, the game's riotous reputation alarmed local authorities, leading to a ban from the streets of Boston in 1657. Thomas Jefferson, one of the Founding Fathers of the United States, was also unimpressed, writing to his nephew Peter Carr in 1785:

> *Games played with the ball, and others of that nature, are too
> violent for the body, and stamp no character on the mind.*

Football in America remained an unruly, anarchic pursuit, frowned upon by the ruling classes, until well into the 19th century. By the 1820s, though, as football was taking shape at England's public schools, it had also arrived at some of the elite universities in the north-eastern United States, which, along with others, would later be known collectively as the Ivy League. The 'rules' were localised and loose, and the game had more in common with the folk football of earlier times than with the more regulated games that were evolving across the Atlantic.

There is evidence of 'foot ball' having been played at Yale University in New Haven, Connecticut, in the late 18th century. At Harvard University, near Boston, a wild game played between first- and second-year students on the first Monday of each academic year had become a regular fixture by 1827. It was known, not without good reason, as *Bloody Monday*. That year, it was commemorated with the epic poem *Battle of the Delta*, written by a student. It has even been suggested that the early Harvard games did not involve a ball.

In New Jersey, students at Princeton University played a version of football known as *ballown* or *balldown*, in which players used their fists and feet to try to direct the ball into their opponents' goal. At Dartmouth College, in Hanover, New Hampshire, *Old Division Football* was established by the 1820s. It was played on a field with goal-lines 185 yards long and 125 yards apart – a goal could be scored by simply kicking the ball over the opponents' line. By the 1840s, football was being played, at least annually, at Columbia University in New York City, Brown University in Providence, Rhode Island, and the University of Pennsylvania in Philadelphia.

The university authorities, with their deeply religious, sombre outlook on life, disapproved of outdoor sport. They saw it as a decadent activity, unbecoming of the 'gentlemen' attending their institutions, and even fretted over the supposed health risks of playing outdoor sports in varying temperatures. Startled by the brutality and chaos of football, and the damage done to university property, Harvard and Yale outlawed the game in 1860, and other universities soon followed suit. Harvard students staged a funeral to mourn the passing of 'Football Fightum', digging a grave and dropping a ball into it.

Needless to say, football in America was not finished. As with British folk football in earlier times, any attempt at banning it proved to be futile. Students needed some way of releasing their youthful energy, and they often did so in the form of fist-fights, or even duels. The more savoury pastime of football began to fight back in the mid 1860s.

A key part in its revival was played by the Oneida Football Club, made up of past and present pupils from some of Boston's elite secondary schools, and named after an Iroquois tribe who had once inhabited the area. Their game, more regulated and less violent than its predecessors, was known as the *Boston Game*.

It had much in common with the football games being played by the upper and middle classes in Britain in this period, when the split between soccer and rugby was still largely unresolved. Kicking was a major part of the Boston Game, but a player could run with the ball in his hands if he was being chased by an opponent, as in the Winchester College rules. Opponents could tackle him by dragging him to the ground, rugby-style.

This was no coincidence: some of the Oneida players had close ties with England, where club captain Gerrit Smith Miller (son of the philanthropist, social reformer and presidential candidate Gerrit Smith) had spent part of his childhood. Oneida played against impromptu 'pick-up' teams on Boston Common, where the club is commemorated today by a granite tablet.

They were unbeaten from 1862 to 1865, with no-one even managing to score against them. The club then disbanded, but some members went on to study at Harvard, and took their game with them. Other Harvard students took a liking to the Boston Game, and the Harvard University Football Club was formed in 1872. The club codified its rules, which had been agreed only verbally until then, and the university soon lifted its ban on football.

Students at other north-eastern universities were also beginning to play organised forms of football, in contrast to the wild rampages that had been stamped out earlier. The rules varied from one college to another, but they were all variations on the soccer rules drawn up by the Football Association in London in 1863, which had been published by Beadle & Company of New York in 1866 (along with a set of rules for rugby, referred to as 'the Handling Game').

Organised sport was increasingly being tolerated, and even encouraged, by college authorities, as they reformed their approach to student life. Rowing had appeared on the Ivy League scene in the 1840s; the first Harvard–Yale race was contested in 1852, starting a strong American tradition of intercollegiate sport. The new, more orderly version of football began to find acceptance at universities in the mid 1860s.

Meanwhile, the end of the Civil War in 1865 gave fresh impetus to the growth of sport in the victorious Union states. Hordes of demobbed soldiers returned north, many of them going to colleges, and were looking for ways of letting off steam. Baseball was booming, and already close to turning professional. On the north-eastern college campuses, the cool autumn climate was ideal for a physical, running-based game, which would also satisfy the demands of the growing cult of muscular Christianity. Football, in one form or another, fitted the bill perfectly.

As the game became more popular, and as the arrival of railways made travel between towns much easier, intercollegiate play was the obvious next step. It was hoped that rivalries between universities would add interest and spice to the game, and that the standard of play would improve as the best players from each college were pitted against each other.

Intercollegiate rivalries were intense in this corner of the country, dating back to the origins of the universities, each with its own religious tradition. Harvard, the first university in the American colonies, was founded by Calvinists in 1636. Yale followed in 1701, as a Congregationalist institution. In 1746, the future Princeton University (initially the College of New Jersey[12]) was established in Elizabeth, near Newark, as a training school for Presbyterian ministers.

Princeton's football players codified their rules in 1867, as did those at Rutgers College in nearby New Brunswick. Two years later, Rutgers challenged Princeton to a series of three games. According to John W. Herbert, a member of the Rutgers team who wrote about the encounter in 1933, they were looking for revenge against Princeton for a 40-2 thumping in a baseball game.

The first game was played on November 6, 1869, in New Brunswick. Rutgers captain William J. Leggett proposed a set of rules, which were accepted by his Princeton counterpart, William S. Gummere, later to become Chief Justice of the New Jersey Supreme Court. Although the rules were quite similar to those drawn up by the FA six years earlier, they did not include all of the changes and clarifications that had been adopted in England since then.

Each team had 25 players, rather than 11. The game had no time limit: instead, it was to continue until one team had scored six goals. Whereas handling had been eradicated from English soccer earlier that year (goalkeepers excepted), players in these Rutgers–Princeton games were allowed to catch the ball, and to 'bat' it with their hands, although carrying and throwing were forbidden.

Around a hundred spectators turned up for the opening game, sitting either on the ground or on a fence surrounding the field. There was even organised cheering, conducted by a group of visiting Princeton students with their 'rocket' cheer: 'Hooray! Hooray! Hooray! Tiger sis-boom-ah [imitating an exploding rocket], Princeton!', a precursor to today's cheerleader squads and college football 'fight songs'.

The game was a contrast in styles and athletic abilities. The Rutgers players, resplendent in scarlet 'turbans', were generally smaller, but quicker and with better kicking skills. Princeton relied more on muscle and height. Rutgers needed just five minutes to score the first goal, but Princeton soon fought back, most notably using Jacob E. 'Big Mike' Michael as a battering ram, bursting through the massed Rutgers defence to create gaps, giving his teammates chances to shoot at goal. With the score tied at 4-4, Leggett told his Rutgers colleagues to keep the ball low, to neutralise Princeton's height advantage. It worked, and Rutgers scored the two decisive goals to win by 6-4.

In the return game at Princeton a week later, the hosts counteracted Leggett's tactics with their own strategy, involving high kicks and catches, and coasted to an 8-0 win. But the final game, to be played at Rutgers, was cancelled. The authorities at both colleges, concerned about the amount of attention that the first two games had attracted, refused to let it go ahead.

The ball from the first game is on show at the American Soccer Hall of Fame in Oneonta, New York. But the occasion is also commemorated, albeit with an asterisk, in the Pro Football Hall of Fame in Canton, Ohio, where it is referred to as both the first 'soccer' game *and* the first 'football' game between two American college teams. Some might find this contradictory, but it simply reflects the state of flux that the football world was in at the time, and the fact that the word 'football' has different meanings in different contexts. Some American historians have disputed the claim that this was the first intercollegiate football game in the US, but the game played on that day certainly *was* football – it just was not the distinctive American brand of football that would evolve later.

A year later, Princeton beat Rutgers on home turf again, and Rutgers introduced Columbia into the fray, defeating them 6-3 at home. Columbia's first captain was Stuyvesant Fish, son of Hamilton Fish, the Secretary of State. But these were the only two intercollegiate games played in 1870, and there were none at all the following year. College authorities were still uneasy about the level of violence in the game. It was safer and better organised than the mob football they had banned in the early 1860s, but was still crude, and largely reliant on brute force, with few rules to control rough play.

Even though intercollegiate football was getting off to a slow start, the game was quietly continuing to develop locally at various colleges. In 1870, a football association was formed at the new Cornell University in upstate New York (where the players soon demonstrated their game to Thomas Hughes, author of *Tom Brown's Schooldays*). Stevens Institute of Technology (usually known as Stevens Tech) of Hoboken, New Jersey, began intercollegiate play in 1872. So did Yale, whose home game against Columbia that year drew a crowd of around 4,000, each paying 25 cents for admission. The revival of Yale football has been credited to David S. Schaff, a student who had spent a year at Rugby School.

The game was also catching on in other parts of the country, particularly the Midwest, although no teams from that region would meet opponents from the north-eastern states for quite a while. Long-distance travel was evidently something of a sticking point. In 1873, the Cornell players hoped to visit Cleveland, Ohio, to play against the team from the

University of Michigan. Cornell president Andrew White, though, was having none of it. 'I will not permit 30 men to travel 400 miles to agitate a bag of wind,' he sniffed, not quite getting into the spirit of things.

As had been the case in England, football's growth was being hampered by the variations in rules. Kick-offs were often delayed by long arguments about which laws would be followed. The problem was solved, up to a point, when delegates from Princeton, Rutgers and Yale met in New York in October 1873, to draw up a simple set of 12 rules. Like the rules used in the Rutgers–Princeton series in 1869, it has been said that these were closely based on those of the FA, but they were actually quite different from the FA rules of the time.

Players were not allowed to carry or throw the ball, but could touch the ball with their hands. There was no mention of goalkeepers. Teams were still large, with 20 players per side, and the game would continue until a team had scored six goals, or until darkness fell. There was no offside rule, and there was an eccentric method of restarting play after a foul, or when the ball went out of play: the player responsible had to throw the ball 12 feet into the air.

It might have seemed that collegiate America was well on its way towards establishing soccer, or at least a form of soccer, as one of its main sports. But there was something missing: Harvard, the nation's most prestigious and influential university, was not at the party. Harvard's football players had taken a liking to the Boston Game, with its carrying, throwing and rugby-style tackling, and had worked hard at developing skills and tactics for it.

Although they liked some aspects of the soccer-oriented game that was emerging at other colleges, they refused to give up the rugby elements which had been essential in shaping the game they enjoyed so much. As a result, the Harvard men did not send a representative to that meeting in New York (neither did Columbia, although they had initially agreed to do so). For the near future, they would be isolated from the intercollegiate football scene – a scene that badly needed them.

The role played by Montreal's McGill University in the history of North American sport has been, to put it mildly, a big one. The first recorded indoor ice hockey game, in 1875, involved two McGill teams; two years later, McGill students formed the first organised club, and drew up the rules for what would become Canada's favourite sport. James Naismith, a McGill graduate, invented basketball in Springfield, Massachusetts, in 1891, and McGill staged Canada's first intercollegiate basketball game in 1904.

When rugby was introduced to Canada by British soldiers and sailors in the early to mid 1860s – a period when it was gradually becoming distinct from soccer, but still had no standard rules – McGill was one of the first Canadian institutions to adopt it. And when the Harvard football players went looking for suitable opponents, after rejecting the soccer-like game of their American peers, they found them north of the border, in the shape of McGill's rugby team.

McGill captain David Rodger challenged Harvard to a pair of games in the spring of 1874, and the 'formal but courteous' challenge was eagerly accepted by his opposite number, Harry Grant. Both games would take place on Harvard soil. The first would be played under the home team's Boston rules, the second under McGill's rugby code. Harvard would pay a return visit to Montreal in the autumn.

The first game was played on May 14 at Jarvis Field, Cambridge. McGill had a wealth of athletic talent at their disposal, with three of Canada's leading sprinters in Duncan E. Bowie, R.W. Huntington and Henry Joseph, but struggled to adapt to the Boston Game's restrictions on running with the ball. In the terminology of the day, vaguely similar to that of tennis, each goal marked the end of a 'game', after which the teams would change ends and start a new game. The first team to win three games would win the 'match'.

Goals were scored by kicking the ball between the goalposts and *over* the crossbar. Harvard won easily, scoring the requisite three goals in just 22 minutes. The next day, even though the Harvard men were unfamiliar with many aspects of rugby, such as offside and drop-kicks, they held McGill to a scoreless tie in the allotted 90 minutes of play.

McGill's version of rugby was similar, but not identical, to the code that the Rugby Football Union had published three years earlier. One notable difference was that touchdowns (as the McGill players called them) were to be used as a tie-breaker if the teams were level on goals scored. Under the RFU rules of the time, results were decided purely on goals, although the tie-break rule would be adopted just a year later.

The Harvard players were encouraged by their performance in the second game, and by the excitement it had generated around the campus. They swiftly put aside their reservations about rugby, which some of them had once dismissed as 'wholly unscientific and unsuitable to colleges'. They would soon forget about the Boston Game, as they embraced rugby wholeheartedly, and hoped to persuade their peers at other American universities to follow suit.

First, though, they happily honoured their agreement to return to Montreal in October, and beat McGill at rugby, 3-0 on touchdowns. The second game, to be played under Harvard's rules, was cancelled. By now, neither team cared much for the Boston Game. Instead, the McGill students treated their visitors to an extravaganza of dining, dancing and fox hunting.

The next American university to take up rugby was Tufts, a neighbour of Harvard's. Tufts and Harvard played against each other in June 1875, the first rugby match between two US college teams. Some historians regard this, rather than any of the soccer-like matches that had been played since 1869, as the first American college football game. Tufts won by a goal to nil, but Harvard are thought to have made another small piece of football history by becoming the first American team to wear uniforms, sporting the university colours: white shirts and trousers, with crimson trimming and socks.

The Harvard students were eager to play against the other elite universities, rather than the lowlier likes of McGill and Tufts. Their prime target was Yale. With a record of six wins and one defeat over the three seasons from 1872 to 1874, they were the team to beat. But, now that Harvard had replaced the hybrid Boston Game with rugby, the gulf between their football code and the soccer-oriented game favoured by Yale, Columbia and Princeton was even wider than before. The argument that had broken out in London a decade earlier, over whether the kicking game or the ball-carrying game best represented what football was all about, was being repeated across the Atlantic.

Despite this, both Harvard and Yale were eager for a game to be arranged. Representatives of the two universities held a meeting, and came up with what became known as the *Concessionary Rules*. Harvard, though, conceded far less than Yale. They backed down on the scoring system, allowing the game to be decided solely on kicked goals, rather than including touchdowns in the scoring. But the game was essentially rugby, with no restrictions on carrying the ball, or on throwing it backwards or sideways.

It would also be played 15-a-side, whereas Yale preferred 11 – a preference that seems to have stemmed from a game against a visiting English team of Eton old boys in December 1873. They believed that the smaller team size would make for a more open game, and would help in persuading the faculty authorities to let them travel to games.

The first Harvard–Yale clash was held on November 13, 1875, on Yale's home turf in New Haven, Connecticut. To nobody's surprise, Harvard ran out 4-0 victors. A crowd of 2,000 showed up, earning a pay day of $500 for each university – in Harvard's case, more than enough to cover their travel costs. The teams met up for a post-game dinner and sing-along, which appears to have got a little out of hand: a newspaper reported that seven Harvard students were arrested that night, for 'creating disturbances and hooting and singing in the public streets'.

This fixture, repeated almost every year since 1875, became such a major event that it came to be known simply as 'The Game'. Yale liked the rugby aspects of the rules, and, although they fulfilled their commitments under the old soccer-like laws for the rest of the 1875 season, they adopted rugby the following year.

Two Princeton students, W. Earle Dodge and Jotham Potter, were among the crowd at this first Harvard–Yale game. Back at Princeton, they raved about rugby, and the word began to spread around campus. In November 1876, with the season still in progress, Dodge and Potter proposed a conference involving representatives of Columbia, Harvard and Yale, along with themselves, to work out a common set of rules, along rugby lines.

The laws agreed at the gathering in Springfield, Massachusetts, were close to those of the Rugby Football Union[13], the only major difference being the scoring system. Yale still wanted results to be decided on goals alone, and Columbia agreed; but Harvard and Princeton insisted that touchdowns should also count. A compromise was reached, with a goal being equivalent to four touchdowns. In a drawn game, a goal from a touchdown conversion would take precedence over four touchdowns. There was still no points system; instead, the score would be recorded by stating how many goals and touchdowns each team had registered (for example, 'Yale 2g, 5t – Columbia 1t').

At the same meeting, Columbia, Harvard and Princeton formed the Intercollegiate Football Association (IFA). Yale, unhappy with the scoring system and the 15-a-side rule, declined to sign up, but continued playing against members of the IFA, which they would eventually join in 1879. After the 1876 agreement, soccer – or, at least, the American universities' version of it – disappeared from the college sports scene. British-style soccer, which essentially became the international version, would not emerge at US universities until the early 20th century, although it was played at amateur and semi-professional levels, mostly by immigrants, throughout the late 19th century and beyond.

We should bear in mind that the 'soccer' which these college students rejected in the 1870s was still a primitive form of the game. Even in England, the concepts of passing and teamwork did not catch on until the middle of that decade, when Scottish innovations were adopted. Given this, along with the crowded field of around 40 players, the lax rules regarding foul play, and the misshapen and poorly-inflated balls that were often used, it is unlikely that the game was particularly attractive to watch. Much of the action in the first Rutgers–Princeton game in 1869 was described in the Rutgers students' newspaper, the *Targum*, as 'headlong running, wild shouting, and frantic kicking'.

It could be argued that soccer arrived in America too early, at a time when it was in a crude, formative state. A more advanced, more appealing form of the game would reach other shores around the turn of the century, with much greater success. The reasons why these American students preferred rugby, though, are open to speculation. In *Offside: Soccer and American Exceptionalism*, Andrei Markovits and Steven Hellerman suggest that the Harvard students might have been trying to emulate their English peers at Oxford and Cambridge, who supposedly regarded rugby as the 'proper' sport for young men of their elite background[14].

Whatever led the Harvard team to choose rugby, perhaps the students at the other Ivy League universities followed suit simply because they wanted to keep up with their Harvard rivals on the social ladder. Another possible explanation lies in the technical differences between the two games. Rugby allowed players to keep firm control of the ball by holding onto it, giving more scope for captains (or, later, coaches) to devise tactics and schemes, in contrast to the less predictable nature of soccer. This might have encouraged the Ivy League students to see rugby as a more scientific game, better suited to such well-educated men as themselves.

Although rugby became the football game of choice at these universities, it seems that the word 'rugby' never found a lasting place in the students' vocabulary. They simply saw the game as a version of football, which, of course, it was. The word 'football' was already firmly established among Americans who played and followed the game, and was not going to go away.

There was something a little contrary about the American universities' adoption of this English game in 1876. It was the centenary year of the United States' independence, and in many aspects of life, the young country was striving to shake off its colonial past and forge its own identity.

Some believe that this sentiment had already made its mark on American sport. In the mid 1850s, cricket was the most popular team sport in the north-eastern US, particularly in New York and Philadelphia (albeit in an era before sport began attracting mass audiences). But the game was fiercely protected by the affluent English migrants who ran the clubs, with Americans largely excluded from playing. In *The Tented Field*, an account of cricket's rise and fall in the US in the 19th century, Tom Melville argues that the game fizzled out because it failed to take on an American identity, something which baseball achieved spectacularly (helped by some mythologising about the game's history, which obscured its roots in English bat-and-ball games).

Perhaps these questions of national identity were of little concern to those Ivy League football players in the 1870s. Many of them had close links with England, and almost certainly would have felt an affinity with their counterparts at Oxford and Cambridge. But the prevailing mood among less privileged Americans was one of independence, with a desire to leave their (mainly) European backgrounds behind, and carve out new lives in a new land.

It seems unlikely that English-style rugby, which the colleges stuck with for the rest of that decade, could have ever have become popular with the wider American public. But there were changes ahead, which is why it is worth bringing up something else that happened in 1876: a student by the name of Walter Camp enrolled at Yale University.

Walter Chauncey Camp was born in Connecticut in 1859. Despite his relatively slight build, he developed a reputation as a fine athlete in his days at Hopkins Grammar School in New Haven. Soon after arriving at Yale, Camp became a half-back in the university football team, proving to be a superb runner, tackler and kicker.

As well as his talent for playing the game, Camp became renowned for his thoughtful approach to it. Historian Parke Davis described him as 'resourceful, courageous, thinking continually in terms of football, swiftly solving new situations, and indomitable.' Rugby football was a new game to these students, and they were trying to develop techniques and strategies without any guidance from coaches. The stage was set for Walter Camp, the thinking football player, to make an impact.

Yale captain Eugene Baker soon began to treat Camp as an equal partner. In Camp's undergraduate years, 1876 to 1879, they won 13 games, tied four, and lost just one. He played a major role in their success, and captained them in the last two of these seasons. After graduating in 1880, Camp stayed on at Yale as a medical student.

Eligibility rules in college football were rather loose at the time, and Camp remained in the team for three more seasons. He had attended college football's annual conventions since 1878, and would stay on the Rules Committee until his death in 1925. At these meetings, he campaigned relentlessly for changes to the rules of the game. By 1880, Camp's seniority was adding weight to his arguments, and Yale had signed up as an IFA member. Now, he began to get results.

The switch to rugby in 1876 hadn't stopped the persistent disagreement and dissatisfaction over the rules, and change was in the air, with Walter Camp leading the way. First on his agenda was the contentious issue of team sizes. He pushed for a reduction from 15 to 11, something which other Yale representatives had long been pursuing.

The Princeton contingent, apparently renowned for a degree of arrogance, were against the idea. The congested 15-a-side game had helped them to grind out scoreless draws against Yale, their strongest opponents, in 1877 and 1879, thereby remaining unbeaten and retaining the championship[15] in each of those years. Their protests drew little sympathy, and the wider view – that a change to 11-a-side would increase scoring and make the game more attractive to watch – won the day, with the rule finally being amended in October 1880.

Another thorny topic was the scrum. Its outcome was too unpredictable for many captains' liking, making it difficult for them to devise schemes for advancing the ball or winning possession. Looking for a more orderly way of restarting play, Camp introduced the idea of a *scrimmage* in 1880.

The change of wording from 'scrummage' to 'scrimmage' may have been subtle, even meaningless, but the new rule was a radical departure. After each tackle, rather than being bound together, rugby-style, in a mass of bodies, the teams would line up on either side of an imaginary *line of scrimmage* at the spot where the tackle took place. The ball would be placed on the ground at that point, and a player from the team in possession would either kick it forwards, or *snap* it backwards with his heel. The man immediately behind him, who would gather the ball after a backward snap, was to be known as the *quarterback*. At first, the quarterback was not allowed to carry the ball forwards after collecting a snap[16.]

Camp's proposal was approved, and the 1880 conference had another major result. The back-heeled snap was soon thought to be a little too awkward, but the rule would stay the same for ten years, until it was changed to allow the ball to be snapped backwards out of the hands.

With the new rules in place, teams began inventing offensive formations and strategies. Each team had a forward line of, typically, six or seven players (*linemen*), who would face their counterparts at the line of scrimmage. Behind them was a quarterback, trailed by some combination of halfbacks and fullbacks, who would do the bulk of the ball-carrying and kicking. Walter Camp devised what became the definitive offensive line-up for decades to come: the *'T' formation* of seven linemen, a quarterback, two halfbacks and a fullback.

Another rule change came about after Princeton had unveiled a new tactic against Harvard in 1879. While one of their players was carrying the ball, others would block opponents with their outstretched arms, helping to clear a path for him. It was against the rules of rugby, as it still is (partly because of its offside law, which appears to have been either ignored or gradually phased out in the collegiate American game). But the referee, one Walter Camp, merely gave them a warning. Camp soon taught his Yale men to use the same tactic, and it became an accepted part of the game.

The first big steps in the evolution of American football, as distinct from English rugby, had been taken, but there were plenty more to come. The idea behind the scrimmage rule was to make the flow of play more predictable; unfortunately it turned out to be *too* predictable.

If a team failed to make good progress after several attempts at advancing the ball, they would usually try either to kick a field goal (if they were close enough to the goalposts), or to punt the ball downfield (conceding possession, but forcing their opponents to retreat). But there was nothing in the rules to enforce this, and it was not always beneficial.

Princeton's strategists realised that the team in possession could keep the ball almost indefinitely, if they wanted to, without moving it far down the field. The quarterback simply had to receive the ball from the snap, take a couple of steps forwards, roughly to the spot where the ball had been snapped; and then go to ground before any opponent could strip it from his hands. Barring any fumbles, this tactic would virtually wipe out any possibility of either team scoring. For a team trying to defend a lead, or to hold out for a tie, it had its obvious attractions. For their opponents, and for the spectators, it was infuriating.

The *safety* rule made things even worse. If a ball-carrier was tackled behind his team's goal-line, that team would then restart play from its own 25-yard line. This effectively allowed a team, when backed up near its own goal-line, to advance a long way forwards by taking a few steps backwards.

When Princeton faced Yale in the 1880 championship decider, they were unbeaten that season, and determined not to lose this record to their strongest rivals. They believed a tie would be enough for them to keep the title, on the grounds that they would finish the season undefeated, although the rules governing all this were a little hazy.

Each time Princeton had the ball near their own end of the field, captain Francis Loney refused to punt it and concede possession to Yale. Instead, on 11 occasions, he carried the ball back over the goal-line and went to ground, taking a safety, which allowed his team to march back up to their 25-yard line. The result: a 0-0 tie, a happy bunch of Princetonians, and a lot of scowling from everybody else. Princeton claimed to have retained their title, but the IFA refused to name anyone as champions that year.

This debacle led the Rules Committee to make more changes. Overtime was introduced, to reduce the chances of a tie. There would be two overtime periods, then known as *innings*, of 15 minutes each. If the score was still tied after overtime, the team which had taken the fewer safeties would win. But Princeton were determined to use stifling tactics when it suited them, and found a loophole in the safety rule. If a ball-carrier was brought down behind his goal-line, but outside one of the sidelines, this would be counted as a *touch-in-goal* rather than a safety, and his team would restart play from their 25-yard line. Unlike a safety, a touch-in-goal would not count against them as a tie-breaker.

A year after grinding their way to that scoreless tie, Princeton again met Yale in their last game of the season. A tie would leave both teams unbeaten, and Princeton again insisted that this would be enough for them to retain the championship (even though they weren't officially the champions to begin with). Needless to say, their view was not widely shared, but they went into the game with a tie in mind.

After securing possession early on, Princeton spent the rest of the first half using their latest spoiling tactic. They exploited the touch-in-goal rule by repeatedly throwing the ball behind their goal-line and wide of the sideline; then restarting from 25 yards out, and running a few short, uneventful plays before doing it all over again. Yale, and the spectators, were unimpressed.

Still, Yale captain Walter Camp, a pragmatist as much as anything else, told his team to take the same approach in the second half, and subsequently through the first overtime period (the second was abandoned because of darkness), leaving the game tied at 0-0. The IFA, possibly tiring of Princeton's antics, awarded the championship to Yale on the strength of their performance in a win over Harvard.

After that infamous 'Block Game' in 1881, it was clear that more changes were needed. Some suggested reverting to the English rugby rules, but Camp had another idea. At the IFA's annual convention in October 1882, he proposed another change which would go a long way towards defining American football.

The team in possession would have three *downs* (attempts at advancing the ball) in which to gain a total of at least five yards. Each down would start from the position where the previous one had ended. If they achieved this, or if they lost at least ten yards, they would keep the ball and start again with a fresh set of three downs. If they failed, their opponents would gain possession at the spot where the third down had ended.

The new rule was agreed. To help officials in measuring the yardage gained or lost, lines were drawn across the field at five-yard intervals. The *gridiron* layout was born, its name coined by Princeton's Ned Pearce at the 1882 convention after he heard Camp's proposal. Suddenly, by accident, American football had become a game of numbers. The seeds had been sown for a profusion of statistics such as rushing yards, yards-per-carry, and many more that would later be devised when forward passing was allowed. In this respect, it found common ground with baseball, the nation's favourite team sport of this era.

This measurability encouraged a more systematic, analytical approach to the game. Camp has been compared with a contemporary of his, Frederick Winslow Taylor, the 'father of scientific management'. Taylor, a Pennsylvania-based industrial engineer, devised production systems to maximise the efficiency of factory workers and machinery, using time and motion studies. Among other things, his methods involved recognising and rewarding the achievements of individuals within a collective framework – an approach that was also becoming evident in American football, with its emphasis on both individual and team statistics.

Camp was breaking football down into its basic elements, and looking to improve each one as far as possible: the same process that Taylor was following for factory production. Both men were revolutionising their respective fields with highly methodical ways of thinking. In *Offside*, Markovits and Hellerman also argue that American football's complex and restrictive rules were necessary in a country whose people had a wide range of national and ethnic backgrounds. They contend that the game could not afford to rely on a common, assumed understanding between players, coaches and spectators about how it should be played – something which was possible in Britain at that time, with its relatively uniform culture.

There was one more bone of contention: the scoring system. Kicked goals were still the primary means of deciding results, but there was confusion and disagreement over how different types of scoring – touchdowns, conversions, field goals and safeties – were to be weighed against each other. Things came to a head in November 1882, when Harvard scored a field goal and an unconverted touchdown, against Princeton's converted touchdown. The referee ruled that Harvard's field goal took precedence over Princeton's touchdown conversion, and declared Harvard the winners. Princeton refused to accept his decision, and claimed victory for themselves.

The next year, Walter Camp (now working at the New Haven Clock Company, but also as an advisory coach for the Yale team) solved the problem with yet another innovation, similar to one that would be introduced in rugby in the British Isles a few years later. Points would be awarded for each type of scoring, ending the confusion once and for all. A field goal would earn five points. Two would be awarded for a touchdown, with four more added for a successful conversion. A safety would score one point, for the team attacking the end where it was conceded.

By now, the other delegates at these conventions were well aware that Camp generally knew what he was doing, and accepted his proposal. One significant feature of this system was that a converted touchdown was worth more than a field goal. Slowly but surely, carrying the ball, in relation to kicking, was becoming more important. Just two months later, the trend continued with another change: a touchdown was now worth four points, with just two for the conversion. The score for a safety was also increased to two points.

Other notable changes were made in the 1880s. The field dimensions were reduced, from 140 by 70 yards to 110 by 53$^{1}/_{2}$. By the middle of the decade, certain types of offences were being punished by moving the ball backwards or forwards by a given number of yards. Timekeeping was tightened up, with referees making allowances for stoppages caused by scoring, injuries and arguments (a game still consisted of two 45-minute halves). From 1889, referees were equipped with stopwatches, a decision possibly brought on by Camp's employment with a clock company; the game's timing rules would become ever more intricate in future years.

Tactics were rapidly becoming more sophisticated. Captains started using coded signals, or *play-calling*, to give instructions to their teammates, a practice first used by the University of Michigan. Soon the quarterback would take over the play-calling duties, and would sometimes use physical signals, such as a tap on the side of the head, instead of verbal ones. *Trick plays* entered the tactical repertoire. The first was Yale's fake field goal against Princeton in 1882: they lined up as if to attempt a kick at goal, but instead, quarterback Henry Twombley shouted the coded signal 'Cheese it!', took the snap, and threw the ball outside to Charles 'Doc' Beck, who ran past the bemused defenders for a touchdown.

With the increased emphasis on tactical planning, players' roles became more specialised and clearly defined. The role of the quarterback – who still was not allowed to carry the ball forwards after receiving a snap (and, like everyone else, couldn't yet throw it forwards) – was still rather limited. Instead, the first stars of the game were mainly halfbacks and fullbacks, renowned for their running and kicking exploits.

One of them was Yale captain Henry Ward Beecher, with 19 touchdowns and 33 conversions in 1887. Princeton had Alexander Moffat, who kicked 32 field goals in 1883, despite his diminutive stature which earned him the nickname 'Teeny-bits'; along with John T. Haxall, whose 65-yard field goal from placement[17] in 1882 remained a collegiate record for 94 years, and has never been equalled in the National Football League.

During the 1880s, teams began holding organised training and practice sessions, and taking care of their diets. Professional coaches were hired, along with medical and physical training staff. Walter Camp had his Yale players training and practising daily; his wife Alice was even known to help out with devising strategies and briefing the players.

Playing equipment, though, was still pretty basic. The players' clothing varied wildly, although a type of laced canvas jacket known as a *smock*, introduced by Princeton in the 1870s, had been widely adopted. Underneath these, the Princetonians wore black jackets with orange stripes on the sleeves, a pattern that was matched on their socks, earning them college football's first nickname, the Tigers. Few players wore padding, and helmets were unheard of. Some used a more natural (but apparently not very effective) way of protecting their heads, by growing thick hair, eerily making some photographs from the late 19th century look almost as if they could have been taken in the 1980s. Others wore nose guards, in the style of soldiers in the Norman Conquest era.

In 1888, Camp was behind yet another rule change. Until now, tackling had been allowed only at waist level or above, but now it was permitted as low as the knees, a change that would dramatically affect the way the game was played. Offensive play had involved plenty of lateral and backward passing, often using the full width of the field. But this change made it easier to force an opponent to the ground, thereby making it harder for the team in possession to use the expansive passing and running style of earlier years.

Instead, teams started using narrower formations, where the main task for a ball-carrier's teammates was to block opponents, creating gaps for him to run through. Rather than trying any intricate passing or lateral running routes, the ball-carrier would simply try to run as far forward as possible, which usually was not very far. The 'three yards and a cloud of dust' approach had arrived, and would dominate the game for decades to come.

Perhaps it would be harsh to say that Camp had lost his magic touch, but this particular development certainly had mixed results. It reinforced football's status as a robust, 'manly' sport. This had its attractions for many of the game's followers (and still does), but came at a terrible price. Heads were now coming into contact with knees, often at high speed, and sometimes with ugly results. Over the next 20 years or so, the level of brutality would escalate to a frightening degree, with serious injuries and even deaths becoming commonplace. Passing and kicking became minor parts of the game; power became more important than skill.

There were no rules governing the number of players at the line of scrimmage, or restricting movement before the snap. This allowed teams to use *mass* and *momentum* offensive plays, where most of the players would line up well behind the line of scrimmage, and then charge forwards. The mass of bodies would bulldoze its way through the opposition, leaving space for the ball-carrier to run through. To achieve this, the players would form a solid line, sometimes by linking arms, but sometimes by more imaginative methods: one team had suitcase handles attached to their uniforms, allowing players to hold on to their teammates.

One of the earliest of these moves was the *V-trick*, or *V-wedge*. This was a terrifying kick-off routine in which the kicker 'inch-kicked' the ball and picked it up himself (there was no minimum distance for kick-offs at the time), then handed it back to a teammate, who was protected by a forward-pointing V-shaped formation as it surged downfield, overpowering anyone in its path.

This led to the *flying wedge*, introduced by Harvard in 1892: a manoeuvre used not only at kick-offs, but also in plays from scrimmage. The various wedge plays were inspired by Napoleonic military tactics, based on a principle of concentrating the maximum force at a given point. Similar defensive schemes were introduced to counteract the wedge plays, making the collisions even more violent.

Players were not only prepared to risk injuring their opponents: teammates were fair game as well. Another particularly reckless move was the *hurdle play*, credited (if that's the right word) to Columbia coach George Sanford, in which the ball-carrier was lifted off the ground by colleagues, and thrown over the opposing defensive line. Some teams even tried to counter this by launching one of their own players into the air as a 'defensive missile'.

Punch-ups at the line of scrimmage became a matter of routine, and biting was not unheard of. Gruesome facial injuries, as well as broken bones, were a regular occurrence. An attempted touchdown would often result in a fierce *maul-in-goal*, as defenders tried to prevent the runner putting the ball on the ground. This led to a rule change in 1889, allowing a 'touchdown' to be scored without the ball actually being touched down.

Perhaps it is surprising to learn that this carnage can be largely attributed to changes proposed by Walter Camp – a comparatively slender man, who had specialised in the more skilful aspects of the game in his playing days, and who reportedly gave up his medical studies because he couldn't stand the sight of blood.

As concern grew over the dangers of the game, Camp's rules committee introduced new disciplinary measures during the 1880s, including one that empowered the referee to dismiss a player from the game after issuing two warnings. More changes came in 1894, restricting mass and momentum plays by requiring the offensive team to have at least seven men at the line of scrimmage, and prohibiting its players from moving before the ball was snapped. But many teams simply came up with new mass and momentum plays, and brute force continued to rule the game.

Although American football's best-known teams were college-based, the game became hugely popular in the 1880s and early 1890s. The annual championship-deciding games, held in New York on Thanksgiving Day, drew particularly large crowds, on a par with the attendances at contemporary English FA Cup finals. There were 24,000 at the 1887 Harvard–Princeton game, and 40,000 saw Yale meet Princeton six years later.

The region's press, particularly the *New York World*, started giving football generous coverage. The high-society excesses of the Ivy League scene already gave popular newspapers plenty of gossip fodder, and college football allowed them to tie this in with their sports coverage. Meanwhile, the game was becoming a lucrative sideline for the universities; the 1893 Princeton–Yale championship game made a net profit of $30,000.

College football was spreading far beyond the north east, with the Los Angeles-based University of Southern California taking it up in 1888, and several teams springing up in midwestern and central states soon afterwards. But it was the 'big four' – Harvard, Princeton, Yale and rising power Pennsylvania – who dominated this period. In 1888, their first season with a coach (inevitably Walter Camp), Yale won all of their 13 games, outscoring opponents by a total of 694-0. The next year, when Camp named the first *All-American* team, judged to be the best college players of the year, all 11 were from Harvard, Princeton or Yale.

In 1890, between them, the big four won 41 of their 42 games against other opponents. Yale's 1888 team was bursting with outstanding players and personalities. At one end of the forward line was Amos Alonzo Stagg, also a talented baseball player, and soon to play an important role in basketball's early development. Stagg would go on to become one of the great names in college football history, with a coaching career that continued until he was 96 years old, spawning a host of tactical innovations along the way.

At left guard was 6ft 3in powerhouse William Walter 'Pudge' Heffelfinger, a farmboy from Minnesota, later to be named regularly in the All-Time All-American selection. Their captain was centre William 'Pa' Corbin, whose sideburns and bushy moustache could be a handicap in a sport where players would impede opponents by grabbing anything they could get their hands on. During a game in 1887 he turned to referee Walter Camp (so highly respected that he was accepted as a referee in his own college's games) several times to complain: 'Mr Referee, this Harvard man is pulling my whiskers!'

In just a few decades, football in the United States had evolved from a chaotic, free-for-all scramble into a well-organised, technically advanced sport, via a period when it resembled the British forms of the game. The gridiron field layout introduced in 1882, for example, would have been unimaginable to those students wreaking havoc on the Yale and Harvard campuses in the 1850s.

By the closing years of the 19th century, the game's popularity was not only spreading across the country, but also among people of all social classes. The rules that had been developed at the Ivy League universities were widely followed, with few, if any, variations. It was still far removed from today's game. Forward passing was not allowed, and substitutions were limited, preventing players from adopting the specialised offensive, defensive and special team roles which would later become the norm. But, with its delineated scrimmage, the system of downs and yardage, and blocking, it was clearly distinct from rugby, and a world away from soccer.

As has been covered, the seeds of the game were planted by the influence of British public school football on the Oneida club in Boston, and, in turn, on the students at Harvard. The arrival of rugby in Canada, followed by the McGill–Harvard encounters in 1874 and 1875, played an important part in the story; as did Harvard's prestige, which encouraged other Ivy League colleges to follow its example by adopting rugby.

But, probably more so than in any other comparable sport in the 19th century, the rules and tactics of American football were influenced by intellectual, scientific thinking, as Walter Camp and his contemporaries relentlessly pursued their ideal of excellence in sport. This was in marked contrast to British sport, where, although tactics were beginning to evolve, there was more emphasis on honest toil and 'playing the game the way it should be played', rather than trying to out-think the opposition.

Also, soccer and rugby were mostly regarded by Americans as British sports; and although they did exist in their British forms in the United States in the late 19th century, they were mainly played by recent immigrants from Europe. Playing American football, or baseball, helped new arrivals to come out of the margins and assimilate into mainstream American society. But it appears that Camp and company did not purposely set out to invent a new sport. Instead, they began with rugby, and then made a series of adjustments, each one intended to remedy some perceived flaw in the game.

Still, when considering the American students' dissatisfaction with rugby, we should bear in mind that they had learned about the game only at second hand, through Harvard's two encounters with McGill, and would have been largely unfamiliar with its traditions and unwritten rules. They had to take the formal rules at face value, interpreting them in their own way, and the resulting style of play was probably less appealing to players and spectators than the British style (and, to some extent, the Canadian one).

It has often been said that American football began as a mixture of soccer and rugby. How anyone could reach this conclusion, though, is hard to imagine. It is true that soccer was the main influence on college football in the late 1860s and early 1870s. It could also be said that the Oneida club's Boston Game was a hybrid of the two English codes. But Harvard completely abandoned this game after discovering rugby in 1874, and it disappeared; as did the soccer-like game that had been adopted at the other universities.

The standard Ivy League football code for the rest of the 1870s was rugby, with no concessions to soccer at all (unless we regard the reduction from 15-a-side to 11-a-side as a concession to soccer, which we probably shouldn't, considering that rugby *sevens* is clearly a form of rugby). As American football became a distinct sport in the 1880s, it moved even further away from soccer, as the kicking element diminished. Other than kicking, which, in any case, is also a feature of rugby, American football doesn't include *any* features of soccer. It would be truer to say that American football is directly descended from rugby, and not at all from soccer.

By this time, American-style football was on its way to becoming a major nationwide sport. The Ivy League universities had taken up rugby, and adapted it into a game of their own. Now this game was breaking out into mainstream society, and eventually it would arguably overtake baseball as America's favourite sport. But not before it had survived a crisis in the early years of the next century; even involving a presidential intervention, forcing more changes which would pave the way for a brighter future.

Chapter 5

Workers' Playtime

'Professionalism in football is an evil and should be repressed.'
– William Pierce-Dix, Sheffield FA Secretary, 1885

*'I object to the argument that it is immoral
to work for a living, and I cannot see why men should
not, with that object, labour at football
as at cricket.'*
– Charles Alcock, FA Secretary, 1885

As outlined earlier, life was no picnic for Britain's working classes in the early 19th century. The Industrial Revolution had left many people cooped up in overcrowded urban slums, working crushingly long hours from Monday to Saturday almost every week of the year. On Sundays, even if they had the energy and the space for any leisure activity, the clergy would condemn them for indulging in it.

Around the middle of the century, though, things started looking up. Humanitarianism was in vogue among the middle and upper classes, and politicians and industrialists began to see benefits in giving workers more rest time. The Ten-Hour Day Act of 1847 set a limit on working hours for women and young men in factories. Three years later, the Factory Act raised this limit by half an hour a day, but also stipulated the earliest starting times and latest finishing times, with a limit of 2pm on Saturdays. In 1874, the maximum working week was reduced from 60 hours to 56½.

For many working people, especially in industries such as engineering, mining, steelworks, shipping and textiles, these changes brought new opportunities for enjoying their spare time. Many were now free on Saturday afternoons, which became a highlight of the week. With the economy booming and wages rising, leisure was no longer the exclusive preserve of the wealthier classes. Workers found new ways of spending their free time: trips to the seaside, visits to music halls, and, of course, sport.

Class relations were improving, and some of the better-off members of society felt a new sense of social responsibility, wanting to help the underprivileged to lead healthier and more satisfying lives. Thomas Hughes, the Old Rugbeian author of *Tom Brown's Schooldays*, helped to found the Working Men's College in London in 1854. Soon afterwards, the Working Men's Club and Institute was created by Unitarian minister Henry Solly, and the Salvation Army by William Booth, a former Methodist clergyman.

Religion, and the muscular Christianity ethos, had a part to play in this. Many churchmen believed that sport, or 'rational recreation' as they sometimes put it, could improve young working men's lives, helping to divert them from less wholesome pursuits such as drinking and gambling. Folk football was a long-lost pastime among urban workers, surviving only in some small towns and rural areas. Now, though, public school old boys were introducing their modern forms of football to the working classes.

Many football clubs began as offshoots of Sunday schools and church-based Young Men's Societies. In 1873, a rugby team was put together by the Young Men's Society at the Holy Trinity Church in Wakefield, to be known as Wakefield Trinity (they would cope without the 'Wildcats' appellation for the next 125 years). Five years later, members of the Sunday school at St Domingo's Church in Liverpool began playing soccer. They soon expanded their membership, and changed their name from St Domingo's FC to Everton FC. Similar stories unfolded in cities such as Leeds, Salford and Southampton.

Schools also played their part. The Elementary Education Act of 1870 introduced universal state schooling in England and Wales. Some teachers at these schools were former public school boys, and introduced their pupils to the joys of football. Grammar schools also helped to disseminate the game, giving birth to soccer clubs such as Blackburn Rovers and Leicester City.

Other clubs were formed as factory or mill teams: Coventry City, Arsenal and West Ham United in soccer, and the St Helens and Hull Kingston Rovers rugby clubs, among others. Manchester United (originally Newton Heath) and Crewe Alexandra began as teams of railway workers. Others, such as Derby County, Sheffield United and Tottenham Hotspur, started as spin-offs of cricket clubs, as had been the case with several clubs in the 1850s and 1860s.

Pubs played a role; by the early 1880s, they provided the headquarters for nearly all Yorkshire's rugby clubs. Unlike church- and company-based clubs, pub-based clubs were not subject to the middle-class religious morals of the day, and working-class customs such as prize-giving and betting crept into their activities. This kind of thing was hardly in keeping with the Corinthian values of their superiors at the Football Association and Rugby Football Union; conflict was around the corner.

Another aspect of late 19th-century life contributed to football's growth: civic pride. Town halls sprang up in many places, becoming focal points of communities. Many towns and cities, especially in northern England, became closely identified with their major employers, mostly owners of factories or textile mills. Local business leaders were seen as symbols of the strength and success of their towns – a phenomenon sometimes known as 'corporate unity'.

Civic pride and corporate unity started influencing the football world, with many clubs being led by businessmen, who saw football as a way of improving their local prestige and popularity. Rather than being private clubs, run by and for their members, football clubs were taking on a new type of identity, as representatives of their towns and cities. In places such as Oldham, Rochdale and Wigan, clubs were formed specifically for this reason, with local dignitaries and entrepreneurs often involved in getting them started. Sam Duckitt, who founded Halifax's rugby club in 1873, summed up the idea bluntly enough:

> *We saw reports in the papers of football matches being*
> *played at Leeds, Bradford and elsewhere, and we*
> *thought that Halifax ought to have a club also.*

It was mainly a middle-class affair at first, involving businessmen, councillors and the like. But as the 1870s wore on, feelings of civic pride and corporate unity began to cut across class barriers – which, in any case, were no longer as rigid as they had been a couple of decades earlier. With this sense of local pride, along with the proliferation of church, factory and pub teams, something was stirring in British football: the working class was starting to take over. In the north, the middle-class ideal of sport, centred around muscular Christianity and a sense of 'fair play', was being overshadowed by a fierce will to win for the sake of a town's honour.

Both codes of football were still governed (in England, at least) by the middle- and upper-class gentlemen of the FA and RFU. They were, for the most part, public school old boys, with conservative views about how football should be played and organised. Most of the committee members of the county and district governing bodies were cut from a similar cloth. Some leaders welcomed the involvement of working-class players, but only on the condition that the higher classes continued controlling the game, and dictating its rules and values. Others were distinctly queasy about the whole idea.

The increased working-class involvement in soccer soon began to make its mark on the FA Cup. For some years after its launch in 1871, the Cup had been dominated by old-boy clubs such as Wanderers, Old Etonians and Royal Engineers. Soon, though, northern teams of humbler origins started finding success. Darwen reached the quarter-finals in 1878–79, three years after switching from rugby. That season, they met Blackburn Rovers at the latter club's ground in the first Lancashire Cup Final, which drew 10,000 spectators, another sign of how much the game had grown in east Lancashire.

Blackburn Rovers became the first provincial club to reach the FA Cup final, facing Old Etonians in 1881–82. Despite their 1-0 defeat, Rovers attended a post-match dinner in London, where Blackburn's two MPs toasted them for their work in raising the town's profile. They then returned north to a warm welcome: civic pride on full display.

But, a year later, it was their neighbours, Blackburn Olympic, who were the first club to take the Cup north, beating Old Etonians 2-1. Whereas the Rovers team had featured some public school old boys, the Olympic players were more of a working-class bunch. They prepared for the final with a training regime and a specially planned diet, showing a level of dedication rarely seen in public school circles, and evoking the disapproval of the Eton old boys.

Not to be outdone, Rovers went on to win the Cup three times in a row. The 12,000 crowd at the Oval for the 1884 final featured a large Lancastrian contingent, described in the *Pall Mall Gazette* almost as if they had descended from another planet: 'a northern horde of uncouth garb and strange oaths.'

The FA Cup's first winners, Wanderers, stopped entering the competition in 1880. So did the Oxford and Cambridge university teams, with Oxford expressing dismay at the competitive nature of cup ties. Old Etonians' defeat in 1883 would be the last appearance in the final by an English public school old-boy club (although the middle-class Glasgow club Queen's Park, also competing for the Scottish FA Cup by now, reached it in the next two seasons). The 'gentlemen' were losing their grip on the game they had nurtured over the last 20 years, in the face of an onslaught from the largely working-class clubs of the north, with their popular support and a burning desire to win.

With the successes of the Blackburn clubs, soccer became even bigger news in Lancashire than before. After Blackburn Rovers had visited Burnley for the 1881–82 Lancashire Cup final against Accrington, the Burnley Rovers rugby club switched codes, also dropping the 'Rovers' tag. Preston North End, also originally a rugby club, adopted soccer in May 1881 after a couple of years of indecision. Both Blackburn clubs also tried to promote the game in Yorkshire, visiting Bradford, Leeds and Dewsbury, but with less success. It faced similar struggles in some Lancashire towns where rugby was the order of the day, notably Wigan.

In its northern heartlands, rugby enjoyed a surge in support in the late 1870s and early 1880s. The Yorkshire Cup, first held in 1877–78, helped to stir up interest in the game. A crowd of 12,000 turned up in Halifax to see Wakefield beat Kirkstall in the 1879 final. Back in Wakefield, the parish church bells rang out in celebration. The players were greeted by a band, and, according to the *Yorkshire Post*, an 'immense concourse' of cheering admirers.

By 1883–84, even first-round Yorkshire Cup ties were drawing attendances of up to 15,000, larger than at any FA Cup final to date (in fairness, soccer fans often faced much longer journeys to their final, having to trek to London from places such as Blackburn and Glasgow). Many of England's international rugby matches of the 1880s were staged in northern cities, mostly attracting bigger crowds than those played in the south.

Like their neighbouring soccer clubs, many northern rugby clubs were now controlled by men from the less affluent sections of the middle class, and were more open to working-class members than clubs had typically been in the past. There were exceptions, though: perhaps most significantly the Liverpool, Manchester and Sale clubs, which remained exclusively middle-class.

It was a similar story in south Wales. Some have suggested that rugby, the more strenuous football code, was preferred by men involved in the more physically demanding industries, particularly coal mining. The harder they pushed themselves at work, the more of a 'physical release' they needed from their sport. If there is any truth in this, it could help to explain how rugby forged ahead of soccer in mining areas of both England and Wales.

As rugby became more popular with the working classes in northern England, the nature of the game there began to change. Blue-collar culture started influencing the way it was played, organised and watched. Teams played to win, and their supporters were loud, boisterous, and sometimes violent. Verbal and physical attacks on players, officials and opposing supporters were not uncommon. Betting was rife, and there were rumours of match-fixing.

This was all a far cry from the RFU's ideal of rugby as a respectable game, which 'gentlemen' would play for the simple pleasure of playing, in front of a polite gathering of like-minded spectators. The atmosphere at a rugby match in Bradford, Wigan or Hull would certainly have felt intimidating to a middle-class player, administrator or journalist. Words such as 'mob' and 'riot' were bandied about in accounts of northern matches. The leaders of the RFU were uneasy about rugby's rising competitiveness, the increasing working-class involvement, and the consequent threat to their control of the game and the supremacy of their conservative values.

The financing and organisation of both football codes in northern England was changing dramatically. Club chairmen started seeing football not just as a form of recreation, but also as a lucrative business. The more successful their clubs, the more people turned up to watch them, and the more they were willing to pay for the privilege. The extra money could then be spent on extending and improving their grounds (allowing crowds to grow even more), on equipment for playing and training, and – whisper it quietly – on luring better players to their clubs.

Although soccer and rugby were thought of as amateur pastimes, neither the FA nor the RFU had clear regulations stating this until the late 1870s. Amateurism was thought to be consistent with the muscular Christianity ethos that had encouraged football at the public schools. It was seen as a game that boys and men should play for their own physical and mental well-being, helping them to develop into well-rounded individuals – not for material gain. This was, supposedly, the way that sport always had been, and always should be.

The truth, however, was not so simple. The idea of offering payments to sportsmen was nothing new. There had been professional cricketers and horseracing jockeys in Britain since the previous century; even in the ancient Greek Olympic Games, winners received prizes, sometimes in the form of cash. But the distinction between cricket's 'amateurs' and 'professionals' (it should soon become clear why these words are in quotes) was a dubious one, and gives us some insight into the roots of the conflict that was about to engulf football.

Each county cricket team featured both 'amateurs' and 'professionals'. The former, mostly specialist batsmen with a carefree, flamboyant approach, were invariably middle- or upper-class 'gentlemen'. The latter, many of whom were brawny fast bowlers, came from lowlier stock. While the 'professionals' were moderately paid, and had to use much of their income to cover their travelling costs, many 'amateurs' treated themselves lavishly to hotel rooms, food and drink, to be reimbursed with expenses that often dwarfed the wages of their 'professional' teammates.

The two classes of cricketers used separate changing rooms, and had little to do with each other off the field. To the 'gentlemen', the 'amateur' tag was a badge of honour, despite the obvious whiff of hypocrisy. The distinction between the two types of players undoubtedly had more to do with social class than with the issue of payments. (In addition, gambling had been endemic in cricket since the early 18th century.) For example, when W.G. Grace went on England's Australian tour in 1891–92, he was paid £3,000, plus expenses covering travel and accommodation for himself, his wife and their two children.

Among northern football clubs, change was brought about by more practical matters. Club chairmen were tempted to offer players money as an incentive to join them, and players were increasingly tempted to grab it. In Britain's economic slump of the 1880s, many players found it difficult to meet their clubs' growing demands while still earning a living.

Manual workers typically finished work at 1pm on Saturdays, making travel to away games especially problematic. Players often had to clock off early, or miss the Saturday shift altogether – resulting in docked wages, and possibly putting them at greater risk of being laid off. The Hull rugby club began funding half of its players' travel costs in 1874, and started paying them in full five years later.

The first rumours of professionalism surfaced in the late 1870s. A rugby half-back, Rufus Ward, left Wakefield Trinity for Halifax in 1877 under suspicious circumstances. According to various accounts, either he had fallen out with the Wakefield committee over an athletics meeting, or he was moving to Halifax to be closer to his girlfriend; but many suspected that Halifax had offered him an inducement to join them.

Darwen's success in the FA Cup and Lancashire Cup was helped by the arrival of outstanding full-back Fergie Suter, from Partick Thistle in 1878. Suter, a stonemason from Glasgow, had written to Darwen asking them to arrange a local job for him. The club happily invited him to move to the town (along with two fellow Scots who happened to be footballers), but he never took a genuine job there, claiming that the local stone was too hard for him to work with. It was widely believed that, in truth, he made his living by playing for Darwen. Although Suter is sometimes cited as the first professional soccer player, it has been claimed that another Scot, James Lang, beat him to it when he joined Sheffield Wednesday in 1876.

As cracks began to appear in football's amateur status, clubs were suspected of using all manner of tricks to reward players without incurring the wrath of the authorities. As well as imaginary jobs, there were rumours of inflated expenses, falsified accounts, payments in kind (legs of mutton were especially popular), unofficial matches with cash prizes, and clubs providing players with accommodation. Some players also benefited financially from testimonial matches.

For the football clubs of the public school old-boy network, these temptations were irrelevant. Their chairmen had little interest in turning them into money-spinning businesses, and their players could easily afford to play for nothing. But the soccer and rugby authorities, both nationally and locally, felt threatened by the rise of working-class interest. Whether they were driven by this fear, or by a genuine belief in the merits of amateurism, is open to debate; they were concerned that material rewards might ruin the spirit of the game, and encourage violent play. Whatever their motives, they soon began clamping down on the professionalism that was creeping into football.

By 1879, in Yorkshire, it was an open secret that some rugby players were being paid by their clubs. Their union, the Yorkshire County Football Club, tried to tackle the issue in November that year, passing a motion stating that 'no player who is not strictly an amateur shall be allowed to play in the Challenge Cup ties, or in any match under the direct control of the County Football Committee.'

But their definition of an 'amateur' was a direct copy of the vague one used by the Marylebone Cricket Club. It appeared to allow almost any expenses to be paid, provided that the player made no *profit* from the game. The rules were not widely understood, and had little effect on the growing practice of paying players over the next few years. It was a similar story in Lancashire, and some clubs in south Wales were suspected of paying excessive expenses. Meanwhile, some of that region's leading players were lured to northern English clubs by supposed offers of employment with local firms.

The FA clarified its stance in 1882, declaring that payments were barred, except for genuine expenses and *broken-time* payments (compensation for lost wages). Any player found to have broken these rules would be banned from the FA Cup and international matches, and his club would be expelled from the association. Soon afterwards, a sub-committee was set up to look into alleged payments, and into the 'importation' of players from Scotland, which was seen as part of the same issue.

Although it was difficult for the sub-committee to prove anyone's guilt in these matters, it was not long before the sparks began to fly. Accrington were expelled from the FA in November 1883, after paying a player to stay with them (having been reported to the FA by Darwen, who were hardly spotless themselves). They were reinstated a month later, but missed out on that season's FA Cup.

In January 1884, London club Upton Park met Preston North End in a fourth-round cup tie. After a 1-1 draw at Preston, Upton Park protested to the FA that some of their opponents were 'undisguised professionals'. Preston were not exactly subtle about their use of paid players: they had a number of Scottish 'imports', who almost certainly would not have moved to Lancashire without a material incentive. A year later, Preston manager Major William Sudell would boldly announce to the FA:

*Gentlemen, Preston are all professionals, but if you refuse
to legalise them they will be amateurs. We shall all
be amateurs and you cannot prove us otherwise.*

Preston were thrown out of the FA Cup, and out of the FA itself. Burnley, another club with several Scots, were also suspended soon afterwards, along with Great Lever. In February 1884, a month after Preston's expulsion, the FA committee considered a proposal to allow professionalism. But, rather than accepting it, they formed another sub-committee to look into the matter further.

There were no limits to broken-time payments, providing a loophole that some clubs exploited. The FA put a stop to this in June of that year, by limiting such payments to one day per week. Sudell led a campaign against the FA's stance, finding plenty of support from the press and public, as well as from other clubs. He played a major role at two meetings in Bolton and Manchester in October 1884, where 31 clubs (mostly from Lancashire, but also including Aston Villa, Walsall Swifts and Sunderland) voted to form a new organisation, the British Football Association. For the moment, at least, these clubs would also remain in the FA.

The FA faced a crisis. Not only were dozens of leading clubs threatening to leave the nest, but the Cup was in danger of degenerating into a farce, with so many clubs being expelled or suspended. Something had to be done, and, not for the first time, it was secretary Charles Alcock who stepped forward.

Although Alcock was a public school old boy of middle-class stock, his background was somewhat different from those of many of his peers. His Sunderland upbringing meant that working-class culture was not completely alien to him; and his experience with cricket had led him to think that professional sportsmen were not the pariahs as portrayed by some of his FA colleagues (and their RFU counterparts).

Just as importantly, Alcock was a pragmatist. He wanted the game to grow in stature and find a wider audience; a wish that seems to have influenced him more than the Corinthian ideal of amateurism. In the 1881 *Football Annual*, issued before the FA had even started disciplining clubs for breaching its amateur code, he wrote:

*There is no use to disguise the speedy approach of a time when
the subject of professional players will require the earnest
attention of those on whom devolves the management of
Association Football.*

It would be wrong to suggest that Alcock was strongly in favour of professionalism. But, although he was decidedly lukewarm about the idea in the early 1880s, his stance softened soon afterwards, as it became clear that continued resistance by the FA would lead to chaos, and possibly to a split.

At a sub-committee meeting in November 1884, facing the prospect of a breakaway by the British Football Association, Alcock suggested that professionalism should be legalised, albeit with tight restrictions. He was supported by one of the game's best-known figures: future FA president Lord Kinnaird, unquestionably one of the public school, muscular Christianity brigade. The committee voted to put the proposal to a special general meeting in January 1885, where it won most of the votes – but not the two-thirds majority needed for the motion to be carried.

Although it would be easy to regard the conflict as a north-versus-south affair, this was far from the case. Many of the proposal's supporters, such as Alcock and Kinnaird, were from southern clubs. Some of its most fervent opposition came from such places as Birmingham, Nottinghamshire and Sheffield. The Scottish and Welsh associations also disapproved – their clubs were already losing many players to English clubs, a problem that was likely to be made worse by overt professionalism in England.

Two months later, at the FA's annual general meeting, Lancashire delegate Richard Gregson put forward another proposal to allow professionalism, provoking the usual backlash. W.H. Jope, of the Birmingham FA, said it would be 'degrading for respectable men to play with professionals'. In reply, Alcock argued that paid players should not be seen as outcasts, claiming that they were necessary for the growth of the game. Again, the proposal failed to win enough votes; this time, though, it came close, with 106 to 69.

The tide was turning in favour of professionalism, and the change finally came at another special general meeting in July 1885. The meeting was poorly attended – perhaps partly because of the time of year, but it has also been suggested that many opponents of professionalism had simply given up the fight. This time, the proposal was moved by Blackburn Rovers chairman Dr E.S. Morley[18], and won enough votes to be carried.

There were restrictions, mainly concerning the FA Cup. Professionals competing in the tournament would have to be registered, and could only play in it for one club in any given season (the latter rule still applies, but now for amateurs as well as professionals). There were also residency rules, and professionals would be barred from serving on FA committees.

Around seven years of conflict in English soccer had, more or less, come to an end. The short-lived British Football Association soon fell by the wayside, having served its purpose in forcing the issue of professionalism onto the FA's agenda. The Scottish and Welsh associations protested fiercely to the FA for making such a radical change without consulting them and the Irish FA. The Scottish FA banned its member clubs from playing against any club that used professionals, effectively ending Queen's Park's involvement in the FA Cup, after two successive appearances in the final. No amateur club would reach the final again.

With professionalism in the open, soccer continued to grow and flourish: not only in Lancashire, but also in the Midlands, where clubs such as Aston Villa, Notts County, West Bromwich Albion and Wolverhampton Wanderers soon turned professional. Clubs became more businesslike and commercially-minded. Players could spend more time improving their fitness and skills, and the quality of play improved rapidly.

But, with the players being paid weekly, the clubs needed a regular diet of attractive fixtures to keep the public, and the money, rolling in. FA Cup ties came along sporadically, and the competitive part of a club's season could be over after one match. The rest of the season consisted of friendlies, which were mostly of little interest, and were often cancelled. Into the breach stepped William McGregor, a man with a big idea.

McGregor was a draper from Perthshire who had moved to Birmingham in 1870, becoming a successful businessman. He got involved in local football, and became a committee member and financial backer at Aston Villa. After a home cup tie against Preston in January 1888 drew a crowd of 26,000, McGregor began thinking up a scheme that could make clubs less reliant on the Cup for their income.

Like professional sport, the idea of a league was hardly new. In the United States, baseball's professional National Association had been launched 17 years earlier. A league table, of sorts, had first been published for what became Australian Rules football in 1877. English county cricket teams had been meeting on a regular basis for some time, and journalists had started compiling an unofficial table in 1887. McGregor envisioned a league structure for English football, which he hoped would become equal in importance to the FA Cup. In March 1888, he sent a circular to the chairmen of Blackburn Rovers, Bolton, Preston and West Bromwich:

> *Every year it is becoming more and more difficult for football clubs of any standing to meet their friendly engagements and even arrange friendly matches. The consequence is that at the last moment, through cup-tie interference, clubs are compelled to take on teams who will not attract the public. I beg to tender the following suggestion as a means of getting over the difficulty: that ten or twelve of the most prominent clubs in England combine to arrange home-and-away fixtures each season, the said fixtures to be arranged at a friendly conference about the same time as the International Conference.*

The chairmen were invited to suggest other suitable clubs, and a meeting was arranged for March 22 at Anderson's Hotel in Fleet Street, London. Some clubs had reservations about the idea: they were wary about the costs of travelling regularly around the country, and concerned that the league might undermine the FA's authority. However, representatives of seven clubs from Lancashire and the Midlands attended the meeting, and approved the plan in principle.

McGregor suggested naming the new scheme the 'Association Football Union', which could have led to confusion with both the FA and the RFU. He was uneasy about the alternative suggestion of 'Football League', apparently because it was reminiscent of the rebellious Irish Land League; but he caved in, and the Football League was born.

Detailed plans were sorted out at another meeting in April, with 12 clubs signing up to a 22-game schedule: Accrington, Aston Villa, Blackburn Rovers, Bolton Wanderers, Burnley, Derby County, Everton, Notts County, Preston, Stoke City, West Bromwich Albion and Wolves. There was little interest from the south, and no clubs from the north-east or Yorkshire were in 'The Ring', as some people called it, just yet.

There was some dispute over the choice of clubs. Nottingham Forest and Sheffield Wednesday were widely thought to have better teams than Accrington, Everton, Notts County and Stoke, but it appears that the latter clubs were preferred because they were drawing bigger crowds[19]. Bolton had suggested inviting Old Carthusians, with their impressive FA Cup record, to join the league; but the inclusion of an amateur 'old-boy' club would have been at odds with the commercial impetus behind the project.

The league got underway in September 1888. There was no league table until November, when a system of two points for a win, and one for a draw, was finally agreed. It seems that the concept of *winning* the Football League hardly occurred to the clubs when the plan was originally hatched – their main objective was to ensure an adequate fixture list. But the competitive element soon developed; *Whitaker's Almanack* (perhaps with some knowledge of developments in baseball) explained that 'these clubs play a sort of American Tournament for the league championship'.

Preston became the first champions in emphatic fashion, staying unbeaten all season and finishing 11 points ahead of Aston Villa – an incredible margin in a season when only 44 points were available. They played in a highly effective, scientific style, while manager Major Sudell took care of off-field matters with a ruthlessness, and, perhaps, selfishness, typical of the way that many successful clubs would operate in future eras. Preston underlined their supremacy by winning the FA Cup, and would repeat their league success the following year. Attendances in the league's debut season were modest, but encouraging, with Preston averaging more than 6,000, and Everton topping the list with over 7,000.

Although the professional game was surging forward, the amateurs were not finished just yet. In 1882, in response to England's regular defeats by Scotland, FA assistant secretary N.L. 'Pa' Jackson came up with the idea of assembling a team of leading English footballers who would play together regularly, helping them to develop a level of teamwork to match that of the Scots.

Jackson formed a new club, Corinthians FC, to bring his idea to life. Most of the Corinthians players also turned out for other clubs, which was just as well, given that the club – faithful to the amateur ideal, even as the professional era began – refused to join any competition that had a prize at stake, including the FA Cup. They were no slouches, beating Cup holders Blackburn Rovers 8-1 in 1884, and providing nine of England's players for their 1-1 draw with Scotland in 1886.

Although Corinthians' profile would diminish as English soccer became ever more professionalised, their name would endure as a symbol of sportsmanship and fair play. Real Madrid's all-white kit was chosen in homage to them, as was the name of one of Brazil's leading clubs, Corinthians of São Paulo. The club merged with Casuals FC in 1939, and Corinthian-Casuals are still with us today in the Isthmian League.

Soccer's continued growth, now fuelled by open professionalism and the birth of the Football League, as well as the FA Cup, continued to pose a problem for rugby. Nowhere was the problem more acute than in Lancashire, where soccer clubs in towns such as Blackburn and Preston had found national fame. Rugby clubs found it increasingly difficult to attract players, many of whom were capable of making a living from the round-ball game; and to attract spectators, who were drawn to soccer by the competitive excitement of cup tournaments and leagues.

At this point, there was no real campaign for full professionalism in rugby. The issue of broken-time payments, however, was looming large. In Yorkshire, although such payments had become a widespread practice by the mid 1880s, for training as well as playing (some considered them to be legitimate expenses, such as Hull, who openly declared an outlay of £18 for 'players' loss of time' in their 1883–84 accounts), the county union would not bring it up formally until 1889.

The RFU, increasingly anxious about what it saw as creeping professionalism, was poised to take action. In 1886, writing in the *Football Annual*, RFU committee member Arthur Budd poured scorn on the current developments in soccer; he was appalled that the recent FA Cup final had featured two professional teams, within a year of the sanctioning of professionalism (or, as he put it, 'legitimisation of the bastard'). Budd doubted whether amateur players could compete on equal terms with opponents who could spend their weekdays training and developing their skills.

Much of the press, typically in the hands of middle-class men with conservative views, supported the RFU and county unions in opposing any hint of professional rugby. A sports writer in the *Yorkshire Post* railed against the alleged tendency of paid sportsmen to play in a rough manner, and to abuse match officials, with little respect for the rules and spirit of the game.

In 1886, an RFU sub-committee drafted a set of rules to clarify the union's stance on payments to players. Crucially, broken-time payments, or 'compensation for loss of time', would not be allowed. In this respect, the proposed regulations were far stricter than those that the FA had adopted in 1882 – perhaps in an attempt to emphasise that rugby must not follow in soccer's footsteps. Some northern clubs were against these proposals, but they were accepted at a general meeting of the union in October 1886, with an amendment allowing players to be compensated for wages lost through rugby injuries.

None of the RFU's leading figures took the kind of pragmatic approach that had been taken by Charles Alcock and Lord Kinnaird at the FA. There was no attempt at reaching a compromise, and no apparent interest in helping to increase rugby's popularity among the wider population. Many working-class clubs, though, were determined to carry on pressing for the rules to be liberalised.

As with the ructions in soccer, although it is tempting to think of the dispute as a simple case of north against south, the actual situation was not so clear-cut. When the stringent new laws on player payments were drafted in 1886, three of the eight members of the sub-committee were from Yorkshire, and only three others were from the south. Some of the staunchest advocates of strict amateurism were northern-based, while some clubs in the West Country and the Midlands (and, outside the RFU's jurisdiction, in south Wales and the Scottish Borders) were accused of professionalism.

But it was in northern England that the campaign for change had the most momentum. It had the biggest concentration of predominantly working-class clubs, and faced a stiffer challenge from soccer than any other region. The northern clubs' sense of grievance was fuelled further by other objections to the RFU: a perceived pro-southern bias in England team selections, and the union's insistence on staging all of its annual general meetings in London, rejecting a proposal to alternate them between north and south.

The RFU leaders were also accused of applying double standards. In March 1888, a squad of British players, many of them from northern

England, visited Australia and New Zealand on an extensive tour organised by two businessmen and professional cricketers, Alfred Shaw and Arthur Shrewsbury. The venture was not authorised by the RFU; but, even though Shaw admitted that its objective was to make money, they made no attempt to stop it. Instead, they just issued a mild warning about sticking to the rules on amateurism.

All of the players were 'lent' some money, as well as being paid expenses. Andrew Stoddart, captain of England in both rugby and cricket at various times, was sent a £50 down-payment cheque, which he never repaid. Other players would receive suspiciously large expense payments.

Among those invited was Jack Clowes, a Halifax forward and factory worker. Shortly before the squad left Britain, Halifax beat Dewsbury in a Yorkshire Cup tie. After the match, Dewsbury president Mark Newsome complained that Halifax had fielded a 'professional', meaning Clowes, on account of his selection for the tour. Conveniently, Newsome had withdrawn two of his own players, who were also due to go to Australasia, from the cup tie.

Clowes was hauled before the county union committee, and admitted to having signed up for a professional tour. By the time the RFU had declared him a professional, though, he had already set sail with the rest of the squad. After the tour, the other players – mostly higher up the social ladder than Clowes – simply had to sign declarations stating that they had not broken the rules. The RFU surprisingly lifted its ban on Clowes, and the affair was largely over with.

Although the union's eventual leniency toward Clowes might appear to suggest they had softened their stance on professionalism, a likelier explanation (according to Tony Collins in *Rugby's Great Split*) is that they were afraid of tarring the rest of the touring party – including the England captain – with the same brush, giving the impression that they had all been hired as professionals. Which, judging by the evidence, they were.

Some members of the RFU and the county unions were unimpressed by the soft treatment of the tourists; none more so than the Rev. Frank Marshall of Huddersfield, an almighty thorn in the side of anyone in Yorkshire rugby who was suspected of breaking the amateurism laws. Marshall was a teacher and parson, with beliefs rooted firmly in muscular Christianity. In the late 1880s, soon after becoming the Yorkshire Rugby Union's treasurer, he took it upon himself to root out all traces of professional rugby in the county, examining clubs' record books, interrogating suspects, and recommending them for punishment by the RFU.

Marshall's first victims were Leeds St John's, forerunners of the current Leeds Rhinos rugby league club, suspended for six weeks in October 1888 for using a job offer to entice a player to join them from Kirkstall. Similar punishments were soon meted out to other clubs, as Marshall continued his rampage. Brighouse Rangers, Cleckheaton, Heckmondwike, Leeds Parish Church and Wakefield Trinity all felt his wrath, and he even gave evidence against his own club, Huddersfield. Before long, Yorkshire rugby was awash with allegations and rumours. The suspensions played havoc with fixture lists, and led many clubs into financial peril. Marshall provoked further antipathy in 1890 by poking his nose into Lancashire rugby, demanding an investigation into Oldham's player recruitment methods.

One of the more prominent cases was that of Dicky Lockwood, one of the early stars of northern rugby. Lockwood, a working-class man from the Wakefield area, was a right-wing three-quarter who made his debut for Dewsbury in 1884 at 16. Three years later, he played for Yorkshire and England. He was quick, and, despite his 5ft 4in stature, a strong tackler. Lockwood was also an inventive tactician, who brought the Welsh system of employing four three-quarter backs into Yorkshire rugby, and pioneered the idea of punting the ball and running after it. His performances turned him into a local hero.

After joining Heckmondwike in 1889, Lockwood became embroiled in accusations of professionalism, levelled at both himself and the club. Huge crowds gathered in the town to show their support for him. He was acquitted, and went on to captain England in 1894, but his career was blighted by run-ins with the RFU. Lockwood's story epitomises the conflict between northern working-class players and the rugby establishment in this period.

Professionalism was not the only contentious feature of soccer that began to rub off on rugby. The success of the new Football League also encouraged some rugby clubs and unions to follow suit. The semi-autonomous West Lancashire and Border Towns Rugby Union formed a league in 1889, and the early 1890s saw increasing pressure for others to be launched. As with cup competitions, many RFU officials considered leagues to be contrary to the spirit of the game, although they did not outlaw them completely.

The Rev. Marshall, by now a Yorkshire representative at the RFU, moved two motions at the union's 1891 annual general meeting: one to put control of player transfers in the hands of the RFU, and another to forbid the formation of 'combinations' (leagues) without the national union's approval. The Yorkshire union adopted the latter rule in June 1892, and soon rejected a plan drawn up by some of its leading clubs to form an 'alliance'.

Other leagues were formed in Lancashire by 1892, one of them even attracting interest from the middle-class Liverpool club. But the lack of a national league, or at least one that covered the whole of the north, meant that rugby had nothing to rival the Football League.

As recounted, rugby's tactics were revolutionised in the 1870s and 1880s, as it evolved from a crude kick-and-run affair into a more scientific game. More thought was given to formations and scrummaging techniques, and passing became a major part of the game. While much of the innovation came from southern amateurs such as the Oxford University team, northern working-class clubs also played their part.

The practice of half-backs passing to three-quarters is thought to have been pioneered by J.H. Payne and Teddy Bartram, playing for the North against the South in 1881. Bradford's Rawson Robertshaw has been cited as the first centre to pass the ball regularly to his wingers, first doing so in 1886. The Yorkshire village team of Thornes FC, as mentioned earlier, developed inventive scrum tactics in the early 1880s.

By the middle of that decade, many northern clubs were holding training sessions, and paying attention to their players' diets and fitness. The RFU thought this kind of thing had no place in an amateur sport. But these advances helped the clubs to raise the standard of their rugby, by improving players' strength, speed, stamina and skills, and allowing them to work on tactics.

Meanwhile, as northern rugby became more business-orientated, club officials became aware of the need to play in an attractive style, as well as the importance of winning. Many games were dominated by congested play among the forwards, with little passing and running, often making for a dull spectacle.

In 1892, Yorkshire Rugby Union secretary James Miller called for teams to be reduced from 15 players to 13, hoping this would make for a faster, more open game. His proposal found some support in the north, but was rejected by the RFU leadership, who had little interest in the crowd-pleasing aspects of the game. Hely Hutchinson Almond, headmaster at Loretto School and a staunch defender of old-style rugby, even suggested reverting to 20-a-side.

This was all happening at a time of social unrest and class conflict in Britain, with the economy slumping and unemployment rising. With the labour and trade union movements emerging, there was a wave of strikes, and clashes between working-class activists and police. There were riots in London's Trafalgar Square in 1886, and Hull dockers staged a violent six-week strike in April 1893. Later that year, troops attacked striking miners in Featherstone, leaving two dead and 16 injured, an event acknowledged today by a sculpture in the town centre. The middle and upper classes grew alarmed at what they saw as a 'mob uprising' by workers.

These conflicts split the northern rugby community down the middle. Some players supported the strikers, while others were members of the police forces that frequently attacked them. Class discord reared its head in other ways: middle-class players sometimes annoyed their working-class teammates by missing training, or by arriving late for matches because of business commitments.

Working-class club administrators, no longer content to obey their supposed social superiors, grew in influence and confidence in the committee room, and were now better organised than in earlier days. Meanwhile, the middle classes needed to keep up a strong presence on the field, to give some credibility to their positions of power; but this became more difficult as the animosity intensified.

By the summer of 1893, rugby's class war had been simmering for years. It was about to come to the boil, with the issue of broken-time payments at the forefront – now an even more pressing matter than before, thanks to the recession. In June, the Yorkshire union passed a motion calling for such payments to be allowed. Three months later, its president, James Miller of Leeds FC, proposed the same motion at the RFU's annual general meeting.

To Miller and many of his fellow Yorkshiremen, broken-time payments were consistent with the amateur ideal. They hoped that the legitimisation of these payments would help to stave off any campaign for 'real' professionalism, which they feared would lead to bankruptcies or liquidation (a common problem in soccer at the time – Bootle, Ardwick, Middlesbrough Ironopolis, Rotherham Town and Accrington all folded, at least temporarily, in the mid 1890s) and ruin the spirit of rugby. They also believed it would help to stabilise the game, by allowing clubs to plan their finances openly, and by reducing the suspensions that were disrupting fixture lists.

Miller and his colleagues hoped the RFU would welcome the move, as a compromise between two extremes: the current, strict version of amateurism, and full-blown professionalism. RFU president William Cail was rumoured to be on their side. The Lancashire union voted to support the change, and northern clubs, mostly in favour, outnumbered southern ones. But the RFU's 1893 AGM, as always, was to be held in London, and the Yorkshire delegates faced a tough task in getting enough sympathizers to attend. A train was chartered, calling at 11 major towns in Yorkshire.

The meeting at the Westminster Palace Hotel attracted more than 400 delegates, the biggest turnout so far. Legend has it that some of the Yorkshire contingent failed to turn up, having lost their way from King's Cross station to the hotel. (In their *Centenary History of the Rugby Football Union*, Titley and McWhirter called them 'country bumpkins'.)

Opponents of broken-time payments had prepared well for the meeting, reportedly securing 120 proxy votes from like-minded club officials, and getting a letter signed by 70 prominent players declaring their opposition.

There was uproar as James Miller, seconded by Mark Newsome[20] of Dewsbury, read out the proposal that 'players be allowed compensation for *bona fide* loss of time'. Miller argued that it was unfair for working men to lose income by playing rugby, making it difficult for them to compete on level terms with wealthier men who could easily afford to do so. Broken-time payments, he reasoned, were just as valid as expense payments.

But William Cail, contrary to rumours, was thoroughly against the idea. In his booming, intimidating voice, Cail moved an amendment: 'that this meeting, believing the above principle is contrary to the true interest of the game and its spirit, declines to sanction the same.' RFU honorary secretary G. Rowland Hill seconded Cail's amendment. Many other delegates, on both sides of the argument, went on to have their say. Unfortunately for Miller and his supporters, the northern clubs were not solidly in favour of the move. Some northern representatives are also thought to have walked out of the room in disgust before the vote was taken, dismayed by the hostile attitudes they had encountered.

Together with the proxy votes their opponents had rustled up, this meant that the Yorkshire proposal was doomed to failure. It was rejected, by 282 votes to 136. Immediately afterwards, the RFU leaders held a special meeting to change the union's constitution, deciding that membership would only be open to clubs whose players were all amateur. Far from seeking a compromise with their opponents, they were rubbing salt into their wounds.

Some speakers at the AGM had warned that the pursuit of broken-time payments could lead to a split in the union's ranks. Two of them, future RFU president Roger Walker of Lancashire, and that arch-purist the Rev. Frank Marshall, openly suggested that the rebels *should* break away and form their own union.

The issue of broken-time payments was not the only bone of contention in the rugby world. In Yorkshire, the county union insisted on a promotion and relegation system between its Senior Competition and Junior Competition, which had been formed in 1892 after some wrangling between the 'senior' clubs and the county union. These clubs, keen to maintain their supremacy, were against the idea, and the dispute soured their relations with both the junior clubs and the county union. Amid all this acrimony, some junior clubs withdrew their support for the campaign for broken-time payments, further damaging its chances of success. Senior clubs grew frustrated at the degree of control that the county union was exercising over them, as well as the RFU's stance on amateurism.

Similar problems were brewing in Lancashire, where soccer fever was raising the stakes even higher, and where the social chasm between the county union leadership and many of the clubs was growing ever wider. In late 1894, Leigh, Salford and Wigan were all charged with making illegal payments, and suspended from the Lancashire championship. Several other clubs were also mired in accusations and rumours. In November, the *Wigan Observer* predicted a split in rugby 'within ten weeks'.

That December, the RFU sent a 'manifesto' on amateurism to all member clubs, asking them to sign a declaration supporting it. One of its more draconian proposals was to shift the burden of proof: any players or clubs charged with professionalism would have to prove their innocence, rather than the union having to prove their guilt. Any clubs found guilty of breaking the rules would be expelled from the union, along with all their members. The manifesto met with opposition, not just from the north, but also from clubs in the Midlands and West Country. The RFU gave up on the burden of proof clause, but William Cail appointed a sub-committee to redraft the laws on the basis of the rest of the manifesto.

The dispute rumbled on into 1895. On January 30, after northern clubs had held a string of meetings to discuss their mounting gripes against the RFU, eighteen club representatives met at Huddersfield's George Hotel. They voted to form a new alliance, with the official, unwieldy title of the Lancashire and Yorkshire Rugby Football Union of Senior Clubs: a 'sort of mutual protection society' under the RFU's umbrella.

Under their planned scheme, each of the two counties would have its own league system, with the champions meeting in a play-off. The plans were submitted to the RFU, minus a secret caveat: if any one of these clubs was punished by the RFU, it would be able to appeal to the Lancashire and Yorkshire union's committee, who would look into the matter and would support the club if they found it to be innocent. But the 'secret' clause became public knowledge, and, to no-one's surprise, the RFU rejected the plans in May.

Two months later, nine leading Lancashire clubs resigned from the county's Club Championship, in protest at the county union's stance. Meanwhile, the argument over promotion and relegation in Yorkshire came to a head, as the county union rescinded the Senior Competition's powers. This left its 12 clubs out on a limb, and they all left the union at the end of July, but the RFU confirmed its support for the Yorkshire union's decision the following month.

Another RFU annual general meeting was looming; and, with it, the expectation of tighter rules on amateurism, based on William Cail's manifesto. Secretary G. Rowland Hill circulated a draft of the rules in August, with the meeting scheduled for September 19. If they were adopted, it would surely spell the end for any lingering hopes of broken-time payments being allowed. One of the changes seems to have been intended purely to alienate the northern rebels: any club that was involved 'in any match or contest where it is previously agreed that less than 15 players on each side shall take part' would be branded as 'professional' – probably a response to James Miller's suggestion of 13-a-side rugby.

Northern clubs were facing the real possibility of leaving the RFU. Some had cold feet, partly because it would damage their counties' prestige on the national rugby scene (since a County Championship had been launched in 1889, only Yorkshire and Lancashire had won it). But they saw no real alternative, and the need for the clubs to 'stick together' must have weighed heavy on their minds. On August 27, there were meetings of senior clubs in both Lancashire and Yorkshire, both resolving to form a northern union as soon as possible.

Just two days later, representatives of 21 clubs came together, again at the George Hotel in Huddersfield: Batley, Bradford, Brighouse Rangers, Broughton Rangers, Dewsbury, Halifax, Huddersfield, Hull, Hunslet, Leeds, Leigh, Liversedge, Manningham, Oldham, Rochdale Hornets, St Helens, Tyldesley, Wakefield Trinity, Warrington, Widnes and Wigan. The clubs passed a resolution to form the Northern Rugby Football Union (often just known as the Northern Union, or NU), 'on the principle of payment for bona-fide broken-time only'. With the exception of Dewsbury, who subsequently withdrew from the group, the clubs agreed to resign from the RFU.

Two Cheshire clubs joined the new union: a telegraphed application from Stockport was accepted during the meeting itself, and Runcorn signed up soon afterwards. The union committee held its first meeting on September 3, to agree on its arrangements and rules, including a home-and-away league format, and a maximum broken-time payment of six shillings per day. The league got underway just four days later, in the face of fierce opposition from the RFU, which duly adopted its new, stricter rules on September 19.

Clubs that had stayed out of the NU faced a fixture crisis, with many of the teams they had planned to meet in the new season having suddenly left the fold. The RFU forbade member clubs from playing against those involved in the rebel union, who, in any case, faced a daunting 42-game league schedule, leaving little time for other matches. English rugby had split itself in two, with no real hope of a reunification.

While the oval-ball game was busy tearing itself apart, soccer was going from strength to strength. Within a year of the Football League's launch, other leagues had sprung up around England: the Midland Counties League, the Football Alliance, the Northern League in the north-east, and the short-lived Second Combination League. Some of the clubs in these leagues, particularly in the Football Alliance, had ambitions to join the Football League, which was widely accepted as the highest level of the game in England.

From its first season onwards, the bottom four clubs in the Football League had to apply for re-election for the right to stay in it. As would usually happen until automatic promotion and relegation arrived, almost a century later, the four clubs facing re-election in the spring of 1889 were all successful. In 1891, though, the league was expanded from 12 to 14 clubs, with Darwen and Stoke joining (the latter having been replaced by Sunderland, the league's first north-eastern club, a year earlier).

A year later, 14 clubs from other leagues were brought into the Football League, which was now split into two divisions. Newton Heath, Nottingham Forest and Sheffield Wednesday joined the league's existing clubs in forming the 16-club Division One, while the other 11 newcomers made up Division Two along with Darwen, demoted after finishing bottom in 1891–92.

Promotion and relegation between the two divisions was to be decided by 'test matches', between the bottom two clubs from Division One and the top two in Division Two (this was replaced by an automatic system in 1898). The second tier grew to 15 clubs in 1893, one of its new members being Woolwich Arsenal, London's first Football League club. By 1898–89, each division had 18 teams – the league's membership had trebled in the first decade of its existence.

Attendances were booming: the first FA Cup final played outside the capital, the Everton–Wolves encounter in 1893, drew 45,000 at Fallowfield in Manchester. Local derbies became big occasions, with 27,000 seeing Sheffield United play Sheffield Wednesday at Bramall Lane in October 1893, and the following season, the first two Everton–Liverpool clashes[21] attracted crowds of 44,000 and 27,000.

By the mid 1890s, soccer was the major football code in most cities and large towns in northern and central England; although rugby was more popular in much of the south, and also had its northern strongholds. Soccer also began to flourish in other parts of the British Isles, as rugby had done a little earlier. The Scottish Football League was founded in 1890, with a strict amateur rule until 1893. The Irish League also began in 1890, with all eight of its clubs based in Belfast. In England, 1894 saw the formation of the Southern League.

Before long, rugby's split would be repeated in Australia and New Zealand. The game would struggle to recover from the damage; while soccer, not burdened by such problems, began spreading throughout the world. But, however harmful the split might appear to have been, it is hard to imagine how rugby could have continued under one umbrella, such was the vast gulf between the sides in the conflict.

The RFU's stance on amateurism was far stricter than that of the FA. The rugby 'rebels' of the mid 1890s were asking for the sanctioning of broken-time payments – something which they (like the FA in the early 1880s) believed to be acceptable in an *amateur* context. In other words, they were not campaigning for professionalism, a point that is often overlooked when the story of the Great Split is recounted. They simply disagreed with the RFU on how to define 'amateur'. The first entry in the Northern Union's original rule book even stated that 'professionalism is illegal'.

Having said that, the NU waited only three years before allowing clubs to pay part-time wages to players, and another seven years before allowing unlimited payments (although full-time professionals would be a rarity until the late 20th century). The RFU, on the other hand, would cling to its amateur stance for a hundred years after the split. In contrast, the FA's attitude was influenced by men such as Charles Alcock, with an approach that allowed room for compromise, eventually leading to full professionalism and the cultural changes that came with it. Other FA leaders, of a more Corinthian persuasion, had simply failed to stem the tide.

Public school old boys would still occupy high positions at the FA for many years to come, but working-class players and fans would stamp their values and culture on the game. Meanwhile, rugby league – as well as evolving into a distinct game from rugby union – would develop its own working-class identity.

Football in the British Isles had come full circle by the end of the 19th century. Working-class folk football had been virtually wiped out by the Industrial Revolution, and by oppression from the establishment. But the middle and upper classes then revived football, in a more regulated form, which was soon embraced by working-class players and fans. While rugby union still remains a largely middle-class affair in most areas, both soccer and rugby league can claim to be 'the people's game' in their respective heartlands.

Chapter 6

The World's Game, Part 1

'Maybe one day everyone here will play this game. It seems to be bringing folks together. It seems to arouse extraordinary curiosity.'
– J. Ugalde, journalist, on Athletic Bilbao v Bilbao FC, 1902.

In the late 19th century, the British were just about everywhere. As well as having political control of large swathes of the planet, Britons were exporting goods, manpower and industrial expertise to all of its corners. Inevitably, many took their favourite sports with them.

In mainland Europe, British businessmen, teachers, textile workers, miners, rail workers, sailors and students formed sports clubs in their adopted home towns. At first, locals often regarded their soccer, rugby and cricket matches as little more than a novelty. Soon, though, they started joining in – especially with soccer. Meanwhile, many continental students discovered the game at British schools and universities, took a liking to it, and introduced it to friends back home. Although many mainland European clubs had middle-class origins, the game quickly became popular with people of all backgrounds.

In Switzerland, British schoolboys formed Lausanne Cricket and Football Club in 1860, although it is not clear what type of football they played at first. Other early Swiss clubs, which definitely fielded soccer teams from an early stage, were FC St Gallen, formed in 1879, and Grasshoppers Zürich, founded in 1886 by English student Tom Griffith. Another claimant to the title of continental Europe's oldest soccer club is Kjøbenhavns Boldklub, in Denmark. Founded in 1876 by British migrants, the club adopted soccer and cricket three years later. A national association, the Dansk Boldspil-Union, was set up in 1889.

In Sweden, British engineers played soccer in Gothenburg in the 1870s, and British embassy staff were known to kick balls around in Stockholm's public parks. A league was set up in Gothenburg in 1896, and was expanded to include Stockholm clubs four years later. Norway's first club was Christiania Footballclub, established in Oslo in 1885; their

(top) The ancient Japanese ball-kicking game of kemari.
(above) Shrovetide football in Ashbourne – a centuries old
tradition very much alive today.

(top) Calcio storico, dating from the 16th century, being played in Florence in 2003.
(above) Eton College pupils playing the Wall Game.

Charles Alcock, driving force behind the birth of both the FA Cup and international soccer.

Yale University's Walter Camp, the 'Father of American Football'.

*Aston Villa committee member William McGregor, prime mover behind the launch
of the Football League in 1888.*

Uruguay players celebrate victory in soccer's first World Cup, on home soil in 1930.

Richmond captain Jack 'Captain Blood' Dyer, a fearsome presence in Australian Rules football in the 1930s and 1940s.

*Sammy Baugh of the Washington Redskins, a pioneer of the modern
quarterback role in American football.*

*(top) Danie Craven (centre), a prominent figure in South Africa's rugby union history, in action for the national side against the British Lions in Johannesburg in 1938.
Ferenc Puskás (no. 10) celebrates after scoring Hungary's third goal in their eyebrow-raising 6-3 win (above) over England at Wembley in 1953.*

(top) Canadian football's heyday, with the Hamilton Tiger-Cats' Vito Ragazzo (foreground centre) about to touch down against the Toronto Argonauts in 1953.
(above) The climax to 'The Greatest Game Ever Played': Alan Ameche clinches victory for the Baltimore Colts in the 1958 NFL championship game, against the New York Giants at Yankee Stadium.

(top) Alfredo di Stefano (right) opens Real Madrid's account in a memorable 7-3 European Cup final win over Eintracht Frankfurt, at Glasgow's Hampden Park in 1960.
(above) Australian Rules legend Ron Barassi (left), playing for Melbourne in 1964.

(top) The first Super Bowl presentation: NFL commissioner Pete Rozelle (left) hands the trophy to Green Bay coach Vince Lombardi, in Los Angeles in 1967.
(above) Leeds (dark jerseys) and Wakefield Trinity players risk drowning in the 1968 Rugby League Challenge Cup final at Wembley.

Rugby union: The powerful Colin Meads leads a New Zealand attack in 1967.

(top) Gaelic football at Wembley Stadium in the 1960s, as Galway (dark shirts) take on Dublin. (above) Wally Lewis, a star of Australia's dominant rugby league side in the 1980s, leads the charge in a Test match against Great Britain.

Oman Biyik (centre) heads Cameroon's goal in a shock 1-0 win over Argentina, which opened the 1990 World Cup.

(top) James Johnson, of the Saskatchewan Rough Riders, leaps into the Winnipeg Blue Bombers' end zone for a touchdown in the 2007 Grey Cup game in Toronto.
(above) Ireland (in green) take on Australia in an International Rules clash at Dublin's Croke Park in 1998.

first game was against a team of British sailors. Several more Norwegian clubs were formed by the end of the century, and an association was founded in 1902.

Britain had close ties with Germany, and the game gained a foothold in Hanover in the 1870s, thanks to German students returning from British schools, along with the influence of British residents. The rules were a little vague in some places. In Braunschweig in 1874, schoolteacher August Hermann simply threw a ball among a group of bemused boys and left them to work out what to do with it. But, with schools playing an important role, various hybrids of soccer and rugby – with soccer gradually taking over – became popular in other cities such as Göttingen, Bremen and Hamburg. Further east, clubs by the name of English FC were formed in both Berlin in 1885, and Dresden in 1890.

The game came up against some resistance in Germany. The Prussian authorities, intent on building their empire's military power, had only one physical activity in mind for young men: a non-competitive form of gymnastics known as *Turnen*. Strength, fitness and discipline were the order of the day. British sporting culture, with its supposedly elitist concept of winning and losing, was dismissed as alien and decadent.

As a result, many German sports clubs began life with an emphasis on *Turnen*, although competitive sports – mainly soccer – would come to the fore by the turn of the century. Traces of these origins can be found in some modern clubs' names. 1860 Munich's full name, for example, is 'Turn- und Sportverein München von 1860': the club started as a fitness and gymnastics association, 39 years before it fielded a football team. Members of the neighbouring MTV 1879 club broke away in 1900, frustrated at their leaders' refusal to adopt football, and created their own club, Bayern Munich.

In Austria, a football scene developed in Vienna in the 1890s, thanks to its large British population. Vienna Cricket and Football Club was formed in 1894 by English gardeners, and eventually evolved into Austria Vienna. Another Englishman, John Gramlick, founded First Vienna FC at around the same time. In 1898, workers at a hat factory formed a club known as 1. Wiener Arbeiter-Fussball-Klub, renamed as Rapid Vienna the following year.

The game was also reaching other parts of the Austro-Hungarian Empire, with SK Slavia of Prague being founded in 1892, followed a year later by AC Sparta, originally known as Athletic Club King's Vineyard. A league was set up in the city in 1896. The following year, Gramlick helped to create the Challenge Cup, a tournament for clubs across the empire, mainly from Vienna, Budapest and Prague.

Pim Mulier, a Dutch-born, English-educated 14-year-old schoolboy, founded the Netherlands' first club in Haarlem in 1879. Although

Haarlemse FC (now known as Koninklijke HFC) played rugby at first, they switched to soccer after four years. Clubs were soon formed in Amsterdam and Rotterdam, and the Nederlandschen Voetbal- en Athletischen Bond, forerunner of today's national association, the KNVB, was established in 1889 with Mulier as president.

Belgium's first club, Royal Antwerp, was founded some time around 1880, as the multi-sport Antwerp Athletic Club. It is believed that two cyclists, Emile Van Migem and Charles Pfeiffer, saw some English student friends of theirs kicking a ball around, and joined up with them to form the club. Over the next two decades, clubs sprang up in cities such as Brussels, Bruges and Liège.

In France, most of the early clubs were formed in port towns alongside the English Channel. Le Havre set up as a rugby club in 1872, but the players also adopted soccer 20 years later, and it soon became their preferred code. A soccer club was also founded in Paris in 1887, by English residents.

Italy's first footballing centres were in the north of the country. In 1896, three years after a group of Britons had founded Genoa Athletic Club, James Richardson Spensley, a doctor from London, set up its soccer team, who would play against visiting sailors. It was soon renamed as Genoa Cricket and Football Club, still the official name of today's Serie A club.

Italian businessmen, returning from trips to Britain, helped to stimulate the game's growth in other northern cities, particularly Milan and Turin. British residents also played a part. Milan Cricket and Football Club, later to become AC Milan, was founded by British expat Alfred Edwards in 1898. Ten years later, though, the club was dominated by Italians – a situation that led some members to form a breakaway club, Internazionale, which would be more welcoming to foreigners.

It has been claimed that Britons helped give birth to Juventus in Turin in 1897, while other accounts suggest that it was all the work of a group of Italian schoolboys, who hatched the idea while sitting on a bench, looking for something to do. At some of these early Italian clubs, soccer and cricket had equal status at first, but cricket began to fade into obscurity as Italian members took greater control.

Spain's first club was Huelva Recreation Club (now Real Club Recreativo de Huelva), founded in Andalucia in 1889. British soldiers, protecting the area after the Carlist War, and British miners and engineers at the Rio Tinto copper mines, had introduced the game to local railway workers.

The Basque country's heavy industry attracted a wave of British workers and businessmen. Along with Basques who had studied commerce and civil engineering in the UK, they created a breeding ground for soccer. At first, locals just watched as the Britons played their strange game; but in the mid 1890s they started joining in, and arranging matches themselves. Juanito Astorquia, a merchant's son, discovered football while studying in Manchester. With friends from a local gym, he formed Bilbao FC in 1898, leading to the birth of Athletic Bilbao three years later.

In 1895, students at Madrid's Open Teaching College formed a football club after studying in Oxford and Cambridge. For reasons best known to themselves, they called it Football Sky. By 1900 it had split into two clubs: New Foot-Ball Club and Español de Madrid. The latter was renamed as Madrid FC, and became the city's dominant club, changing its name again to Real Madrid after gaining royal patronage in 1920. Atlético Madrid, an offshoot of Athletic Bilbao, was formed in 1903 by Basque migrants.

The game took longer to catch on in Catalonia, where people in high places tended to find the idea of men running around in shorts a bit distasteful. The region's first club was Palamós CF, formed in 1898 by Gaspar Matas, yet another man who had learned the game while studying in England. One of FC Zürich's founders, Hans Kamper, arrived in Barcelona that year, en route to Africa on a business trip. But he liked the city and stayed there, taking a job as an accountant. He scoured local gyms for potential teammates, and placed an advert in a newspaper. The ensuing meeting in November 1899 gave rise to FC Barcelona, featuring Catalan, Swiss and British players. The Witty family, Anglo-Catalan shipping merchants, soon became involved, improving the game's respectability in the eyes of the local gentry.

Another club, Español, was set up in 1900, to represent Barcelona's non-Catalan population. Its founder, student Ángel Rodríguez, made the intention pretty clear: 'We create this club to compete with the foreigners of Barcelona' – injecting a political element into the rivalry between the clubs from the start, at a time when Catalan nationalism was on the rise. Barcelona soon had an even more intense rivalry with Real Madrid, as the latter came to be identified with the federal Spanish establishment.

Portugal was another of Britain's important trading partners, and British sailors played football in the Lisbon area as early as the 1870s. Portuguese boys also learned the game at British schools, and brought it home with them. A football scene began to develop in the 1890s, and the following decade saw the formation of four major clubs: Benfica, Porto, Boavista and Sporting Lisbon, the last created by a split in the Benfica ranks.

The British textile industry helped to introduce the game in Russia, Poland and Romania. Two Lancastrian brothers, Clement and Harry Charnock, formed a club at a textile factory that they ran in Orekhovo-Zuevo, near Moscow, in the 1890s. They imported playing strips from Blackburn Rovers, and even placed an advertisement in *The Times* of

London, looking for 'engineers, mechanics, and clerks capable of playing football well.' The club, known initially as Morozovtsi Orekhovo-Zuevo Moskva, would later move to the capital. After the 1917 communist revolution, it came under the control of the secret police, and was renamed as Dynamo Moscow.

Life was not easy for footballers, or for their followers, in corners of Europe that were under authoritarian control, such as Poland, Serbia and northern Greece. The Tsarist, Prussian and Austro-Hungarian rulers were nervous about anything that attracted large, boisterous crowds in rebellious parts of their empires. Just as the British establishment had cracked down on folk football in earlier times, they stamped their authority on soccer, imposing tight restrictions on crowd sizes. It was a similar story in Turkey. Today's major Istanbul clubs, Beşiktaş, Galatasaray and Fenerbahçe, were founded in 1903, 1905 and 1907 respectively; but the Ottoman authorities did not legalise sports clubs until 1912.

Soccer was not only spreading across Europe, but also Latin America, especially in the growing industrial cities along South America's eastern seaboard. British sailors, businessmen, railway workers, gas workers and diplomats were setting up sports clubs in these cities, nowhere more so than along the banks of the River Plate.

As early as 1865, a British sporting club was formed in Buenos Aires. Argentina's first recorded football match was played in 1867 by British migrants, members of the newly-formed Buenos Aires Football Club. Another sports club in the city, Gimnasia y Esgrima la Plata, was set up by middle-class Argentines in 1887. The club adopted soccer 13 years later, and still operates in the upper reaches of the Argentinian game today, clinging to a name which suggests its main activities are gymnastics and fencing.

The River Plate club was formed in Buenos Aires in 1901, mainly by locals who had seen British sailors playing the game in the Boca district. Racing Club was born two years later, and Italian immigrants founded Boca Juniors in 1905. Further afield, British railway workers established Rosario Central in 1889. Ex-pupils of that city's English High School formed Newell's Old Boys, named after teacher Isaac Newell.

In Montevideo, British railway workers formed the Central Uruguayan Railway Cricket Club in 1891. Locals and Italian migrants began to dominate the club, though, and football had become its main sport by the time it was renamed as Peñarol in 1913. Their rivals, Nacional, were the result of an 1899 merger between Uruguay Athletic Club and Montevideo Football Club. As early as 1889, matches were being played between teams from Buenos Aires and Montevideo. A Scotsman, Alexander Watson Hutton, was instrumental in forming the Argentine

Association Football League, later renamed as the Argentine Football Association, in 1893. A Uruguayan equivalent was set up in 1900.

The first match in Brazil is thought to have been played by visiting British sailors in 1884, but things did not really get going until the next decade. An important role was played by Charles Miller, whose British father, John, had emigrated to São Paulo in the 1870s to work in railway construction, at a time when around 3,000 British families lived there.

The younger Miller learned football at school in Hampshire, and played for Southampton and Corinthians, as well as playing cricket with the MCC. After returning to Brazil in 1894, inevitably finding a job in the railway business, he helped to set up the football branch of the São Paulo Athletic Club; and, later, the local league, the Liga Paulista. When another club was founded in the city in 1910, by migrants from various European countries, it is thought that Miller suggested its name: Corinthians.

Oscar Cox, son of a British diplomat in Rio de Janeiro, learned his football while studying at Lausanne in Switzerland. After returning to Rio in 1897, he tried to promote the game there, and eventually formed a club, Fluminense, five years later. Flamengo was founded in Rio in 1895, but initially as a rowing club, hence the name (still its official one) Clube de Regatas do Flamengo. The club adopted football in 1911, giving birth to the intense 'Fla–Flu' rivalry, a highlight of the Rio state league (Campeonato Carioca), which had begun in 1906 after a team of British sailors had played a match in the area. British sailors also inspired the creation of Santos in 1912.

In other parts of Latin America, which lacked close trading links with Europe, the game took a little longer to catch on. Chile's oldest club is Santiago Wanderers, formed in the port of Valparaiso in 1892. The Federación de Fútbol de Chile was established three years later. The game was introduced in Ecuador, some time around 1899, by the Wright brothers, Juan Alfredo and Roberto, who had picked it up in England.

A Dutchman, William Paats, got things started in Paraguay after moving to Asunción in 1888. He brought a ball back from a trip to Buenos Aires, and taught the game to locals. Tournaments were being played in the capital by 1900, and Paats formed its first club, Olimpia, two years later. Mexico's first club, Pachuca, was set up by Cornish miners in 1901.

Across Latin America, soccer was a thoroughly British phenomenon in the early years. Local people would mostly just look on with amusement at the 'crazy English' chasing a ball around a field. Playing equipment and rule books were imported from Britain, and Spanish was initially forbidden at meetings of the Argentinian FA. These roots can still be detected in the names of many leading clubs, featuring English words and names, such as River Plate and Newell's Old Boys in Argentina,

Corinthians in Brazil, Liverpool in Uruguay, and Santiago Wanderers and Everton in Chile.

But, as the game became more popular with the wider population, its British connections quickly faded into irrelevance, just as its public school origins had been obscured when the working class took it over in Britain. Good playing facilities and equipment may have been hard to come by, but the locals learned to improvise – playing in streets and alleyways, or on beaches, often using rolled-up socks as makeshift balls.

All sections of society learned to love the game: indigenous peoples, descendants of African slaves, and newer arrivals from southern Europe. Employers saw the benefits of supporting, and sometimes owning, local clubs, realising that the game could help to boost their standing in their communities. Perhaps even more so than in Europe, intense local rivalries developed quickly in cities such as Rio and Buenos Aires, as people from different districts, or different ethnic or social backgrounds, latched onto different teams.

As the locals took control of the game, they began playing it their own way. The typical English style, with an emphasis on hard work, hard running and physicality, gave way to an approach based on ball control and possession. But there was some British influence behind this: Scottish football leaned towards short passing, rather than the long-ball approach, and a Scot, John Hurley, encouraged this style in Uruguay.

In the hands of South Americans – especially in Brazil – soccer became an even more skilful game, featuring feints, swerves and flicks. Some believe that *capoeira*, a 'fight-dance' developed by slaves in the 17th century, helped to shape the Brazilian style of play, particularly when black players came to the fore in the middle of the 20th century.

In other regions of the world, though, the game was not exactly spreading like wildfire. Around the turn of the century, the English FA tried to promote it in Britain's past and present 'white settler' colonies – the USA, Canada, Australia, New Zealand and (white) South Africa – perhaps thinking their cultural ties with Britain would help the game to grow. English teams were sent on missions, such as a Corinthians tour of South Africa in 1897. But other cool-weather sports had already become established in these countries – mostly other forms of football, along with ice hockey in Canada – and soccer made little impression.

It did find some popularity in black Africa, but it would be decades before the region had the urban infrastructure and playing facilities necessary for it to develop substantially. There were small signs of activity in Asia – the Philippines played against China in Manila in 1913, and the Japanese FA was founded in 1921 – but the game would make little progress there until much later in the century.

On a worldwide scale, although it was not yet a truly global game, soccer had forged well ahead of Britain's other main sporting exports, rugby and cricket. No-one can say, for certain, why this happened; the most likely explanations are that it was cheap to play, needing little equipment; and that it was relatively simple, helping it to cross cultural and linguistic barriers.

Although local working-class people across Europe and South America quickly made the game their own, displacing the mainly middle-class British founders of their clubs, the FA's rules were widely accepted, with few variations. The British model of national associations, leagues and knockout 'cup' tournaments was adopted in most, if not all, of the nations that the game reached.

By the turn of the century, the Home International tournament had become an annual highlight of the game in the UK. The idea of international soccer had not yet caught on elsewhere, but this was about to change. The national teams of Argentina and Uruguay made their debuts against each other in Montevideo in 1901. It was the first of their 14 meetings in that decade, a period in which neither team played against anyone else.

Austria and Hungary were the first mainland European countries to have national teams, which met in Vienna in 1902. The next to appear was Bohemia and Moravia, playing against Hungary a year later. Over the next few years, Belgium, France, Germany, Holland and Switzerland all joined in the fray.

The International Football Association Board (IFAB) had been set up in 1886, with representatives of the English, Scottish, Welsh and Irish associations, to govern the game's rules, at least for matches played in the British Isles. The IFAB's rules were generally accepted abroad, but there were some variations in the laws used in different countries, causing difficulties when national teams met. Players were also starting to move between clubs in different nations, sometimes leading to disputes, and it became clear that cross-border regulations were needed.

In 1902, Robert Guérin, of the Union des Sociétés Françaises des Sports Athlétiques, decided it was time for action. With support from Carl Hirschmann of the Dutch FA, he invited the English association to take the lead in creating an international governing body. But the men running the English game had an insular outlook, and little appetite for getting involved in such a venture. FA secretary Frederick Wall was not against the idea, but decided it would need approval from the FA executive committee, the IFAB, and the Scottish, Welsh and Irish associations. Their deliberations proceeded painfully slowly, and Guérin's patience eventually ran out:

A Develyshe Pastime

Tired of the struggle and recognising that the Englishmen,
true to tradition, wanted to wait and watch, I undertook
to invite delegates myself.

The result was a meeting in Paris on May 21, 1904, featuring representatives from Belgium, Denmark, France, Holland, Spain, Sweden and Switzerland. They agreed to form the Fédération Internationale de Football Association (FIFA), and elected Guérin as president. Some of the federation's statutes, agreed at this meeting, have had a lasting impact on the way the game is run. For example, FIFA would recognise just one national association in each member country; and a player suspended in one country would be ineligible to play in others. Even though the British associations were not involved, it was agreed that all member nations would follow the IFAB's playing rules.

The following April, after some persuasion from Baron Edouard de Laveleye of Belgium, the FA finally gave FIFA its stamp of approval, and joined up. Scotland, Wales and Ireland followed suit in June, along with Austria, Germany, Hungary and Italy. An Englishman, Daniel Burley Woolfall, even became FIFA president in 1906. He stayed in office for 12 years, a brief spell of harmony between the British associations and FIFA. Woolfall made a particular effort to standardise the laws of the game worldwide, a cause that was helped when two FIFA delegates were admitted onto the IFAB in 1913.

FIFA soon expanded beyond Europe, with South Africa joining in 1909, followed by Argentina and Chile in 1912, and Canada and the USA[22] a year later. FIFA had tried to organise an international tournament in 1906, without success. Ten years later, though, Argentina staged the first South American Championship: a four-team, round-robin competition that would evolve into the Copa America. The continent's own federation, CONMEBOL (a highly selective abbreviation of 'CONfederación SudaMEricana de FútBOL'), was founded during the tournament.

When the first modern Olympic Games were held in 1896, soccer was not yet sufficiently well known, worldwide, to earn a place in the schedule. It was an exhibition sport in the 1900 Paris games, and in St Louis in 1904, but was barely noticed. Both tournaments were contested by club teams, with London's Upton Park the winners in Paris, followed by Galt FC of Canada four years later.

Soccer became an official Olympic sport in 1908, with the FA taking charge. Great Britain won the tournament in London that year, and did likewise in Stockholm in 1912. Belgium claimed gold at the 1920 Antwerp games, albeit with the help of a walk-off by Czechoslovakia in the final, unhappy with the performance of 72-year-old English referee John Lewis.

By now, the Olympic tournament, although restricted to amateurs, was becoming something of an unofficial world championship. FIFA took control of it in 1924, the year when Uruguay became the first South American entrants. As professionalism had not yet been legalised in Uruguay, this Olympic team was effectively the full national side. En route to Paris, they played a series of warm-up matches in Spain, where they dazzled spectators with their close passing, fast dribbling and changes of pace. Among them was José Leandro Andrade, believed to have been the first black footballer to appear in mainland Europe[23]. Uruguay won the tournament, and repeated their success in Amsterdam four years later, establishing themselves as a powerful force in the football world.

While the game was catching on around mainland Europe and South America at the start of the new century, its following in the UK continued to grow. It had become an integral part of working-class life, mostly in northern and central England and in Scotland, but increasingly in southern England as well. It was also becoming a highly competitive business. Transfer fees were escalating (Alf Common's move from Sunderland to Middlesbrough in 1906 caused shock waves by breaking the £1,000 barrier), and there were rumours of match-fixing and illegal payments to players.

Southern clubs were starting to make their mark. Southampton reached the FA Cup final in 1900, while still in the Southern League – as were Tottenham when they went one better a year later, beating Sheffield United in a replayed final, prompting wild celebrations in north London. In Scotland, professionalism had been legalised in 1893, with the Celtic–Rangers rivalry soon taking centre stage in both league and cup.

Attendance figures kept on going up. Tottenham and Sheffield United's draw in the 1901 FA Cup final, at the Crystal Palace stadium, was seen by 110,820 fans. Twelve years later, 120,081 saw Aston Villa beat Sunderland at the same venue. Some grounds were ill-equipped to cope with such large crowds, and safety standards were poor. When 70,000 turned up at Ibrox Park in Glasgow for the Scotland–England match in 1902, a wooden stand collapsed, leaving 25 people dead and 537 injured.

When war broke out in the summer of 1914, rugby union was suspended almost immediately in England. But the Football League and FA Cup continued for another season, to the disgust of many press commentators, who argued that the nation's young men had a more important task on their hands than playing football.

More than 2,000 professional British players signed up for duty, and many clubs contributed to the war effort, helping to recruit volunteers among their local communities, and making their stadiums available for use as drill grounds. But the critics would not be appeased, and this episode widened the class divide between soccer and rugby union. Fee-paying schools largely abandoned soccer for many years, and the FA's upper-crust committee men began looking increasingly remote from the vast majority of players and supporters.

English soccer's growth resumed after peace had been restored, with each of the Football League's two divisions expanding from 20 clubs to 22 in 1919–20, the first post-war season. The next summer, the League swallowed up 22 clubs from the Southern League, forming the new Third Division. Just a year later, 20 northern and Midland clubs joined the league to become the Third Division North, while the existing Third Division was renamed as the Third Division South. Soon, the league would have 92 clubs.

Despite the economic slump of the 1920s, crowds of more than 60,000 were commonplace. The 1923 FA Cup final between West Ham and Bolton was scheduled for the huge Empire Stadium, newly built in what was then the Middlesex village of Wembley. The FA grossly underestimated the level of interest in the match, and declined to make it an all-ticket event. The result was a scene of massive overcrowding, with thousands spilling onto the pitch. They were ushered back to the edges of the field, largely thanks to the efforts of Billy, a white police horse, and the game somehow went ahead. The 'White Horse Final' was officially seen by 126,047 fans, but the real figure was undoubtedly far higher. Despite this near-disaster, Wembley became the regular venue for FA Cup finals and many England home matches.

Scotland already had a major stadium of its own, in Glasgow's Hampden Park, opened in 1903. Hampden has always been the home of Queen's Park (still an amateur club today, but they were in the First Division at the time), but began hosting Scottish Cup finals and internationals in its first few years, effectively becoming the national stadium. For some time leading up to World War II, it had the highest capacity of any soccer stadium in the world.

By the late 1920s, British soccer was spawning all kinds of paraphernalia. Cigarette cards of famous players were hugely popular, and millions began trying their luck at the football pools, first introduced by Littlewoods in 1923. Media coverage was on the rise: the first radio match broadcast took place in 1927, and the first televised game came ten years later. Cinema-goers could see match highlights in weekly newsreels.

All this, though, was happening in almost total isolation from the outside world. The post-war political climate had soured relations between the UK's four associations[24] and those on the continent – in particular, the English FA refused to let its team play against Germany or Austria. British football was inward-looking, oblivious to the advances that the game was making overseas. Few Britons took much interest in what was happening abroad, feeling sure that their footballers were superior to foreigners. It was a belief that would persist, despite strong evidence to the contrary, until being punctured by a series of rude awakenings in the 1950s.

FIFA president Daniel Burley Woolfall died in August 1918, further weakening the fragile bonds between the British FAs and FIFA. The four associations withdrew from FIFA soon afterwards. Although they rejoined in the early 1920s, the relationship remained decidedly uneasy, especially over the issue of changes to the laws of the game. They left again in 1928, after a dispute over the amateurism regulations to be applied to footballers in the Olympics.

Despite British football's aloofness in the inter-war years, many continental clubs turned to Britons when looking for coaches. There were two main schools of tactical thought, both influenced by coaches from the UK. One was the typical English approach, based on speed, directness and physical strength. Wingers played an important role, supplying crosses for tall, powerful centre-forwards. Midfield was largely bypassed, as half-backs tried to spray the ball out to their wingers as soon as they got it.

This was known in Spain as the '1-2-3', or as *la manera inglesa* – the English way. It still had its Spanish advocates as late as the 1990s, particularly in the Basque country, including Javier Clemente, national coach for much of that decade. It also found favour in Germany, mainly in the north, where some called it the 'Flying Hussar'. One of its disciples was Otto Nerz, Germany's militaristic coach from 1923 to 1936.

The other main style was based on short, quick passing, emphasising ball control and movement off the ball. This approach had been evolving in Scotland, arguably since the early 1870s, but the major figures who promoted it abroad were from south of the border.

Jimmy Hogan was a Lancastrian who played for Fulham in the 1900s, where his understanding of the game was influenced by Scottish coach Jock Hamilton. Hogan later embarked on a coaching career of his own, which took him to Switzerland, Austria, Germany, Hungary and Holland. Along with the influential Hugo Meisl, Hogan coached Austria's outstanding national side, the *Wunderteam*, arguably Europe's best in the early 1930s. Among other things, Hogan was one of the first coaches to advocate a controlled diet for players.

Hogan eventually found a management job in England in 1934, returning to Fulham; but was sacked within a year, having perturbed some players with his unfamiliar training methods (using a ball, for example) and his un-English tactics. The club's board dismissed his progressive ideas, claiming that 'seasoned professionals did not need coaching', which gives us some idea of where English football's head was buried in those days. Still, Hogan had a happier time at Aston Villa between 1936 and 1939, leading them to promotion into Division One and an FA Cup semi-final.

The quick-passing game reached Germany's Ruhr industrial belt, where soccer was booming in the 1930s. Schalke 04 developed it into their own 'spinning top' style, with players continually moving around the pitch, looking to pass to teammates in better positions than themselves. Otto Nerz, though, was unmoved, dismissing it as 'fiddling and dribbling around'.

Another much-travelled English proponent of the short-passing game, Fred Pentland, bounced back after an unfortunate start to his coaching career. His first position was with the German Olympic team, taking over in May 1914. Germany was hardly the ideal place for a Briton to be when war broke out a couple of months later; sure enough, Pentland soon found himself in a detention camp (along with several other former footballers, including Derby's legendary Steve Bloomer), where it is thought that he spent much of his time coaching German officers in the finer points of football.

Pentland managed France's Olympic side in 1920, but soon moved on to Spain, where he became something of a hero. After a short spell at Racing Santander, he began the first of two hugely successful spells with Athletic Bilbao. He also had three stints with Atlético Madrid, and one with Real Oviedo. Fred Pentland was affectionately known as *El Bombín*, a reference to his ever-present bowler hat. He appears to have been something of an eccentric; in English football circles, with his alien sense of tactics, he was considered a maverick.

Meanwhile, in Italy, Cheshire-born William Garbutt, a former winger with Woolwich Arsenal and Blackburn Rovers, made a big impact as Genoa's coach between 1912 and 1927. Thanks to him, to this day, coaches in Italy are often known as 'Mister'.

Although soccer's laws had become fairly stable by the mid 1920s, there was a creeping problem that needed to be addressed, perhaps more so in England than elsewhere. The offside rule still required an attacker to have at least three opponents (which could include the goalkeeper) between himself and the goal-line, in order to be in an onside position.

Some teams had developed offside traps, notably Newcastle. One of their full-backs, Bill McCracken and Frank Hudspeth, would move up to the halfway line, leaving just the other full-back and the goalkeeper behind him. A forward pass beyond the halfway line would usually result in an offside flag. Even if their opponents managed to spring the trap, they would still have a defender to beat, as well as the goalkeeper, giving the offside trappers a safety net.

Games were often littered with offsides, sometimes as many as 40. The trap was widely seen as cynical, and there was a clamour for change. In the summer of 1925, the IFAB made a simple adjustment to the rule: only two players, not three, would be enough to keep an attacker onside.

The immediate effects were spectacular. In 1925–26, 6,373 goals were scored in the Football League, compared with 4,700 the previous season. (Two years later, Everton's Dixie Dean would score 60 league goals in a season, a record unlikely to be threatened in the modern game.) Newcastle, having done much to instigate the change, were among the first teams to adjust their defensive tactics to stem the flood of goals. Centre-half Charlie Spencer retreated from his roving midfield position, becoming a third defender: the *stopper*, whose main role was to counteract opposing centre-forwards, who, along with wingers, had been running rampant since the rule had been changed.

At Arsenal, veteran forward Charlie Buchan had been signed in the summer by new manager Herbert Chapman. From the start of the season, Buchan had been trying to persuade Chapman to adopt a three-man defence, without success. After a 7-0 thumping by Newcastle, the manager relented, and the new formation helped them to a 4-0 win over West Ham in their next match.

Herbert Chapman is sure to loom large in any account of English football in the 1920s and early 1930s. In an age when most teams were picked by committee, while their managers apparently did little more than puff on a cigar and utter a few words of encouragement before each game, the Yorkshireman revolutionised the role in countless ways. After spells in charge at Northampton and Leeds City, Chapman joined Huddersfield in 1920. Over the next five years, he led them to an incredible run of success.

Money was hard to come by, in a town where rugby league drew large crowds, but Chapman assembled a defensively sound, counter-attacking team, making good use of wingers. They became the first club to win the league title three times in a row, starting in 1923–24. The third of these triumphs, though, was achieved without Chapman, who had been lured to the capital by ambitious Arsenal chairman Sir Henry Norris. With spending power that he could not have imagined at Huddersfield, he built a team to fit his tactical vision, eventually winning league titles in 1930–31 and 1932–33.

Unlike his contemporaries in England, but in common with some overseas coaches, Chapman recognised the importance of fitness, diet, teamwork, discipline, man-management and motivation. He had a flair for publicity, and strove to improve the game as a spectacle: he was an early advocate of such things as floodlights, stadium clocks, numbered shirts, and white balls. Chapman's work ethic eventually got the better of him: he died after catching pneumonia while watching Arsenal's third team in January 1934, with his senior side on their way to another championship.

Although many English fans welcomed the glut of goals that followed the change in the offside rule (the scoring rate diminished only gradually, as many teams were slow to adopt a three-man defence), some observers complained that the quality of play had suffered, with pace and power becoming more valuable than skill and sound defence. While many continental and South American teams were adopting more sophisticated styles, English football was still a rather crude game. Austria's *Wunderteam* lost 4-3 to England at Stamford Bridge in 1932, but amazed the home spectators with their ball control and short passing.

The Olympics had started to pose a problem for FIFA by the late 1920s. Many national associations were now letting clubs pay their players in some way or another, even if they did not allow full professionalism. FIFA claimed that players who only received 'broken-time' payments should be classed as amateurs, and pressed the International Olympic Committee (IOC) to let such players take part in the Olympics, but the IOC refused to budge.

FIFA secretary Henri Delaunay believed that football had outgrown the Olympic tournament, and that the IOC's strict rules on amateurism were out of step with the way the game was developing. There were possibly also doubts over whether there would be a soccer tournament at the 1932 games in Los Angeles, a city that would be difficult for European teams to reach, and where soccer was almost unheard of.

Along with another Frenchman, FIFA president Jules Rimet, Delaunay put forward a proposal at FIFA's 1928 congress: that the federation should arrange a tournament of its own, open to both professionals and amateurs. The idea was agreed, and plans were made for the first World Cup, to be held in 1930.

Uruguay was chosen as the host nation, partly in recognition of its Olympic titles in 1924 and 1928, and also to honour the centenary of its independence. The decision was not to everyone's liking: many of FIFA's member nations were European, and their delegates were unhappy about the long sea journeys their teams would face. Although the Uruguayan government offered to cover their transport and accommodation costs, some European associations refused to enter the tournament. Others, having initially agreed to enter, then pulled out at short notice. Only four European teams turned up – Belgium, France, Romania and Yugoslavia – and they were hardly the continent's finest.

The World Cup was originally planned as a 16-team knockout competition. But the late withdrawals reduced the field to 13 entrants, and instead of giving byes to some teams, the organisers decided to solve the problem by arranging the entrants into four groups. All the games were played in Montevideo, in just three stadiums.

Not everything went smoothly: there were countless refereeing disputes and other complaints, a mass brawl in the Argentina–Chile game, and even a snow shower just before the opening match between the USA and Belgium. Overall, though, the tournament was regarded as a success. The hosts became the champions, beating Argentina 4-2 in the final in front of 93,000 at Estadio Centenario. Both teams had trounced their opponents, Yugoslavia and the USA respectively, 6-1 in the semi-finals.

The next tournament, in 1934, was to be held in Italy. The Uruguayan FA, still seething over the European snubs in 1930, refused to send a team. But, with 31 countries wanting to take part this time (21 of them European), a qualifying system had to be used for the first time. In a fairly chaotic process, littered with withdrawals, 12 European teams reached the finals, along with two from South America (out of four contenders), one from North and Central America and the Caribbean (from four), and one from a combined Afro-Asian group of just three teams. The final tournament had a simple knockout format; Argentina, Brazil and the USA faced long trips back across the Atlantic after just one game each.

By this time, football's popularity had been noticed by political leaders, as well as businessmen. International matches, especially in the competitive, highly-charged environment of the World Cup or Olympic Games, provided a platform for politicians to appear in front of large, nationalistic crowds, revelling in patriotic pride and – so they hoped – basking in the glory of their teams' success.

Italian dictator Benito Mussolini grasped the opportunity that the 1934 World Cup presented to him, using the event to promote his National Fascist Party and stir up jingoistic feelings. (Adolf Hitler would follow suit two years later, when Germany staged the Olympics in Berlin.) Success for the Italians would, of course, help Mussolini's cause; and there were numerous rumours of match-fixing in their favour. One of the games under suspicion was their 2-1 extra-time win over Czechoslovakia in the final, at the Stadium of the National Fascist Party in Rome. Italy raised eyebrows with their physical approach to the game, which went largely ignored by referees.

The World Cup took place in Europe again in 1938, in France this time – to the further fury of the Uruguayans, who stayed away again. Argentina also pulled out, leaving Brazil as South America's only representatives. These were dark days in Europe, and politics inevitably interfered with the tournament. Spain withdrew before the qualifying stage because of the country's civil war. Austria qualified for the finals, but did not appear in them, owing to the country's annexation by Germany.

For the 15 remaining teams, the tournament was again arranged on a knockout basis (with Sweden getting a bye to the quarter-finals) – the last World Cup to be organised this way. Italy retained their title, beating Hungary 4-2 in the final in Paris. In both 1934 and 1938, Vittorio Pozzo, Italy's Anglophile coach, who had learned the game as a student in Manchester and Bradford, had adopted the *metodo* formation. This was a variation on the 2-3-5 system that most teams had employed until the mid 1920s, but with the inside-forwards dropping back to help the half-backs – sometimes described as a 2-3-2-3 line-up.

Just over a year later, much of the world was at war again. Soccer competitions around Europe were either suspended, or drastically altered to suit the harsher conditions of everyday life. But the game still had a strong appeal, and was widely played as a way of entertaining troops. In Britain, the government initially imposed tight restrictions on travel and public gatherings, including spectator sport. But these were loosened just a few weeks into the war, and football bounced back impressively.

Attitudes had changed since World War I, and sport was no longer frowned upon as an unsuitable frivolity in wartime. Instead, it was seen as a way of helping to keep up the public's morale, and encouraging them to co-operate in the war effort. Again, British football's authorities and clubs made their grounds available for military training. Players and coaches also helped with the armed forces' physical training[25].

Regional leagues were set up in England and Scotland, along with the War Cup. Teams were often of a makeshift nature, with many players either away on military duty overseas, or stationed far away from their usual clubs. They regularly featured guest players and amateurs, sometimes plucked from the crowd at the last moment. Despite this, attendances were healthy, some as high as 60,000. It is thought that the custom of post-match handshakes began in Britain during these years, perhaps a reflection of how the game had temporarily lost some of its intensity.

Football in wartime Germany came under the direct control of the Nazi regime. Trying to convince the German people, and the outside world, that life was carrying on as normal, they did their best to keep the regional leagues, the end-of-season championship tournament and the German Cup running. To some extent, they succeeded. Large crowds still turned up for important games, such as the 90,000 or so who saw Rapid Vienna beat Schalke 04 in the 1941 championship final in Berlin. The national side also continued playing, although teams willing to face them were a little thin on the ground. This all carried on until the late summer of 1944, when the football scene fell apart as the hardships of a losing war campaign began to bite.

Soccer had enjoyed a boom period after the First World War, and was about to experience another. This time, with varying degrees of success, the Brits would finally throw themselves into the international fray.

Chapter 7

The Gaelic Game

*'The game is Gaelic in its very essence. All the consequences
of this Gaelic nature combine to give it character.'*
– Joe Lennon, *Coaching Gaelic Football*, 1964

Just as in Britain, the early history of football in Ireland is little-known, other than a series of violent incidents and attempts at banning it. Hurling, its sister sport, features in a rich litany of Irish folklore tales, perhaps going back several thousand years. In contrast, although some football-like activity is thought to have been going on for over two millennia, little was written about it until the 17th century.

When the River Liffey froze in 1338, Dubliners played football on it. Unlike hurling and Irish handball (similar to modern American handball and the Basque game of pelota), football avoided a ban when the Statutes of Galway were declared in 1527. Locals were ordered not to play 'hurlings of the littill ball with hockie sticks or staves, nor use no hands ball to play without the walls, but only the great footballe.' But it fell foul of the Sunday Observance Act in 1695: anyone caught taking part in various games on a Sunday, including *'foot-ball playing'*, faced a 12 pence fine. On a slightly more positive note, English writer John Dunton, who travelled in Ireland in 1677, described games of football in Fingal, near Dublin, 'where the people use it much and trip and shoulder verie handsomely.'

For some of the more vivid stories of Irish football from the 18th century, we can be thankful to the island's poets. An epic poem by Matt Concannon the Elder described a game in Fingal in 1720, featuring teams from nearby Swords and Lusk, in some detail. The ball was made from oxhide stuffed with hay, the goals were fashioned from bent sally-rods (long wooden sticks, normally used as weapons), and each team had just six players, a remarkably low number for this time. They were allowed to carry, kick and catch the ball, and to wrestle and trip each other.

Twenty years later, Redmond Murphy an tSléibhe wrote of a 12-a-side match in Omeath, County Louth, in *Léana an Bhábhúin*, again with players carrying the ball and seizing it from each other. One of the poet's relatives, Patty an tSléibhe, was wrestled onto a pile of stones during the game, and died from his injuries 16 days later.

A 'match of football between married men and bachelors' was played in Dangan, County Meath, in 1731. Nine years later, another game was played on the frozen River Liffey in Dublin. Football had become a regular sight in the Dublin area by the end of that century, as well as in other Leinster counties such as Meath, Wexford and Kildare.

The game in 18th-century Ireland seems to have had much in common with some of Britain's most refined forms of folk football, such as *hurling to goales* in Cornwall, *cnapan* in west Wales, and East Anglian *camp-ball*; but with more emphasis on kicking. Large sums of money were often wagered on results, with some of the spoils being handed out to the winning players.

A variety of football known as *caid* had become popular in County Kerry by the early 19th century, particularly on the Dingle peninsula; although the word 'caid' is often used to refer to early Irish football in general. In Kerry, it is sometimes used today as a name for modern Gaelic football. Caid was described in a thesis by Father W. Ferris of Glenflesk, near Killarney, early in the 20th century, based on the recollections of an 80-year-old who had played it as a young man.

It came in two forms, much like the Cornish games of *hurling to goales* and *hurling over country*. *Field caid* had a small playing area, with arch-shaped goals made from the boughs of trees. *Cross-country caid* was a long-distance game, stretching between two neighbouring parishes; play began after the church service each Sunday in the winter, and went on until sunset – or until an argument brought it to an early close. The ball was made from an animal bladder wrapped in animal skin; the word 'caid' means the scrotum of a bull.

Like most forms of football at this time, caid had few rules. Wrestling and tripping were accepted as parts of the game. Rucks would form around the ball, with fast runners waiting nearby, hoping to gather the ball when it broke loose[26]. Around the middle of the century, caid developed into what was descriptively known as the *rough-and-tumble game*.

The Great Famine, in the mid and late 1840s, devastated much of Ireland, particularly rural areas in the west. Populations of towns and villages were ravaged by starvation, disease and emigration. Many everyday activities, including sport, practically ground to a halt. But Irish-style football survived, and was still being played regularly in the 1860s and 1870s, even in western counties such as Cork, Kerry and Limerick.

By this time, though, traditional Irish sports were facing new threats. They were often banned, or at least discouraged, by the authorities, and by other establishment figures such as clergymen and landlords – either because of fears about violence and disorder, or because of suspicions that games were being used as a cover for political meetings, as the nationalist movement gathered momentum.

After rugby became established in Dublin in the 1850s and 1860s, and soccer in Belfast soon afterwards, they both began to spread around the island, as did cricket, a favourite of local government officials, police and the armed forces. British-style athletics also became widespread in the 1860s. These sports were largely run in Ireland by British organisations, or by middle-class Irishmen, mostly of a conservative, unionist persuasion. The Victorian concept of the 'gentleman amateur' was much in evidence, and working-class nationalists barely got a look-in.

Some Irish sportsmen and journalists grew frustrated with the British and unionist stranglehold on sport, and began suggesting that something should be done to preserve and promote native games. As early as 1858, Denis Holland, editor of the nationalist newspaper *The Irishman*, proposed forming a network of local clubs to organise Irish-style sporting activity. Holland moved to the United States, and his idea lay dormant for more than two decades; but the baton was eventually picked up by Michael Cusack, a fiery character from a Gaelic-speaking area of County Clare.

After working as a teacher in various parts of Ireland, Cusack founded the Civil Service Academy, often known as Cusack's Academy, in Dublin in 1877. He encouraged its students to play sports such as rugby, cricket and athletics (and possibly Irish-style football), often joining in himself. He became a familiar figure around the city, known as a powerful orator.

Cusack is thought to have been a nationalist of some sort – mostly favouring the Home Rule movement, which wanted limited autonomy for Ireland, but sometimes appearing to lean towards the more radical end of the scale. But he happily engaged with people of all political affiliations, and was more concerned with promoting Irish culture than espousing political causes; among other things, he was involved in the Gaelic Union for the Preservation and Cultivation of the Irish Language.

By the late 1870s, Cusack had become disenchanted with the Dublin athletics scene. Despite being predominantly middle-class, it was hardly staying faithful to the 'gentleman amateur' ethos. Winners often received cash prizes, betting was rife, and there was even a drunken riot at an athletics meeting in 1878. Traditional Irish jumping and throwing events were often left out of the schedules.

Cusack's views were shared by Pat Nally, a leading athlete from Balla, County Mayo. Nally was a prominent member of the Irish Republican

Brotherhood (IRB), often known as the Fenians, a secret fraternity advocating armed revolt against British rule. He wanted Irish athletics to come under nationalist control, and met Cusack in 1879 to discuss their ideas. Cusack went on to vent his frustrations through articles in the *Irish Sportsman* journal in the early 1880s. He started organising athletics meetings, and founded the Dublin Athletic Club in 1882.

Soon, though, Cusack began turning much of his attention towards team sports. Hurling had practically died out in the Dublin area, replaced by the milder game of hurley, which was more like hockey. Cusack set up the short-lived Dublin Hurling Club in 1882, hoping to bring hurling back to the forefront. He wanted the game to be revived all over Ireland, with standard rules, and found support from like-minded men in Cork and Galway. That same year, Cusack was involved in launching the *Gaelic Journal*, a bilingual publication that was later acknowledged as a crucial influence behind the revival of the Irish language.

It might well have been his involvement in hurling, and his contact with sympathisers around the island, that gave Cusack the idea of forming an Irish sports association. He argued the case for such an organisation at a meeting in Loughrea, County Galway, in August 1884. On October 11, an anonymous article, later found to have been written by Cusack, appeared in both *The Irishman* and another nationalist newspaper, *United Ireland*. Titled 'A Word on Irish Athletics', it called for the birth of a movement to preserve sport with an Irish identity, creating new opportunities for working-class, nationalist sportsmen; and to contribute to a wider campaign to rekindle interest in Irish culture.

Both newspapers soon featured letters of support for the article from Maurice Davin, a former athlete of international standing from Carrick-on-Suir, County Tipperary, who had been at the August meeting. Davin suggested drawing up nationwide rules for football and hurling, partly in the hope of reducing violence and injuries. His letters were followed by one from Cusack himself, proposing a meeting in Thurles, County Tipperary, on November 1.

At least seven men turned up for the meeting at Miss Hayes's Commercial Hotel, although some accounts suggest that there were several more. Maurice Davin took the chair. As well as Michael Cusack, the others known to have been present were Tipperary stonemason J.K. Bracken, Kerry policeman Thomas St George McCarthy, Belfast journalist John McKay, local solicitor Joseph O'Ryan, and Waterford journalist John Wyse Power. Bracken and Wyse Power were both IRB members[27].

After Cusack had opened the meeting, Davin gave a short speech, criticising the state of Irish sport. He called for a new governing body to wrest control from British hands, to draw up revised rules for Gaelic games, and to make sport accessible to ordinary Irishmen. Cusack followed this with a longer, typically vitriolic speech, attacking the press for ignoring Irish sports. He also read out 60 messages of support for the movement, and suggested staging a national athletic festival, based on the Tailteann Games, which had been held in Ireland from 1829 BC until around 1180 AD.

The Gaelic Athletic Association for the Preservation and Cultivation of National Pastimes was duly founded (thankfully, its name would soon be shortened to the first three words, often abbreviated to 'GAA'). Maurice Davin was elected as president, with Cusack, McKay and Wyse Power as secretaries. They were keen to enlist support from the Catholic church, and Archbishop Croke of Cashel, a moderate nationalist, soon agreed to become the association's first patron. Support was also offered by Home Rule Party leader Charles Stewart Parnell, Land League founder Michael Davitt, and Irish migrants in the United States and Australia.

With some help from John McKay, Davin drew up the GAA's rules for hurling, and for what would become known as Gaelic football, in January 1885. Like the Football Association's original laws, the football rules – essentially a codification of the 'rough-and-tumble game' – were few in number (only ten of them), were brief, and left some aspects of the game unclear to the uninitiated.

The playing area was to be at least 120 yards long and 80 yards wide, with goalposts 15 feet apart, joined by a crossbar eight feet from the ground. Each team could have between 14 and 21 players. Play would last for an hour, with the teams switching ends at half-time, and would be officiated by a referee and two umpires. As the referee started the game by throwing the ball into the air, all the players would be in the middle of the field, each holding hands with an opponent.

Results would be decided purely on goals, scored by kicking the ball between the goalposts and under the crossbar. If the ball crossed a sideline, or was put over the goal-line (but not into the goal) by a defender, an opponent would throw it back into play. If an attacker forced it over the goal-line without scoring, the opposing goalkeeper would take a free kick from near his goal.

Pushing, tripping and holding were not explicitly prohibited, except when done from behind, in which case the guilty player was to be sent off. The same punishment applied to head-butting, presumably from any direction. The rules said nothing about whether players could carry the ball (and, if so, how far), or throw it (apart from sideline throw-ins), or about legal methods of tackling. These points would be clarified over the coming years.

There was no offside rule of any kind, as is still the case. The absence of offside has helped to set Gaelic football (along with Australian Rules) apart from both soccer and rugby. As well as allowing players to remain spread out around the field, rather than being bunched together, it makes long kicking, combined with catching, into a powerful attacking weapon.

Although Michael Cusack was clearly no Anglophile, he did admire both the way that England's Amateur Athletic Association ran its affairs and the county-based structure of English cricket, which had also been adopted in Ireland. From the outset, GAA sportsmen were required to be amateurs. Each county was to have a GAA board, and there would be local representation at parish level. This was all part of the plan for the GAA to become a grass-roots organisation, reaching out to working-class Irishmen in rural areas as well as cities and towns.

The results were impressive. Recalling the GAA's first two years, Cusack later wrote that 'the Association swept the country like a prairie fire.' Nationalists all over the island joined up, along with some unionists. Cusack claimed that the GAA had 50,000 members just 18 months after its foundation, which suggests that there were more than a thousand clubs. Its presence was especially strong in the Munster and Leinster provinces, and there was even an English-based branch in Wallsend, near Newcastle-upon-Tyne, as early as March 1885.

Athletics was the GAA's main priority in these early days, and it held its first athletics meeting in Macroom, County Cork, just ten days after its inaugural meeting. Several GAA events were held in 1885, and many more the following year, with football and hurling gradually becoming major attractions. The first hurling match under GAA rules took place in Tynagh, County Galway, in January 1885.

On February 15, the new football rules were first tried out in three games: Callan v Kilkenny Commercials in Callan, County Kilkenny; St Patrick's v St Canice's in Kilkenny town; and Naas at home to Sallins, in County Kildare. All three games ended in 0-0 draws, and the lack of goals soon led to calls for a secondary method of scoring.

The rules were revamped in 1886, with *points* introduced as a tie-breaker for drawn games. At first, a point could be scored by simply forcing the ball over the opposition's goal-line anywhere outside the goal, but *point posts* were soon added, 21 feet either side of the goalposts, and a point was scored if the ball passed between a goalpost and a point post, or over the crossbar – somewhat similar to a *behind* in modern Australian Rules football. In response to concerns that the game was too rough, the GAA outlawed wrestling and 'handigrips'.

The new organisational framework and standard rules breathed fresh life into Gaelic football and hurling. By 1886, both were being played far more widely, and more often, than in the years before the GAA was founded. A football tournament was held in Kilkenny in March of that year, with six teams from Kilkenny, Dublin, Tipperary and Waterford.

The All-Ireland championships, for both sports, were first staged the following year. Each county would have a 'champion club' (and could choose its own way of determining which club this would be), which would enter a provincial knockout tournament. The four provincial winners would play in the All-Ireland semi-finals, which would be followed by a final.

There was little interest in the All-Ireland championships at first, and the first football tournament was plagued by withdrawals and delays, with only around a quarter of the 32 counties entering teams. Dundalk Young Irelands, the Louth champions, were the first club to reach the semi-finals, beating Ballyduff Lower of Waterford to clinch the Leinster title in July 1887. The All-Ireland final was not held until the following April, when the Dundalk side lost to Limerick Commercials.

Despite the explosion in activity, the GAA went through a string of crises in its early years, several of which threatened its existence. It was widely seen as part of the Irish nationalist movement, which was gathering pace in the 1880s. Some other sporting organisations, such as the rugby section of the Irish Champion Athletic Club, which had counted Michael Cusack as a member just a few years earlier, accused it of being a political body. Cusack and John McKay both denied this, as did GAA patron Michael Davitt, who insisted that, when it had been founded, 'the idea was national, not political.'

October 1885 saw the imposition of 'The Ban': if any GAA member was caught playing a non-Gaelic football code, his club would be banished from the association. Some saw this as evidence of the GAA being anti-British; others argued that it was a necessary part of its campaign to protect Irish sports.

Cusack, though, was not around to defend the GAA's position for long. His often tactless, confrontational style had made him few friends and many enemies. The man who had founded the GAA was unseated as its secretary in July 1886, after barely 18 months, ostensibly on the grounds of poor accountancy. If the association really had been apolitical up to this point, this was all about to change.

Two months later, P.T. Hoctor, of the Irish Republican Brotherhood, became the GAA's vice-president, while John O'Leary, president of the IRB's Supreme Council, was elected as a patron. A power struggle broke out among the GAA leadership, between radical and moderate nationalists. Meetings often degenerated into shouting matches, and sometimes into fist-fights.

Maurice Davin was marginalised by the IRB contingent, and resigned as president in April 1887, leaving the IRB holding even more power, as Hoctor became its *de facto* leader in the absence of a replacement. The GAA's nationalist links drew the attention of the Royal Irish Constabulary

(RIC), which was accused of appointing spies to infiltrate it; the GAA consequently banned RIC staff from joining up. Catholic clergymen also criticised the association, for staging games on Sundays.

Davin was re-elected to the presidency in January 1888, ushering in a quieter period of a year or so. But 1888 did not pass without its problems: it was the year of the 'American Invasion', when around 50 hurlers and athletes visited the United States to demonstrate their sports. The tour was intended as a fund-raiser for a Celtic cultural festival planned for the following year; in the event, it *lost* almost enough money to sink the GAA.

As if this were not bad enough, only around two thirds of the touring party returned to Ireland, and the ensuing disruption led to that year's All-Ireland football championship being abandoned. However, the tour did help to generate interest in Gaelic games in the US. The New York GAA was formed in 1891, followed by branches in Chicago, Detroit, Philadelphia and San Francisco.

In January 1889, Maurice Davin walked out of a GAA central council meeting during an argument over finances. His departure was taken to mean that he had resigned, again, as president. This time, the hard-line republicans became even more dominant than before. IRB member Peter Kelly took Davin's place, and the few remaining Protestants and unionists jumped ship.

The nationalist movement was split even further in the early 1890s, when Home Rule Party leader Charles Stewart Parnell became embroiled in a divorce scandal. The GAA leadership generally stayed loyal to Parnell, a stance that cost them much support. Another period of calm arrived in 1893, when the largely apolitical Dick Blake, of Meath, became a powerful member of the central council.

After becoming secretary in April 1895, Blake declared the GAA to be neither political nor sectarian, and prohibited political discussion at its meetings. The ban on GAA members playing 'foreign' football was lifted in 1896; the police ban had been scrapped two years earlier. This was a brighter spell for the association, after years of turmoil, with the number of member clubs rising from 217 to 360 between 1895 and 1897. In January 1898, though, radical nationalism came back to the fore, as the GAA's IRB faction forced Blake out of office. Matters had been brought to a head by the upcoming centenary of the 1798 uprising against British rule, which gave fresh impetus to the movement.

The GAA council was split over whether or not to join in the commemorations, but many GAA members did get involved. The next three years saw more internal unrest, verbal attacks from the clergy, and doubts over the GAA's survival, before the appointments of two younger men in 1901 – president Jim Nowlan and secretary Luke O'Toole – gave it a new lease of life.

As the new century began, the GAA was becoming increasingly linked with the nationalist movement, and was even thought to be playing a leading role in it. Some members of a new nationalist party, Sinn Féin, launched in 1905, were prominent on GAA county boards, and some GAA leaders supported the party. In a fresh move to 'de-anglicise' sport in Ireland, the GAA restored its ban on members playing 'foreign games' in 1905. Around the same time, another rule was introduced to prohibit policemen, soldiers and sailors from taking part in GAA sports.

Back on the field, Gaelic football was beginning to take shape. The GAA adjusted its rules, hoping to cut down on violence and create a more free-flowing game. Some points had been clarified in 1888: the ball could not be thrown (but could be struck with the hand), it could be caught, and free kicks were to be awarded for fouls. Additionally, if a defender put the ball out of play over his team's goal-line, the opposition would get a free kick 40 yards from the goal (this was moved to 50 yards out in 1895).

During his spell in office in the mid 1890s, Dick Blake pressed for the rules to be made even more specific, believing them to be 'crude and imperfect and unworthy of the GAA'. Blake was an unashamed soccer and rugby fan, willing to adopt some features of those codes if it would help to improve the Irish game.

The number of players in a team, having previously been anything from 14 to 21, was fixed at 17 in 1895; it would be reduced to 15, the present number, in 1913. From 1896, substitutions could be made without needing the opposing captain's approval. Whereas points counted initially only as tie-breakers, a rule introduced in 1895 made a goal worth five points, with results determined by total points. A year later, a goal was devalued to three points, another rule that has remained unchanged[28]. The first explicit rule on ball-carrying was also published in 1895, stating that the ball could be held for no more than four steps, and for no longer than was 'necessary to kick or fist it away'.

From 1892 onwards, clubs taking part in All-Ireland tournaments were allowed to select players from other clubs in their counties. Gradually, the teams would evolve into representative county sides, particularly when county boards began to take control of selection.

Dublin and Cork clubs dominated All-Ireland football in the early years, with Dublin Young Irelands winning the 1891, 1892 and 1894 titles. The last of these was won by default: the Dubliners walked off the pitch after an invasion by spectators in a replay at Thurles, and their opponents, the Nils club from Cork, refused another replay. It was the second consecutive All-Ireland final to end in disarray, a reflection of the slightly chaotic state of affairs in the GAA's formative years. Until well into the 1920s, it was quite normal for a final to take place the year after the tournament started, or even two years later.

By 1900, a London GAA board had been formed, and the All-Ireland finals of 1900 to 1903 (actually taking place between 1902 and 1905) each pitted London's champion club against the winners of the 'home' tournament. London's representatives each time, always soundly beaten, were the Hibernians club. Among their number was a Cork-born civil servant named Sam Maguire, later to play an important role in the Irish independence campaign. In 1928, soon after his death, a new trophy for the All-Ireland football champions was commissioned: the Sam Maguire Cup, the most treasured prize in Irish sport today.

Kerry emerged as a leading power in the 1900s, with Kildare, Dublin and Louth as their main rivals. As the game became more disciplined, and training methods improved, counties developed distinctive styles of play. Dublin specialised in the 'catch-and-kick' game, while Kerry and Kildare were early exponents of the *hand-pass*, a technique that got around the rule against throwing the ball: instead, it was held in one hand and struck with the other, using an open palm or a closed fist.

The 'scoring space' was altered dramatically in 1910, when a rugby-style H-shaped goal structure was introduced, but with a net attached to the crossbar and the lower part of each goalpost. Point posts were scrapped – a single point could now only be scored by kicking the ball between the goalposts and over the crossbar. As some compensation, the gap between the goalposts was widened from 15 feet to 21.

A tournament between teams representing Ireland's four provinces, the Railway Shield, was introduced in 1905, but was abandoned after just three seasons. The game was adopted at many schools around this time, and the Sigerson Cup, for universities, was launched in 1911. Meanwhile, the GAA wanted to establish a major stadium and headquarters, and looked to the Jones's Road sports ground in Dublin, which had already staged many football and hurling finals since 1895. The association bought the ground in 1913, renamed it as Croke Park in memory of its first patron, Archbishop Croke, and soon decided that all future All-Ireland finals would be staged there.

The Home Rule movement had recovered from the Parnell scandal by now, and was finding support in the British parliament. The House of Commons passed a series of Home Rule bills, only to see them rejected by the House of Lords, or, in one case, postponed because of the outbreak of World War I. After militant northern unionists had formed the Ulster Volunteer Force to fight against Home Rule, radical nationalists responded by forming the Irish Volunteers, and many GAA members, including secretary Luke O'Toole, signed up. This left many GAA men with little time for sport, and both football and hurling saw a slump in activity.

The nationalist campaign intensified in 1916, the year of the Easter Rising, when Patrick Pearse of the Irish Volunteers read out the 'Proclamation of the Irish Republic' outside Dublin's General Post Office. The British authorities reacted with fury, executing the leaders behind the Rising and imprisoning many other nationalists, including some GAA members. A Royal Commission investigation concluded that the GAA was 'anti-British'. In response, the association denied being a political body, while acknowledging that some of its members were involved in nationalist activity.

The government even outlawed the GAA for a short time, in the summer of 1918. Soon afterwards, public meetings in Ireland – including spectator sports events – were prohibited, except with official permits. The GAA refused to accept the ruling, and ordered its clubs not to apply for permits. A day of mass defiance known as 'Gaelic Sunday' was arranged for August 4, when Gaelic games were played simultaneously around the country, with an estimated 100,000 players involved. Only one match, at Croke Park, saw any attempt at police intervention.

The following January, two events on the same day marked the start of the Irish War of Independence: an ambush of policemen in County Tipperary by members of the Irish Republican Army (a new incarnation of the Irish Volunteers), and Sinn Féin's unilateral launch of an Irish parliament, the Dáil Éireann, in Dublin. By the summer of 1920, everyday life in Ireland was being badly disrupted. The police were now supplemented by two paramilitary forces, the Auxiliaries and the Black and Tans, both with reputations for brutality against civilians.

That autumn, with the war at its peak, republican leaders believed that a network of Dublin-based British intelligence agents, known as the Cairo Gang, were plotting to have them killed, and decided to strike first. In the early hours of Sunday, November 21, led by Sinn Féin's Michael Collins, republican forces assassinated 14 people in Dublin. Whether *all* of them were spies isn't entirely clear, but it certainly spelt the end for the Cairo Gang.

A Gaelic football match between Dublin and Tipperary was scheduled for Croke Park that afternoon, as a fund-raiser for relatives of republican prisoners. There was a tense atmosphere in Dublin, as news of the killings spread, and the GAA considered cancelling the match. But it went ahead, watched by a crowd of around 10,000.

Just after the game had started, a British military plane flew over Croke Park and fired a red signal flare. Forces of some sort – either Black and Tans, Auxiliaries, or even regular RIC policemen, depending on which account we believe – climbed over a wall into the ground. They fired shots onto the pitch and into the stands, prompting spectators to run to the far end of the ground. A police officer went onto the pitch and announced that everyone present would be detained and searched. Some fled into nearby houses, and hid under beds. Some accounts even suggest that the players were all lined up for execution, before a modicum of sanity was restored.

When the dust had settled, 12 spectators lay dead, along with Tipperary captain Michael Hogan. Another player, Jim Egan, was wounded. In front of a large crowd back home in Grangemockler, Hogan was buried in his football kit. One of Croke Park's stands would later be named after him.

It appears that the raid on the stadium was not officially authorised, and was carried out by rogue (and possibly drunk) elements of the British forces. But it was widely seen as a misplaced reprisal for that morning's killings, and led to widespread condemnation, at home and abroad, of the way that Britain was conducting the war. The loss of the Cairo Gang was also a major blow to the government. Before long, it was rumoured that negotiations for a truce were underway. The events of November 21 would go down in Irish history as 'Bloody Sunday', and would highlight how closely Gaelic sports had become identified with the push for independence.

The war had almost crippled the GAA, and it was saved from bankruptcy only by a loan from the Dáil in January 1921. Six months later, though, a truce was called, and life started to return to normal. The Anglo-Irish treaty, splitting the island into the Irish Free State and the British-ruled province of Northern Ireland, was signed in December that year, and ratified by the Dáil the following month.

Suddenly, the GAA found itself in a different world. In 26 of the 32 counties, there were no British-backed politicians, police or armed forces. But these were still tough times for the association: some of its leading staff had perished in the war, while many of the survivors were busy in the Irish Free State's political scene. Worse was to come in June 1922: a split between nationalists supporting the treaty, and those who objected to its terms, led to a civil war.

Most members of the GAA council were either pro-treaty or neutral. They generally enjoyed good relations with the fledgling pro-treaty government, provoking threats from anti-treaty forces. For a year or so, Gaelic sports in Munster and Connacht practically stopped altogether, while GAA activity in Northern Ireland still faced hostility and suspicion from the authorities. In January 1923, Irish government forces executed two anti-treaty Clare GAA officials, Con McMahon and secretary Patrick Hennessy. Clare soon had both a pro-treaty GAA board and an anti-treaty one – a situation that lasted until the summer of 1925, two years after the civil war ended.

Early in 1923, there was an attempt at using the GAA to help broker an agreement between the warring factions. The association has been credited with helping to heal the country's divisions after the war. As Gaelic sports began to pick up again in peacetime, army and police teams started springing up, an unthinkable idea just a few years earlier. The GAA largely shook off its political affiliations, as a new generation of younger leaders began to take control.

During those troubled times in the early 1920s, one of Gaelic football's most distinctive features had been born. Playing for Mayo against Dublin in 1921, Seán Lavan – a gifted all-round sportsman who would represent the Irish Free State as an Olympic sprinter in 1924 and 1928 – unveiled a new way of overcoming the restrictions on carrying the ball. Since 1907, a ball-carrier had been allowed to bounce the ball on the ground after taking four steps, and could then take another four steps; but it was thought that he could go no further.

Lavan ran towards the Dublin goal, bouncing the ball *on his foot* after finishing his second set of four steps. This foot-tap was technically a kick, which he thought would entitle him to catch the ball directly (as if a teammate had kicked it to him) and start another sequence of four steps, a bounce on the ground and four more steps, and so on. At the end of his run, Lavan kicked what he thought would be a point. The referee ruled it out, but the *solo run* soon found acceptance, and would eventually become an integral part of the game.

The hand-pass was well established by now, and was crucial to Kildare's 'combination' playing style, which helped them to six consecutive Leinster titles between 1926 and 1931. They reached the All-Ireland final in five of those seasons, winning it twice. Kerry returned to the fore, having undergone more turmoil than most counties in the civil war, becoming All-Ireland champions four times in a row from 1929 to 1932. Two of their leading players, Con Brosnan (pro-treaty) and John Joe Sheehy (anti), had played senior roles on opposing sides in the war.

The Kerry footballers visited the United States several times in the early 1930s, playing in New York and Chicago in front of crowds of up to 60,000, larger than any domestic attendance to date. They also found success in the early years of the National Football League (NFL), a winter competition launched in 1925. The league provided the county teams with a regular programme of games, with a knockout format in the later stages. It has gathered a reasonably strong following over the years, but has never quite rivalled the All-Ireland championship for prestige.

The inter-provincial Railway Shield, abandoned 20 years earlier, was revived as the Railway Cup in 1927, with the final taking place on St Patrick's Day. Attendances were encouraging at first, but the competition's status has dwindled, and, although it still survives, it seems unlikely to last much longer. Another new arrival was the 'minor' All-Ireland championship, for under-18 players, established in 1928.

Until 1925, players had only been allowed to represent the counties in which they lived. The *non-resident* rule, introduced that year, also gave them the option of playing for their counties of birth. Meanwhile, radio commentary began in 1926, helping to bring big games to a wider audience. Twelve years later, a teenage Michael O'Hehir made his commentating debut, going on to become the much-loved 'voice of Gaelic sports' over the coming decades[29].

The main story of the 1930s was the rivalry between the Connacht giants, Mayo and Galway. Mayo won six NFL titles in a row from 1933–34 to 1938–39, and an All-Ireland championship in 1936, while Galway weighed in with All-Ireland titles in 1934 and 1938. Kerry had yet another spell of success, reaching five consecutive All-Ireland finals from 1937 to 1941, and winning four of them. The finals were drawing huge crowds by now, with nearly 70,000 seeing Kerry's 1938 victory over Galway.

Ireland, or at least the Irish Free State, was enjoying its new-found political stability, and the new sense of national pride helped to sustain the public's interest in Irish culture, including indigenous sports. As the GAA celebrated its fiftieth anniversary in November 1934, it had nearly two thousand affiliated clubs, with a membership estimated at around a quarter of a million. Croke Park was being expanded and improved, with the double-decker Cusack Stand, named after GAA founder Michael Cusack, opening in 1937. There was some unease over the 'foreign games' rule, though – particularly when the GAA expelled Irish president Douglas Hyde, one of its patrons, for attending an international soccer match in Dublin in 1938.

Although the Free State stayed neutral in the Second World War, daily life was affected by shortages of coal and petrol, making it difficult for supporters to travel to games. Sports fans are a resourceful lot, though, and many were happy to cycle long distances to follow their teams.

By 1947, interest in Gaelic sports in the United States had waned a little since the successful tours by Irish county teams in the early 1930s. In an effort to revive it, the GAA broke its own pledge to stage every All-Ireland final at Croke Park. Instead, that year's Kerry–Cavan final was played at the Polo Grounds, home of baseball's New York Giants. The idea met some resistance in Ireland, but the GAA, keen to reach out to the Irish diaspora while marking the centenary of the Great Famine, approved it at its annual congress.

Conditions were hardly ideal, with a rock-hard field, and the pitcher's mound still in place, but a respectable turnout of 35,000 made the venture something of a success. The game was broadcast live on Irish radio. Its start was held up by various formalities, and Michael O'Hehir spent much of the closing stages pleading on-air with the station's management to keep the broadcast going until the game finished (which they did). Cavan won by 2-11 to 2-7, the first of their three titles in six years.

Like many sports, Gaelic football enjoyed a boom in the 1950s. Some proof of this can be gleaned from the attendances at All-Ireland finals, from the 76,174 who saw Mayo v Louth in 1950, up to the 87,102 crowd for the Dublin–Kerry final of 1955. The 1950s also saw renewed interest in the traditional language and music of Ireland, helping to forge an atmosphere in which Gaelic games could flourish.

There was still much debate over the football rules, especially over the hand-pass. Many purists thought – as some do today – that hand-passing was contrary to the spirit of the game, preferring to see the more traditional 'catch-and-kick' method of moving the ball. A rule change in 1956 forbade players from hand-passing with an open palm, but they could still do so with a closed fist.

The GAA had decided in 1935 that the rules could only be changed at intervals of at least five years, hoping to keep some stability. In 1945, throw-ins from the sideline were replaced by kick-ins, with the ball being kicked from the ground. Sixteen years later, goalkeepers were allowed to pick the ball up off the ground, within the square in front of the goal (outfield players have never been permitted to do this in any part of the field).

Nearly four decades after Ireland had been partitioned, the All-Ireland title went north of the border for the first time in 1960, when Down beat Kerry. A year later, Down retained the Sam Maguire Cup with a win over Offaly in front of a 90,556 crowd, still the record All-Ireland attendance. Down played in a fast, fluent style that has often been described as 'total football', epitomised by Seán O'Neill, widely rated as one of the best forwards ever to play the game.

Other county sides had other ways of getting results. Galway and Dublin developed new styles of forward play, while Kerry still made much use of the old 'catch-and-kick' method. The game was becoming more team-oriented than in earlier days; it was now more of a running game, rather than a display of individual kicking and catching skills.

Television first reached Northern Ireland, and some parts of what was now the Republic of Ireland, when the BBC installed a transmitter near Belfast in 1955. Ulster Television was launched in 1959, and the Republic's own public service station, Télefis Éireann, later to become part of RTÉ, was opened two years later.

The GAA leaders were wary of TV at first, fearing that coverage of Gaelic games would lead to a fall in attendances. But there were other reasons for concern, as 'foreign' sports became more visible, and other leisure options became available in an increasingly urbanised society. Soccer's 1966 World Cup was shown extensively on RTÉ, giving the sport a boost in Ireland. Still, although British soccer clubs such as Celtic and Manchester United became popular on the island, Gaelic sports survived the onslaught relatively unscathed.

The late 1960s saw the start of a challenging period for Gaelic sports in Northern Ireland, with the sectarian unrest of 'the Troubles'. Once again, the authorities viewed the GAA – which still banned members of the British army and the Royal Ulster Constabulary from joining – as a part of the nationalist movement. Some players were harassed by the police, or interned, and British forces attacked and occupied GAA buildings.

The Troubles provided a stern test for the GAA's claim to be non-political. In 1971, after years of debate, it lifted 'The Ban', which had prohibited GAA members from playing or watching soccer, rugby, cricket or hockey. Croke Park, though, was still closed to 'foreign', or perhaps more specifically English, sports.

Although the All-Ireland championship had originally been a tournament for the champion clubs of the counties, the club element had vanished early in the 20th century, as full-blown county teams took over. Clubs' profiles had subsequently diminished, and county boards often got the better of clubs in wrangles over the availability of players. An idea cropped up in the 1960s, in the hope of reviving the club scene: all All-Ireland *club* championship. Provincial inter-club tournaments began in the mid 1960s, and a national competition was launched in 1971.

The club All-Irelands got off to a quiet start, with only around 200 people turning up to the first final at Croke Park. But the competition eventually found its feet, and became a source of huge local pride for the successful clubs. The final is held on St Patrick's Day (a slot vacated by the struggling Railway Cup), after the clubs have played through the winter. With the main All-Ireland championship taking place between spring and early autumn, and the NFL having recently shifted from a long winter schedule to a shorter period between February and April, the club tournament now takes centre stage for several months in late autumn and winter.

By the mid 1970s, there was some frustration at the way in which Gaelic football was being played. Players often marked their opponents tightly, and the 'pull-and-drag' method of tackling was a regular sight. Frequent fouling was lightly punished, thanks to weaknesses in the rules, and there was little flow to the game. The rules were revamped in 1974 and 1975, largely to try to counteract these trends.

One new law prohibited the 'third-man tackle'; another stated that only a player holding the ball could be tackled. The concept of the 'personal foul', for offences such as tripping or pulling down an opponent, was introduced. A player's second personal foul would earn him a caution, and a third would result in a dismissal. Two rectangles were drawn in front of each goal (replacing a single square), one 15 yards wide and five yards deep, and another 21 yards by 14.

A personal foul inside the larger rectangle would lead to a soccer-style penalty kick from the edge of that area, 14 yards from the goal. The goalkeeper could not be charged within the smaller rectangle. Hand-passing with an open palm, banned since 1950, was now allowed again. Soon it would become common practice to score a goal from a palmed 'pass', much to the dismay of purists. The rules would later be tightened again, to restrict scoring with the hand.

After decades with little football success for the island's most populous county, the Dublin GAA board made sweeping changes towards the end of 1973, with former star player Kevin Heffernan taking charge of the team. Heffernan oversaw a vast improvement in fitness, skills and tactics. Gaelic football quickly became big news in Dublin, as the side reached every All-Ireland final from 1974 to 1979, winning three of them, and also took NFL titles in 1976 and 1978. Among their players in 1976 and 1977 was Kevin Moran, soon to find further fame in soccer with Manchester United and the Republic of Ireland.

Dublin soon came up against a stiff challenge from Kerry, never a team to stay out of contention for long. Kerry manager Mick O'Dwyer trained his players hard, demanding high levels of speed and stamina, and used some innovative attacking tactics. Their rivalry with Dublin dominated the All-Ireland championship for a decade, with the two sides meeting in six of the 11 finals from 1975 to 1985.

Kerry came out on top in five of these finals, as their hard-running, all-round game often got the better of Dublin's more predictable, short-passing style of play. In *A History of Gaelic Football*, Jack Mahon described this Kerry side as 'the greatest football team in the history of the GAA'. Their late 1970s forward line featured five of the game's all-time greats in John Egan, Eoin Liston, Ger Power, Mikey Sheehy and Pat Spillane. Meath and Cork were the next teams to dominate, taking eight of the ten All-Ireland final berths between 1987 and 1991; although, at a time when the game was generally cleaning up its act, Meath's physical approach was not to everyone's liking.

By this time, the GAA leadership had overcome its aversion to television, now seeing it more as a potential source of revenue than as a threat, and allowing more coverage than before. Advertising hoardings had become commonplace by now, and around the time of the GAA's centenary celebrations in 1984, it began allowing competitions and trophies to bear sponsors' names; which also started appearing on players' shirts in 1991. These developments raised eyebrows, in a not-for-profit organisation which expected its players to remain amateur, but they became useful ways of raising funds.

Gaelic football faced another surge of competition from soccer as the Republic of Ireland suddenly rose to prominence with Jack Charlton at the helm, reaching major tournaments for the first time: the 1988 European Championship, and the World Cups of 1990 and 1994. Inevitably, many Irish sports fans jumped at the chance to celebrate the success of an Irish national team on a global stage. Yet again, the GAA feared that its sports might fade into obscurity; but the intense competition for the All-Ireland title helped to keep Gaelic football in the headlines.

In 1991, the Sam Maguire Cup found its way to Ulster for the first time in 23 years, as Down won the title. It was the start of a spectacular run for Ulster sides, with both Donegal and Derry claiming their first-ever titles in the next two years, followed by another Down victory in 1994. Tyrone almost kept the sequence going in 1995, losing by a single point to Dublin. The traditional powerhouses of Kerry, Galway and Meath soon re-asserted themselves, but Armagh and Tyrone put Ulster back in the limelight in the 2000s with their first All-Ireland titles.

Women began playing organised Gaelic football in 1974, generally meeting a dismissive response. Gradually, though, the women's game, basically under the same rules as the men's, but with less tolerance of rough play, attained some respectability. Even some old-timers found it more enjoyable to watch than the modern men's game, with more free movement and less gamesmanship. Senior and junior All-Ireland championships are run on roughly the same lines as the men's tournaments; the finals have been staged at Croke Park since 1986.

Since the GAA's earliest years, Gaelic games have been played by Irish migrant communities elsewhere in the world. The GAA has encouraged this, and today it has 'county' boards in London, Gloucestershire, Hertfordshire, Lancashire, Warwickshire, Yorkshire, Scotland, Canada and New York, with others covering continental Europe and the remaining parts of North America. Some clubs in London, such as Dulwich Harps, have started attracting young players without Irish backgrounds, including many from ethnic minorities. Although this is clearly a promising sign for Gaelic football's future in the wider world, it remains little more than a recreational game beyond Ireland's shores.

In the mid 1990s, the GAA launched a major expansion and improvement programme for its spiritual home, Croke Park. It now has a capacity of more than 82,000, making it one of Europe's largest stadiums, complete with a GAA museum on the premises and a GAA library nearby. Soon after its completion in 2005, the Lansdowne Road rugby and soccer stadium was due to be shut for a long period of renovation. The Irish RFU and the FA of Ireland turned to Croke Park as their best option for a temporary home. After much soul-searching and lengthy debate, the GAA suspended the 'foreign games' rule that prohibited the use of its showpiece stadium for such sports.

The question of whether to 'open' Croke Park raised bigger questions about the GAA's place in the modern world. Back in 1884, when it was founded, the overriding issues in Irish politics and culture surrounded the island's relationship with Britain, and questions about whether to seek full independence, Home Rule, or neither.

Today, Ireland occupies a very different place in the world. The Republic is not only an independent nation, but also part of the European Union; while Northern Ireland has entered a more conciliatory era since the 1998 Good Friday agreement. Economic progress practically stopped the exodus that had been draining the island's population for so long, and also encouraged an influx of immigrants from continental Europe and beyond; although the picture changed again in the late 2000s, as the economic downturn hit the Republic hard.

The new-look Ireland presents challenges to the GAA: can it attract players and spectators among the island's newcomers, largely unfamiliar with Gaelic sports, and among northern Protestants? Although the GAA's constitution declares it to be non-political and non-sectarian, it states the association's aims in terms that could easily be interpreted as Irish nationalist sentiment, and requires all members to support those aims. Some unionists have taken this to mean they are effectively banned from joining, although this is not stated explicitly.

Not surprisingly, the GAA is still strongly linked with the Catholic, nationalist population in many people's minds. It has been criticised for having stadiums, stands and trophies named after militant Irish republicans, unlikely to be seen as heroes by those of a unionist persuasion (although one of them, Sam Maguire, was a Protestant). This was highlighted in 2006, when the Antrim county board allowed its Casement Park stadium in Belfast to be used for a rally commemorating the republican hunger strikes of 1981, in defiance of the GAA central council.

The following year, Darren Graham, a protestant footballer and hurler who had played football for Fermanagh, retired at the age of 25, complaining of sectarian abuse from opponents. The GAA condemned the way he was treated, but clearly has some work to do if it is to avoid being labelled as parochial, prejudiced and backward-looking in today's world.

Amateurism is another thorny issue that seems unlikely to go away. Gaelic games are almost unique, in being played in front of such large crowds by players who earn no material reward. There have been suspicions of pseudo-professionalism, with players sometimes allegedly accepting offers of dubious 'jobs' which have led them to move to other counties, allowing them to play in those counties' teams. Players have also been allowed to earn money from endorsements. The Gaelic Players' Association has been pushing for government grants to be awarded to county-level players, similar to those given to Olympic athletes, rebuffing warnings from GAA officials that this would be the start of a slide into professionalism.

As long as the amateur rule stays in place, Gaelic football is in danger of losing more players to Australian Rules football, following in the footsteps of Jim Stynes in 1985, Tadhg Kennelly in 1999, and others. However, full-blown professionalism appears unlikely. It could seriously damage the structures of the GAA's competitions, and, consequently, that of the GAA itself. With 32 counties involved, there may not be enough money for all county-level players to be paid equally; the result could be an elite group of counties, with the better players from other counties being allowed to join them. Additionally, the (modified) knockout format of the All-Ireland tournaments is hardly conducive to professionalism, as it gives each team an unpredictable number of games.

Gaelic football also has problems in its rules and their enforcement, with many observers unhappy with the prevalence of the hand-pass, the unclear definition of tackling, and the many unsavoury off-the-ball incidents. Still, the GAA survives in reasonable health, with around 800,000 members worldwide, and a strong following for its two major sports. Its strength lies largely in its grass-roots make-up, which gives small communities across Ireland the chance to become involved, and to achieve their own moments of glory – a democratic set-up that would be difficult to sustain if the players were to turn professional.

We should not forget that hurling has also played a significant part in the GAA's story; but Gaelic football is the more popular game in most counties; it lays a strong claim to being Ireland's number-one sport, as well as being a part of its identity. Whether it can make an impact beyond Irish nationalist circles will depend, to some extent, on how the GAA presents itself to the rest of the world.

Chapter 8

The Men of Mark

*'Australian Rules football might best be described as a game
devised for padded cells, played in the open air.'*
– Jim Murray, American sportswriter

Nobody knew it at the time, but August 1835 was quite a month for Australian Rules football. Farmers from Tasmania built a settlement at the northern tip of Port Phillip Bay, on what was then the south coast of New South Wales. The town would later be named 'Melbourne', after the British prime minister. The same month, somewhere in New South Wales (it isn't clear exactly where), a boy named Tom Wills was born. Twenty-three years later, Wills would be in Melbourne, sowing the seeds for Australia's own football game.

As the town grew, some of its more affluent residents, with time on their hands for leisure, found the conditions perfect for sport. The summer heat was less stifling than in places such as Sydney and Brisbane, and the winters were milder and drier than in Britain, the old home of many of the newcomers. The area was blessed with vast open spaces, ideal for field games. British migrants clung to their old customs and pastimes, including their sports, as they tried to create a 'home from home' in new surroundings. Melbourne Cricket Club was founded almost as early as the town itself, in 1838; horse racing, rowing and athletics were also organised.

Sporting opportunities were more limited for working-class settlers, most of whom had to work all day on Saturdays. Religious beliefs meant that playing games on a Sunday was out of the question, leaving public holidays as the only chances to let off some steam. Some sort of football, probably a form of British-style folk football, was being played in Melbourne on holidays at least as early as 1840. The Old White Hart Inn's Christmas festivities in 1849 ended with a 'Grand Match at the old English game of Football', and other matches were played in Melbourne the following year, as well as one in Geelong, 45 miles to the south-west.

The southern part of New South Wales became a separate colony, Victoria, in 1851. Around the same time, gold was discovered near towns such as Ballarat, Bendigo and Castlemaine, between 50 and 100 miles north-west of Melbourne. Prospectors flocked to the goldfields from other parts of Australia, and from further afield, particularly the British Isles. Many gave up the hunt before long, with little to show for their efforts, and gravitated to Melbourne, now growing into a frantic, bustling city. Its population mushroomed from around 25,000 in the early 1850s to 125,000 a decade later. Victoria, as a whole, attracted more than half a million migrants in this period, many of them British.

Church-based grammar schools sprang up in and around Melbourne. Some of their teachers, having attended British public schools, were well versed in the creed of muscular Christianity and its relationship with sport. The movement was boosted in Australia by the arrival of Thomas Hughes's *Tom Brown's Schooldays* in 1857, with its account of football at Rugby School.

Hull-born Uppingham School old boy Dr John E. Bromby became headmaster of Melbourne Church of England Grammar School (a.k.a. Melbourne Grammar) in April 1858, and soon had his pupils playing football. Bromby found kindred spirits in his counterpart at St Kilda Grammar School (in an eastern Melbourne suburb) and fellow Cambridge University graduate, William C. Northcott; and Alexander Morrison, a former teacher and school rector from Scotland, now the head at Scotch College in central Melbourne.

These men had come from different footballing backgrounds, and when they discussed arranging inter-school matches, they faced a problem that many football organisers were getting used to: which rules should they use? Bromby and Northcott came up with some sort of answer, early in the southern winter of 1858, when teams representing their schools played against each other, although it is not clear what rules they followed.

Melbourne Grammar went on to face Scotch College on August 7, in a 40-a-side contest on a huge field next to the Melbourne Cricket Ground (MCG), where they had to contend with gum trees, pebbles and steep slopes. Again, no-one can be sure of the rules that were in force, but they were most likely based on those of Rugby School.

The match went on all afternoon, and continued over two subsequent Saturdays. A plaque on an outer wall of the MCG commemorates it as 'the first game of Australian Football'. Each team nominated an umpire. Scotch College chose John Macadam, a Glaswegian chemist and teacher, in whose honour the macadamia nut was named; Melbourne Grammar plumped for a young man named Thomas Wentworth Wills.

Wills was the son of a wealthy sheep owner, Horatio Spencer Wills. The family settled in the western part of what would soon become Victoria, and the ten-year-old Tom was sent to school in Melbourne in 1846. Four years later he was in England, finishing his education at Rugby School. While Horatio Wills was unimpressed by reports of his son's faltering academic progress there, it was a different story on the playing fields.

The youngster built a reputation as an outstanding cricketer and (Rugby-style) footballer. This was common knowledge in Melbourne when he returned in December 1856, finding a job in a solicitor's office. Cricket was the primary sport in south-eastern Australia, and Wills was soon being hailed as Victoria's best player. He joined Melbourne Cricket Club, and served as its secretary in 1857–58.

Tom Wills became one of a group of affluent, sports-mad young men in the city, largely based around the cricket club. Among them were two British-born Cambridge University alumni, William Hammersley and J.B. Thompson; and an Irishman, Thomas 'Red' Smith, once of Trinity College, Dublin. Wills had already come across Hammersley in England. They were joined by Wills's step-cousin, and soon to be brother-in-law, Henry Colden Antill (H.C.A.) Harrison, known to Wills as 'Coldy'. Unlike the others, Harrison had lived in Australia since birth, spending much of his childhood in rural Victoria.

Wills was a prolific, if eccentric, letter writer, and his ravenous appetite for sport led him to write a letter to the sporting journal *Bell's Life in Victoria* in early July 1858. He suggested that local cricketers should take up a sport during the winter, ostensibly to keep themselves fit (or, as he put it, to 'keep those who are inclined to become stout from having joints encased in useless superabundant flesh') – although it seems likely that he was simply bored with waiting for the cricket season. His main proposal was to form a 'foot-ball club', with a committee to draw up a set of rules. As alternatives, he suggested a rifle or athletics club.

A number of men responded to Wills's letter, showing an interest in playing football. Despite his enthusiasm, Wills was possibly not the ideal man to make the arrangements: his season as secretary at Melbourne Cricket Club had ended with all the club's possessions crammed into a tin box, a sign that organisational skills were hardly his strong point. Instead, Jerry Bryant, a publican, took the initiative. Using *Bell's Life in Victoria* to spread the word, he arranged a practice at Yarra Park near the MCG (and, conveniently, near his hotel) on July 31.

Some practices and games took place over the next few Saturdays, with an awkward mix of footballing styles. There was no clear consensus on the rules, although the players gradually began to agree on certain elements of the game that they preferred. By the end of the winter, they had formed Melbourne Football Club, albeit on a loose basis (it would be formally constituted at the start of the next season), and played their first inter-club match, against South Yarra, a club from a prosperous area in the south of the city. Melbourne FC, now in the guise of the Australian Football League's Melbourne Demons, can lay claim to being the world's oldest surviving *major* football club (although Sheffield FC, now a low-profile amateur side, beat them by a year[30]).

On July 31, 1858, the day when Wills and co. held their first practice, a team of men from St Kilda had played against a side made up largely of schoolboys. The St Kilda men struggled to adapt to the rugby-like rules being used that day, and, frustrated at getting few chances to kick the ball, some of them 'began to fisticuff'. Clearly, it was time for some common rules to be sorted out.

The problem arose again at Melbourne FC's first game of the 1859 season, blighted by confusion over what was, and was not, acceptable. The question of running with the ball, which would cause so much acrimony in London four years later, was perhaps the most disputed topic. A number of influences were coming into play, some of them conflicting with each other.

Some players, including Tom Wills, saw the Rugby School rules as a good basis for the local game, while some preferred the Cambridge-style kicking game, and others looked to develop styles and skills of their own. The embryonic Melbourne game was partly shaped by its surroundings: the wide-open spaces around the city encouraged an expansive game with a large playing area, while the hard ground (thanks to a series of dry winters) discouraged anything that would cause players to fall down often, such as scrummaging and tripping.

The players elected a committee of seven to draw up a set of rules, which they did at a meeting on May 17 at Jerry Bryant's Parade Hotel, most likely chaired by Wills. The others at the meeting, all members of Melbourne Cricket Club, were William Hammersley, J.B. Thompson, Thomas Smith, Alex Bruce, T. Butterworth and J. Sewell.

They studied the public school rules from Eton, Harrow and Winchester. Hammersley later recalled that 'Tom Wills suggested the Rugby rules, but nobody understood them except himself'. They also considered informal 'rules' which they thought had worked well in their matches and practices so far. As well as ball-carrying, there were differing views on the method of scoring, and the degree of physicality that should be allowed.

The committee came up with ten rules, recorded on a document found in a trunk in a storeroom at the MCG museum in 1980. They stated that the playing area could be up to 200 yards wide (with an unspecified length), with the side boundaries being marked by posts. In these early days, the pitch was usually rectangular. A goal could be scored by kicking the ball between the goalposts, at any height, without it touching another player along the way.

Either side of each goal, 20 yards from each goalpost, there would be a *kick-off post*. If the ball went behind the goal, without a goal being scored, a member of the defending team would kick it downfield, from 20 yards in front of an imaginary line joining the kick-off posts. (It appears that no lines were required to be drawn; the edges of the playing area were marked out by the goalposts, kick-off posts and boundary posts.)

In a rule reminiscent of the British public school codes, and the Cambridge University and Sheffield rules of the time, if a player caught the ball 'on the full' from a kick, he could call 'mark', entitling him to kick the ball without being impeded. The ball could also be caught, but without claiming a mark, if it had bounced once after a kick. It could not be picked up off the ground; if it rolled, or bounced more than once, it could only be kicked[31].

If the ball crossed one of the side boundaries, it would be thrown back into play at a right angle (the rules did not specify which team would do so). Other than this, throwing was forbidden. Pushing and tripping were allowed at first, provided that the victim was running or holding the ball, although tripping would soon be banned. Hacking was outlawed. Many aspects of the game were left undefined: the length of the pitch, width of the goals, game duration, team sizes, and even the issue of carrying the ball – either because the players couldn't agree on them, or because they wanted the rules to be flexible, allowing room for experimentation.

The Melbourne Rules, as they became known, closely resembled those used at Cambridge University and Sheffield FC. Perhaps the most striking similarity with the Sheffield game, in relation to other British football codes, was the lack of an offside rule; although it has been suggested that both the Melbourne and Sheffield footballers might have followed an unwritten offside convention in the early days, at least in some matches.

In *More Than a Game: The Real Story of Australian Rules Football,* Robin Grow ponders whether the Melbourne Rules might have influenced the original Football Association laws of 1863. The FA's rules, though, were copied from those used at Cambridge, with which Hammersley and Thompson were probably familiar[32]; and Grow presents no evidence that the FA knew anything of the Melbourne rules.

Another speculative thought comes courtesy of Brendan Murphy in his history of Sheffield FC, *From Sheffield With Love.* Henry Creswick, a migrant from Sheffield to Melbourne who probably knew the likes of Wills, Hammersley and Thompson, could have been related to Sheffield FC co-founder Nathaniel Creswick, and might have told the Melbourne footballers about the Yorkshire club's rules as they were formulating their own.

There have also been claims that Melbourne football was based on Gaelic football, while some have dismissed this as a myth. The truth seems to lie somewhere between the two extremes, but probably closer to the 'myth' end of the spectrum. As already mentioned, Gaelic football was not codified until 1885, although its informal predecessors, *caid* and the 'rough-and-tumble game', were much older. The people and institutions who shaped the Melbourne game were mostly from Anglo-Scottish, Protestant backgrounds; and, in their written accounts of its birth, Wills and Hammersley gave no indication of an Irish influence. It is true that an Irishman, Thomas Smith, was among the game's founders; but he had attended the mainly Protestant, rugby-playing Trinity College in Dublin, which hardly suggests he came from a background where Gaelic sports were played.

On the other hand, many working-class Irish migrants, gold prospectors and convicts were based in Victoria in the mid 19th century, and may have brought a Gaelic influence to the early football games in Melbourne, particularly the 'kick-and-catch' element. Some accounts suggest that Irishmen (other than Smith) took part in the early kickabouts that led to the birth of Melbourne FC, adding Gaelic-style punting to the chaotic mix of styles.

A converse theory suggests that Gaelic football might have been influenced by the Victorian game, as Irishmen returned home from Australasia. Archbishop Croke, the Gaelic Athletic Association's first patron, is thought to have seen some Melbourne-style football during a spell in New Zealand.

Another disputed version of the game's origins is that it was derived from an Aboriginal game, *Marn-Grook*. Richard Thomas, Victoria's Protector of Aborigines, saw Marn-Grook being played in Western Australia in 1841. In a brief account of it, he wrote of players punting the ball (made from possum skin) to each other, and leaping to catch it. Forty years later, James Dawson described it as a team game involving between 50 and 100 players; those who kicked the ball the furthest and highest were acclaimed at the close of play.

Tom Wills mixed with indigenous children as a boy in the countryside, and might well have seen, and even played, either Marn-Grook itself or a children's version known as *pando* or *bidi*. If he did, the experience might have encouraged him to make punting and high-catching an important part of the new game. Then again, the 'high mark' did not become a major feature of Victorian football until at least the mid 1860s, by which time Wills had become a marginal figure.

The Aboriginal theory, like the Gaelic one, is not supported by written evidence from the men who created the Victorian game. Whether they intentionally kept quiet about Irish-Catholic or Aboriginal ingredients of the game, to avoid alienating their white, middle-class, Protestant peers, or whether there simply was no such influence, is something we shall probably never know.

Melbourne FC was soon joined by other clubs nearby. Many were named after suburbs, parks or streets; others were linked with cricket clubs or hotels. Collingwood, Emerald Hill (later to become South Melbourne, and, much later, the Sydney Swans), Prahran, Richmond[33], South Yarra, St Kilda and University were all up and running by 1860. Down the coast in Geelong, which was now linked to Melbourne by rail, a club was formed in July 1859. Tom Wills moved there the following year, and captained the team a number of times.

Further afield, clubs were founded in Ballarat and Bendigo in the early 1860s. The new game, with only minor variations in rules between different cities and towns, gradually became known as Victorian Rules football. In Melbourne itself, Carlton, Essendon, Royal Park and an early incarnation of Fitzroy were all established by 1864, along with many school and college teams. Games were arranged on an adhoc basis, and were often spread out over several Saturdays[34], making it tricky to plan fixtures. In many cases, the first team to score twice would win the match, however long it took.

Soon, the clubs wanted something to play for. Melbourne and University contested a Silver Cup in 1862. The following year, the Caledonian Society donated a Challenge Cup, which would be competed for on a 'challenge' basis: a team could claim it by defeating the current holders. Gradually, some clubs became recognised as 'senior' and others as 'junior'. Clubs began building identities as representatives of their towns or suburbs, with nicknames, songs and distinctive colours; and developing intense rivalries with their neighbours.

For some years, Victorian football's rules remained brief, loose and open to interpretation. A revision in May 1860, this time with a number of clubs involved, gave a captain the right to award a free kick to his team if their opponents broke a rule, except where umpires were present. There was also a clarification of one of the more contentious issues, although it wouldn't last: '[the ball] shall not be run with in any case.'

The mark was becoming a major part of the game, as a useful way of advancing the ball and creating scoring opportunities. Without the constraints of an offside rule, it was a far more useful attacking weapon in Victorian Rules football than in most British codes. Players could kick to teammates further downfield, and a series of marks could quickly turn defence into attack.

The game soon attracted large crowds (even as early as 1859, around 2,000 are thought to have watched a Melbourne v South Yarra match), and not everybody approved of the mark. Some spectators became frustrated by the frequent hold-ups, as players took their time over kicking after claiming marks. Others saw it as a fair reward for intelligent and skilful play, and a welcome chance for the players to draw breath.

Another unloved aspect of the game was its habit of breaking down into lengthy scrummages, often starting when a player held on to the ball after being tackled. Each team would have a large pack of players, trying to force the ball forwards and their opponents backwards, until the ball either came loose or was driven into the goal. Until the mid 1860s, a round ball was normally used, and dribbling was not uncommon. When rugby-style balls came into use, though, dribbling inevitably went out of favour, and drop-kicks became more frequent; although most players usually preferred to punt.

The game was mainly played on public parks, with little, if anything, being done to make the conditions suitable for it. Play was often hampered by trees, ditches, rocks and swampy ground; and by excitable spectators spilling onto the playing field, sometimes to be pushed back by players and policemen. These hazards, together with the long playing area (often around 300 yards), made scoring difficult, and many games were drawn.

Victorian Rules football in the 1860s was a rough, anarchic game. Although there was a rule against hacking, it was hard to enforce, particularly in scrummages, and had little effect. A player holding the ball could be charged, or knocked to the ground. Spicing things up even further, some players wore spikes on their boots, and it was not unusual for players to drink alcohol before a game and during breaks in play.

The rule against carrying the ball was another that often went ignored. Players had their own preferences about how to play the game, based on their strengths and their earlier footballing experiences, which were often more influential than the formal rules. One of the game's more forceful characters, the aforementioned H.C.A. Harrison, played a part in resolving the ball-carrying debate.

Although he probably had no involvement in founding Melbourne FC and drawing up the initial rules (and his first recorded appearance in a game was not until the end of the 1859 season), such was Harrison's influence on the game in the 1860s that he was later dubbed the 'father of Australian football', a title he happily accepted in his old age. Harrison took over the Melbourne FC captaincy in 1861, and soon became known as the game's outstanding player, and one of its best tacticians. He was also one of its more aggressive players, with an approach once described by a rival as 'a little vicious'; as well as having a knack for exploiting loopholes in the rules, and getting them changed to suit his team's strengths.

Running with the ball had become widely accepted by 1864 – despite being against the written rules – and many spectators enjoyed watching it. There was a vague agreement that a player running with the ball should bounce it, but it was unclear how often he should do so. Things came to a head in a match between Royal Park and Melbourne in 1865. Royal Park captain Theodore Marshall was unhappy with Harrison's habit of carrying the ball over long distances, and asked one of his quicker players, J.E. Clarke, to retaliate by carrying it as far as possible, without bouncing it.

Clarke duly ran for more than 40 yards with the ball, and scored a goal, provoking a rather hypocritical protest from Harrison. The captains eventually agreed that, for the rest of the match, anyone who carried the ball should bounce it at least once every ten yards. A variation on this agreement appeared in an 1866 review of the rules, which Harrison drafted. They stated that 'no player shall run with the ball unless he strikes it against the ground every five or six yards' – although, confusingly, this clause came just after one which said the ball should not be carried 'further than is necessary for a kick'.

Now that the practice was openly allowed, expert ball-carriers known as 'dodgers' began to emerge, even though bouncing the ball became a tricky proposition as oval balls replaced round ones. Defenders fought back against the trend by grabbing dodgers, or pushing them from behind. If a player tried to keep hold of the ball while under attack, his teammates would help him out, inviting more intervention from the defending side; the inevitable result was a ruck or scrummage. In another feature of the 1866 rules, the size of the pitch was specified as 200 by 150 yards, making it narrower and generally shorter than before, but still larger than in most forms of football.

By 1867, a large contingent of British troops had become stationed in the Melbourne area. Some of them took an interest in the city's football scene, and challenged local clubs to matches. The soldiers' scant knowledge of the Victorian rules, and their inclinations towards various British football codes, led to some chaotic games – often particularly rough, even by the standards that Melburnians were used to[35]. But the locals enjoyed these wild, rough-and-tumble games, which gave them their first chance to see international football, of a sort, and were sorry to see the troops leave in 1870.

It would be hard to deny that Melbourne, around 1870, was the football capital of the world. Soccer and rugby in Britain were still almost exclusively middle-class affairs, barely noticed by the general population. Elsewhere, including other Australian cities and North America, football as a spectator sport had barely got off the ground, if at all. Perhaps it was only Melbourne's geographical isolation (at a time when even a trip to or from Sydney usually involved a long trip by sea) that prevented its football scene from getting the recognition it deserved.

By now, most manual workers were free on Saturday afternoons, allowing many working-class players and spectators to get involved. Some crowds in the early 1870s were estimated at around 10,000, with matches between Carlton and Melbourne usually the biggest draws. They included people from all social backgrounds, including many women. By 1876, the journalist 'Vagabond' was claiming that 'football is followed by all'. Among its followers were some wild young things (male and female) known as *larrikins*, who often threw missiles onto the field or at opposing supporters, and attacked players and umpires.

As the crowds became bigger and more excitable, it became clear that something had to be done to keep them off the playing fields. Carlton built a fence in 1876, and started charging an admission fee to cover its cost. After more than a decade of free football, many people were aghast at the idea of having to pay to see it, and there was further resentment when the club carried on charging a fee after the fence had been paid for.

Most clubs were regularly using cricket grounds by now, with their ready-made fences, stands and pavilions. Melbourne FC had played a match at the MCG in 1869; but, with the cricket club concerned about damage to the turf, several years passed before this became a regular event. The football rules did not specify the shape of the pitch, and now that games were being played in oval-shaped arenas, it made sense to use the entire space available; hence the shape of today's pitches.

Play was often slow and congested, frequently breaking down into tedious scrummages. The rules committee tried to improve the flow of the game in 1874, deciding that a player who was tackled must drop the ball, after which it could not be picked up until someone had kicked it.

There was some concern about the level of violence, and the numerous injuries. J.B. Thompson had written a plaintive letter to Tom Wills in 1871, bemoaning the brutality in the once 'noble and manly' sport they had helped to create – and this was from a man who had once recommended 'running straight at [the opponent], regardless of the consequences', and tackling a ball carrier by kicking him to the ground. The rules committee of 1874 tried to cool things down by banning *rabbiting*, the practice of felling an opponent by charging at him below hip-level. These were also the first rules to suggest that a match might have a time limit, although it was left to captains to decide what it would be.

Helped by the rule changes, the game became more fluent, allowing teams to develop techniques and tactics. Some started training, despite complaints that it violated the spirit of the game. Team positions were becoming more clearly defined, typically including a goalkeeper, backs, half-backs, centres, centre-forwards, a centre-forward on goal, a *goal sneak* (a term for a goalscoring specialist, harking back to the Eton term for offside, 'sneaking'), and possibly a pair of 'wing-forwards on goal'. Some of the heftier players were designated as *followers*, who would join in with rucks all over the field; while faster ones were employed as *rovers*, or *quicks*, whose role was to collect the ball and run with it when it came loose.

Spectacular *high-marking*, as practised by Aboriginals in Marn-Grook, where players leapt high to catch kicks and claim marks, had become an important part of the game by the mid 1870s. Many spectators loved it, but it was not without its hazards: defenders would often 'capsize' or 'buffet' opponents as they leapt, sometimes causing serious injuries; even death, in the case of John Mills of the Ballarat Imperials in 1883. Much safer, but less popular with fans, was the *little mark*, where the ball was kicked just a few yards to a teammate, who would then make a mark. Some teams, notably Carlton, used it as a way of gradually moving the ball into scoring positions.

The balls were now made from rubber, rather than a pig's bladder encased in leather, allowing players to kick them further and more accurately. Kicking techniques evolved, such as the long drop-kick, and the *torpedo punt* or *screw-kick* (where the ball is held at an angle to the body), which helped to gain more distance than the conventional *end-over-end* method. Place-kicking was a common way of shooting for goal after making a mark.

As the game became more advanced, it also became more competitive. The format of the Challenge Cup, which had faded into irrelevance somewhat, was revamped in the early 1870s. Each season would now end with a 'grand match' to decide the year's cup winners: the forerunner of today's Grand Final in the Australian Football League.

While Melbourne remained the epicentre of Victorian Rules football, the game also began to stir into life in other Australasian colonies. Much of this was down to migrants from Victoria who played it in their new environs, often having to contend with Britons who were trying to establish rugby or soccer as the local code.

Some form of football was played in Adelaide as early as 1860. It is not clear what rules were being followed at first, but some matches attracted such distinguished spectators as the Governor of South Australia and the Anglican Bishop of Adelaide. By the early 1870s, a game similar to Victorian Rules was being played there. One notable difference was that the goalposts were joined by a crossbar eight feet from the ground, and a rope eight feet higher up. Goals were scored by kicking the ball through the space bounded by the goalposts, crossbar and rope. Arguments over the rules nearly destroyed the game in

Adelaide, but a meeting of clubs in 1876 led to the adoption of rules closer to those followed in Victoria.

In Tasmania, football clubs started popping up in the mid 1860s, including Hobart Town FC and their local rivals New Town, but a north–south split hampered the game's progress. Southern clubs, such as those in Hobart, preferred Victorian-style football, while those in the north, centred around Launceston, had a code that was somewhere between Victorian Rules and rugby, including a rule that allowed for a 'touchdown' followed by a free kick at goal.

Victorian migrants in Sydney played their old colony's form of football at some time in the 1860s, but were outnumbered by devotees of rugby, better suited to Sydney's soft ground than to the harder surfaces in Melbourne. The Southern Rugby Union (later to become the New South Wales Rugby Union), founded there in 1874, worked hard at improving and promoting its game, seeing a potential threat from Victorian Rules. Up in Queensland, a schoolboy Victorian Rules match was played in 1870 in the Brisbane area, but the game made little progress, and was soon overtaken by rugby.

It would be some time before Victorian football caught on in remote Western Australia, still a penal colony at the time. British soldiers played some sort of football in Perth in 1868, possibly inspired by the game they had learned in Melbourne; but little else happened until the 1880s.

Things looked more promising in New Zealand, which saw an influx of gold-diggers and other migrants from Victoria in the 1860s; especially on the South Island, which had close economic ties with Melbourne. A football match was played, at least partly under Victorian Rules, in Nelson in 1869, the year before that town staged New Zealand's first rugby match. By 1876, Dunedin had both a rugby club and a Victorian Rules club. The Wellington rugby club flirted with Victorian Rules, and the one in Auckland nearly introduced a rule in 1877 requiring a ball-carrier to bounce the ball.

For nearly the first 20 years of its existence, Victorian Rules football had no governing body – just a loose alliance of leading clubs which met occasionally to revise the rules. By 1877, there was a widespread feeling that Victoria needed a formal association, to take ownership of the rules, control the game, administer discipline, and arrange matches against teams from other colonies.

In May of that year, delegates from the most powerful clubs, Melbourne and Carlton, along with others from St Kilda, Albert Park and Hotham (soon to become North Melbourne) formed the Victorian Football Association (VFA). Geelong joined soon afterwards, as did Essendon, South Melbourne and West Melbourne over the next two years. Some 'country' clubs also signed up, although they had little influence. A number of junior clubs came under the VFA's wing, but had no voting rights.

Sir William Clarke, a prominent Melbourne landowner, was chosen as the VFA's first president. One of its vice presidents was H.C.A. Harrison, now retired as a player; but his step-cousin and brother-in-law, Tom Wills, no longer played a major role in the game. Since his father had been killed in an Aboriginal attack on his sheep station in Queensland in 1861, Wills's life had gradually been taken over by alcoholism, depression and erratic behaviour, which would culminate in his suicide in 1880.

The VFA published a new set of rules, with an emphasis on closing loopholes and clarifying some of the game's murkier points. A new rule prohibited handing the ball off to a teammate, and the ball-carrying law was spelt out more clearly: a player could not carry the ball further than was necessary for a kick, *unless* he bounced it every five or six yards. At the end of the 1877 season, the *Australasian* newspaper printed the first unofficial league 'ladder'. Carlton were declared as the champions, as the senior club with the most victories against other senior clubs.

One of the VFA's aims was to promote the game outside Victoria, and to get intercolonial football up and running. The most promising territory was South Australia, largely thanks to a young Englishman, Richard Twopeny, who had arrived in Adelaide in the mid 1870s. Twopeny quickly took a liking to Victorian Rules football, which he later said he had found to be more 'scientific' and 'amusing' than soccer and rugby. After joining the Adelaide club and becoming its captain, he suggested setting up an association.

Nine clubs duly formed the South Australian Football Association in May 1877, the same month that the VFA was set up. There were several matches between clubs from the two colonies over the next few years, and 1879 saw the first representative game, as Victoria beat South Australia 7-0 in front of around 5,000 spectators in Melbourne.

Queensland was the next colony to have an association, founded by Victorian migrants in 1879. But the only suitable grounds were soon monopolised by rugby, which also offered the attraction of inter-colonial contests with neighbouring New South Wales. After a brief heyday in the mid 1880s, with four representative matches against New South Wales, the game began to peter out in Queensland.

In 1877, the VFA tried to arrange two games between Victoria and New South Wales, one each under Victorian and rugby rules. They were rebuffed by a representative of the New South Wales rugby clubs, ostensibly because of concerns over offside rules (or the lack of them), but perhaps also because there was some unrest in the Sydney rugby scene. Some clubs were agitating for changes which would make the game more free-flowing – even the elimination of scrums – and exposure to the Victorian game might have fanned the flames even higher. Still, the Waratah rugby club invited Carlton to play twice in Sydney that year, and this time the idea came to fruition, with both games arousing plenty of local interest.

In 1881, soon after the New South Wales Football Association (NSWFA) was founded, its team was thrashed twice by Victoria, 9-0 in Melbourne and 9-1 in Sydney, in the first representative games between the two colonies. Melbourne FC toured the Sydney area that year, beating everyone in sight. These results seem to have demoralised those who were trying to develop the game there, and matters were made worse by the NSWFA's failure to secure use of the Sydney Cricket Ground. The Southern Rugby Union even banned its players from playing Victorian Rules.

The name of the game was seen as a handicap – in the *Melbourne Punch*, a reporter by the name of 'Orange and Blue' wrote:

> *The great objection to the rules in New South Wales was*
> *that they were styled 'The Victorian Rules of Football'.*
> *Had they been dubbed the Scandinavian rules, well*
> *and good; but Victorian – perish the thought!*

By the 1890s, except in the Riverina region near the Victorian border, the game had almost disappeared in New South Wales. Another colony where it faced stiff competition from rugby was Western Australia; but the game did start to make progress there, with an association of four clubs being formed in the mid 1880s.

A Tasmanian representative side toured Victoria in 1887, getting some impressive results, including a relatively close 7-4 loss to a VFA select team. New Zealand's association was formed in 1880, but the game was in decline there by this time. The North Island, closely tied with Sydney, was becoming the more powerful half of the colony, helping rugby to become the more prominent football code.

Looking further afield, the VFA recognised that rugby had an international dimension – with British teams touring Australasia and vice versa – and tried to emulate it. In 1879, a proposal to invite English football teams to Victoria came to nothing (it is not clear whether they would have been rugby or soccer teams, or both). When an unofficial British rugby squad toured Australia and New Zealand in 1888, they were scheduled to play several games in Victoria under the local rules; but this part of the tour was hardly a success, and was cut short.

Perhaps Victorian Rules football was not set to take over the world, or even Australia. But in the 1880s, in its booming heartland of Melbourne, nothing could touch it. The city continued to grow at a dizzying rate, with over a quarter of a million people in 1880 (just 45 years after its foundation), and nearly half a million by the end of the decade.

Old suburbs expanded, new ones were built, and local industry thrived. Cable trams served the inner suburbs, and steam trains covered the outer ones, helping football fans to flock to games in greater numbers than ever before. In 1880, big matches often drew crowds of around 15,000 (compared with the 6,000 at that year's English FA Cup final). Later in the decade, South Melbourne regularly attracted more than 25,000 fans, with a reputed 34,000 at their home game against Geelong in 1886.

The VFA started appointing neutral umpires in 1883, paying them £1 a week, a generous fee at the time. They were helped, at least in theory, by goal umpires – still chosen by the teams, and not noted for their impartiality. The field umpires were also equipped with whistles by this time, and were relieved of one of their burdens in 1887 as timekeepers were introduced, using large bells to signal the end of each quarter.

As in cricket, there was no rule allowing an umpire to dismiss a player from the game. He could punish a serious offence by awarding the match to the opposing team; but this would clearly have been a tough decision to make against the home team, in front of a large, belligerent crowd.

Umpires were improving, and so were the players, particularly in their goal-shooting skills. The unpopular *little mark* was countered slightly by a rule change in 1886, requiring the ball to travel at least two yards before being marked. Tall forwards began to dominate the game, although Geelong found success by making good use of smaller, nippier players who would wait for the ball to emerge from rucks. The club became unofficial champions seven times out of nine from 1878 to 1886, and went unbeaten in their 27 games in the last of those seasons.

The VFA took a tighter grip on proceedings in the run-up to the 1889 season, taking control of fixture planning. The idea was to ensure that every club – especially the poorer ones – had a 'fair' schedule. An official league ladder was finally introduced, with four points awarded for a win and two for a draw.

As the VFA clubs' coffers were filled by the growing crowds, some sceptical observers started to wonder where all the money was going. Some had their suspicions. As competition intensified, clubs came under pressure to hire the best players they could get, and often did so by dubious means. All kinds of inducements were offered to players in attempts to lure them into moving between clubs, or to persuade them to stay where they were. There were spurious or inflated expenses, offers of houses and notional jobs (Fitzroy player Alf Bushby was officially employed by the club as, among other things, a comedian), prizes for turning up at training, and many other ruses.

Rumours of these goings-on drew the same response as elsewhere in the sports world: condemnation from middle-class 'gentlemen' who preached amateurism, and a more sympathetic view from the game's working-class followers. The VFA tried to clamp down on these signs of professionalism, particularly when the zealously pro-amateur Thomas Marshall became its secretary in 1885, but with little success.

Victoria found itself in an economic slump in the early 1890s. Unemployment soared, attendances dropped, and some players struggled to make ends meet, fuelling their resentment over the amateurism rules. Many Victorians fled to Western Australia, lured by yet another gold rush, and some footballers were among those who looked for new pastures. Albert Thurgood, widely seen as the game's leading player – tall, strong, quick, versatile, and an expert high-marker and kicker – left Essendon for Fremantle of the Western Australian Football Association (WAFA). After leading the VFA's scoring chart three times, Thurgood was the WAFA's top scorer in the first three of his four seasons with Fremantle.

The game itself went into something of a slump; play was often congested, and goals were hard to come by. Some clubs started pushing for rule changes, such as a reduction in team sizes, and the inclusion of *behinds*, where the ball passed between a goalpost and a kick-off post, in the scoring (behinds had been recorded on scoresheets for some time, but made no difference to the outcome of a match, which depended purely on goals); but the VFA was slow to act.

The more powerful clubs, such as Melbourne and Essendon, were also unhappy with the fixture lists, wanting to play money-spinning matches against each other more often. The VFA was also accused of being weak in its control over player transfers, illicit payments and on-field discipline. As early as 1889, Geelong and Essendon mooted the idea of leaving the VFA to form a new league, and there were more talks along these lines in the mid 1890s.

The final straw came at the end of the 1896 season, when the VFA sparked anger by postponing a championship decider between Collingwood and South Melbourne (who had finished level on points), to allow other fixtures to be completed first. The night before the match was finally played, delegates from Collingwood, Essendon, Geelong, Fitzroy, Melbourne and South Melbourne met to make plans for a breakaway organisation: the Victorian Football League (VFL). The league got underway the following season, with Carlton and St Kilda also on board.

The VFA limped on with just five clubs – Footscray, North Melbourne, Port Melbourne, Richmond and Williamstown – and found itself on the losing side of a power struggle with the VFL. But it did introduce rule changes in 1897, perhaps a few years too late. Teams were reduced from

20 players to 18, the minimum kicking distance for a mark was raised from two yards to ten, and a new scoring system was introduced, with six points for a goal and one for a behind.

The VFL soon copied these changes, and came up with an innovation of its own. Each season's 'premiers' would be decided by a round-robin finals tournament, rather than the title going to the team on top of the ladder. The 1897 finals were something of an anticlimax, with some poorly-attended 'dead' games, but the format was revamped the following year to ensure a winner-takes-all Grand Final, which soon became a major event.

The VFL finals helped to revive the public's interest in the game, and the Victorian press started lavishing praise on its star players. Much of the attention was focussed on leading scorers such as Mick Grace of Fitzroy, and Albert Thurgood, now back at Essendon. Thurgood beat Collingwood almost single-handedly in the 1901 Grand Final, with a performance that featured a place-kick measured at 93 yards.

It often took something out of the ordinary to beat Collingwood. Now an established powerhouse, with an effective tactical system and strong team spirit (and some outstanding individuals such as the brilliant, if often difficult, Dick Condon), they reached every finals series from 1897 to 1911. Carlton also shone in the early years of the new century, becoming premiers in 1906, 1907 and 1908, after appointing Jack Worrall as the game's first coach (officially the 'secretary-manager') in 1902.

The VFL expanded to ten clubs in 1908, when Richmond jumped ship from the VFA, and University transferred from the Metropolitan Junior Football Association. Umpiring standards were still improving, but the officials' limited powers allowed players to get away with something approaching murder, and the game still drew criticism for its rough play.

There were fears that all this aggression might drive many spectators away from the game, and towards rugby – particularly women, who made up around 40 per cent of the attendances. Collingwood even opened a Ladies' Pavilion in 1900, and it was not unusual for women to be involved in running the clubs. The game was an important part of many women's, as well as men's, social lives. An item in the 'Smart Girl's Calendar' in the 1903 *Melbourne Punch Annual* pictured a young woman at a match, and read:

> *In June she thinks it quite a lark*
> *To sit and watch the 'men of mark'.*

A new era dawned on New Year's Day, 1901, as the Commonwealth of Australia Constitution Act came into force: the key moment in Australia's evolution from a group of British colonies into a unified, largely independent country. The former colonies were now states. The 'federal spirit' of the times inspired both the VFL and VFA to renew their efforts to make their game a national one, and to take it overseas as a symbol of the young nation.

Collingwood toured Tasmania in 1902, and played Fitzroy the following year in Sydney in front of more than 15,000 spectators. Carlton and Geelong also met in Sydney that year, and the New South Wales Football League was formed, replacing the New South Wales Football Association, which had fizzled out a decade earlier.

Inter-state representative football moved up a gear, having disappeared for several years in the 1890s, when it had been 'inter-colonial'. A group of administrators formed the Australasian Football Council (AFC) in November 1906, trying to create a national – and, to some extent, international – framework for the game, which was now becoming known as Australian (or even Australasian) Rules football.

As the AFC's name suggests, it had New Zealand in its sights. Transport and communication links between Australia and New Zealand had improved greatly, and Dunedin had a large Australian population. By 1900, although it had been overtaken by rugby, the game was being played by more than a hundred clubs in New Zealand. The AFC's early meetings involved delegates from the VFL and other state associations, as well as one from the New Zealand League of Australian Football. The VFA, though, was left out in the cold, a sign of its declining power.

The Melbourne Carnival, in August 1908, celebrated the half-century jubilee of the game's (notional) birth date, with a tournament featuring representative teams from the six Australian states and New Zealand. Guest of honour at the opening match was H.C.A. Harrison, one of the game's pioneers. The VFL and Tasmanian teams finished on top of the two mini-leagues. Crews from visiting US warships put on a demonstration of American football at the MCG, drawing a mixed reaction: an observer from the *Melbourne Punch* likened them to 'a herd of swine digging for worms'.

The VFL and AFC were even bold enough to try to exploit the current turmoil in the American game, writing to US president Theodore Roosevelt and 69 American universities and colleges to extol the virtues of their own football code. They also hoped to take advantage of the split in the rugby world, which hit Australia in 1907; there were discussions with the newly-formed New South Wales Rugby League over merging Australian Rules and rugby league into one code.

All these efforts to promote Australian Rules in New South Wales and Queensland were to little avail, and rugby league became the dominant game there. Meanwhile, the AFC's relationship with the New Zealand association hit the rocks, mainly because of disputes over travel expenses.

The New Zealanders were voted off the council in 1914, and the game again went into decline in that country.

At least Australian Rules football was still going strong in Victoria (not to mention South Australia, Tasmania and Western Australia), but not altogether smoothly. As well as the violence and injuries, the game was under fire over rumours of professionalism and match-fixing, and its links with gambling. Carlton suspended three players from their 1910 semi-final against South Melbourne, believing they had taken bribes to throw the match. Two of them, Douglas Fraser and Alex 'Bongo' Lang, were found guilty by the VFL, and banned for five years.

The Carlton scandal helped to convince the league that the lure of money was an inescapable element of the game. The following year, it began allowing clubs to pay their players. Most, though, retained other jobs, using football merely to supplement their income. The one team that remained fully amateur, University, dropped out in 1914, after struggling to compete with the semi-professionals.

The First World War was bitterly divisive in Australia, with arguments raging over how much support the nation should give to Britain, and over the question of conscription. Football continued, to the disgust of many observers, who accused it of hampering recruitment efforts. Others argued that the game provided some light relief for the public; but, in 1915, news of the Battle of Gallipoli shocked the nation, and made pursuits such as football seem trivial.

All but four of the VFL clubs stopped playing in 1916, and some players offered to forego their wages. The VFA had shut down in 1915. So had the Western Australian Football League (WAFL), before being ordered to resume by the Supreme Court. In South Australia, the league was suspended for much of the war, prompting the working-class Port Adelaide club to stage a rebellion, launching the Patriotic Football Association. Things were almost back to normal by 1918, with only Melbourne still missing from the VFL.

Soon after peace had returned, the VFL launched a 'second 18' league, which would help clubs to develop their younger players. Footscray, Hawthorn and North Melbourne defected from the VFA to the VFL in 1925, expanding the league to 12 clubs. The VFA was not dead yet, though, as it grew from eight teams to 12 in the late 1920s, gaining a foothold in the outer Melbourne suburbs.

Among the stars of the 1920s was ruckman Roy Cazaly, a non-smoking teetotaller with an approach to fitness that was ahead of its time. After a low-key stint with St Kilda from 1910 to 1920, Cazaly's heyday came in his seven seasons with South Melbourne. His leaping ability gave rise to the regular cry of 'Up there, Cazaly!', which inspired a song of that title, later used as a battle cry by Australian soldiers in the Second World War.

In his wake came the Collingwood duo of full-forward Gordon 'Nuts' Coventry, the first VFL player to kick a hundred goals in a season, scoring 118 in 1929, and the versatile Albert Collier. It was another golden era for Collingwood, with four consecutive titles from 1927 to 1930. Collier left for Cananore in the Tasmanian league in 1931, at a time when the sport was enjoying a boom period on the island.

The game was still violent, and was now being played at a faster pace than before. Injuries inevitably became a serious problem, prompting the VFL to start allowing substitutions in 1930, with just one replacement allowed per team. Two would be allowed in 1946, three in 1994, and four in 1998.

When the Great Depression arrived in 1929, it hit Australia hard. Amid fears of a decline in attendances, clubs were encouraged to tighten their belts. The VFL imposed a maximum player wage of £3 per game, less than a typical manual worker's weekly wage. Players who had no other employment, of whom there were many, could be paid an additional £3 a week. Despite the hard times, fans still flocked to football games in large numbers, looking for cheap entertainment to help lift the gloom. A crowd of 75,754 saw Richmond and South Melbourne contest the 1933 Grand Final, and there were 96,834 at the Carlton–Collingwood final five years later.

The Hollywood era helped to bring about a cult of celebrity, which soon pervaded Australian football. Some players were idolised, notably Fitzroy rover Haydn Bunton, who cultivated a film-star image. Goalscoring full-forwards usually drew the most attention, at a time when a new, more streamlined ball design helped them to refine the art of kicking. As well as Gordon Coventry, there was South Melbourne's Bob Pratt, who smashed Coventry's record with 138 goals in 1934, Jack 'Skinny' Titus of Richmond, Carlton's Harry 'Soapy' Vallence (this was clearly a golden era for nicknames), and Billy Mohr at St Kilda.

Some of the less prolific scorers also found fame, none more so than centre-half-forward Laurie Nash, who also played for Australia in two cricket Tests. Modesty was not one of Nash's better qualities (when asked who was the greatest player he had seen, he replied, 'I see him in the mirror every morning when I shave'), but he was far from alone in admiring his aerial and kicking skills.

After making his name in Tasmania with the City club in Launceston, Nash joined South Melbourne, who had a knack for finding talented players from beyond the Melbourne area. Another leading light in the 1930s was Jack Dyer, the fearsome but highly skilled Richmond captain, whose powers of intimidation earned him the nickname 'Captain Blood'.

The VFL's maximum wage led some players to seek their fortunes elsewhere in the late 1930s, and some of the wealthier clubs in the VFA and WAFL took the opportunity to do some poaching. Bunton went west to join Subiaco in the Perth area, while Nash, Vallence and Pratt all moved to VFA clubs.

The Australian National Football Council (ANFC, a successor to the Australasian Football Council) tweaked the playing rules in 1939, hoping to improve the flow of the game. After being tackled, a player had to kick or hand-pass the ball, rather than dropping it. At the same time, despite protests, the *flick-pass* – a hand-pass with the open palm, rather than a closed fist – became legal.

Days before that year's finals were due to begin, Australia declared war on Germany. For the first two years of the Second World War, there were few calls for football to be suspended, and the game carried on pretty much as normal. But Australia's situation suddenly became more grave as Japan entered the war in December 1941, with its forces soon bombing Darwin and piloting submarines into Sydney Harbour. Prime minister John Curtin called for restrictions on crowds at sporting events, and many football grounds were taken over by the military.

The VFA and the Tasmanian league shut down from 1942 to 1944, while the WAFL ran only a junior competition, and South Australia had a scaled-down tournament. The VFL kept going, although Geelong pulled out in 1942 and 1943, facing problems with transport as well as a shortage of players. With Japan on the retreat in 1945, near-normal service was resumed.

The crowds came flooding back, with 73,743 at the Essendon–Melbourne Grand Final in 1946. A decade later, 115,802 would pour into the MCG, recently expanded for the Olympic Games, for the final between Melbourne and Collingwood. The VFL's dominance over the VFA and WAFL was restored, as the economy recovered and rich clubs found ways of circumventing the maximum wage rule.

The brighter mood in the post-war years inspired another effort to promote the game in areas where it was still a minor interest. A Footscray–Richmond match was staged in Brisbane in 1948. The ANFC launched what it called a 'propaganda' campaign, and, together with the VFL, held a successful National Day in 1952, with VFL games staged in Sydney, Brisbane, Hobart, Albury (in New South Wales, near the Victorian border) and the eastern Victorian towns of Euroa and Trafalgar.

The game's profile was also boosted in 1960 by the introduction of the ANZAC Day match, still a big occasion today, honouring the exploits of Australian and New Zealand troops. But, when a centenary Carnival was held in Melbourne in 1958, the VFL select team was predictably dominant, reinforcing the idea that this was essentially Victoria's game rather than Australia's.

Radio commentary was well established by now, having started in 1925. Along with press coverage, it had helped the game to become a major part of Melbourne life. When television arrived in Australia in 1956, though, the game's authorities took a cautious approach, typical of many sports around the world, worried about a possible fall in attendances. After some closed-circuit experiments that year, some games were partially televised on Melbourne stations in 1957. A bigger deal was struck the following year, but with only the last quarter of each live game being aired. Live coverage stopped altogether after the 1961 season, not to return until well into the next decade.

Coaches were playing an increasingly visible role in the game by now, as team tactics began to overshadow the efforts of individual players. One of the leaders in the field was Melbourne's Norm Smith, who used innovative ideas involving decoy runners and intelligent use of space. Smith led the club to five titles out of six between 1955 and 1960, and another in 1964.

Smith's brother, Len, developed a style at Fitzroy based on quick movement, keeping possession, and rotating players between positions. This approach, which he also used in a later spell with Richmond (where his successor Tom Hafey would keep his methods alive), was comparable with the 'total football' of Down in Gaelic football around this time, and that of Ajax in soccer a few years later.

A more pragmatic, less attractive approach was taken by Hawthorn in the early 1960s, under coach John Kennedy, with an emphasis on power, stamina and denying space to the opposition. Violence was still rife; Collingwood's Murray Weideman raised a few eyebrows by boasting of his 'enforcer' role in a 1963 *Sporting Globe* interview.

Since the game's early years, Melbourne clubs had been closely identified with various districts near the city centre. By the 1960s, though, population shifts had weakened these ties, with many residents having moved to the eastern and outer suburbs. St Kilda relocated to Moorabbin, ten miles south-east of central Melbourne. North Melbourne moved to the northern suburb of Coburg, but soon returned after an ill-fated spell.

The VFL had used a system of 'metropolitan recruiting zones' since 1915, with each club allowed to recruit players from certain parts of Melbourne. Players from 'the country' could be signed by anyone, a situation that the wealthier clubs were now exploiting by simply waving their chequebooks at the best prospects from outside Melbourne. 'Country zoning', covering Victoria and the Riverina region of New South

Wales, was introduced in 1967 in an attempt to even things up. Players from elsewhere, though, were still up for grabs.

The growing influence of money was plain to see in 1964, when Melbourne star Ron Barassi left the club for a player-coach role with Carlton, signing a contract worth £20,000 over three years[36]. Many were shocked by the deal, at a time when most players were still earning less than the average manual worker. It was an early sign of a difficult period for the game, when its traditions and values came under threat.

Transfer fees were introduced in 1971. Players campaigned for a bigger share of VFL revenues, and more power in running the game, leading to the birth of the VFL Players' Association, also in 1971. The sport also had to compete with a growing range of leisure choices, and the first real threat of a soccer boom, fuelled by immigration from southern Europe and Australia's qualification for the 1974 World Cup.

The VFL continued tinkering with the rules, trying (again) to speed up the flow of play, and to cut down on stoppages. Defenders often kicked the ball to the sides of the field when caught in tight situations – often putting it out of play, or into an area where 'followers' would close in on it, leading to a spell of dull, congested play. This tactic was discouraged by a rule introduced in 1968, making it an offence to kick the ball out of bounds 'on the full'.

The game was becoming largely based around short passing, much of it by hand, with players overlapping and running into space; in contrast with the earlier style, where the ball was often kicked over a long distance into a pack of players. The main pioneer of this style, in the mid 1960s, was Geelong's Graham 'Polly' Farmer, an Aboriginal (although few people knew it at the time) from Western Australia. Playing against Collingwood in the 1970 Grand Final, Carlton – coached by Ron Barassi – made frequent use of the hand-pass all over the field, even near their own goal, where most teams would usually kick the ball as far away as possible.

All this fast-paced action was becoming a little too much for the central umpires, struggling to keep up with play as it moved from end to end on these vast ovals. Help was at hand in 1976, when the VFL ruled that games should be officiated by two field umpires, rather than one.

The late 1960s brought the first signs of a growing commercialisation, with sponsorship creeping in, and TV coverage becoming more extensive (although still not live). Early in the 1970s, North Melbourne president Allen Aylett overhauled his club's structure, with an emphasis on the business side of football. Sponsors, rich supporters and off-field commercial ventures led to a huge increase in the club's income, helping to fund improvements in the team. In 1975, after 50 years in the VFL, they were champions for the first time.

Other clubs followed their lead: Carlton was formed into a company, CFC Ltd, complete with four subsidiaries. Aylett took up the VFL presidency in 1977, a sign of the league's new business-oriented direction. Colour TV had reached Australia the previous year, boosting the audience for televised football and the subsequent revenue. That year's Grand Final, between Collingwood and North Melbourne, was the first to be shown live.

The VFL leadership studied the business side of American sports, particularly the National Football League. Soon it had a Properties Division and a corporate logo, and even launched a travel agency and insurance company. Aylett pushed for the VFL to take full control of the game, taking over the remit of the former ANFC, now itself renamed as the National Football League. All this money-chasing led to battles over TV audiences, and a rash of new competitions tied to TV deals.

Coaches continued strengthening their grip on the game. David Parkin, a physical education lecturer who coached Hawthorn from 1977 to 1980, later joining Carlton and Fitzroy, brought a thoughtful, systematic approach to tactics. Like the league's marketing men, he turned to the United States for inspiration, using American coaching methods as a basis for his own.

Another leading coach was Essendon's Kevin Sheedy, one of the best-known figures in the game's history. Sheedy was inventive, if sometimes eccentric, and liked to use versatile players. After taking the job in 1981, he led Essendon to premierships in 1984 and 1985, after a 19-year drought; the 1985 side has sometimes been hailed as the best the league has ever seen. Sheedy would stay on until 2007. Some players also managed to stand out in the 1980s, notably Geelong's Gary Ablett, a powerful, elusive wingman turned full-forward; and Tony Lockett, St Kilda's colossal, high-scoring full-forward.

By this time, the game's links with Gaelic football (with a number of series having been played under compromise rules) had brought Irish talent to the attention of VFL clubs. Melbourne coach Ron Barassi, who had captained and coached the first Australian side to visit Ireland in 1968, persuaded the club's management to offer scholarships to Gaelic footballers. Jim Stynes joined from Dublin in 1985, and became a huge success. Sean Wight, who had only played at a junior level for Kerry, also established himself in the Melbourne side.

The 'Irish Experiment' was shelved, though, as rosters were limited to 42 players, and clubs became reluctant to take on anyone who would need some time to learn the game. But it was revived in the late 1990s, and by 2007 the trickle of Irishmen was threatening to turn into a flood, prompting the GAA to negotiate an agreement with the Australian league to limit the number of transfers.

As the free-market ethos of the 1980s permeated football, some clubs found themselves in financial trouble. South Melbourne, having seen their fan base eroded as their heartland became gentrified, asked the VFL for approval to stage all of their 1982 home matches in Sydney on Friday nights, hoping to land a TV contract. This was welcome news to the league's leadership, who had already been looking into the idea of setting up a Sydney team. The short-term plan was agreed, but soon became a permanent one, and the club morphed into the Sydney Swans.

It was a big move for the VFL, establishing its first full-time presence outside Victoria; but the club struggled for years to overcome Sydneysiders' indifference to the game, and faced animosity from other clubs, who were effectively subsidising the venture. The problems were eased in 1985 as the Swans became the first VFL club to be taken into private ownership, bringing a cash injection that helped to attract star players, such as Greg Williams from Geelong. But the stock market crash of October 1987 hit the club's owners hard, and they sold it back to the VFL Commission.

The league carried on looking into possible relocations, as part of a radical restructuring plan which also included proposals for club mergers, expansion, elimination of financially weak clubs, and more use of large stadiums. Two new out-of-state clubs, the Brisbane Bears and the Perth-based West Coast Eagles, were created in 1986, following the American expansion model. The Bears had a difficult time at first, before merging with Fitzroy in 1996 to become the Brisbane Lions. The launch of the Eagles finally brought some national recognition for Western Australia's strong Aussie Rules pedigree, and they won a title as early as 1992.

Inevitably, the VFL was renamed as the Australian Football League (AFL) in 1989. Two years later, the recruitment zoning system was replaced by an open national draft (another Americanism), further eroding the links between Melbourne clubs and their traditional localities. Many fans were angry at the effects of the game's corporate revolution, and some launched a 'Fight For Football' protest campaign in 1991.

Undaunted, the AFL continued expanding, and two more new clubs, the Adelaide Crows and Fremantle Dockers (the latter becoming local rivals for the West Coast Eagles), were set up in 1991 and 1995 respectively. Port Adelaide, an existing club from the South Australian league, joined the AFL in 1997, having been overlooked in favour of the Crows. The same year, Footscray were renamed as the Western[37] Bulldogs, after being taken over by businessmen who believed their old name suggested they were 'underprivileged, third-rate, lacking success'.

Clubs with roots in Melbourne's inner suburbs began sharing larger stadiums in the city, using their old grounds merely as practice facilities. North Melbourne, renamed as the Kangaroos in 1999 (as if to shed any connections with their city, let alone their district), played some 'home' games in Canberra, before turning to the Gold Coast area, south of Brisbane. (Tradition struck back in 2007, as 'North Melbourne' was re-instated as the club's primary name, with 'Kangaroos' as a nickname.) At the time of writing, nine Melbourne clubs share just two grounds: the MCG, and the Telstra Dome in the docklands. Another sign of the game's commercialisation came in 1999 when, as part of a cat-food promotion, Geelong player Garry Hocking was persuaded to change his name by deed-poll, briefly, to 'Whiskas'.

By the mid 1990s, the VFA was hopelessly overshadowed by the big-money AFL. The Victorian State Football League, a junior competition, effectively swallowed it up, adopting it as an open-age league that was confusingly named the Victorian Football League.

Australian Rules football is a popular recreational sport in much of the country, particularly in Aboriginal communities. A national survey by the Australian Sports Commission in 2005 found that 387,000 people were regularly playing organised Australian football, an increase of 42 per cent since 2001. The AFL-supported *Auskick* programme has helped to increase participation among children.

Although the game had long been popular with women, they were rarely seen playing it until 1981, when the Victorian Women's Football League was formed, with four teams. By 2006 it had grown to 26 teams (run by 20 clubs), in three divisions. Women's leagues were set up in Western Australia in 1987, South Australia in 1990, and later in New South Wales, Queensland and the Australian Capital Territory. The AFL also now runs a women's championship.

For much of the game's history, there were only tentative, ineffective attempts at developing it overseas, perhaps a symptom of Australia's so-called 'cultural cringe': an inferiority complex about its own cultural creations, rooted in the colonial era. Things began to change in the 1980s, as Australian sportsmen, celebrities and TV programmes became well known internationally. Soon, Aussie Rules was being televised in Europe and North America, and exhibition matches were staged in Britain, Canada, the US and Japan.

Meanwhile, mostly without the help of the VFL/AFL, grass-roots leagues began to emerge around the world. Unlikely as it may seem, Denmark was one of the first success stories. Australian expat Mick Sitch placed an advertisement in a Copenhagen newspaper in 1989, looking for players to join him in a training session. The healthy response, and Sitch's enthusiasm, led to the birth of the Danish Australian Football League in 1991. Today it has 22 teams, grouped into four divisions, with many Danish players as well as Australians.

The British Australian Rules Football League was formed in 1989, and is going strong today, mainly in the London area. Other leagues have been created across Europe, in Canada, and in the US, where former Essendon coach Kevin Sheedy has become something of an Aussie Rules missionary.

Less surprisingly, the game has made steady progress in countries closer to Australia, such as New Zealand, Papua New Guinea and Samoa. The AFL has targeted South Africa as a promising market for the sport, and has started staging pre-season games there. The game had been played in South Africa over a century earlier, by Australians fighting in the Boer War or prospecting for gold.

The International Australian Football Council was formed in 1995, to oversee global developments in the game, before being usurped by the power-hungry AFL's new Development Committee in 2002. The first International Cup was held that year (without an Australian team, in the interests of competitive balance), with Ireland as the winners. New Zealand took the title three years later, followed by Papua New Guinea in 2008. Despite all this progress, though, Australian football – like Gaelic football – has not grown into a major spectator sport anywhere outside the land of its birth.

Today's game is drastically different from the one that was played in the late 19th century. Pack play was eliminated long ago, and the game has become faster and more skilful, with far more goals being scored. Violence has been virtually wiped out, other than the odd high tackle and some alpha-male jostling, with TV cameras on hand to capture indiscretions, and the AFL perhaps wary of having its image tarnished in the eyes of sponsors and 'media partners'. Most AFL players are fully professional, which was not the case until the late 20th century. They are directed by teams of coaches in booths in the stands, armed with headsets and video equipment.

The league has gone more-or-less nationwide, with possible expansion into Canberra and Tasmania being mooted. Along with commercial forces and demographic changes, this has created something of an identity crisis for the game in its spiritual home of Melbourne, as clubs have drifted away from their local roots. In today's money-driven professional sports world, perhaps the truth is that a city of under four million simply cannot support nine teams in a top-tier league, making further relocations, mergers or closures inevitable.

Meanwhile, the AFL's recent attempts at promoting the game outside its heartlands seem to have been geared towards finding new markets for its 'product', and enlarging the talent pool for its clubs to recruit players from – hardly surprising, but hardly helping to foster a genuine love of the sport.

Whatever may be happening elsewhere, though, Aussie Rules is undoubtedly the number one sport in Victoria, South Australia, Western Australia, Tasmania and the Northern Territory. The AFL Grand Final regularly has the highest attendance of any annual single-day event in the nation, drawing a full house of around 100,000 at the MCG. The game might never become a global one, but it certainly isn't going away.

Chapter 9

Carrying the Union Flag

'I prefer rugby to soccer. I enjoy the violence in rugby, except when they start biting each other's ears off.'
– Elizabeth Taylor, actress, 1972

For some years, rugby's split in 1895 was a serious blow to the game governed by the Rugby Football Union[38]. Yorkshire had won the County Championship every year since its inception in 1889, except for Lancashire's 1891 title. They won it again in 1896, but further defections to the Northern Union, by the likes of Hull Kingston Rovers and Salford, spelt the end of Yorkshire and Lancashire's dominance; neither would be champions again until Yorkshire's victory in 1926.

The Yorkshire Cup had once had 132 entrants in its heyday, but was down to just 11 by 1901. RFU membership was nearly halved, slipping from 481 clubs in 1893 to just 244 a decade later. The England team was also depleted, having had a large northern contingent in the years just before the split, many of whom were now out of the picture. It was no coincidence that the national team's fortunes plummeted after 1895.

The RFU's draconian rules made pariahs out of players and clubs who had any link, however tenuous, with rugby league. Its guilt-by-association approach was comparable with that of the Gaelic Athletic Association in its war on non-Irish sports, although it is unlikely that either party would have appreciated the comparison. It made life tricky for the remaining rugby union clubs in Lancashire and Yorkshire, who could hardly avoid having some sort of contact with their NU neighbours. Some Yorkshire clubs even considered forming another breakaway body, to be known as the Northern Amateur Union.

Making things worse, the game was losing ground to soccer in some of its strongholds in the Midlands and south-west, such as Coventry and Bristol. Wales also felt the effects of the split, with many of its working-class players fleeing to the NU; this seems to have influenced the English members of the International Board into giving the Welsh Rugby Union some leeway in following the amateurism rules.

The Scottish and Irish unions, though, were not so lenient, and protested furiously when the WRU contributed £50 to a testimonial fund for Newport's Arthur Gould in 1896. Gould had been the outstanding Welsh player of his day: a quick, skilful three-quarter who pioneered the attacking, running style that would dominate Welsh rugby for decades to come. Accusing the Scots and Irish of applying double standards, the WRU withdrew from the IRB, scuppering the 1897 and 1898 championships, before returning to the fold after Gould's retirement. The Scottish union soon had something else to get steamed up about, when a group of largely working-class clubs formed the Border League, against its wishes, in 1901–02.

South African rugby started taking shape in 1889, as the South African Rugby Board (SARB) was set up, and Eastern Province, Western Province, Griqualand West and Transvaal contested the first inter-provincial championship. Two years later, shipping tycoon Donald Currie presented an eponymous trophy to Griqualand West, for giving a British Isles team[39] the toughest match of their tour, losing only 3-0. From 1892 onwards, the Currie Cup was awarded to the inter-provincial champions. Another touring British Isles team got the better of the South African national side in 1896, although the hosts did win one of the four test matches.

The Boer War, of 1899 to 1902, played a part in spreading the game's appeal among Afrikaners. Around 24,000 Boers and sympathisers were held in prisoner-of-war camps, where many passed much of their time playing rugby. The war gave Afrikaners a cause to rally around, and rugby gave them a means of affirming their identity to the world, especially to the British.

South Africa were strong opponents by the time the next British Isles tourists arrived in 1903, winning a three-test series by a game to nil. Three years later, they went on their first overseas tour, winning 26 of 29 games in the British Isles and France, with full-back Arthur Marsberg and wing J.A. 'Bob' Loubser among their leading lights.

The South Africans wore green jerseys with a springbok emblem; on their arrival in Britain, captain Paul Roos told the press that they wanted to be known as the Springboks. None of this meant a lot to South Africa's non-white players, who were ignored by the SARB, and had no hope of selection for the national team. Meanwhile, the South African Coloured Rugby Football Board set up its own tournament, the Rhodes Cup, in 1898.

In Australia, the game was still largely divided along colony or (after independence in 1901) state lines, with most of the action happening in

New South Wales and Queensland. A union was formed in Melbourne in 1888, but Victorian Rules remained the dominant code there. A combined Australian team first appeared in 1899, playing four tests against a British Isles side in Sydney and Brisbane. Four years later they met New Zealand for the first time, losing 22-3 in Sydney. After hosting the British and Irish again in 1904, Australia – now known as the Wallabies – first toured England and Wales in 1908–09.

In 1901, Lord Ranfurly, New Zealand's Governor-General, donated a trophy to be awarded to its leading rugby team. The Ranfurly Shield – initially featuring soccer-style goalposts – was to be contested on a challenge basis, with the holders keeping it until they lost to a club who challenged them. Auckland were the first holders, and would often dominate proceedings in years to come.

The British Isles squad that visited Australia in 1904 also toured New Zealand, losing their match against the national side: a sign that the hosts were becoming a real force. The RFU's strict regulations had deterred the NZRFU from asking its players to make the long trip to the British Isles. When a tour finally came about in 1905, it became a defining chapter in New Zealand's rugby history; and, arguably, the nation's history.

Nicknamed the All Blacks for the first time, but later also known as the Originals, the tourists astounded their hosts with a relentless, almost unstoppable brand of rugby. Marshalled by captain Dave Gallaher, and starring the likes of attacking full-back Billy 'Carbine' Wallace, they won all but one of their 33 matches in the British Isles and France, outscoring their opponents by a ratio of nearly 20 points to one. The exception was a 3-0 defeat to Wales in Cardiff, featuring a disallowed All Black try that still rankles with Kiwis today.

The tourists' success helped to establish rugby as a symbol of New Zealand's identity, at a time when it barely had one (independence as a 'dominion' was still two years away). As All Blacks coach Graham Henry put it a century later, 'They left home as colonials and returned as New Zealanders'. Ironically the Originals tour helped to bring about the launch of rugby league in the Antipodes, which would do immense damage to rugby union in Australia (although far less in New Zealand).

Meanwhile, the game's popularity in Wales was strengthened by the national side's win over the otherwise all-conquering All Blacks. It faced a brief threat from rugby league, with six clubs from south Wales joining the Northern Union in 1907 and 1908. But they did not last long, and, although Welsh rugby union clubs lost many players to the rival code, there were plenty of others to take their place; while the sense of pride in the national team helped to keep the game buoyant.

Paris was the early centre of French rugby, with Racing Club de France and Stade Français at the forefront. The latter hosted London club Rosslyn Park in 1892 (a fixture that led a British journalist to worry that 'it might lead to international complications'), and a combined Paris team paid a return visit the following year. An Edinburgh select side played in Paris in 1896, with the Parisians visiting Scotland two years later.

By this time, though, the balance of power was shifting to the south and south-west of the country. Clubs sprang up in cities such as Bordeaux, Perpignan and Toulouse, and in a host of smaller towns. The region's close links with Britain, through shipping and the wine trade, undoubtedly helped the game to grow there.

By 1910, France had around 100 clubs. It also had a national team, making its bow with a 38-8 defeat to New Zealand at the Parc des Princes in Paris in January 1906, at the end of the first All Blacks tour. Three months later they faced England, again in Paris, and over the next few years they began meeting all the home nations regularly. The French struggled in these early years, having to wait until 1911 for their first win, against Scotland.

The annual internationals between the home nations were officially friendlies, but had become known informally as the International Championship, with the press publishing an unofficial table. The games against France were hardly taken seriously at first, but were gradually afforded the same status as other matches, and the championship evolved into the Five Nations tournament.

With England reeling from the schism in the north, Scotland and Wales dominated in the early years of the new century. But the opening of the RFU's own stadium in 1909, at Twickenham on the south-western outskirts of London, helped spark an English revival. Like the Welsh at Cardiff Arms Park, and later, the Scots at Murrayfield, England became tough to beat at their home fortress, remaining undefeated there until 1926.

The RFU and WRU suspended play within weeks of the outbreak of war in 1914, and the Australian unions cancelled their premierships the following year. British rugby union officials got involved in military recruitment, and supported the National Relief Fund. The game was sometimes played on battle fronts; and gradually resumed on a more normal basis in 1916, with a short-lived amnesty for rugby league rebels. Hundreds of past and present players lost their lives in the war, including many internationals, among them the 1905 All Blacks captain Dave Gallaher.

The Belfast-based, rugby-playing North of Ireland Football Club stopped play for a different reason in 1916: to let its players join the Ulster

Volunteers, the loyalist paramilitary force that opposed the nationalist uprising (which, as outlined earlier, was linked with Gaelic sports). In Dublin, on the other hand, prominent nationalists such as Éamon de Valera, future Taoiseach and president of the Irish Free State, and Kevin Barry, who died in the Easter Rising, were keen rugby players. Through the turmoil of the War of Independence, partitioning and the Civil War, the Irish RFU stayed in one piece, with a single team still representing the whole island.

Rugby union flourished in England after the war, with the game being played at many grammar and private schools; as explained in chapter 6, soccer had fallen out of favour at many of these schools, after continuing in 1914–15. The number of RFU-affiliated clubs rose to 485 by 1924–25, higher than before the 1895 split. The national side achieved Grand Slams (beating all opposition in the Five Nations) in 1921, 1923, 1924 and 1928, under the shrewd captaincy of Wavell Wakefield.

By this time, England certainly needed a captain such as Wakefield (several decades would pass before British rugby union accepted the notion of a coach), with intelligent, progressive ideas about tactics. Since the turn of the century, the All Blacks had been playing a more advanced game than the home nations. They used an analytical approach, with planned manoeuvres designed to win possession at scrums and line-outs, as well as pioneering various ploys, such as off-loading the ball while being tackled. They also trained regularly, another alien concept in the British Isles. It was not entirely one-sided, though: the Welsh try that beat New Zealand in 1905 came from a planned move.

The usual scrum formation at the start of the century had three men in the front row, two second-rowers, and three at the back (3-2-3), helping the back-rowers to wheel the scrum and heel the ball away. A 3-4-1 line-up, used globally today, evolved in South Africa in the 1920s, allowing the flankers in the second row to break away quickly.

The All Blacks preferred a seven-man scrum, in a 2-3-2 formation, with an emphasis on heeling the ball quickly towards their backs. The spare man, a wing-forward, would put the ball into the scrum, and then – according to New Zealand's detractors – loiter alongside it, obstructing the opponents' scrum-half. Under the rules of the day, the offside line at a scrum was determined by the position of the ball, rather than the back-rowers' feet, allowing players to stay alongside the scrum. All Black captain Dave Gallaher, their wing-forward on the 1905 tour, was labelled a 'cheat' by British observers.

The issue flared up again during the British Lions' 1930 tour of New Zealand. Two years later, a new law required the front row to have three players, effectively forcing the All Blacks to revert to an eight-man scrum without the 'rover'. By now, forwards usually had specialised roles in the scrum – an idea introduced by the humble Yorkshire club Thornes back in 1882, but which was developed further, particularly in the back row, by Wavell Wakefield in England's side of the 1920s.

As tactics became more advanced, they also became cynical and defensive in some aspects of play. Most of all, backs began intentionally kicking the ball into touch ('working the touchline'), hoping their team would win possession from the ensuing line-out, and therefore gain territory. It was effective, but hardly enthralling to watch.

In New South Wales and New Zealand, the game faced a threat from rugby league, and the unions were anxious to do something about it. They experimented with a rule change: if a player kicked the ball into touch 'on the fly' from more than 25 yards beyond his team's goal-line, a penalty would be awarded (or, at one stage, there would be a line-out from a position level with the spot where the ball was kicked, rather than where it crossed the line).

The RFU sanctioned the experiment in 1921, as did the IRB three years later. But the rule was not applied globally (New Zealand and Australia, like France and South Africa, still had no representation in the IRB), and the likes of South Africa's Bennie Osler continued happily belting the ball into touch. Some other rule variations were tried out in the rugby hotbed of Auckland, including one that required the referee to put the ball into the scrum.

Rugby union's growth in France helped it to reach other parts of mainland Europe in the early 20th century. Italian students returning from France, mostly to northern cities such as Milan and Turin, started playing the game in 1910. After a slow start, Italian rugby picked up in the mid 1920s, by which time around ten clubs had been formed. The Federazione Italiana Rugby (FIR) was founded in 1928. The next year, a national championship was launched, and the national side made its debut against Spain, where the game had made some progress in Barcelona.

Romanian rugby got underway just before the First World War, again thanks to students returning from France. The Bucharest-based Romanian Tennis Club played the country's first match in 1913, and became its first champions the following year. It grew steadily over the next 30 years or so, and the Federatia Romana de Rugby was set up in 1931. There were also French connections when rugby reached Czechoslovakia, Poland and Russia in the 1920s. A German federation was formed in 1900; the initial impetus came from British links (with RFU president William Cail playing a part in the 1890s), but French encouragement helped it to make progress in the 1920s and 1930s.

British expats in Argentina, mainly in and around Buenos Aires, played rugby, as well as soccer, in the late 19th century. In 1899, the River Plate Rugby Union was created, with an affiliation to the RFU, and a four-club championship was first held. The union would evolve into today's Unión Argentina de Rugby. By 1905, there were enough Argentine-born players for an *Argentina v Extranjeros* match to become an annual fixture. A strong British select squad toured in 1910, and other teams soon followed. Argentina became renowned for producing fast, powerful forwards, among them Olympic heavyweight boxing champion Arturo Rodriguez Jurado.

Although rugby in the United States had mutated into American football in the 1880s, the game had a brief heyday in California from around 1906 to 1915, when a crisis in the American game led some universities to abandon it in favour of rugby. They found rivals up the coast in British Columbia, where the game was relatively popular.

A Canadian side visited Britain in 1902; a Californian student squad toured Australia and New Zealand in 1910, and hosted a return visit by the Wallabies two years later. In 1913, though, a full All Blacks team went to California and embarrassed their hosts with a string of easy wins – perhaps one reason why they reverted to American football soon afterwards.

Universities also played an important role in Japan, where Britons had been playing rugby since the 1870s. In 1899, a mainly Japanese club was formed at Keio University in Tokyo, partly thanks to Edward Clarke, a Yokohama-born lecturer. Regional unions started springing up in the 1920s, and the Japanese Rugby Union was set up in 1926. University matches became big attractions, often drawing crowds of more than 20,000.

Rugby's strong presence in Australia and New Zealand, along with British colonial ties, inevitably rubbed off on the islands of the south-west Pacific. The first match in Fiji was played in Ba in 1884, between British and local soldiers. Regular play started around 1900, and a club competition was started four years later. Paddy Sheehan, a plumber from New Zealand, was behind the creation of the white-dominated Fiji Rugby Football Union in 1913. Native Fijians soon became more involved, forming a separate union in 1915, which was merged into the original union in 1945.

Australian teachers introduced rugby in Tonga around 1900, and Tongans also brought the game home after learning it overseas. The Tongan Rugby Union was set up in 1923. Samoa (then known as Western Samoa) came under New Zealand's control in the First World War, after a period of German rule, and rugby soon sprang into life there, with a union being formed in 1924. Inter-island rivalries started developing that year, as Fiji played against Tonga and Samoa.

Rugby union crept into the Olympic Games, almost unnoticed, with a series of low-key tournaments between 1900 and 1924. France won gold in Paris in 1900, when Great Britain and Germany were the only other teams involved. There is some dispute as to whether this was an official event or an exhibition tournament, and there was no rugby at all in the 1904 Olympics in St Louis. Four years later in London, the Australians, already on British soil for a tour, had only to beat Great Britain (who were really Cornwall) to become champions.

After another non-appearance by the sport in 1912, and a further hiatus caused by the First World War, the United States were the unlikely winners in Antwerp in 1920, and again in Paris in 1924. After this, there was just an exhibition contest in 1936. None of these tournaments involved more than three teams, and few of those could have been considered to be full national sides.

In any case, in the inter-war years, South Africa and New Zealand were so far ahead of the pack that each Test series between them was seen as something of a world championship. Although both teams were drawn from small populations (taking South Africa's all-white selection policy into account), the players' backgrounds help to explain their success in rugby. Many European settlers in these countries had led tough lives – building their own homes, and working in manual industries such as farming and mining, while their northern hemisphere counterparts lived in relative comfort. This undoubtedly helped New Zealanders and South Africans to develop the physical and mental toughness so valuable in a sport such as rugby.

The two first met in New Zealand in 1921; each team won a test, with another ending in a draw. The tour became notorious for a hard-fought match in Napier between a Maori side and the visitors. A South African journalist cabled a racially-charged report back home, condemning the 'Europeans' in the crowd for cheering on the Maoris against 'members of their own race', and suggesting that the Springboks themselves were 'disgusted' by this. The report was leaked in New Zealand, causing uproar. (What the journalist thought of the Zulu war cry, which his countrymen used as a response to the Maori *haka*, is unclear.)

One of New Zealand's leading lights of the decade was a Maori: George Nepia, a ferocious tackler, prolific kicker and shrewd reader of the game. With Nepia at full-back, New Zealand won all 28 matches of their British tour in 1924–25, as well as winning both of their games in France. This All Black team would be remembered as the 'Invincibles'.

When choosing their squad to tour South Africa in 1928, the New Zealand selectors caved in to pressure from the hosts, leaving out Nepia and other Maori contenders. Again, neither side could come out on top, with each winning two tests. Nine years later in New Zealand, the South

African strategy, based around their forward play and Bennie Osler's relentless kicking, helped them to a 2-1 series win.

Two of the most powerful figures in South African rugby history, both products of Stellenbosch University, were prominent on the 1937 tour. One was A.F. 'Mr Mark' Markötter, an influential coach and selector from 1921 to 1938, notorious for kicking players, or hitting them with his walking stick, if they made mistakes. The other, scrum-half Danie Craven, an early exponent of the dive-pass, later became known as South Africa's 'Mr Rugby'.

Non-white rugby in South Africa came back to life in the 1930s, after fading somewhat in the previous two decades. Cape Town's Malay population became especially renowned for their knowledge and love of the game. The Rhodes Cup was revived in 1928, after floundering for some time, and the South African Bantu Rugby Union was formed in Port Elizabeth in 1935. A non-white 'Springboks' team toured the country three years later, but a planned overseas tour was scrapped when war broke out.

While rugby union flourished in New Zealand and South Africa, it was a different story in Australia, where it struggled to compete with rugby league, and became mainly a middle-class affair. It practically died out in Queensland, before re-emerging in the late 1920s, when some schools switched back from rugby league, the state union was re-formed, and club competitions got underway again. The picture was only slightly healthier in New South Wales: Sydney was reduced to six clubs by 1919, and the influential Sydney University almost converted to rugby league. Contacts with New Zealand and South Africa helped the game to stay on its feet.

The New South Wales 'Waratahs' team of the 1920s often featured Queenslanders and Victorians, and some of their matches were later recognised as full Australian internationals. They won two of their four tests on a British Isles tour in 1927–28, impressing spectators with their attacking play. By 1931, Australia again had an official national side, and the Bledisloe Cup was introduced as a prize for the winners of their test series against New Zealand.

The resurgent England team of the 1920s soon found stiff competition from the Scots, whose Murrayfield stadium in Edinburgh opened in 1925, giving them an answer to Twickenham. The Scotland team that year revolved around a three-quarter line of Oxford University graduates, featuring the Australian-born Johnny Wallace and Ian Smith, and George Aitken, a former New Zealand captain (Phil Macpherson was the sole Scot). They also had a powerful pack, and an outstanding full-back in Dan Drysdale.

The inter-war era was a less happy one for the Welsh, beset by economic struggles, class conflict, and a continuing exodus of players to rugby league. On the brighter side, the launch of the Secondary Schools Rugby Union in 1923 helped to keep the supply line of players flowing; and both Swansea and the national side beat the visiting All Blacks in 1935.

The game's administrators were still staunchly conservative, remaining zealously opposed to major rule changes, to anything that hinted at professionalism, and to any links with rugby league. This was particularly true in the British Isles, and nowhere more so than in Scotland, where even the smallest concessions to spectators were too much for SRU secretary James Aikman Smith to contemplate. At an England–Scotland match in the 1920s, King George V asked Smith why the Scots were not wearing numbers (as England and Wales were doing by now). The exact wording of his reply varies between different accounts, but it was along the lines of: 'Sir, this is a game for gentlemen, not a cattle market.'[40]

In England, the RFU's paranoia even led to Bristol's international full-back Tom Brown being suspended indefinitely in 1933 for 'discussing the advantages of rugby league', a sport he had never seen, let alone played. Other than the knockout County Championship, the union still refused to allow nationwide league or cup competitions.

Things were a little less restrained across the channel, as rugby union enjoyed a boom period in France. The Fédération Française de Rugby (FFR) was formed in 1919, and the number of clubs tripled to around 800 between 1920 and 1923, mostly in the south and south-west. The national championship became intensely competitive, with local and regional rivalries fuelling some fierce action on the field, along with spectator violence and intimidation of referees. A number of players died from injuries sustained in matches, prompting questions in the National Assembly. While the French game was governed by middle-class administrators in Paris, it was taking on a life of its own in its southern heartlands, dominated by rural working-class men with little regard for the FFR's conservative ethos.

The French national side made great strides in the 1920s, becoming genuine contenders in the Five Nations. But relations with the 'home' unions were souring, with suspicions of professionalism and player poaching among French clubs, as well as concerns about the hard-fought nature of the championship. Eyebrows had been raised as early as 1912, when Stade Bordelais advertised in the Scottish press for a stand-off half, offering a 'good business situation'; the club's committee members were banned for life.

In January 1931, 14 clubs left the FFR in protest at their rivals' alleged sins, forming their own short-lived Union Française de Rugby Amateur. This attracted the attention of the IRB, which took action a month later, refusing to sanction matches against France or French clubs, 'until we are satisfied that the control and conduct of the game has been placed on a satisfactory basis in all essentials.' This turmoil helped bring about the launch of rugby league in France.

The French would be allowed back into the fold in July 1939, after scrapping their club championship, but the war would delay their return to the Five Nations stage for another eight years. During their time in exile, the FFR nurtured relations with other continental unions, helping to form the Fédération Internationale de Rugby Amateur in 1934 along with Belgium, Catalonia, Czechoslovakia, Italy, Germany, the Netherlands, Romania and Sweden.

The late 1920s and 1930s saw a surge of activity in some of the game's other outposts. The New York Rugby Football Club was formed in 1929, and soon became affiliated to the RFU. Other American unions were soon formed, in the Midwest and southern California. Japan toured British Columbia in 1930, and a Canadian squad paid a return visit two years later. The sport was nearly banned in Japan during a clampdown on foreign influences, and was renamed as *tokyu* ('fighting game') in an effort to avoid censure.

No sooner had the Wallabies arrived in the British Isles for their planned tour in September 1939, than war broke out again. They soon sailed back to Australia, and the English and Welsh unions both suspended play before the month was out.

Unofficial rugby soon got underway, though, including a game between France and the British Army in February 1940. Troops from New Zealand and South Africa played in various parts of the world, and American forces played in New Zealand, giving their hosts food for thought with their running patterns and overarm, one-handed throwing.

The French club championship was restored in 1943. Japanese rugby petered out that year, but came back to life in September 1945, just weeks after atomic bombings on Hiroshima and Nagasaki that signalled the end of the war. The first months of peacetime also saw a British tour by a New Zealand army team known as the Kiwis, which helped to revive the game, and the Five Nations championship returned in 1946–47.

The home nations finally loosened their grip on the game in 1948, when Australia, New Zealand and South Africa were each given a seat on the IRB. The RFU gave up four seats, leaving England, Ireland, Scotland and Wales with two each. This finally led the Australian state unions to join forces, forming the Australian Rugby Union (ARU) in 1949. Other unions applied to join the IRB, including those of France and (in the absence of a national Canadian union) British Columbia, but were turned down.

The scoring system was tweaked in 1948, with drop goals falling in value from four points to three. The ARU, facing tough competition from rugby league, was given approval to continue with the rule against kicking into touch from anywhere between the 25-yard lines, and also for a law that barred players from moving past the centre line of a scrum before the ball came out.

Ireland emerged after the war as a real force in the Five Nations, with a Grand Slam in 1948 and a Triple Crown the year after. Jack Kyle was one of the stars of the era: a versatile outside-half, with great acceleration and a deceptive running style. Wales also found some success, achieving a Grand Slam in 1950, and contributing 14 players to that year's Lions squad to tour Australia and New Zealand. (It was also a golden age for the domestic Welsh game, with around 40,000 often turning out for club matches at Cardiff, and 30,000 in Newport.) In contrast, England's chances were hampered by the RFU's arcane selection methods, while Scotland were mired in outdated tactics, sticking with a 3-2-3 scrum formation long after most sides had switched to 3-4-1.

France bounced back strongly after returning to the Five Nations, thanks in part to the FFR having seen off the threat from rugby league (with the help of some dubious friends in high places). Lourdes flanker Jean Prat played a leading role, captaining his country to their first win at Twickenham in 1951, a shared Five Nations title in 1954, and a memorable home victory over the All Blacks that year.

Lucien Mias, once described as a 'bulldozer with a brain', led a powerful forward line, which, in 1958, helped France to become the first tourists to win a Test series in South Africa since 1896. Their first outright Five Nations title came the following year. But the rumours of professionalism persisted, and the French were nearly expelled again in 1952 and 1957. An offer to scrap the club championship (again) was withdrawn after clubs protested.

New Zealand and South Africa, the latter coached by Danie Craven for much of this period, were still some way ahead of the rest. Air travel now gave them more chances to prove their superiority, as well as helping the game domestically. Among New Zealand's stars were Richard 'Tiny' White, a mobile forward with great ball-handling skills, and full-back Bob Scott, who had switched from rugby league on joining the army in 1942. Scott's South African contemporary Hennie Muller would describe him as 'altogether, the greatest footballer I've ever played against in any position'.

One of the All Blacks' strengths was a relentless rucking game, developed by the Otago provincial side. South Africa's success was largely based around winning possession at line-outs and scrums. The laws still allowed players to loiter near a line-out, and Muller often took advantage by running into opposing players as they stood in the line.

With New Zealand being the only major team to feature non-white players, tours involving the two nations still had political overtones; especially after the National Party came to power in South Africa in 1948, and started implementing the apartheid system of racial segregation. Before their South African tour the following year, the NZRFU again appeased their hosts by excluding Maoris; some were sent on a 'consolation' second-string tour of Australia.

The home side won the test series 4-0, a result that many Kiwis blamed on biased refereeing. New Zealand's revenge came on home soil in 1956, as they won a brutally-fought Test series, littered with brawls, by three games to one. The touring Springboks beat all four home nations, and France, in 1951–52. The Lions, though, showed signs of progress in South Africa in 1955, with a 2-2 series draw.

Rugby union was often a dull game in the 1950s, with many teams favouring negative, stifling tactics. It was livened up by a rule change in 1958, helping the play to flow more smoothly: after a tackled player had released the ball, it no longer had to be kicked before being picked up. Six years later, the offside line at scrums was redefined, to prevent players creating congestion by lurking alongside the scrum (a favourite tactic of South Africa). It was now defined by the position of the feet of the player furthest back in the scrum, rather than the position of the ball. Another change, in 1964, required players not involved in a line-out to retreat by at least ten yards.

Kicking the ball into touch was still a widely-used ploy. A Scotland–Wales match at Murrayfield in 1963 featured 111 line-outs, mostly thanks to the boot of Welsh scrum-half Clive Rowlands. The Australasian rule against kicking directly into touch from between the 25-yard lines was finally implemented by the IRB as an experiment in 1968, and permanently in 1970 – half a century after it was first proposed.

The change transformed the role of full-backs, forcing them to find other ways of playing themselves out of trouble. Some, such as Scotland's Andy Irvine and J.P.R. Williams of Wales, became expert runners as well as kickers, and contributed far more in attack than previous full-backs had done. Another Antipodean suggestion from the 1920s was adopted worldwide in 1968: injured players could now be replaced by substitutes (up to two per team).

The Springboks slumped in the 1960s, leaving the All Blacks almost untouchable. From 1961 to 1970, New Zealand won 42 tests and lost only five, a sequence that featured 17 consecutive wins from 1965 to 1969. Backed up by Don Clarke's prolific goal-kicking, their main strength was an imposing forward line, including captain Colin Meads – a tremendously powerful, competitive leader, and a towering figure in New Zealand's rugby history.

Australia made progress in the 1960s, with promising results against South Africa in 1963 (away) and 1965 (at home), and on their 1966-67 British Isles tour. Outside-half Phil Hawthorne and scrum-half Ken Catchpole were their key players. Both were lost in 1968, though: Hawthorne to rugby league, and Catchpole to an injury sustained in a ruck, when the fearsome Meads nearly pulled off his leg.

South Africa's international matches were increasingly overshadowed by the race issue. The Sharpeville Massacre in 1960 raised global awareness of apartheid, and 162,000 New Zealanders signed a 'No Maoris, No Tour' petition before that year's tour by the All Blacks. The *Broederbond*, a conservative Afrikaner fraternity, had a strong presence in both the ruling National Party and the South African Rugby Board (even English-speaking whites were often thought to be unjustly overlooked for the Springbok captaincy and other leading roles), and the government had formally banned inter-racial sport in 1956.

The 'home' unions generally showed little concern about the SARB's racial policies; but a Springboks tour of Ireland and Scotland in 1965 encountered anti-apartheid protests in Dublin, the WRU nearly voted to boycott South Africa two years later, and there were more demonstrations when the Springboks visited the British Isles in 1969–70. Even the NZRFU made a stand in 1967, cancelling that year's planned All Blacks tour of South Africa when it became clear that the host board would not accept Maori players. In 1970, though, a dubious compromise allowed a tour to go ahead, with some Maoris and Pacific Islanders being counted as 'honorary whites'.

On the field, the home nations were still struggling to compete with those in the southern hemisphere. Some southern observers thought they needed a more competitive attitude; others blamed the lack of coaching, an issue that Welsh rugby, in the doldrums in the early 1960s, was the first to tackle. The Newbridge club appointed a coach in 1961. The WRU hired its first coaching organiser in 1965, and finally made Clive Rowlands the national team coach three years later. In 1968–69, the Welsh union started arranging training sessions for the national squad, a move that needed approval from the IRB. Even the ultra-conservative Scottish union appointed Bill Dickinson as coach – officially an 'adviser to the captain' – in 1971.

But it was the Welsh who showed the first fruits of this modern approach, as an outstanding national side emerged, becoming either

197

outright or joint Five Nations champions 11 times from 1964 to 1979. As well as the attacking full-back J.P.R. Williams, the team featured outside-half Barry John, a superb runner and goal-kicker; and versatile scrum-half Gareth Edwards, one of the most compelling players the game has produced. The Wales team of the 1970s played with great flair and energy, and became familiar figures across Britain, as the BBC's generous TV coverage brought rugby union to a wider audience.

Along with the likes of Scotland's Andy Irvine, and Mike Gibson and Willie John McBride from Ireland, Welshmen also played important roles in a successful spell for the Lions, who won their series in New Zealand in 1971 and South Africa in 1974. The latter tour highlighted a trend towards a more aggressive style of rugby. Expecting rough treatment from the Springboks, the Lions decided to strike first, by planning and executing their notorious '99' call in Port Elizabeth, where each player attacked his opposite number. France and Australia also played with a robust approach; for the All Blacks, it was nothing new anyway.

Some light relief came from the Barbarians, an invitation-only side made up mostly of leading British and Irish players. Formed in 1890, the 'Baa-Baas' began playing end-of-tour matches against visiting international sides, becoming something of a surrogate Lions team that could be seen first-hand in the British Isles (with a few isolated exceptions the Lions have only ever played abroad). The Barbarians are known for an open, expansive style of rugby, best remembered for a spectacular, sweeping move against the All Blacks in 1973 that ended with a Gareth Edwards try.

Although the 'big eight' nations dominated the game, Argentina showed signs of progress when they began playing regularly in the 1960s. On a tour of South Africa in 1965, they won 11 of their 16 matches. Meanwhile, the first Asian Rugby Football Tournament was held in 1969, largely organised by the Japanese union, whose team met their first major opponents, France, four years later. Fiji made a strong impression in France and Wales in 1964, as did Tonga in Australia in 1973.

The Rugby Union of Canada was formed in 1965, and started fielding a national team, who played against a Lions side en route from New Zealand in 1966. The IRB insisted that anyone who had played professional Canadian football must be banned. The United States of America Rugby Football Union (now USA Rugby) was set up in 1975, at a time when the game was growing at college level in the US.

While international rugby hogged most of the limelight, developments at club level were helping to shape the game's future. Gradually, in the 1960s and 1970s, its domestic structures came to resemble those of professional sports. The Floodlit Alliance was launched in Wales in 1964, staging mid-week club matches. The RFU rejected a proposal for an

English league in 1968, but agreed to launch the national Knockout Cup in 1971–72, a century after the FA Cup had begun.

The union also showed signs of accepting a more commercial approach, as perimeter advertising was first allowed at Twickenham in 1973, and the Cup was named after sponsors John Player two years later. In 1976, it agreed to the publication of 'merit tables' (league tables, under a more acceptable name).

Scottish Rugby Union president David Thorn had dared to utter the 'L' word as early as 1965, suggesting that informal 'league tables' would help to liven up the game. An official Scottish league was eventually set up in 1973–74. Border clubs dominated it for some time, with Hawick winning ten of the first 14 titles. The NZRFU also created a league, the National Provincial Championship, in 1976, with teams representing New Zealand's 27 provincial unions. Its top 11 sides were in Division One, with Division Two split into North Island and South Island sections.

By the early 1980s, the game's amateur status was under serious threat. The increasingly competitive domestic game, together with international matches, meant that the leading players were facing ever greater demands on their time. Like the working-class players of northern England a century earlier – but now with the added burden of frequent, lengthy overseas tours – they struggled to combine their rugby 'careers' with other jobs. There was also the usual danger of losing players to rugby league, a major problem in Australia and Wales in the 1980s.

The South African issue cast another shadow over the game. South Africa was driven out of international cricket after prime minister B.J. Vorster cancelled England's 1968–69 tour, objecting to the selection of a 'coloured' player, South African-born Basil D'Oliveira, in the English squad. It was also banished from the Olympic Games in 1970, having been suspended six years earlier. In 1971, the United Nations endorsed sporting boycotts of South Africa, and the Springboks faced protests on tour in Australia.

Politicians in New Zealand and Australia began speaking out against the SARB's racial stance. New Zealand prime minister Norman Kirk cancelled the Springboks' planned visit in 1973. A year later, Kirk stated that no racially-selected teams should be invited to the country. In 1975, though, New Zealand's own National Party, more sympathetic to its South African namesake, came to power. This paved the way for the All Blacks to tour South Africa the following year, prompting many African nations to boycott the Olympic Games in protest at New Zealand's inclusion.

In domestic South African rugby, though, there were small signs of a move towards racial integration. Two non-white unions were partly merged into the SARB in 1977, under the leadership of Danie Craven, who also invited some non-white school teams to a rugby festival in 1980.

Black and coloured players were even considered for Springbok selection. One of them, Errol Tobias, played for South Africa against Ireland in 1981 and England in 1984, although critics saw his selection as a token gesture.

The Springboks' 1981 tour of New Zealand was something of a turning point, with the host nation deeply divided over whether the tour should go ahead. New Zealand has rarely seen such scenes of mayhem as those that followed the South Africans around the country. Demonstrators tried to disrupt the tour, leading to the cancellation of a match against Waikato in Hamilton, and were sometimes attacked by rugby fans. During a test match at Auckland's Eden Park, a protestor repeatedly flew a light aircraft overhead.

Four years later, a return visit by the All Blacks was cancelled, after New Zealand's High Court upheld an injunction submitted by two Auckland lawyers, claiming the tour would not be in the NZRFU's 'constitutional interest of promoting the game'. However, some of the players met South African contacts, and arranged an unofficial tour for the following year.

The New Zealand Cavaliers, coached by Colin Meads and featuring many first-choice All Blacks, played 12 matches against all-white opposition, four of them against the full South Africa side. Adding more fuel to the fire, there were rumours that the rebels were paid for their efforts. Still, the NZRFU took a lenient stance on the venture, banning each player for just two test matches, and retaining Meads as a selector.

A cynic might suggest that the NZRFU had a good reason to keep the leading All Blacks in the fold in 1986: there would be a World Cup the following year. The idea had first been mooted in the 1950s, and was proposed again by the New Zealand union in 1979. The IRB had rebuffed it each time, concerned that it would lead the game into commercialisation and professionalism. By the mid 1980s, though, there seemed to be little choice. Australian businessman David Lord had announced plans for an international, professional rugby union 'circus' in 1983, claiming to have signed more than 200 players to lucrative contracts.

Lord's scheme never materialised, but it stirred the IRB into holding an emergency meeting, to discuss how to respond to such threats to their control over the game. The ARU and NZRFU proposed a World Cup, and were asked to look into the idea. An agreement was reached at the IRB's annual general meeting in 1985: the first Rugby World Cup would be held, in Australia and New Zealand, in 1987.

Sixteen teams were invited to take part, with South Africa excluded on political grounds. The two host countries were joined by the Five Nations contestants and nine 'second tier' nations, which became associate members of the IRB: Argentina, Canada, Fiji, Italy, Japan, Romania, Tonga, the United States and Zimbabwe (France had finally been admitted, as a full member, in 1978).

Both the host sides were expected to mount strong challenges. Australia had continued to improve, despite the drain of talent to rugby league, and had won all four tests in the British Isles in 1984. Coach Alan Jones had moulded the Wallabies into an exciting side, typified by brilliant wing David Campese. Other stars of the team included fly-half and trusty kicker Michael Lynah, and outside-half Mark Ella, one of the first Aboriginals to make a mark on the game.

Much of New Zealand's strength lay in the contingent from Auckland, who were in the midst of a 62-game, eight-year defence of the Ranfurly Shield; including outside-half and kicking specialist Grant Fox, and Michael Jones, a flanker in a typically dominant All Black pack. France were also highly fancied, having achieved a Grand Slam earlier that year, with full-back Serge Blanco and centre Philippe Sella standing out. The home nations, in contrast, were bogged down in defensive tactics, and short on attacking power.

The teams were split into four groups of four. Canada surprised many with their good performances in the first round, but the favourites soon came to the fore. New Zealand hammered Wales 49-6 in the semi-finals, before comfortably beating France (who had narrowly edged out Australia in their semi-final) by 29-9 in Auckland to become world champions.

Like its equivalent in soccer, the World Cup would be held every four years. The 1991 tournament was to be staged in the British Isles and France; this time, only the quarter-finalists from 1987 were admitted automatically, with the other eight places allocated via a qualifying system.

England were a much stronger side in 1991. The national Courage League had been set up in 1987–88, with Bath dominating in the early years, and coaching and conditioning were finally being taken seriously. With a solid forward line, and other outstanding players such as fly-half Rob Andrew and wing Rory Underwood, England were among the favourites. Wales, meanwhile, were going through a difficult spell, having lost the likes of Jonathan Davies to rugby league. They were knocked out in the group stage, even losing to Samoa at Cardiff Arms Park. New Zealand began an enduring habit of under-achieving at World Cups, losing in the semi-finals to Australia, who cemented their place among the elite by beating England 12-6 in the final at Twickenham.

As the World Cup grew into a major event, South Africa's absence from mainstream rugby became even more glaring than before. But the times were changing: in February 1990, the African National Congress was legalised, and its figurehead Nelson Mandela released from prison, signalling the start of apartheid's demise. Some SARB members, including the eminent Danie Craven, had held talks with the ANC in 1988, to the fury of white hard-liners, and the ANC agreed to support South Africa's return to world rugby.

The SARB and the South African Rugby Union (formerly the South African Coloured Rugby Football Board) merged in January 1992, forming the non-racial South African Rugby Football Union (SARFU). Craven was chosen as its president, but died a year later, aged 82. The boycotts were lifted: within the SARFU's first year, the All Blacks and Wallabies toured South Africa, and the Springboks visited England and France. South Africa's rehabilitation was sealed the following year, when the IRB chose it to host the 1995 World Cup.

Sport, having played a part in bringing down apartheid, now contributed to South Africa's healing process in the post-apartheid years, and helped to reshape the country's image, despite its national rugby and cricket teams still being almost totally white. The 1995 World Cup was its coming-out party. Many black South Africans found themselves supporting the Springboks, once seen as a symbol of white supremacy, for the first time.

The tournament saw some embarrassingly one-sided games, with the giants proving to be far too strong for the minnows: New Zealand crushed Japan 145-17, while Scotland piled 89 points on the Ivory Coast without reply. The All Blacks were a real force again, largely thanks to their giant wing Jonah Lomu, whose power, pace and elusive running helped them to beat all four home nations. They reached the final in Johannesburg, along with the hosts, who had found their feet after making a shaky return to the international stage. South Africa countered the Lomu threat by smothering the midfield, cutting off his supply line. Joel Stransky's drop goal in extra time gave them a 15-12 win, followed by the memorable sight of a beaming President Mandela, in a Springbok jersey, handing the trophy to skipper Francois Pienaar. New Zealand were weakened by a bout of illness, believed to have been caused by food poisoning, sparking inevitable conspiracy theories.

With South Africa back in the fold, and the World Cup well established, rugby union was growing rapidly as a business. The day before the 1995 final, a body known as SANZAR (South Africa, New Zealand and Australia Rugby) announced itself to the world, with plans for a Tri-Nations tournament, and a trans-national league known as the Super 12. Both were backed by a huge television deal with Rupert Murdoch's News Corporation.

The Super 12 was a revamp of the former South Pacific Championship, or Super 6, launched in 1986, featuring state teams from Australia and provincial ones from New Zealand, along with Fiji. The addition of three South African sides and Samoa in 1993 had expanded it to a Super 10. Now, though, the Pacific Island teams were being jettisoned, as commercial factors started to dictate matters: the Super 12 would have five teams from New Zealand, four from South Africa, and three from Australia.

One of the catalysts behind SANZAR's launch was the danger posed by Murdoch's Super League plans for rugby league, which threatened to lure many players away from rugby union. There was also another plan for a worldwide professional rugby union circuit. This time, the man behind the proposal was former Wallaby and IRB member Ross Turnbull, who managed to sign up over 400 players – many of them well known – for his unappealingly-named World Rugby Corporation.

Murdoch's scheme did not quite work out as intended, and Turnbull's fell apart without a match being played, but they had spurred the southern unions into action. The game's amateur façade had become something of a joke, with some players blatantly making money from their rugby careers in some way or other. The SANZAR deal was the final blow, with the IRB fearing it would lose control of the game if it stuck with its amateurism rule.

The Olympic movement had given up the fight against professionalism; it seemed only a matter of time before rugby union would follow suit. With a great degree of reluctance among some delegates, at a meeting in Paris on August 26, 1995 – a hundred years, almost to the day, since the Northern Union was formed – the IRB voted to allow professionalism.

In Australia, New Zealand and South Africa, rugby union was already being run as a commercial operation, and adapted easily enough to this drastic change in the game's regulations. Things went less smoothly in England, where the club and league structures, and the RFU, were less business-orientated, and struggled to cope with the new world in which they found themselves. The game was ravaged by financial losses and instability, with famous old clubs such as Richmond, Bristol and Coventry falling upon hard times and almost disappearing. There were also continual wrangles between clubs and the RFU over television money and player availability.

The game in Wales was boosted by the return of some prodigal sons from rugby league, but its clubs lost many players to the greater riches on offer in England. In Scotland, commercial forces saw much of the attention switch to Glasgow and Edinburgh, and away from the game's thinly-populated, working-class heartland in the Borders. It was a similar story in France, with the game's traditional structure, based around villages and small towns, under threat from the lure of money in the larger cities.

The Heineken European Cup was launched in 1995–96, with a mixture of club and provincial sides split into four pools of three in the opening stage, followed by semi-finals and a final. The English and Scottish unions refused to let their teams compete at first, but relented a year later. Toulouse were the first champions, beating Cardiff in the final at Cardiff Arms Park. The Super 12 kicked off in 1996, with an open, high-scoring brand of rugby, and a brash style of presentation that would have been unthinkable just a few years earlier. The Auckland Blues won the first two titles, averaging nearly 39 points a game.

The World Cup entered the professional era in 1999, when it was nominally hosted by Wales, although most of the games were actually played elsewhere in the British Isles and France. New Zealand had been dominant in Tri-Nations play and against European opposition, but failed in the World Cup yet again, losing to France in the semi-finals. Instead, it was Australia who came out on top, captained to a second title by their superb lock John Eales.

Despite their poor performance at the tournament, including a 101-3 thrashing by the All Blacks, Italy's progress since the 1980s earned them a place in the Five Nations – turning it into the Six Nations – in 2000. After beating Scotland in their first match, Italy reverted to their 1999 World Cup form, losing their next 14 games.

In 2001, a collection of Welsh clubs, Scottish district teams and Irish provincial sides came together to form the Celtic League. Irish rugby was on the upturn, highlighted by Leinster and Munster becoming the league's first two champions. The Welsh clubs had trouble adapting to the changing times, and were demoted to semi-professional status in 2003, effectively becoming feeder clubs for five regional professional 'superclubs' in the Celtic League, which became the Magners League three years later.

That year's World Cup, held in Australia, saw England become the first northern hemisphere side to land the trophy. Despite the discord between the RFU and the clubs, they had advanced impressively under the leadership of innovative coach Clive Woodward and their imposing, ultra-competitive captain Martin Johnson. England's triumph sparked a media frenzy, largely focussing on fly-half Jonny Wilkinson, whose drop goal had decided the final against Australia. Excited columnists, showing a poor understanding of sports fan culture, claimed that rugby union was set to overtake soccer as England's favourite sport. But injuries and loss of form, along with the failure of Woodward's English-dominated Lions in New Zealand in 2005, soon dampened the hysteria.

As commercial forces continued to reshape the game, international tours became shorter, with visitors playing far fewer games against club sides than before. In 2006, European tours by the southern hemisphere teams effectively merged into a single event, known (in the northern hemisphere) as the autumn internationals. The SANZAR competitions expanded in 2006, with more fixtures being added to the Tri-Nations schedule, and the Super 12 becoming the Super 14.

The professional era has not been kind to the second-tier nations, lacking professional leagues and struggling to compete with the stronger teams in international play. The IRB helped to improve their prospects in 2005, providing extra funds for their facilities and management, and launching the Pacific Five Nations tournament involving Fiji, Japan, Samoa, Tonga, and a junior New Zealand team. When Australia's second-string side joined the tournament a year later, it was renamed as the Pacific Nations Cup. The junior All Blacks were replaced by an all-Maori team in 2008.

The World Cup was mostly held in France in 2007, helping to promote the game in parts of the country where it had never made a big impression, as crowds of around 40,000 turned out in places such as Lyon and Nantes. The hosts surprisingly beat New Zealand, who had looked almost invincible a year earlier, in the quarter-finals; before losing to England, who in turn were beaten by South Africa in a forgettable final.

More memorable was the success of Argentina, beating the French in the opening match and progressing to the semi-finals. The domestic Argentinian game has remained strictly amateur, with most of the national side playing for European clubs; but their strong form has led to calls for their inclusion in the Six Nations or Tri-Nations. The IRB has also held talks with the national union about the possibility of setting up a professional structure in Argentina.

In 1991, just four years after the first World Cup took place, a women's equivalent was launched, with the United States becoming the first champions in a tournament held in Wales. The women's game had only existed sporadically until the 1970s, when the French took the lead, forming a federation in 1970. France played in the first international, against the Netherlands in 1982, by which time women were playing regularly at colleges and universities in Britain and the US.

The Women's' Rugby Football Union (WRFU), covering Britain and Ireland, was founded in 1983; within five years, there was a Great Britain team, a cup competition and a league. By 1994, the WRFU had split into four national bodies, affiliated to the men's unions. England won the second World Cup that year, held in Scotland, before the New Zealanders took over, winning the next three tournaments in the Netherlands, Spain and Canada.

The changes in rugby union since 1995 have dramatically altered the game's character, and its place in the sporting world. Particularly in the SANZAR nations, it is now packaged and presented in much the same way as other major team sports. Much of the old elitism has been eroded; but, in countries such as England and Australia, none of this has led working-class sports fans to embrace the game to any great extent.

In countries where the game has a lower profile, growth is unlikely to come easily. As Huw Richards points out in *A Game for Hooligans*, the variety and complexity of its skills make it difficult for new players to learn to play at a high level; the intricate rules can also be a barrier to attracting mass audiences. Particularly in the northern hemisphere, many matches are decided largely on penalty kicking; while negative tactics, time-wasting, collapsing scrums and lengthy rucks also detract from the game's appeal to newcomers.

At least the Super 14 offered a livelier brand of rugby, helped by some experimental rules, some of which the IRB has decided to try out globally. For example, if the ball is kicked into touch from inside the 22-metre line, the line-out takes place in a position level with the spot where the ball was kicked, rather than where it crossed the touchline. Other changes that would help to open the game up, such as reducing team sizes to 14, might improve its chances of reaching a wider audience, but could also alienate some of its devotees.

The World Cup has helped to democratise the international game, allowing any nation with a rugby union set-up to challenge the established countries. Some other competitions, though, face uncertain futures. The geographical isolation of some countries has caused problems: the time differences between South Africa and Australasia have put future South African involvement in the Tri-Nations and Super 14 in doubt; while Argentina, lacking any serious opponents in the Americas, can't easily slot into either the Tri-Nations or Six Nations. Another tricky issue facing South African rugby is the question of racial quotas in Springbok selection – favoured by some politicians, but not so popular within the game.

Back in the land where rugby began, there have been concerns about the relentless stream of injuries in the English league, largely blamed on modern tackling methods (the two-man tackle has become commonplace, and defenders tend to run at a ball-carrier, rather than waiting until he reaches them), and the pressure exerted on spines and necks during scrums.

Meanwhile, the increased demands on international players, along with the intensity of the Premiership, continue to provoke squabbles within the English game. The RFU tried to put things right in November 2007, agreeing to pump more than £100 million into the domestic game over eight years, in exchange for access to players picked for the national side. It also set up a Professional Game Board, including some ex-players, to oversee the top level of the game. This was all a far cry from the dying days of the amateur era, when England captain Will Carling famously dismissed the RFU committee as '57 old farts'.

Perhaps another sign of how the game's nature has been affected by professionalism was the 2009 'Bloodgate' scandal, in which Harlequins back Tom Williams was persuaded to bite on a blood capsule in order to allow a substitution during a Heineken Cup match. Such a trick would have been unimaginable in the amateur days, when winning was more of an aspiration than an obsession.

With so much having changed in recent years, rugby union's future is hard to predict. One thing *is* clear, though: whether for better or for worse, it will be largely dictated by marketing and media moguls, rather than tweed-jacketed committee members. At its higher levels, the game is no longer a gentlemen's pastime, but simply another 'brand' in the world of big-money sport.

Chapter 10

Gridiron Glory

'Two rigid, rampart-like lines of human flesh have been created, one of defence, the other of offence, and behind the latter is established a catapult to fire through a porthole opened in the offensive rampart a missile composed of four or five human bodies globulated about a carried football with a maximum of initial velocity against the presumably weakest point in the opposing rampart.'
– Benjamin Ide Wheeler, president of the University of California, describes one of American football's more dangerous manoeuvres, 1906.

Glendale, a suburb of Phoenix, Arizona, might seem an unlikely setting for American football's oldest professional club. But it does hold that distinction, as the home of the National Football League's Arizona Cardinals, although they took some time to get there.

The Cardinals relocated to Arizona from St Louis in 1988. Up to 1960, they had been the Chicago Cardinals – founder members, in 1920, of what would become the NFL. Earlier still, they were the Racine Cardinals, and before that, the Racine Normals (named after their home field in Normal Park, on Chicago's Racine Avenue), having begun life as the football team of the Morgan Athletic Club in 1898.

Athletic clubs were a product of changes in middle-class society in the victorious Union states, after the American Civil War of 1861 to 1865. Many people found themselves with plenty of leisure time, as well as money, and were looking for healthy, enjoyable ways of using both.

Three affluent young men, John Babcock, William Curtis and Henry Buermeyer, formed the New York Athletic Club in 1868, aiming to promote and develop organised amateur sport. Similar clubs soon appeared around the Northeast and Midwest. The main focus was on track and field athletics, but other sports were organised – including, from the 1880s, the brand of football that was evolving at the Ivy League universities. As the game's popularity grew, it was inevitable that some college players would want to continue playing after graduating, and that people would be keen to watch them. Athletic clubs provided the ideal platform.

As the clubs became increasingly competitive in the 1880s and 1890s, especially in football, their thirst for success created a dilemma. As well as sporting opportunities, the clubs provided a means of social climbing. Class distinctions formed part of their identities, and many of the talented football players available to them were not considered socially suitable to be accepted as members.

Some clubs found a way around this problem by giving 'special athletic memberships' to these players, letting them use their facilities and play in their teams, without being full members. The clubs sponsored them, and covered their expenses. Nobody wanted to admit it, but professional football was a short step away.

As in other sports, various tricks were often used to reward the best players without making them openly professional. Some clubs arranged spurious 'jobs', or paid inflated expenses, while others used an intricate scam involving gold watches (as 'trophies') and pawnbrokers. Without a governing body for non-college football, there was no-one to keep an eye on this chicanery.

Strictly speaking, there were no anti-professional rules before 1888, simply because there was nobody to make them. But there was an understanding, at least in public, that football players should not be paid. In an attempt to fill the vacuum, the Amateur Athletic Union (AAU) was formed that year, as an umbrella group encompassing the Intercollegiate Football Association (IFA), the Intercollegiate Association of Amateur Athletes of America, and various clubs and colleges.

The AAU had plenty of clout, particularly with the Olympic movement just starting. It could isolate clubs and colleges that broke its rules on amateurism, by banning them from competing against other AAU members. Track and field athletics came under the most scrutiny at first. In the early 1890s, though, football began taking up much of the AAU's time.

By now, the upper and middle classes of south-western Pennsylvania's industrial belt, in and around Pittsburgh, had garnered immense wealth through the steel industry, and a number of athletic clubs had sprung up in the area. American football had not been on their agenda as yet (although soccer and rugby were often played in the area), but that all changed very quickly.

The Allegheny Athletic Association (AAA), featuring two leading Yale players from the late 1870s – club president John Moorehead and O.D. Thompson – became the first club in the area to field a football team, in the autumn of 1890. The Pittsburgh Athletic Club (PAC) soon followed suit, and an intense rivalry rapidly developed between the two. Other, humbler clubs were also formed in small towns nearby, such as Latrobe, Greensburg and Jeannette, where football was becoming a large part of civic and social life.

In south-western Pennsylvania, and in other burgeoning football centres such as Chicago and Detroit, it was common practice for clubs to field a core of local, working-class players, along with a handful of 'stars' with college pedigree. In 1892, both the AAA and PAC had their eyes on a crop of outstanding Chicago Athletic Association players, notably ex-Yale forward William 'Pudge' Heffelfinger.

After a bidding war between the two clubs, the AAA discreetly offered Heffelfinger the tidy sum of $500, which he accepted, to play against the PAC in November that year. The AAA had recently accused the PAC of using player-coach William Kirschner as a professional player, on the grounds that the club employed him as a physical education instructor, whose salary increased, while his workload decreased, during the football season.

The PAC contingent were shocked to see Heffelfinger lining up against their team in AAA colours. Manager George Barbour called his players off the field, largely because PAC members had placed sizeable bets on their team to win. After much bickering, the game went ahead as an exhibition match, with all bets cancelled. The AAA won by 4-0, courtesy of a Heffelfinger touchdown.

Pudge Heffelfinger had secretly become America's first professional football player. His payment for this appearance was not common knowledge until 1963, when the Pro Football Hall of Fame discovered an AAA accounts document that clearly listed a $500 'game performance bonus'.

In the Hall of Fame's list of the first seven professionals – presumably such an odd number was chosen because Latrobe's John Brallier, long regarded as the first, turned out to be the seventh – the first five were AAA players. Brallier earned his first fee in 1895, as a 16-year-old quarterback receiving ten dollars, plus expenses, for one game. The AAA turned fully professional in 1896, as did Latrobe a year later. However, professional football soon went into decline in the Pittsburgh area, and would make no major impact anywhere in the US for some time to come.

While athletic clubs embraced professionalism, the college football establishment remained staunchly against it. Their attitude, as with their British peers at Oxford and Cambridge and in the Rugby Football Union, was based on a distinction between middle- and upper-class 'gentlemen', who supposedly could never accept money for playing a sport, and working-class professional sportsmen, such as baseball players, whom they often regarded with disdain.

College athletes were expected to play purely for the pleasure of the game, the nobility of the struggle, and the honour of their colleges. In 1889, the IFA declared that anyone who had been paid to play *any* sport would be ineligible to play football for a member institution. College football, though, was hardly spotless. In any case, the Ivy League-based IFA was falling apart, and its influence was waning. After numerous squabbles over eligibility and other issues, Harvard and Columbia left the IFA in the early 1890s. By 1893, only Princeton and Yale remained, and the association was soon disbanded, to be replaced by the Intercollegiate Rules Committee (IRC).

Meanwhile, college football was blossoming in the Midwest, particularly Michigan and Illinois. Seven colleges in the region formed an association, which would evolve into today's Big Ten conference, in 1895. A more open, less violent style of football was developing there, with an emphasis on *end runs*, where a ball-carrier would try to run around the mass of bodies formed by the offensive and defensive lines, rather than burst through it.

Midwestern teams began eclipsing eastern ones in the early years of the new century, none more so than the 'point-a-minute' University of Michigan side, unbeaten in their first 56 games under head coach Fielding Yost between 1901 and 1905. In Yost's first season, Michigan became the first team from outside Ivy League circles to be crowned national champions.

San Francisco staged the west coast's first intercollegiate game, between Stanford University (managed by future US president Herbert Hoover) and the Berkeley-based University of California, in 1892. Their annual meeting became known as the 'Big Game', complete with all the festivities that had come to adorn big games in the east. Later that year, American football pioneer Walter Camp spent some time in California, sharing his expertise with Stanford.

By 1900, more than 250 American colleges had football teams. Many were drawing large crowds, and raking in substantial sums of money, allowing them to pay their coaches handsomely. Some university presidents encouraged the game, pleased by the sense of identity and solidarity it helped to generate among students and alumni. Others, notably Harvard's Charles Eliot, voiced concerns over such issues as rough play, the use of non-student 'ringers', alleged payments to players, dubious recruitment methods, and a fear that football mania was distracting students from their academic pursuits.

While arguments raged over how college football should be governed, the rules of the game itself were remarkably consistent. The fledgling professional game simply copied the college rules. The substitution rules were loosened in 1897, allowing players to be replaced for any reason; until 1905, a substituted player could later rejoin the game. The value of a touchdown was raised from four points to five a year later; a conversion now added only one point, rather than two. Field goals were devalued from five points to four in 1904.

In an attempt to stamp out the dangerous *V-wedge* routine, it was agreed in 1894 that the ball must travel at least ten yards from a kick-off (preventing the kicker from tapping the ball into his own hands, becoming a ball-carrier backed up by a charging phalanx of teammates). By 1896, the offensive side could only have one player in motion when the ball was snapped, and he could not be running forwards. Both rules still apply today.

None of these changes, though, were very effective in making football safer. In fact, things got far *worse* in the mid 1890s, at least on the east coast. Since blocking had been legalised in 1888, the play had become increasingly concentrated around the ball, with little running, passing or kicking – often making it dull for spectators, as well as dangerous for players. Players often pushed or pulled teammates, or appeared to injure opponents intentionally, sometimes by jumping onto them or poking their eyes.

A brutal Harvard–Yale clash in 1894, which left Yale lineman Fred Murphy in a coma, was seen as a blow to the game's reputation, and, in the eyes of Harvard president Charles Eliot, to that of his university. Appalled by the apparent win-at-all-costs attitude, the risks of death and serious injury, and even the use of deceptive tactics, Eliot called for tighter controls and changes in the playing rules. Earlier that year, a debate between professors Burt Wilder of Cornell and Princeton's Woodrow Wilson (yes, another future US president) had pondered the question: 'Ought the Game of Foot Ball to be Encouraged?'

November of that year also saw a fateful grudge match in Washington, DC, between local rivals Georgetown University and the Columbia Athletic Club (at this stage, college and non-college sides often played against each other). Georgetown quarterback George 'Shorty' Bahen's vertebrae were broken, paralysing him, and leading to his death the following January.

The Georgetown authorities reacted by banning football. Their counterparts at the Alabama and Columbia universities did likewise, at other times in the 1890s. The death of the University of Georgia's Richard 'Von' Gammon in 1897, caused by a pushing-and-pulling move in a game against the University of Virginia, nearly led to the game being outlawed in both states.

By now, most players were wearing protective gear, such as padded clothing and, in many cases, leather helmets (although some ball-carrying backs found that headgear restricted their vision, and preferred to go without). But the toll of deaths and major injuries reached crisis point in 1905, when 18 college players are thought to have died. This was the Progressive Era in American society, a time when there was little tolerance for such danger and disorder, and the campaign to reform football was gaining momentum.

That year, none other than president Theodore Roosevelt took up the cause. It has been suggested (but disputed) that the problem grabbed Roosevelt's attention when he saw a photograph of the mangled face of Swarthmore College's Bob 'Tiny' Maxwell after an injury. It seems more likely that the catalyst was an article in *McClure's Magazine*, written by Henry Beach Needham, a friend of the president, revealing that Princeton players were routinely told to 'take out' their opposition's key players in the first five minutes of a game.

Roosevelt was no football-hater. In the muscular Christian tradition, he admired its spirit of 'manly' competition, and even used a football metaphor as one of his guiding principles in life: 'Don't foul, don't shirk, and hit the line hard'. But he was alarmed by the game's increasing violence, and its often devastating results. He expressed his concerns in a speech at Harvard in June 1905, and summoned representatives of Harvard, Princeton and Yale to a White House meeting four months later. Although it has been claimed that Roosevelt threatened to outlaw football, there is no real evidence to back this up. But he did insist on reforms, and persuaded his guests to issue a statement of intent to clean up the game.

As the catalogue of tragedies kept growing, it soon became clear that something more effective was needed. The death of Union College's Harold Moore, from a kick on the head in a game against local rivals New York University in November 1905, prompted the latter's chancellor Henry MacCracken to arrange a conference in New York for early December. At the conference, attended by delegates from around a dozen colleges, a proposal to abolish football was outvoted. Instead, there would be another, larger, gathering on December 28.

This time, around 60 colleges were represented, but many of the major football powers were absent, including the 'Big Three' of Harvard, Princeton and Yale. Those who did turn up agreed to form a new body, the Intercollegiate Athletic Association of the United States, which would be renamed as the National Collegiate Athletic Association (NCAA) in 1910. It became the main controlling body of American college sport, as it still is today.

A committee was formed, hoping to co-operate with Walter Camp's IRC in overhauling the rules of the game. The two met in January 1906, with Harvard coach Bill Reid emerging as the leader of the combined group. A month later, they came up with a set of rule changes, some of which would change the game enormously over the coming decades.

Most drastic of all was the decision to allow forward passing. The intention was to make the game more open, encouraging teams to use spread-out formations, rather than having everyone bunched together around the ball. But the idea was strongly opposed by purists, including veterans of the 1870s rugby era (even for Camp, the great innovator, this was a step too far), and was accepted only after severe restrictions had been agreed.

If a forward pass hit the ground before being touched, the defending team would take over possession, at the position of the throw. This would be replaced by a 15-yard penalty a year later. A touchdown could not yet be scored by catching a pass beyond the goal-line; instead, there would be a *touchback*, with the opposition gaining possession on their 20-yard line. As with today's rules, the ball could only be thrown forward once on each play, and only from behind the line of scrimmage.

A passer could be hit, even after releasing the ball. A thrown ball also had to cross the line of scrimmage at least five yards wide of the point where the play started. To help officials in judging this, lines were drawn along the length of the field at five-yard intervals, in addition to the existing lines drawn parallel with the goal-lines, giving the field a chequer-board look.

Another important change concerned how far the offence needed to advance the ball, in three downs or less, in order to keep possession. Rather than five yards, they would now have to gain ten, as Camp suggested after seeing such a rule in action in Canada. It was another attempt at opening up the game, by forcing teams to take a more adventurous, creative approach towards moving the ball downfield, with less reliance on short, predictable runs with the ball.

To cut out the sparring, punching and other unsavoury acts at the line of scrimmage, a *neutral zone* was established, separating the opposing groups of linemen by a distance equal to the length of the ball. Tough penalties were introduced for personal fouls, 'unsportsmanlike conduct' and 'unnecessary roughness', and pushing-and-pulling plays were prohibited. The game's duration was cut from 70 minutes to 60, to reduce the fatigue that was thought to be partly to blame for many injuries.

With the 1906 season seven months away, there was a long wait before anyone could see what impact the rule changes would have, and there was still unease about football in some quarters. Northwestern University, in the Chicago area, suspended it in March. The same month, lecturer Frederick Jackson Turner faced protests over his anti-football campaign at the University of Wisconsin. Gun-toting students marched towards his residence, chanting 'Death to the faculty'. After arguing with Jackson as he stood on his doorstep, and threatening to throw him into a lake, they settled for burning him in effigy instead.

Out west, the Stanford–California rivalry had become so intense that the universities' presidents were desperate to cool things down. At Stanford, David Starr Jordan denounced American football as 'fundamentally a battle between hired gladiators'. Jordan wanted his students to switch to soccer or rugby union, as did his California counterpart Benjamin Ide Wheeler, who believed them to be 'the heartiest and manliest of the Anglo-Saxon sports.' Harvard's Charles Eliot advised them against adopting soccer, fearing that 'our American college boys would spoil it in five minutes'.

After they had seen visiting Australian and New Zealand teams in action, both Jordan and Wheeler plumped for rugby in February 1906. The prospect of international competition helped to tempt them away from the American game, as well as a belief that rugby would be safer, and would bring about a calmer atmosphere. Stanford coach James F. Langan travelled to British Columbia to learn the finer points of the game. Some other western colleges took it up, as did most Californian high schools.

Stanford and California stuck with rugby until 1915, but it aroused little interest. After a dispute between the two, California reverted to American football that year, and Stanford followed suit two years later. (As mentioned in chapter 9, some heavy defeats by the touring All Blacks probably also discouraged the colleges from continuing with rugby.) As well as being remote from the east coast and Midwest, California was still thinly populated, and its dalliance with rugby had barely been noticed elsewhere.

Coaches from more than 100 colleges attended another New York conference in September 1906, where the new rules were clarified and discussed. Many were unsure about when to employ the forward pass, what would be the ideal throwing technique, and whether three downs would be enough to gain ten yards. For some years, most teams would use the forward pass sparingly, usually as a last resort. The tight restrictions made it a risky proposition, and the size and shape of the ball (still the same as in rugby) made it difficult to throw one-handed.

When the forward pass was used, it generally helped to relieve the congestion at the line of scrimmage. It also helped teams to change the direction of play, using the element of surprise to outfox opponents. Some younger coaches, such as Harvard's Percy Haughton, pushed for the rules about forward passing to be loosened; some of the old guard, notably Walter Camp, wanted it scrapped.

For three seasons, the changes also appeared to be making the game safer; but this did not last. The 1909 college season saw 26 fatalities, eight more than in 1905, and the critics came out in force again. The *New York Times* called for football to be suspended. In a tone reminiscent of 16th-century English puritans condemning folk football, the *Washington Post* asked:

> *Does the public need any more proof that football is a brutal, savage, murderous sport? Is it necessary to kill many more promising young men before this game is revised or stopped altogether?*

The game was banned or suspended at some colleges, amid fresh concerns that it might be outlawed. Stanford president David Starr Jordan dismissed the 1906 changes as a 'farce', calling the game 'rugby's American pervert'. More reform was inevitable, and there would be plenty of it over the next few years.

Several changes were made in 1909. Games were to be divided into quarters rather than halves, and a substituted player could return to the game in a later quarter. Field goals were now worth only three points, as they are today, rather than four. The next year, mass and momentum plays were further limited, by requiring the offence to have seven men standing at the line of scrimmage when the ball was snapped. Forward passes no longer had to cross the line of scrimmage five yards wide of the position of the snap (eliminating the chequer-board field layout), but were reined in by new provisions: they could only be thrown from at least five yards behind the line of scrimmage, and could travel no more than 20 yards beyond it.

The two rules committees – Camp's IRC and the NCAA's reform committee – merged in 1912. The combined group pushed through another raft of changes, mainly intended to open the game up further, and to encourage more scoring. As many had feared, it had proven overly difficult to gain ten yards in three downs. Instead, there would now be four downs. A touchdown would score six points (still with one point for a successful conversion) rather than five, another rule that has survived to this day.

The 20-yard limit for forward passes was scrapped, and it became possible to score a touchdown by catching a forward pass beyond the goal-line. But it had to be caught within the *end zone* – a new feature of the field layout, stretching for ten yards between the goal-line and the new *end line*. To help make room for the end zones, the distance between the goal-lines was reduced from 110 yards to 100.

By now, some coaches were using the forward pass as a major part of their strategies, rather than a last resort. West Virginia Wesleyan College used it extensively in 1912, surprising some of their more renowned rivals as they went unbeaten all season. Jess Harper used it successfully as coach at Wabash College in Indiana, and took his methods to the University of Notre Dame in South Bend, Indiana.

Notre Dame quarterback Gus Dorais and end Knute Rockne practised passing and catching during the summer. In November 1913, their little-known team shocked the college football world with a 35-13 win over the mighty Army side, with Dorais throwing 17 attempted passes, five of them producing touchdowns. Suddenly, Notre Dame was a force to be reckoned with, and so was the forward pass.

The American involvement in World War I almost brought college football to a standstill, thanks to shortages of manpower and fuel. However, many soldiers learned the game in military camps, helping to bring about a post-war boom. Meanwhile, the armed forces hired some coaches, including the still-ubiquitous Walter Camp, to help with military strategy.

The NCAA was growing rapidly in size and influence, mostly under the leadership of Palmer Pierce, president from its inception in 1905 to 1913, and again from 1917 to 1929. By 1919, it had 170 member institutions, and covered 11 sports. The 1920s saw college football blossoming into a lucrative, hugely popular spectacle. Newspapers were giving it more and more space, radio commentary began in 1922, and vast stadiums started to spring up, such as the 52,000-seat Rose Bowl in Pasadena, near Los Angeles.

The Rose Bowl's roots lay in the Tournament of Roses, a New Year festival held in the town since 1890 to celebrate southern California's mild winter weather. In 1902, the festivities included a football game between Stanford and Michigan, nominally the respective western and eastern 'champions' of the season that had just ended.

The game was not a great success, and was replaced by chariot racing the next year; but football returned to the schedule in 1916, now attracting more interest. The Rose Bowl stadium was opened in 1923 – so called because it was built by digging a bowl-shaped hole in the ground, and using the excavated soil as the foundations for the stands, an idea first used by Yale a decade earlier. Gradually, the term 'Rose Bowl' came to refer to the game itself, as well as the venue; the word 'bowl' would also be applied to other post-season football games. The stadium would eventually host two soccer World Cup finals – for men in 1994, and women in 1999.

As the crowds grew, so did the controversy over college football's ethics. Many university officials, and other observers, were uneasy about its commercialism, and its prominent role in collegiate life. Students with a talent for football were being subsidised via loans, slush funds, bogus 'jobs', and waivers on accommodation, food and tuition fees. There was intense competition to hire the best coaches, with generous salaries on offer. Some coaches and trainers were thought to be too ruthless in their treatment of players – some even gave them strychnine as a stimulant, or cocaine as an antidote to pain.

While college football started the new century with a turbulent couple of decades, the professional game was just beginning to find its feet. It still had a presence in south-western Pennsylvania in 1902, when Latrobe manager Dave Berry formed a league. Although its teams were all in the same state, Berry was bold enough to dub his venture the 'National Football League'. Latrobe was too small a town for such a project; instead, the league featured three newly-formed big-city teams: the Pittsburgh Stars, Philadelphia Athletics and Philadelphia Phillies.

Baseball was big news in both cities, and Berry tried to hitch a ride on its bandwagon, forging links between his league's Philadelphia sides and the city's two major-league baseball clubs, even going as far as to adopt their names. The Stars featured renowned baseball pitcher Christy Mathewson at fullback, while the Athletics were coached by Connie Mack, then in the early stages of his 50-year stint managing their baseball namesakes. The league was something of a shambles, and fizzled out after one season, with all three teams claiming the title.

Also in 1902, a mini-tournament billed as the 'Football World Series' was held indoors at New York's Madison Square Garden, with five teams from around the Northeast, and an exhibition of Gaelic football after the final. It was repeated the following year, but, like the first National Football League, the World Series made no lasting impact.

Football was being played widely at (non-collegiate) amateur level around the Northeast and Midwest, mainly in 'sandlots' – rough playing areas with little in the way of field markings. Many teams were formed by companies, neighbourhood associations and athletic clubs. They generated intense local pride and rivalries, and helped to foster a working-class culture, in what had started out as a middle-class sport.

There were also hosts of semi-professional teams in these regions, some of them drifting towards full professionalism. North-eastern Ohio was a prime example, with several small cities becoming engrossed in their local teams' fortunes. Local businessmen saw the game as a vehicle for entertaining the public and raising their own profiles. Akron and Massillon had emerged as the leading clubs by 1905, when the newly-formed Canton AC (later known as the Canton Bulldogs) joined them as contenders for the state's unofficial championship.

Gridiron Glory

Pro football in Ohio was a messy business, with players often moving between teams at a dizzying rate. Until the forward pass came into regular use in the 1910s, the game offered little entertainment, with tactics remaining simple and predictable. (College teams, who could stay together for a whole season or more, and get plenty of practice time, were able to develop more sophisticated moves.) Attendances relied heavily on results, and losing teams rarely stayed in business for long. In turn, the desperate need for success led clubs to pay inflated salaries to players, often digging themselves into deep financial trouble.

The professional game had a low profile and a seedy reputation, living a twilight existence as American football's dirty little secret. Some players would turn out for college teams on a Saturday, and then, using pseudonyms and disguised by face masks (which were ostensibly protective), for professional sides the next day. Even as late as 1911, the *Encyclopedia Britannica* baldly stated, in relation to American football, that 'professional football is not played in America.'

Whatever the purists may have thought of the professionals, no-one could have doubted their commitment. When Canton Bulldogs centre Harry Turner suffered a fatal spinal injury in a 1914 game against Akron, his last words, referring to the opposition's star quarterback, were: 'I know I must go, but I'm satisfied, for we beat Peggy Parratt.' Canton were devastated by Turner's death, but were boosted a year later by the signing of Olympic pentathlon and decathlon champion Jim Thorpe, perhaps the outstanding player, and surely the world's leading all-round sportsman, of his day. Thorpe soon became their player-coach, and the Bulldogs became unofficial Ohio champions in 1916, 1917 and 1919.

The Midwest's economy boomed in the early years of World War I, thanks to a rise in demand from Europe for its foodstuffs and other products. Crowds at professional football games grew, not only in Ohio, but also in Indiana and Michigan. A business-fuelled form of civic pride known as 'boosterism' cranked up the intensity of competition, particularly between teams from neighbouring towns. The game was also becoming more refined and entertaining, thanks to the increase in forward passing and the growing presence of former college players.

Most clubs, though, were losing money, as salaries spiralled out of control. In 1919, there was some talk of creating a formal league, to regulate payments, prevent poaching and bidding wars, ban the use of current college players, arrange fixtures, and determine the champions. The idea finally came to fruition in August 1920, when Canton owner Ralph Hay hosted a meeting at his Hupmobile car dealership in the town. Representatives of the Akron Pros, Cleveland Indians and Dayton Triangles agreed to join Hay in forming the American Professional Football Conference.

Other team owners soon became interested, and another meeting was held a month later. Six new teams were represented, all from outside Ohio: three from Illinois, two from Indiana, and one from upstate New York. This time, Hay's office was too small, and the delegates sat on the running boards of cars in the sweltering showroom, staying cool by drinking beer from buckets suspended from the fenders. The league was renamed as the American Professional Football Association; two years later it would become the National Football League (NFL). More teams would join up, before, or even after, the season got underway.

Jim Thorpe was named as league president, more for his fame than for any business or organisational acumen he may have been thought to have. The embryonic NFL could barely be called a 'league' in the modern sense – more a loose alliance of clubs. Scheduling was left for the teams to sort out among themselves, and the champions would be decided by a vote. There were apparently no agreements on the main issues that had been behind the league's formation in the first place, such as salary control, player movement and the use of college players. Akron, unbeaten in their 11 games, were confirmed as champions the following April, four months after the season had ended.

As the league tried to get its act together after an untidy first season, the ineffective Thorpe was replaced as president by Joe Carr, Columbus Panhandles manager and part-time sportswriter. Carr took a more businesslike approach to the job, most likely trying to emulate baseball's major leagues. A constitution and by-laws were drawn up, with limits on player movements and eligibility. Still, the league was hardly any more stable in 1921 than it had been the previous year. Some of its 21 teams were laughably short-lived: the Tonawanda Kardex, for example, based in a Buffalo suburb, announced their arrival with a 45-0 thrashing by the Rochester Jeffersons in November, and duly dropped out of the league without having played at home.

Others would be far more durable. The Green Bay Packers, a small-town Wisconsin club formed in 1919 (the name was based on their sponsors, the Indian Packing Company), joined the league in 1921. The club was taken over by a public non-profit corporation two years later, and, after coming through some difficult times, with occasional threats of being moved to Milwaukee, has remarkably stayed in the NFL to this day.

Among the league's founders were the Decatur Staleys, from central Illinois, formed to promote the A.E. Staley Starch Company. During their title-winning 1921 season, player-coach George Halas, having been granted control of the team by A.E. Staley, moved them 180 miles to Chicago; a year later, they became the Chicago Bears. Halas, later known as 'Papa Bear' and 'Mr Everything', would stay with the team almost continuously, as coach, owner, or both, until his death in 1983.

Throughout the NFL's early years, many clubs struggled financially, thanks mostly to small crowds (typically a few thousand) and travel costs. Few sports fans felt strong affinities with professional football teams, and the press coverage was meagre and often dismissive, particularly in big-city newspapers and nationwide journals. The pro game still had a shady image, linked in many people's minds with drinking and gambling, and its playing style was widely considered inferior to that of college football.

If the clubs really did want to generate some loyalty among their local public, some went about it the hard way. Home teams were required to pay a fixed 'guarantee' fee to their visitors, which some clubs found to be more lucrative than playing in front of their paltry home crowds. As a result, with scheduling still on a free-for-all basis, some chose to play most of their games away from home.

Some of these 'road teams' had the air of a travelling circus. The Kansas City Cowboys, for example, promoted themselves by performing roping and spinning tricks, and once wandered around downtown New York dressed in Wild West gear, handing out tickets. The Oorang Indians, nominally based in LaRue, Ohio, were assembled by Walter Lingo for the sole purpose of promoting his Oorang Dog Kennels business. As pre-game and half-time entertainment at their games, the all-Native-American team (featuring a declining Jim Thorpe) performed tribal dances, tomahawk-throwing, and even bear-wrestling. Such silliness would have been unthinkable in baseball or college football, and reinforced professional football's reputation for tawdry, low-rent gimmickry.

Joe Carr had big-time ambitions for the NFL, and saw little future in a league stuffed with small-town, suburban and short-lived teams. Instead, Carr used (and, in some cases, arguably abused) the league's regulations to favour clubs in the major cities. Among his favourites were the New York Giants, that city's first stable NFL team and the league's first serious presence on the east coast, joining the league in 1925; and the Chicago Bears, the more popular team in the Midwest's major city, easily outdrawing the Cardinals by the mid 1920s.

Perhaps the most blatant example of Carr's big-city bias came in November 1925, when he let the Bears sign star half-back Harold 'Red' Grange just days after his last college appearance – hardly in keeping with the league's policy on recruiting college players. Grange, a spectacularly agile runner who had honed his muscles by delivering ice, had made a big impression in 1923, his first year at the University of Illinois. Dubbed the 'Galloping Ghost', he had his finest hour the following season in a game against Michigan, scoring five touchdowns and passing for another[41].

Grange's abrupt signing with the Bears, which meant he would leave university without a degree, provoked outrage in the college sports world, mostly directed at his reviled agent C.C. Pyle. Grange himself was hardly coy about his motives, admitting that 'I'm out to get the money, and I don't care who knows it.' The demand for his services was certainly there. This was the 'Age of Heroes' in American sport: baseball had Babe Ruth, boxing had Jack Dempsey, and the men running the NFL wanted to find their own.

After joining the Bears, Red Grange was whisked around the country on a tour involving 18 games in two months, sharing half of the gate receipts with Pyle, while also earning a film contract and a string of product endorsement deals. But Grange's contract expired at the end of the season, and, together with Pyle, he applied to set up a New York Yankees franchise in the NFL. When the league rejected their plan, Grange and Pyle reacted by creating the American Football League, with their Yankees team intended as its star attraction; but the venture failed dismally, barely lasting a season[42].

Grange rejoined the Chicago Bears in 1927, but missed the next season through injury, and was never quite the same again. Some historians have suggested that Grange transformed the NFL from its ramshackle early self into a 'major league'. Others, such as Craig R. Coenen in *From Sandlots to the Super Bowl*, argue that the result of his arrival was more of a blip than a revolution, as attendances quickly slipped back to pre-Grange levels after the initial rush of interest had died down.

Other team owners were keen to promote their own star players, sometimes to the point where team identities barely seemed to matter. Ernie Nevers, an exceptional runner, passer, kicker and defender who had made his name at Stanford, joined the Duluth Eskimos. The team rarely played at home, and were sometimes billed in posters as 'Ernie Nevers' Eskimos', with no mention of the Minnesota town that they nominally represented.

The Grange affair, where a student's feats in college football brought him almost instant riches in the professional ranks, along with an early exit from university, intensified the debate over the rights and wrongs of the college game. The American Association of University Professors savaged it in a 1926 report, denouncing its attendant 'hysteria', its effect on studies, and the huge sums of money involved. The same year, the Carnegie Foundation launched an extensive three-year investigation into college sport, looking at issues such as recruitment, subsidies and safety, culminating in a scathing report that provoked angry denials from coaches and administrators.

There was now also a fear that college football would be overshadowed by the professional game (on the other hand, this could have helped bring about the 'de-emphasis' that some of its critics were calling for).

But the big crowds kept rolling in, such as the 117,000 who saw Notre Dame take on Navy in 1928.

College football was taking on a distinctive flavour in the Deep South, where the amateur tradition was being broken even more brazenly than in the north. The game helped the region to assert itself as it recovered from the long-term ruinous effects of the Civil War, and was pursued with an aggressive, rebellious zeal, both on and off the field.

In Alabama, Auburn University won nearly three quarters of their games under Walter Camp protégé Mike Donahue between 1908 and 1922, helped by offers of scholarships and dubious employment to players. Big victories for southern teams, particularly the 'flagship' state university sides, were seen as badges of state pride and southern honour. When the Alabama team returned from their Rose Bowl success over Washington in January 1926, their train was greeted by crowds at each station in their home state, and finally by 15,000 admirers in Tuscaloosa. Georgia's 1927 and 1929 wins over Yale triggered wild celebrations across the state.

The Great Depression subdued the mania surrounding college football, with attendances and income slumping between 1929 and 1933. Meanwhile, a rise in death and serious injury figures in high school football was widely blamed on poor equipment, training and supervision, resulting from the economic squeeze. But the mid 1930s brought a revival, with the start of regular radio coverage, and a rash of new post-season 'bowl' games in sun-belt cities, such as the Orange, Cotton and Sugar Bowls in Miami, Dallas and New Orleans respectively.

After slowly finding its feet in its first decade, the NFL made bigger strides in the 1930s, evolving into a more credible, professionally-run league. Fixture scheduling was assigned to a central committee in 1931. From 1936, it ensured that each team would play an equal number of games. Starting in 1934, the league champions played against a college all-star team each year, helping to raise the league's profile at a time when it was still in the college game's shadow. The NFL launched a public relations campaign that year, and set up a publicity department in 1938.

The annual draft, a brainchild of Philadelphia Eagles owner Bert Bell, was instituted in 1936, allowing teams to select college leavers in an orderly procedure, in contrast with the bidding wars of previous years. The Pro Bowl, with the champions meeting an NFL all-star team, was first staged in January 1939, in Los Angeles.

The NFL's success inspired the launch of another rival league in 1936, again named the American Football League. This AFL collapsed amid financial ruin after just two seasons, but at least held the distinction of featuring the first professional west coast team, the Los Angeles

Bulldogs. Yet another AFL sprang up in 1940, also folding in its second season.

NFL president Joe Carr continued trying to rid the league of small-town and financially weak teams, using league entrance fees and 'forfeit guarantees' (penalising teams that failed to last a whole season) as deterrents. Its membership was slashed from 22 teams to 12 in 1927, and, as the Depression saw off the likes of the Frankford Yellow Jackets (from a Philadelphia suburb) and the Providence Steam Roller, down to just eight by 1932. By 1934, the Green Bay Packers, with their fervent support and unique not-for-profit structure, remained as the league's only small-town club, as they have been ever since.

The league was also helped by changes in its playing rules and season structure, which came about largely by accident. When Ohio's Portsmouth Spartans (soon to become the Detroit Lions) and the Chicago Bears were tied for first place in 1932, an extra game was arranged as a decider. To avoid the effects of the brutal December weather, the NFL staged it at the indoor Chicago Stadium, normally used for ice hockey and circuses. The circumstances forced alterations to the playing area and rules: the goal-lines were just 60 yards apart, the field was only 45 yards wide, and field goals were eliminated.

The cramped conditions highlighted a weakness in the normal rules. If the ball went over a sideline, it would be moved halfway across the field for the start of the next play. However, if a play ended inbounds, *near* a sideline, the game would restart from that same position (or a yard infield, if the play ended within a yard of the sideline), resulting in lop-sided formations. This made things so difficult for the offence that they would often deliberately run the ball out of play, allowing themselves to start the next down from a central position, hardly making for exciting viewing.

At Chicago Stadium, the narrow gaps between the sidelines and fencing could have led to farcical scenes; but the NFL found a solution. Broken lines known as *hashmarks* were drawn along the length of the field, ten yards from each sideline. If the ball went dead between a hashmark and a sideline, it would be re-spotted on the hashmark, ensuring plenty of room for the players to line up on either side.

Chicago came out on top, by nine points to nil. The extra game was such a hit that the NFL decided to have one every year, rather than awarding the title to the team with the best record. The league was split into Eastern and Western divisions, with the two winners meeting in a championship game. The restructuring helped to cut travel costs and intensify rivalries, as well as providing an end-of-season showpiece.

The NFL also responded to the play-off by drawing up its own rules for the first time, having simply followed the college rules until now.

Hashmarks became a permanent feature, initially ten yards infield, but later gradually moving closer to the centre. The ball was to be placed on the hashmarks if it was downed between the sideline and hashmarks, or if it went out of bounds.

Thanks to a dispute over the Bears' crucial touchdown in the 1932 play-off, it was agreed that a forward pass could be thrown from anywhere behind the line of scrimmage, rather than at least five yards behind it. The passing game got another boost from reductions in the width of the ball in 1929 and 1934, making it easier to grip. In 1933, the goalposts were moved from the back of the end zone to the front, reversing a change that had been made in 1927 in an effort to discourage field goal attempts.

By the early 1930s, most teams had abandoned the *'T' formation* for offensive plays, where the quarterback stood just behind the centre, with three other backs side-by-side behind him. The more unbalanced *single-wing* system had come into favour, with the quarterback playing a blocking role, while the centre usually snapped the ball back several yards to the fullback.

The Chicago Bears, though, brought the 'T' formation back into fashion under new coach Ralph Jones in 1930, helping the quarterback to dictate play from just behind the offensive line. It now featured variations such as *split ends* (forerunners of modern wide receivers), end runs, and a back in motion before the snap. Although their scheme was largely geared towards passing, the Bears still had a potent running game, featuring the fearless, head-down ball-carrying style of fullback Bronko Nagurski, who once ran the ball into a brick wall before telling a teammate, 'That last guy hit me pretty hard.'

The art of passing was developed further by Green Bay under coach Earl 'Curly' Lambeau; and by Sammy Baugh, quarterback of the Washington Redskins, a team that had found a warm welcome in the capital after moving from Boston. Baugh emerged in an era when the quarterback became the primary passer, and is widely seen as the original star in the role. But his team was torn apart by the Bears in the 1940 championship game, as Chicago's advanced tactics, partly modelled on German military strategies, helped them to a 73-0 win. The 'T' formation soon took over. The Pittsburgh Steelers would be the last NFL team to abandon the single-wing offence, in 1952 (although the *wildcat offence*, with the ball being snapped directly to a running back, swept the league in 2008, and is often likened to the single-wing).

The NFL, following Major League Baseball's example, appointed its first commissioner in 1941, replacing the role of president. After FBI director J. Edgar Hoover had been considered, the job went to respected former Notre Dame player and coach Elmer Layden.

On December 7 that year, stadium announcers at three NFL games told servicemen present to report to their units, as news broke of the Japanese attack on Pearl Harbor. As America found itself at war again, football continued at both college and professional levels; but teams were depleted, and fuel shortages made things difficult. Some NFL teams merged temporarily: the Philadelphia Eagles and Pittsburgh Steelers, for example, joined forces under the official name of the Phil-Pitt (or Pittsadelphia) Eagles-Steelers, although many knew them as the Steagles.

As in World War I, the armed forces harnessed the expertise of some football coaches, such as Navy coach Tom Hamilton, who helped with the navy's military training. One side-effect of the war was the emergence of female cheerleaders in college football. Until now, cheerleaders, or 'pep squads', had largely been male; but war call-ups left the nation short of young men, paving the way for women to step into the role.

After the war ended, having claimed the lives of 21 NFL players, normal business was quickly resumed in professional football, with some clubs now drawing larger crowds than many leading college teams. As the league became more profitable, many big-city businessmen grew envious of team owners, and longed to get in on the act. But the owners were reluctant to share the spoils with newcomers by expanding the league, and their would-be rivals' only option was to create a new one.

The birth of the All-America Football Conference (AAFC) was announced in 1945, with play starting the following year. The new league initially had a friendly attitude towards the NFL, with a policy that ruled out poaching NFL players. Its leaders suggested a post-season 'World Series of Football' between the two league champions, and a combined draft.

The NFL, though, ignored the AAFC's overtures. The leagues soon fought a bidding war, which caused serious financial damage to both, accompanied by a flurry of lawsuits. The AAFC had teams in the burgeoning cities of Los Angeles and San Francisco; the NFL tried to compete head-on, with its Cleveland Rams moving to Los Angeles in 1946 (thus becoming the first west coast team, in any sport, in an established major professional league[43]).

The AAFC was the NFL's first serious rival. For three years, the leagues enjoyed similar levels of quality and popularity. The NFL was concerned enough to dismiss Elmer Layden as commissioner in 1946, replacing him with Philadelphia owner Bert Bell.

By 1949, though, the AAFC was in far worse shape than its rival. Poor management, a lack of adequate coaches, and the overwhelming supremacy of the Cleveland Browns (champions each year from 1946 to 1949, winning 47 of their 54 regular-season games), left it struggling to survive. But the NFL had an eye on its more successful clubs, and the leagues reached an agreement in 1949: the Browns, Baltimore Colts and San Francisco 49ers joined the NFL, while the AAFC's four other teams were disbanded, with their owners receiving compensation. The NFL was reorganised, on a non-regional basis, into the American and National Conferences. With teams in Los Angeles and San Francisco, it was now a more genuinely 'national' league.

The post-war years saw a drastic change in American football, although its seeds had been sown during the war itself. A rule allowing unlimited substitutions was introduced in college football in 1941, to help teams that were short of talented players; the idea was to allow lesser players, lacking in all-round skills, to specialise in certain roles. Nobody made much use of this new freedom until 1945, when Michigan coach Fritz Crisler, with the luxury of a large squad, unveiled a new strategy in a game against Army.

Most of Crisler's players would only feature in either offence or defence – allowing them to focus on specialist roles and skills, and to rest during much of the game. Although the highly-fancied Army side won by 28-7, their coach, Earle 'Red' Blaik, liked Michigan's idea. Blaik referred to the separate units as 'platoons', thus helping to coin the term 'two-platoon football'. The change met some resistance from traditionalists who maintained that football should be an 11-versus-11 affair (except in the case of injuries), and was reversed in 1953. But the limits on substitutions were gradually loosened again over the next 12 years, until there were none left.

The NFL also adopted free substitution in 1943. It imposed a limit of three changes at a time in 1946, but scrapped this restriction four years later. By 1960, Chuck Bednarik, of the Philadelphia Eagles, was the only 'two-way' player in the league.

The two-platoon system evolved in the 1950s and 1960s, with roles becoming more specialised. A 1951 NFL rule barred linemen from catching forward passes, leaving offensive linemen with little more than a blocking role. As offensive and defensive schemes grew in sophistication, former halfbacks evolved into wide receivers, running backs, or cornerbacks.

Defensive lines began to split into two rows, with the rear players becoming *linebackers*, one of the game's most prominent positions today. While the defensive linemen battled with their offensive counterparts, the linebackers would either stay back to defend against a pass or run, or look for a way of getting to the quarterback.

New York Giants player-coach Tom Landry established the 4-3 formation (four linemen and three linebackers), which he later used successfully when coaching the Dallas Cowboys. A new breed of linebacker soon emerged, with speed as well as strength, and became a key factor in the *blitz* – a defensive gambit developed by the Chicago Bears in the late 1940s, where several linebackers and defensive backs would charge at the quarterback.

A third platoon also began to develop: the *special teams* employed in kicking situations. Place-kicking and punting became specialised tasks, each usually covered by one player in each squad, who was rarely expected to do anything else. Their colleagues in the special teams were (and still are) generally offensive and defensive back-ups, responsible for fielding kick-offs and punts, pressuring the opposing kick receiver, blocking opponents, or trying to block kicks.

Until the mid 1960s, place-kickers used a crude 'straight on' technique. Now, free substitution gave them more scope to hone their kicking skills. The Buffalo Bills' Pete Gogolak introduced the soccer-style kick in 1964, using an angled run-up and striking the ball with his instep. Gogolak was soon eclipsed by Jan Stenerud, a Norwegian who stumbled upon American football while attending Montana State University on a ski-jumping scholarship. Stenerud used his soccer experience to get into the varsity team as a kicker, and went on to find professional fame[44].

Coaches were playing an increasing role, helped (in the NFL) by a 1944 rule change that allowed them to direct operations from the sideline. The Cleveland Browns' dominance in the AAFC, and further success in the NFL, was largely down to the innovative work of coach Paul Brown – so revered in the area for his record with Massillon High School and Ohio State University that the new team was named after him. Brown was intensely methodical, preaching discipline and good organisation. He was the first coach to use playbooks, to hire specialised position coaches, and to use substitutes as messengers. In his other role as general manager, he also secured the services of some of the era's stars, such as quarterback Otto Graham and fullback Marion Motley.

Despite all these advances, American football still had a rough edge in the 1950s. Players were often hit in the face after releasing the ball, and sometimes had their necks twisted or spines bent, not necessarily by accident. Tighter rules were introduced to curb the use of hands and legs on opponents, and more officials were put onto the field, bringing the total to six by 1965 in the NFL, and by 1972 in the college game (today, both have seven).

Protective gear also helped to limit the damage, with helmets becoming mandatory in college football in 1939, and in the NFL four years later. Initially they were made from leather, lined with felt on the inside; but plastic helmets became the norm after the war, despite fears that they could cause injuries as well as prevent them. Face masks were first allowed in college football in 1951, and gradually became common at all levels of the game. Paul Brown saw an opportunity in the improved headgear: he secretly had radio equipment fitted into his quarterback's plastic helmet in 1956, allowing instructions to be given from the sideline. But the device was soon discovered and banned, not becoming legal until 1994.

College football was still coming under fire over recruitment methods and financial aid to its players, with gambling now also entering the picture. Alarm bells had been raised in 1939 when football was abolished at the University of Chicago, a member of the high-profile Big Ten conference. Days later, the NCAA toughened its stance, announcing a new definition of amateurism and new rules about subsidies, and empowering itself to expel offenders. But there was little support for these measures, and little money available to fund investigations.

More conferences were being formed, with varying attitudes towards these matters. At the elite institutions where the game had been born – the likes of Harvard and Princeton (soon to be officially known as the 'Ivy League') – the regulations were tightened in 1945 and 1953, in an attempt to control the game's excesses. But these universities no longer had much influence on the college football scene, and most of the major conferences had no real appetite for self-restraint.

With such a wide range of football cultures under its umbrella, the NCAA had a tough task in drawing up a universal set of rules. The first serious attempt came in 1947 with the *Purity Code*, soon to be better known as the *Sanity Code*. But these revamped regulations about subsidies, expenses, employment and recruitment had little effect. Many colleges flouted them, but proposals to expel these colleges were outvoted, and no other punishment was available. Some colleges openly announced that they would ignore the rules. In the south, the scholarship system was so deeply ingrained that there seemed to be little hope of eradicating it.

Looking for stronger leadership, with support staff and real powers, the NCAA installed its first executive director, Walter Byers, in 1951. Byers, who would stay in office for 36 eventful years, assembled a full-time staff, and set up a national headquarters in Kansas City. A string of college sport scandals in 1951 and 1952 put him and his team to the test. But, a few years later – after half a century of tame finger-wagging – the association was finally showing its teeth, punishing or censuring such football powerhouses as Michigan State and Notre Dame.

Another challenge facing post-war college football was the growing presence of television, which threatened to commercialise the game even more. The businessmen running the professional game, of course, had no such worries; but they did fear that TV coverage could reduce attendances. In 1947, with TV ownership rising rapidly, the NFL and AAFC let team owners make their own decisions on the matter. But when the NFL's L.A. Rams became the first team to have their home games shown regularly on local TV, in 1950, their attendances nearly halved.

The league office soon took more control over TV contracts, but most teams struck deals with local broadcasters, often for away games only. The NCAA banned coverage of college football in 1951, but soon started making exceptions, and got into a spate of wrangles over the issue with conferences, colleges and even the Justice Department.

Regular national NFL coverage began in 1956, on CBS. Football was ideal for TV – more so than baseball – with viewers getting a perfect vantage point (looking along the line of scrimmage, with all or most of the players in the picture), and with the frequent stoppages allowing plenty of time for replays, analysis, and, of course, commercial breaks. Televised football was especially lucrative in the New York market, as highlighted by the 1958 championship decider between the New York Giants and Baltimore Colts. This game, later dubbed 'The Greatest Game Ever Played', drew enormous media attention and more than 40 million viewers, and produced a thrilling finish, the Colts winning in overtime after drawing level with seven seconds left.

This game proved to be a landmark in the NFL's ascent as a form of mass entertainment, at a time when it was learning to use TV as a powerful promotional tool. Professional football was finally overtaking the college game, and baseball, as the nation's main sporting attraction. By 1960, it was not uncommon for 50 million viewers to tune in on a Sunday in the regular season.

College football, with a more cautious approach to TV, and a less attractive style of play (which the NCAA tried to remedy by gradually adopting NFL rules, such as free substitution), was now seen in some quarters as merely a training ground for future professionals. As early as 1954, NFL commissioner Bert Bell gave the colleges a paternalistic pat on the head: 'We have their best interest at heart. They're our farm system.' College football, though, was still in rude health, with millions of Americans having deep-rooted allegiances to their former colleges and flagship state teams.

The NFL's remarkable rise in the late 1950s caught the eye of a new cluster of businessmen who wanted a piece of the action. As in the 1940s, though, the NFL team owners were reluctant to allow expansion. Instead, a group led by two Texan oil billionaires, Lamar Hunt and Bud Adams, announced plans in the summer of 1959 for yet another American Football League (AFL). It was due to start play the following year, with franchises in Boston, Buffalo, Dallas, Denver, Houston, Los Angeles, Minneapolis and New York.

Like the men behind the AAFC, Hunt and Adams wanted to co-operate with the NFL, but were rebuffed. AFL commissioner Joe Foss would later propose a 'world's championship' game between the respective champions, only to be ignored by NFL bosses. But they did secure a substantial TV deal with ABC, worth $8.5 million over five years, to be split evenly among the clubs.

NFL commissioner Bert Bell died from a heart attack in October 1959. His replacement, former public relations man Pete Rozelle, was more open to expansion; the Dallas Cowboys franchise was added in 1960 (to compete with the AFL's Dallas Texans), followed by the Minneapolis-based Minnesota Vikings a year later (led by the same people who had intended to run an AFL team there).

The AFL's first season, with the Houston Oilers coming out on top, suffered from poor attendances and heavy financial losses. The TV ratings, though, were encouraging, and the ABC deal helped the league to survive in the hope of seeing better days. It tried to cultivate a more exciting, high-scoring style of play, and steadily gained credibility.

The game was still growing in popularity, with NFL players such as Jim Brown, Bart Starr and Johnny Unitas becoming household names. The AFL gave some cities a chance to get in on the act, boosting their civic pride by putting them on the 'major league' map. San Diego was a prime example: when the L.A. Chargers moved to his city, mayor Charles Dail enthused, 'I've never seen such universal enthusiasm for anything here.'

Another TV deal for AFL coverage was agreed in 1964, this time with NBC, securing around $40 million for the teams over five years. It helped the New York Jets to achieve the league's biggest coup so far: the signing of star University of Alabama quarterback Joe Namath in 1965, on a three-year contract worth a staggering $427,000. The NFL responded by trying to outbid the AFL on salaries; and, despite the TV income, both leagues began spending beyond their means, a situation that could not carry on for long.

After years of acrimony, the AFL and NFL finally held secret talks, and an agreement was announced in June 1966. Because of TV commitments, a full merger would have to wait until 1970; but, in the meantime, the leagues would hold a combined draft, and would not poach each other's players. The two champions would meet, in what was initially labelled the 'AFL-NFL Championship Game'. Rozelle became commissioner of both leagues, and, later, of the merged league.

The first AFL-NFL Championship Game saw a 35-10 win for the Green Bay Packers over the Kansas City Chiefs, in front of 61,946 in Los Angeles in January 1967. It was known in some quarters as the 'Super Bowl' (in the tradition of post-season college games such as the Rose Bowl), a name that would become official two years later. The media took a huge interest in the big game; both CBS and NBC televised it, with half of the nation's television sets tuned in.

Legendary Green Bay coach Vince Lombardi cut a fearsome figure, and had moulded the Packers into an imposing outfit, with an emphasis on team spirit, mental toughness and an immense will to win. They repeated their Super Bowl success against the Oakland Raiders a year later, having become NFL champions for the fifth time in seven years, by beating the Dallas Cowboys at home in a title game now known as the 'Ice Bowl', with temperatures plunging to minus 28°C. Lombardi then stepped down to become general manager. After his death from cancer in 1970, the Super Bowl trophy would be named in his honour.

NBC got a taste of the nation's growing mania for pro football in 1968, when it abandoned a New York Jets v Oakland Raiders game a minute from the end, to begin showing its production of the children's story *Heidi*. The Raiders scored two late touchdowns to grab a dramatic win, prompting a flood of complaints to the network when viewers realised what they had missed.

Super Bowl III, that season's finale, became perhaps the most talked-about game in the sport's history. Many still saw the AFL as an inferior upstart league, a view reinforced by the NFL's Packers having easily won both Super Bowls to date. This time, though, the AFL's Jets approached the game, against the Baltimore Colts, with a swaggering self-belief.

Quarterback Joe Namath famously 'guaranteed' a Jets win during the build-up. It was a clash between the old and the new, in an era of culture wars: the brash, long-haired Namath against his more conventional, clean-cut opposite number Johnny Unitas. The Jets backed up their bravado with a 16-7 win, a shot in the arm for the AFL's reputation and confidence. Namath, nicknamed 'Broadway Joe' for his colourful lifestyle, soon had his own TV chat show.

The full AFL–NFL merger went ahead as planned in 1970, with the combined entity known as the National Football League. The former AFL teams, along with the Baltimore Colts, Cleveland Browns and Pittsburgh Steelers, formed the American Football Conference (AFC), with the National Football Conference (NFC) encompassing the rest. Each conference was split into Western, Central and Eastern divisions, and the regular season featured some inter-divisional and inter-conference games. The AFC and NFC champions would meet in the Super Bowl. The next year, the Pro Bowl was reorganised into an AFC v NFC all-star game.

Until now, professional football had been played almost exclusively on Sundays, with Saturdays reserved for college games. In 1970, though, some NFL games were played on Monday nights, in front of ABC's TV cameras; the next year, *Monday Night Football* became a weekly event, and televised sport would never be quite the same again.

Sports coverage on American TV had previously been a bland affair. Presenters, commentators and analysts shied away from saying anything remotely contentious, for fear of upsetting the management of the teams or the league (this is still largely true in local and regional coverage, where the on-air staff are generally employees of the teams, rather than the TV companies). But the *Monday Night Football* team, assembled by innovative ABC Sport producer Roone Arledge, and led by caustic commentator Howard Cosell, took a more irreverent approach, trying to entertain viewers rather than toe the league line. The show became one of the most-watched on American TV, with a style that would influence other sports coverage around the world[45].

By the early 1970s, NFL games across the country regularly drew huge crowds, regardless of the home teams' fortunes. Some teams outgrew the baseball stadiums they were using, and moved into larger, purpose-built homes of their own. Outstanding teams, players and feats went into American lore, not least the Miami Dolphins' 'perfect season' in 1972, when they won all 14 regular season games and went on to victory in the Super Bowl.

The NFL continued tinkering with the game's rules and presentation, trying to improve the experience for those watching both 'live' and on TV. In 1970, the stadium clock became the official timing instrument, and players began wearing their names on the backs of their jerseys (a baseball innovation, which some AFL teams had adopted before the two leagues came together). Referees were equipped with microphones in 1975, allowing them to explain decisions to spectators and TV viewers.

Another effort to discourage field goal attempts was made in 1974: goalposts were returned to the back of the end zone (ten yards behind the goal-line), and a missed field goal attempt would give the opposition possession at the line of scrimmage, rather than on their 20-yard line. The next season, field goal attempts dropped by a third. *Pass interference* rules were established in 1978, forbidding contact with a pass receiver who was at least five yards beyond the line of scrimmage.

While professional football went from strength to strength in the late 1960s and early 1970s, things were less rosy for the college game. It was a time of political, social and racial unrest, and student rebellion. Some liberal observers saw college football as overly violent, and condemned coaches' authoritarian treatment of players as 'dehumanising'. There was also a drop in student enrolment, which, along with inflation, rising tuition fees, and large squads, put a squeeze on many budgets. The NCAA imposed cost-cutting measures in 1971, including limits on scholarships; but another blow came a year later with the arrival of Title IX, a law requiring schools and colleges to give male and female students equal access to sporting facilities and activities.

The exposure and income generated by television had widened the gap between the major and minor football colleges. Some of those at the top of the pile were looking to follow the NFL's lead in maximising profits, and in staging a national end-of-season title game, provoking another hail of criticism over college football's principles. In 1973, with football as the driving force, the NCAA acknowledged the disparities by splitting its member institutions into three tiers – Divisions I, II and III – mainly based on stadium sizes and attendances. There was still some disquiet, with many thinking that Division I, with around 250 colleges, was too large to suit the needs of its 'biggest' members. As a result, it was split up in 1978, with the top 105 forming Division I-A, and the others becoming Division I-AA.

In recent decades, perhaps the closest thing that there has been to a tactical revolution came in the 1980s, courtesy of the San Francisco 49ers. Bill Walsh became their head coach in 1979, with the team at a low ebb, having made his name as an assistant coach for various NFL clubs, and as head coach at nearby Stanford University. Walsh rebuilt the team, making expert use of the draft to acquire the likes of quarterback Joe Montana, and, several years later, wide receiver Jerry Rice, possibly the best players ever to occupy their respective positions.

Rather than the usual mix of long passing and a conventional running game, Walsh used a scheme that became known as the *West Coast Offence*, making regular use of short forward passes, many of them thrown to running backs. Receivers were spread around the field, forcing defences to open up, and there was an intricate set of passing routes, with the quarterback having a range of options on each play. The 49ers won three Super Bowls during Walsh's ten seasons at the helm, before George Seifert continued his work with equal success, with Steve Young replacing Montana in the early 1990s. The West Coast Offence would form the basis of many other NFL attacks in the years to come.

Tactics have become more complex in recent times, as offences and defences – organised by offensive and defensive co-ordinators – have tried to outdo each other in increasingly subtle ways. Special teams, largely overlooked in the past, now attract more attention from head coaches, hoping to gain valuable yards from kick-off and punting situations.

Another latter-day development is the mobile quarterback, using his agility and running ability to make unexpected gains with the ball still in his hands, or to escape from trouble. The idea emerged in the late 1980s and 1990s, through the likes of Randall Cunningham and Steve

Young, paving the way for the explosive Michael Vick to make his mark with the Atlanta Falcons.

Teams tried almost anything to get an edge over their opponents, sometimes hovering around the boundaries of acceptability. The 2007 NFL season saw a spate of controversies. There was the 'Spygate' affair, where the New England Patriots were caught videotaping the New York Jets' sideline signals, violating league rules. Coaches began trying to unsettle opposing kickers, by calling timeouts just as they were about to attempt field goals; while Baltimore Ravens coach Brian Billick accused Jets defenders of calling out fake signals, trying to confuse his offence.

Performance-enhancing drugs became a serious issue in the 1970s, together with the use of recreational drugs by players. The problem reached crisis proportions in 1986, when Cleveland's Don Rogers died from heart failure brought on by cocaine use. The NFL introduced a drug-testing policy two years later, and has garnered much praise for its tough stance ever since, under Pete Rozelle and his successors as commissioner, Paul Tagliabue and Roger Goodell. Still, the frequency of suspensions for drug offences (usually reported casually in the media, as if nothing much had happened) suggests that the policies have hardly made for an effective deterrent.

NFL players have been involved in a litany of crime cases in recent years, often involving guns or domestic violence, sometimes murder. The spring and summer of 2007 brought shocking revelations about a dog-fighting ring run by Michael Vick, one of the league's star attractions. Vick was given a 23-month jail sentence, leaving the Atlanta Falcons in turmoil.

Despite the many stains on its reputation, though, the NFL has had a remarkable success story over the last half-century, becoming something of a role model for leagues in various sports worldwide. Its 32 teams are all financially stable and well supported, the Super Bowl has become a phenomenal event, and the league's draft, salary cap and revenue-sharing scheme have helped to keep it competitively balanced.

More rival leagues have come and gone since the AFL merger. The World Football League began in 1974, but failed to complete its second season. The United States Football League, launched in 1983, fared slightly better, attracting involvement from property tycoon Donald Trump, but only lasted three seasons.

Vince McMahon, owner of what was then the World Wrestling Federation, unleashed the XFL in 2001, with TV coverage on NBC. It had looser rules regarding foul play (on the assumption that many sports fans thought the game had gone 'soft'), and cheerleaders of an even more overtly sexual nature than those in the NFL. The XFL, though, was widely ridiculed, and collapsed after its first season.

In any case, new leagues would have to compete not only with the NFL, but also with the enduring appeal of college football. While the controversy continues over its commerciality and its questionable place in collegiate life, along with a string of scandals involving drugs, violence and financial wrongdoing (particularly in the 1980s), the game still has a massive audience. Big games are played in an atmosphere of near-hysteria, with huge bands leading the massed singing of 'fight songs'. Michigan, Pennsylvania State, Ohio State and Tennessee regularly draw crowds of more than 100,000, more than any NFL stadium can hold.

The search for a collegiate equivalent of the Super Bowl led to the birth of the Bowl Championship Series (BCS) in 1998, featuring four (later five) games, one of which is regarded as a national championship decider. But the complex method of deciding which teams are to play in each game, using a mixture of voting and computerised rankings, has been the subject of intense debate. The BCS is outside the NCAA's control, instead being run by a committee of conference commissioners and bowl organisations, along with a representative of the unaffiliated Notre Dame.

Some observers, including former long-time NCAA leader Walter Byers, have suggested that the ethical arguments over college football should be ended by simply letting the colleges pay their players, stamping out the alleged hypocrisy over amateurism at a stroke. Others fear that this would lead to such issues as contract disputes and free agency, which could tear apart the whole structure of college sport. In *College Football: History, Spectacle, Controversy*, John Sayle Watterson suggests allowing big-time football colleges to 'spin off' their teams into commercial franchises, with no requirement for the players to pursue degrees.

College football aside, there is a chasm between the NFL and the grass-roots. Unlike baseball and ice hockey, American football has no professional minor leagues, leaving sub-NFL players with little choice but to switch to indoor arena football or Canadian football, both of which we shall look at in later chapters. There are many semi-professional and (non-college) amateur leagues dotted around the US, with around 800 teams in all. Considering the country's size, this figure may seem small compared with, say, the number of soccer teams at similar levels in England. American football, though, is largely a spectator sport, which most Americans have never played, at least in its full-contact form.

At many high schools, particularly in southern states, football players are treated as an elite group, carrying the hopes of local communities on their shoulders. H.G. Bissinger captured this phenomenon superbly in *Friday Night Lights*, following the fortunes of a Texan team in the 1988 season – summed up in the words of local estate agent Bob Rutherford:

'Life really wouldn't be worth livin' if you didn't have a high school football team to support.'

Away from the schools, youth football has a thriving scene under the Pop Warner scheme, conceived in Philadelphia in 1929 as a way of keeping teenagers out of trouble. It was named after Glenn 'Pop' Warner, a renowned coach who was involved in the project in its infancy, having earlier helped to nurture Jim Thorpe's talents at Carlisle Indian School in southern Pennsylvania. After starting with four teams, it had 157 within a decade; there are now more than 5,000, organised into local leagues around the US, in various age and weight categories.

American football, arguably the most overtly macho of all football codes, may seem to be the least likely to be played by women. But, in a wealthy, entertainment-hungry nation of 300 million, just about anything can happen, and probably will. So, perhaps, it should come as no surprise to learn that there is an eventful, albeit mostly obscure, history of women playing the game.

A newspaper report in 1896 told of a masked ball in a New York casino, whose main attraction was a five-a-side football game played by women – some dressed in sailor suits, others in short dresses or skirts and stockings, in Princeton and Yale colours. At the opening kick-off, the ball strayed into the audience. Some players ran after it, mingling a little too closely with the spectators, and the game was cut short before things could get out of hand.

A 'girls' football' game[46] was reported to have been played at San Jose State Teachers' College in 1925; but, despite the NCAA's diversity programmes, and the gender-equality provisions of Title IX, women's college football has never become firmly established. A year later, the NFL's Frankford Yellow Jackets staged women's games as half-time entertainment. Two female teams based in Toledo, Ohio, went on barnstorming tours in 1930 and 1931, but the venture folded after attracting criticism, including accusations of exploitation from the First Lady, Lou Henry Hoover.

Things began to pick up in the mid 1960s, when promoter Sid Friedman launched the Women's Professional Football League (actually semi-professional), again in Ohio. The league grew in the early 1970s, and briefly generated a good deal of interest. The more wide-reaching National Women's Football League followed in 1974, but struggled financially.

Three new leagues were formed in 2000: the National Women's Football Association, the Independent Women's Football League, and a new Women's Professional Football League. On a different note, perhaps the most visible form of women's American football today is the Lingerie Bowl – a pay-per-view TV event staged during half-time of the Super Bowl, featuring models wearing pads, helmets and little else. First held in 2004, it was expanded into the Lingerie Football League a year later. Looking back at the bawdy events reported in New York in 1896, perhaps things have come full circle.

Much has been said about baseball's colour bar – the 'gentlemen's agreement' among team owners that kept the major leagues all-white until 1947. It would be easy to believe that American football never had such problems, but this is far from the case: it has its own history of racial strife.

In the game's early days, black students were a rarity at the main football-playing colleges, especially in the south. At many colleges, only the most exceptionally talented black players had a chance of being selected; and those who did make it often faced racist abuse, disproportionate levels of violence, and off-field segregation. Black players were often dropped for games against teams who objected to the prospect of facing them.

Paul Robeson (Rutgers University) and Frederick 'Fritz' Pollard (Brown University) overcame these barriers to achieve All-America recognition, as leading college players, in the 1910s. Robeson later found further fame as a singer, actor and civil rights campaigner; his political leanings led to his name being dropped from the All-America lists during the US government's anti-communist crackdown in the 1950s.

Following in the footsteps of the first black professional, Charles Follis (with Shelby AC of Ohio in 1904), Robeson and Pollard found success in the professional ranks. Pollard even co-coached several NFL teams in the 1920s. But the NFL was hardly any friendlier to African-Americans than the college scene, and things soon became even worse.

At the NFL meeting in 1933 that led to a rash of rule changes, it is widely believed (although it was never officially admitted) that the team owners also agreed to exclude black players. None would appear in the league for the next 13 years. The official explanation, that none were up to NFL standards, is scorned by historians who argue that the likes of Joe Lillard (Chicago Cardinals) and Ray Kemp (Pittsburgh Pirates, later to become the Steelers) had been performing well enough. Among the more credible theories are that the owners wanted to make the league supposedly more 'respectable', on a par with baseball's major leagues; and a fear that white fans, suffering the effects of the Depression, would resent black players earning more money than them.

After World War II, many white Americans softened their attitudes towards blacks, largely out of respect for their war efforts. The Brooklyn Dodgers broke baseball's colour bar by fielding Jackie Robinson, while AAFC teams, particularly the superb Cleveland Browns, welcomed black players.

The NFL's L.A. Rams came under pressure to integrate after moving from Cleveland, under threat of being denied use of the L.A. Coliseum. In March 1946, they signed outstanding black halfback Kenny Washington, previously ignored by NFL clubs. The league gradually became more integrated, although the Washington Redskins – still owned by George Preston Marshall, thought to be the main instigator of the alleged 1933 agreement – remained all-white until 1962.

College football also became more integrated in the 1950s and 1960s, although it came slowly in many southern and western states. In 1951, Johnny Bright, star tailback for Drake University of Des Moines, Iowa, was twice punched in the face by Wilbanks Smith of Oklahoma A&M (now Oklahoma State) in the early minutes of a game. Drake's protests were rebuffed, and they withdrew from the Missouri Valley Conference. Bright, fearing more of the same in the NFL, later turned to Canadian football for his professional career. The fallout from the incident, including a broken jaw for Bright, helped bring about changes in the rules concerning blocking, and also encouraged many players to wear face masks.

Four years later, Georgia Tech considered pulling out of the Sugar Bowl, objecting to opponents Pittsburgh having a black player. Georgia state governor Marvin Griffin threw himself into the fray, backing the calls for a boycott. Possibly unaware that the Civil War had ended 90 years earlier, Griffin thundered:

> *The South stands at Armageddon. The battle is joined.*
> *We cannot make the slightest concession to the enemy*
> *in this dark and lamentable hour of struggle.*

Griffin lost the argument, and the last bastions of segregated college football finally fell in the 1960s, under pressure from the Civil Rights movement and federal government. Both college and professional football were widely integrated by the late 1970s; today, the majority of NFL players are African-American. Although the equality of opportunity has helped to raise standards of play, there have been concerns over apparent 'stacking' – a tendency to typecast black players as being best suited to certain positions, such as running back, wide receiver and the defensive backfield roles. Only in very recent years have significant numbers of blacks become quarterbacks or head coaches; the NFL now forces clubs to interview black candidates for coaching jobs.

Until satellite TV became a powerful force in the 1980s, American football was largely unknown outside North America. Its first overseas appearance may well have been the exhibition game played by crews of two US warships in Melbourne in 1908, mentioned in chapter 8. The game appeared in Britain two years later, when American sailors demonstrated it in Kent. It returned during World War II, and a European league for US armed forces was set up in 1946.

American university professors introduced the sport in Japan in 1934. A Japanese association was formed that year, and teams sprang up at high schools and colleges. An East v West college game in 1937 drew a crowd of more than 25,000, and became an annual event, known as the Rice Bowl, 11 years later. A South Korean association was also founded, in 1945. Around 1970, many companies in Japan started fielding semi-professional sides, which became the basis for the Japan American Football League, launched in 1985 and later renamed as the X-League. Today, the Rice Bowl features the X-League champions and their college counterparts.

Televised NFL coverage hit Europe in the early 1980s. At first, much of it was sporadic, coming in the form of week-old highlights packages; but the game became familiar to many Europeans, and such names as Joe Montana, Jerry Rice and Dan Marino became well known. The NFL, well versed in the art of marketing, wasted little time in trying to exploit the interest that this exposure had generated. It staged pre-season games at London's Wembley Stadium in 1983 and 1986, as it had done in Tokyo and Mexico City, in 1976 and 1978 respectively. More overseas exhibition games followed in 1989 and 1990.

Some of the new armchair fans got the urge to organise the sport locally, or to strap on the pads themselves. A host of leagues and associations were formed in the mid 1980s, in countries such as France, Germany and the UK, and also in Australia. A European international championship was first held in 1983. The International Federation of American Football was eventually founded in 1998, and launched a quadrennial World Championship the following year. Japan were champions in 1999 and 2003, and staged the 2007 tournament, losing in the final to the first USA team to enter (made up of amateurs with recent college experience).

As well as sending teams to play exhibition games abroad, the NFL soon started setting up foreign-based teams. The World League of American Football started play in 1991, under the NFL's auspices, with teams in Barcelona, Frankfurt, London and Montreal, plus six in the US. After a hiatus in 1993 and 1994, it returned as an all-European affair in 1995, and was renamed NFL Europe two years later. The league was largely used as a vehicle for developing unproven players, with its spring season allowing them to compete for places in the following autumn's NFL squads. Home-grown players were thin on the ground, and were mostly kickers with soccer or rugby backgrounds.

NFL Europe failed to attract the expected crowds in Britain and Spain, and, by 2005, five of its six teams were based in Germany, where there was far more interest. After the 2007 season, when the league had been renamed again as NFL Europa, the NFL pulled the plug. The European league no longer fitted into its global strategy, as it shifted its focus towards staging regular-season games abroad, starting with a Wembley appearance by the New York Giants and Miami Dolphins in October 2007. Wembley was again chosen as a venue in 2008 and 2009, and the Buffalo Bills agreed to play a 'home' game in Toronto each year from 2008 to 2012. Other venues, in countries such as Germany, Italy and Japan, are being considered for the future.

Still, as in the US, American football in the outside world remains predominantly a spectator sport, relying heavily on TV. The game's complexity, and the costs of playing the full-contact version with a reasonable level of safety, have undoubtedly limited its global growth as a participation sport, perhaps along with a perception that it is a game for Americans.

The NFL's international audience is generally in the minority, as the game has failed to overtake sports with deeper local roots. US college football, meanwhile, remains in almost total obscurity outside North America. The sport is often mocked by foreigners, mostly for peripheral aspects such as the protective gear, frequent stoppages and supposed gimmickry (the British media seem almost incapable of mentioning American football without referring to 'razzmatazz', as if it were an integral part of the game) – which is unfortunate, as it has much to offer to sports fans who are willing to learn about its intricacies and its long history.

From its beginnings as an Ivy League version of rugby, American football has evolved into a mass spectacle, making huge technical and tactical advances, arguably unmatched by any comparable sport. While baseball might still justify its claim to be America's 'national pastime' (thanks largely to its grass-roots scene), on autumn weekends – from high-schoolers on Friday night, through collegians on Saturday, to the pros on Sunday – football is its favourite sport.

Chapter 11

In a League of Their Own

'*Rugby league is more than just a game, it's a belief,
a way of life and, at times, it's like being part of
an oppressed minority.*'
– Terry Wynn, Member of European Parliament, 2002

When the rugby rebels of the Northern Union began their 1895–96 league programme, just days after leaving the Rugby Football Union, nobody knew quite what to expect. Many sympathetic clubs were taking a wait-and-see approach, delaying a decision on joining the NU.

As it turned out, that first season was quite a success. Manningham pipped Halifax to the title by a single point on the final day, having been helped to the top of the table by their powerful forward pack – still an important element of NU rugby, which remained essentially the same game that was being played elsewhere. By the time of its first annual general meeting, the NU's membership had more than doubled, to 50 clubs.

Not surprisingly, there were teething problems. Travelling around the north of England stretched the clubs' meagre budgets to breaking point; so, from the next season, Lancashire and Yorkshire would have separate leagues, with 14 and 16 clubs respectively (the NU's other member clubs played in 'junior' leagues). There were also grumbles about the style of play, with a great deal of scrummaging and little try-scoring. Even with the players receiving only broken-time and expense payments, bigger crowds were needed, and the entertainment value had to be improved. Just a week into the first season, Leeds committee member Harry Sewell told the *Yorkshire Post*:

We want to do away with that scrummaging, pushing and thrusting game, which is not football, and that is why I propose to abolish the lineout and reduce the number of forwards to six. The football public does not pay to see a lot of scrummaging.

Sewell was not alone in wanting to scrap the line-out. The idea was debated early in the 1895–96 season, along with reducing teams from 15 players to 13 (already suggested four years before the split), and even using a round ball to allow more accurate passing. The changes were put to the test in a trial match that autumn, with some encouraging signs. But the NU still had a conservative streak, and shied away from making drastic changes in its first two years. Some small adjustments were made during the 1895–96 season: a penalty would be awarded for a deliberate knock-on, and the ball had to be put into a scrum on the referee's side, after which the scrum-half had to retire behind the scrum until the ball re-emerged.

The union took a bolder approach in 1897, replacing the lineout with a punt-in from the touchline (the kick could be in any direction, but the usual offside rule for kicking applied). A drop goal or penalty kick would only earn two points, down from four and three respectively. A try still only scored three points, but was now more valuable than any kicked goal. Other changes followed in the next few years: despite the complaints about excessive scrummaging, the punt-in was replaced by a scrum, and a scrum would also be awarded if a tackled player could not release the ball.

By splitting the league into two, the NU had cut the number of games from 42 to 26 for Lancashire clubs, and to 30 for those in Yorkshire. This left room in the schedule for the NU's answer to soccer's FA Cup: the Challenge Cup, which also built on the tradition of the popular Lancashire and Yorkshire cup tournaments of earlier years. It was first held in March and April of 1897, with 52 entrants. Batley beat St Helens 10-3 in the final, watched by 13,492 at Headingley in Leeds. They retained the trophy against Bradford at the same venue a year later, in front of the biggest attendance at any English club rugby match to date: 27,941.

As well as tweaking the playing rules, the NU was having to rethink its attitude to professionalism. With broken-time payments limited to six shillings a day, clubs had trouble attracting players, particularly from south Wales, where many were on higher (although illicit) incomes in rugby union[47]. Some clubs simply flouted the regulations, and it became clear that something had to change. In 1898, the NU sanctioned regular wages for players – but with tight restrictions that required every player to have another job outside the game, effectively allowing nothing more than semi-professionalism.

The approach may have reflected a degree of conservatism, but the NU also wanted to use wage controls to keep the leagues competitive, and to avoid the wage inflation that was crippling some soccer clubs. It set up a Professional Subcommittee, which embarked on extensive investigations that led to a glut of suspensions, recalling the chaos that had preceded the 1895 split.

The Lancashire–Yorkshire league split was another bone of contention. Some of the major clubs wanted to play against their peers from across the Pennines, rather than lesser opponents within their own county. Twelve of them met in April 1901 to discuss forming a breakaway Northern Rugby League, but later reached an agreement with the NU, which restored a single 14-club top tier the following season. The lowlier clubs were still organised into Lancashire and Yorkshire leagues, but these were combined into a national Second Division a year later.

One reason behind all this discontent was soccer's popularity in northern England. It was seen as a more spectator-friendly game: simpler, with more flow, and with the ball always visible to fans, rather than being buried under a scrum, ruck or maul. It also had a national dimension, appealing to people of all classes, in all regions.

As early as 1896, some NU clubs were fielding soccer teams. Stockport, overshadowed by Stockport County, folded in 1903. A cross-code saga began unfolding in Bradford that year, when Manningham – the NU's first champions, but now in the Second Division – formed a soccer team, Bradford City (who were admitted to Division Two of the Football League before they had even kicked a round ball), and resigned from the NU. Holbeck followed Manningham's lead in 1904, by morphing into Leeds City, forerunners of Leeds United. It was a different story in Wigan, where the local NU team drew bigger crowds than soccer's Wigan United, who shut down in 1903. Still, the union's committee was sufficiently worried to issue a ruling in June 1905, forbidding clubs from involvement in other football codes.

Despite being Bradford's only NU club after Manningham's defection, Bradford FC still struggled to attract spectators, with Bradford City quickly gathering support. In 1907, they followed Manningham into the soccer world, becoming Bradford Park Avenue. Soon afterwards, rugby league followers filled the gap by forming a new club, Bradford RFC; who duly signed all of Bradford FC's former players, took their place in the NU's league system, and changed their name to Bradford Northern.

The NU scrapped its wage and work regulations in 1905, after a largely futile seven-year battle to enforce them. In theory, players could now become fully professional. In reality, though, the clubs could not afford to pay a living wage, and players still generally kept up some other form of employment.

Also in 1905, Divisions One and Two were combined into a 31-team league – too large for a full home-and-away schedule, which would have meant 60 matches per team. Not all clubs played the same number of games, and league placings were now decided on percentages rather than points. From 1906–07, the top four teams took part in play-offs to determine the champions.

The battle with soccer forced the NU to take another look at the rules of the game, particularly after a dull Challenge Cup final in 1903, with Halifax grinding out a 7-0 win over Salford. There was still a widespread feeling that scrums were occurring too often, and lasting too long. As with American college football in the 1880s, the central issue was the question of how to resume play after a tackle. Traditionally, the struggle for possession was a vital part of rugby. But, for the commercially-minded NU, the elements with the biggest appeal to spectators – running, passing, tackling and try-scoring – were the ones that mattered most.

Some club officials suggested reverting to the RFU rules, citing the All Blacks' spectacular play in 1905–06 as proof that attractive rugby was possible under those laws. But most preferred a more radical approach, and they got their way in the summer of 1906.

Teams were reduced from 15 players to 13, with six forwards rather than eight. Additionally, after a tackle, the players involved would have to stand up; the tackled player would then put the ball down, and either he or an opponent could play it with the feet. This mini-scrum became known as the *play-the-ball*, perhaps rugby league's most distinctive feature to this day. It eliminated rucking and mauling, and full-blown scrums became a lesser part of the game.

The results were dramatic: play became much faster, with forward packs playing a less dominant role, and more space for backs to exploit. Scoring averaged 26.5 points per game in 1906–07, compared with 14.4 the previous season (partly helped by the haplessness of Liverpool City who in their one and only season lost all 30 games, while conceding an average of 46.6 points per match).

An *Athletic News* headline declared 'The New Rules Completely Vindicated'; while the changes were widely welcomed in NU circles, and were even praised by rugby union officials in Coventry. Then again, *The Times* dismissed the NU's game as 'an incoherent parody of rugby football', and members of South Africa's rugby union tour party were equally unimpressed. The gulf between the two codes had just grown a good deal wider.

By this time, rugby league had an international dimension, of sorts, thanks mainly to an influx of Welsh rugby union converts to NU clubs. A match between England and 'Other Nationalities' – 13 Welshmen and two Scots – was staged in Wigan in April 1904. Bad weather and questionable scheduling (on a Tuesday afternoon) hardly helped the occasion, and only 6,000 spectators turned up. The fixture was repeated in 1905 and 1906, still attracting little interest, before being scrapped as a more significant international scene suddenly developed.

A Develyshe Pastime

Despite their triumphant British Isles tour, and the accolades that came with it, the 1905–06 All Blacks were not an altogether happy bunch. Many of them were working men of modest means, and could barely afford the long break from their jobs. Although the tour made a profit for its organisers, and was supported financially by their government, the players were given just three shillings a day for expenses (enough to outrage the arch-conservative Scottish Rugby Union, leading to a frosty relationship between it and the New Zealand union for the next few decades).

Some of the All Blacks watched rugby league matches during the tour, and were impressed by the standard of play and large crowds, not to mention the fact that the players were openly paid. On the way home, one player, George Smith, is thought to have met Australian contacts in Sydney, to discuss the possibility of following the NU's example in the Antipodes.

There was an appetite for such an idea in the Sydney area, where rugby had attracted a large contingent of working-class players and spectators by now. Many players were angry over the lack of help from the New South Wales Rugby Union (NSWRU) with insurance and compensation for injuries.

Little happened over the next year or so, until Albert Baskerville, a young postal worker and rugby player from Wellington, contacted the NU to suggest arranging a British tour by a professional New Zealand squad. Well aware of the impact that the All Blacks had made in 1905–06, NU officials welcomed the idea, on the condition that it would involve some of the leading players from that tour. Despite strong opposition from the New Zealand union, a tour was arranged for 1907–08.

Perhaps spurred into action by the prospect of a professional New Zealand side, some powerful figures in Sydney – businessman James Giltinan (one of George Smith's contacts), cricket hero Victor Trumper and politician Harry Hoyle – took Australia into the rugby league fold. The trio suspected that working-class sympathy would lie with the players in their battles with the NSWRU. Trumper had recently led a failed attempt by Australian cricketers to take control of national team affairs; now he empathised with his rugby counterparts, and wanted to help to free them from the union.

At a meeting at Bateman's Crystal Hotel in Sydney, on August 8, 1907, around 50 players, and delegates from eight senior clubs, founded the New South Wales Rugby League (NSWRL). They also announced a series of matches against the New Zealand professionals, which went ahead soon afterwards; the NSWRU expelled the Sydney players who took part.

Next stop for the New Zealanders was England, where thousands greeted them in the city square in Leeds. The tour party featured only four members of the 1905–06 All Blacks squad. But it did include *Australia's* leading player: H.H. 'Dally' Messenger, the goal-kicking three-quarter, who had secretly agreed to play in the NSWRL, in return for a place in the New Zealand tour squad and a £50 fee. Messenger was hugely popular in Sydney. As large crowds flocked to see him, many people wondered where the money was going – a question that fuelled the growing resentment towards the NSWRU.

After a crash course in the rules and tactics of rugby league, the tourists – dubbed the 'All Golds' on account of their financial rewards – played 35 matches, winning 19. Among these games were the first genuine rugby league internationals, as the visitors faced Wales in Aberdare, and England in Wigan, as well as three matches against a Northern Union representative side. In contrast with the rugby union tour two years earlier, the profit of £5,641 was split between the Kiwi players. Some were signed up by NU clubs.

En route home, the squad played ten games in Australia, a visit marred by Baskerville's death from pneumonia in Brisbane. Some rugby league matches were played in New Zealand in 1908, and the New Zealand Rugby League (NZRL) was formed in Auckland the following year. But the All Blacks' popularity, along with intense pressure from the NZRFU, which had the government on its side, meant that the breakaway code would face a difficult future in New Zealand.

It hardly got off to a great start in Australia. A rugby league tour of Britain in 1908–09, with the team nicknamed the Kangaroos, was fraught with difficulties, and financially disastrous. The following September, though, the team played four charity matches back home against their rugby union counterparts, who were then banned by their union and duly joined the rugby league ranks. This self-inflicted blow knocked the stuffing out of rugby union in Australia, giving the new code the upper hand.

The NSWRL set up an eight-team Sydney competition, with its champions decided via a complex play-off system that would see many changes in the coming years. South Sydney were the first winners, in a 1908 season that was plagued by poor refereeing, a dearth of star players, and apathy in the press.

Rugby purists lashed out at the rebel league. Players were threatened with being sacked from their day jobs, a newspaper railed at 'the serpent of professionalism', and a man told colleagues at a rugby union club meeting that he would rather see his son dead than have him play professionally.

But, as had happened in England when the 13-a-side and play-the-ball rules were implemented two years earlier, many rugby followers enjoyed the faster, more free-flowing game, with more running, less scrummaging, and fewer kicks into touch. Spectators could see the ball far more often than before, helping them to feel more involved in the game. A *Sydney Morning Herald* correspondent enthused that 'the difference between the new rugby and the old rugby is as a motor car compared to the bullock wagon'.

Outside Sydney, 'country' competitions soon sprang up around New South Wales, and rugby league soon reached Queensland, Australia's other rugby heartland. Disaffected Brisbane rugby union players formed the Queensland Rugby Association, later to become the Queensland Rugby League (QRL), in March 1908, and two months later one of the All Golds' matches en route home from Britain was against a representative Queensland side. The first inter-state rugby league game, a 43-0 stroll for New South Wales, was played in July, and a Brisbane league was started the following year.

The first Australasian tour by an England team (for the next 38 years, the team would generally be known as 'England' even though it often featured Welshmen, and occasionally Scots), in 1910, was crucial in establishing the game's supremacy in New South Wales and Queensland. The NU, eager for its game to be seen as 'respectable', insisted that clubs should only nominate 'players who will do honour to the union both on and off the field' for selection. The squad was captained by Salford's James Lomas, a Cumbrian back with a prolific scoring record in both tries and goals.

The clashes between 'home' and 'colonial' players captured the public's imagination, with 42,000 seeing the first test match at the Sydney Showground. Another was staged in Brisbane, followed by two games in Sydney between England and a combined Australasian side. In the first of the latter matches, Maori star Albert 'Opae' Asher showed off his trick of hurdling over would-be tacklers while carrying the ball. One of his victims, Hunslet crowd-pleaser Billy Batten, tried to imitate him, but mistimed his leap and left Asher with a gashed head.

A possible visit by the England squad to the United States was mooted for the return trip, but the idea came to nothing. This was the brief period when rugby union was the preferred football code at some Californian colleges, and it is tempting to wonder how events might have unfolded had 'the new rugby' thrown itself into the mix. (British and Australian Test squads did play exhibition games in the US in later years, when it was arguably too late for the game to make a real impact there.) Another missed opportunity came in 1912–13, when the NU rejected a proposed British tour by a coloured South Africa team, advising them to spend more time learning the game instead; the plan was never revived.

There were other unhappy rugby union players closer to the NU's doorstep: in south Wales. As it was relatively easy for them to move to northern England, there was little incentive for the NU to set up a Welsh league. However, some local businessmen were keen to develop rugby league in south Wales, and attracted some support from the NU leadership. Clubs were formed in Ebbw Vale and Merthyr Tydfil, joining the NU league system in 1907. The NU helped them, and their opponents, with travel costs.

The first Wales–England international was played in Tonypandy in April 1908, a 35-18 Welsh victory in front of a 12,000 crowd. The Wrexham-based Welsh Northern Union had been formed during that season; but the NU had its eye on the south of the country, and declined to affiliate the new union, which soon folded. Four more south Walian clubs joined in 1908–09: Aberdare, Barry, Mid-Rhondda and Treherbert. But rugby union was thriving in the region, and the new clubs struggled to build up support. The NU's financial backing dwindled, and all six clubs had vanished by the autumn of 1912.

By this time, though, rugby league in northern England and eastern Australia was in its strongest position yet. It arrived in Australia with perfect timing, with the rule changes of 1906 helping it to make an instant impression. In 1911, more than 50,000 saw New South Wales face New Zealand at the Sydney Cricket Ground, more evidence that the new code had won the 'rugby war' in New South Wales and Queensland. Meanwhile, the game's international expansion enhanced its credibility in Britain.

The rule changes, and their effects on the way rugby league was played, had also given it a distinct identity, helping it to emerge as a sport in its own right. Its affinity with working-class culture helped to strengthen this identity, but also encouraged its middle- and upper-class detractors – including much of the press – to pour scorn upon it. Still, rugby league's establishment credentials were boosted in 1911, as Edward Stanley, the 17th Earl of Derby, was named as the NU's honorary president, and King George V as its patron (then again, the latter never went so far as to attend a match).

A sign of the game's new confidence came in 1911–12, when an Australasian[48] tour of Britain took in such unlikely venues as Birmingham, Bristol, London, Newcastle and Edinburgh. The return tour in 1914 saw one of the game's legendary matches. With the series squared at 1-1, the third and final Test, originally to be played in Melbourne, was rescheduled and switched to Sydney at short notice, infuriating the England party. A spate of injuries left England down to ten men just after half-time, but they hung on for a 14-6 win. The match became known as the 'Rorke's Drift' test, named after a battle in the Zulu War in 1879.

Even the local press hailed the visitors' efforts that day, especially those of captain Harold Wagstaff. Along with Antipodean stars such as Albert Rosenfeld and Douglas Clark, and several Welshmen, Wagstaff was a central figure in Huddersfield's success in the 1910s. From 1911–12 to 1913–14, the 'Team of All the Talents' won nine of the 12 available trophies[49], while their fast, open style helped them to draw bigger crowds than the town's soccer team.

In Australia, South Sydney, Eastern Suburbs and Balmain dominated the Sydney competition in its first decade. Fortitude Valley, a suburban Brisbane side, won seven of the first 11 Queensland titles. The game made stuttering progress in New Zealand, with premierships being set up in Auckland in 1910, and in Wellington and Canterbury three years later.

When the British squad returned from their Australasian tour in August 1914, the country was already at war. Three players immediately joined their regiments. The NU committee voted to go ahead with the upcoming season; and, along with the Football League and FA, were duly pilloried by journalists and RFU officials, despite pledging to support the war effort.

Many clubs were badly affected by the loss of players and spectators to the armed forces, and by the decrease in leisure time for those who were still around. In June 1915, play was suspended for the rest of the war. The spirit of national unity temporarily thawed relations between the rugby codes, with NU players being allowed to play in military teams under RFU rules.

Club competitions in New South Wales and Queensland continued throughout the war, prompting accusations from rugby union circles that the leagues were deliberately exploiting the war to press home their advantage over the rival code. NSWRL secretary Ted Larkin was among the thousands of Australians to perish in the Gallipoli campaign in 1915.

The post-war years saw rugby league making great progress in Queensland, so much so that the Queensland Rugby Union folded in 1919, not reforming until 1928. The game was taken up by many schools, and became popular in towns such as Ipswich and Toowoomba. The state's representative side shocked New South Wales with a 25-9 inter-state victory in 1922, starting a run of 17 wins in 24 games up to 1928. Queenslanders also became prominent in the national team.

However, a power struggle between the QRL and the Brisbane league sparked an exodus of players to Sydney clubs, weakening the Queensland team (back then, players represented the states where their clubs were based, regardless of birthplace). The Sydney premiership remained Australia's elite club competition, with South Sydney its dominant team for some time, clinching seven out of eight titles between 1925 and 1932.

Meanwhile, the Australian Rugby League (ARL) was formed in 1924, taking charge of the national team.

In 1922, under pressure from the Australian and New Zealand leagues, the Northern Union relaunched itself under the less parochial-sounding name of the Rugby Football League (RFL). The word 'union' was now exclusive to 15-a-side rugby, while 'league' was synonymous with the breakaway code; the terms 'rugby union' and 'rugby league' soon became convenient labels to distinguish the two.

Another reason for dropping the 'Northern' tag was the re-emergence of south Wales, as Welsh rugby union converts joined English clubs in their droves in the 1920s and 1930s, and contributed greatly to the successes of clubs such as Swinton and Wigan. The national side drew 13,000 spectators for a match against Australia in 1921, and 23,000 for one against England in 1926, both in Pontypridd. A club was formed in the town that year, and joined the RFL; but, in a familiar story, economic hardships forced it to collapse after little more than a season.

The Challenge Cup final was becoming a major event, with 41,831 turning up in Rochdale for the 1924 Wigan–Oldham contest. The 1927 final was broadcast on the radio – the start of a troubled relationship between rugby league and the BBC. Two years later, with club grounds no longer big enough, the RFL boldly moved the final to London, choosing Wembley Stadium as the venue.

The first Wembley final, with Wigan facing Dewsbury, was heavily promoted in London, with leaflets even being cheekily handed out at a rugby union match at Twickenham. Some supporters were unhappy about the final being moved far away from the game's heartlands, but many began to treasure their 'pilgrimage' to the capital. The switch to Wembley, with its symbolic value as a national stadium, also raised the game's profile in the south, and helped to swell the RFL's coffers.

A year later, order was restored to the league format, with all teams now playing the same number of games, and placings based on points rather than percentages. Again, the rules of the game were being debated. It was widely felt that there were still too many scrums, and that scrum-halves and front-row forwards were taking too many liberties in their execution. The NU (as it still was) issued guidelines for scrums in 1921. The front-rowers had to stay in a straight line, with the two nearest to the put-in keeping their feet on the ground; while the scrum-half had to put the ball in by either rolling it along the ground or pitching it underhand.

None of this had any great effect, though, and eventually more substantial changes were made. The current 3-2-1 scrum formation became mandatory in 1930. Two years later, it was decided that scrums must take place at least ten yards from the nearest touchline (probably by coincidence, this was just months before the NFL introduced hashmarks, ten yards from the sidelines, for a similar reason). The play-the-ball rule was adjusted in 1926, to state that only one player from each team could try to kick or heel the ball.

Rugby league was treated as a simple game in this era. Training generally meant little more than two nights of running each week. The concept of a coach, though, did begin to develop, although most of the men performing the role were officially either managers or players. The tactics used to great effect by Salford in the 1930s were largely devised by manager Lance Todd (one of the 1907–08 New Zealand tourists) and captain Gus Risman.

Dai Rees, Halifax manager in the early 1930s and later with Bradford Northern, preached discipline, and often studied his team's upcoming opponents. North Sydney half-back Duncan Thompson had strong ideas about teamwork, advocating a strategy based on off-loading the ball when being tackled; his intelligent approach was even acknowledged by Brisbane Broncos coach Wayne Bennett in the 1990s.

While the arguments continued about how to improve the domestic game, British fans had few complaints about the entertainment on offer when the Kangaroos came to town. Their attacking play and ball-handling skills had helped make test matches a huge attraction by the 1920s. Anglo-Australian test series, known as the 'Ashes' in the cricket tradition, had also become notoriously violent. On the 1929–30 Kangaroos tour, the brutality of the third Test in Swinton alarmed a *Yorkshire Post* correspondent: 'To call it a game is a misnomer. War is a more appropriate term.'

Another Test, in 1932, became known as the 'Battle of Brisbane', with injuries forcing the hosts to finish with only ten players. Their manager-coach Harry Sunderland called some of the incidents 'disgusting', while also marvelling at how the combatants drank and joked together just hours later. The 'stiff-arm' tackle, a recent trend in England, was copied by Australians after that 1932 series, but was outlawed by the RFL two years later.

The 1933–34 Kangaroos squad was littered with exceptional players, such as stand-off Vic Hey, speedy forward Wally Rigg, and high-scoring centre Dave Brown. The home side featured Wigan full-back Jim Sullivan, a former Welsh rugby union prodigy, who became rugby league's all-time leading goal-kicker with 2,687 in first-class matches.

The game was essentially an amateur one in New Zealand, whose touring side, still known as the All Blacks, enjoyed far less success than the Australians. Their 1926–27 British tour was blighted by internal disputes, fights and desertions, as well as defeats in all three Tests. The NZRL branded the venture a 'fiasco', and banned seven squad members for life.

After a brief boom just after the war, the domestic British game faced tough times in the 1920s and 1930s. The economic depression devastated some of the industries, such as textile-making and coal-mining, which most rugby league towns relied on, spelling serious trouble for many clubs.

Despite the hardship, supporters' clubs staged fund-raising events, and Featherstone miners even donated three pence from their weekly wage to help keep the local club afloat. Some clubs turned to other sports, such as greyhound racing, speedway, and even baseball, to generate income. Most clubs in New South Wales were on a firmer footing, largely thanks to the well-used poker machines in their social clubs ('leagues clubs') – still a vital source of revenue today, although recent concerns about the social effects of gambling have led some clubs to consider scrapping them.

The Challenge Cup final's move to Wembley raised hopes that regular rugby league could catch on in the capital. In 1933, Wigan Highfield were bought by the owners of White City Stadium, and became London Highfield. But they only stayed there for a single season, thanks to heavy financial losses, and returned north to become Liverpool Stanley[50].

Undeterred, Sidney Parkes, owner of Wandsworth Greyhound Stadium, proposed a six-team southern section of the league, hoping to attract northern migrants. His plan was not fully realised, but Parkes did set up two London-area clubs, Acton & Willesden, and Streatham & Mitcham, who entered the RFL's top tier in 1935. Streatham & Mitcham managed to sign former Maori rugby union star George Nepia. Still, neither club attracted much local interest, and both vanished within two years. The north-east was another target for expansion, with a Newcastle club joining the RFL in 1936, before suffering the same fate as the London clubs.

As mentioned earlier, French rugby union hit a crisis in 1931. Fourteen clubs left the Fédération Française de Rugby (FFR), accusing rivals of professionalism, and the International Board cast France adrift.

Early in 1933, two journalists from the sports paper *L'Auto* (forerunner of *L'Équipe*) brought the FFR's plight to the attention of RFL secretary John Wilson, seeing an opportunity for rugby league to take root in France. However, Wilson, a former Olympic cyclist, then contacted an old French friend from his cycling days, Victor Breyer, now the editor of rival paper *L'Echo des Sports*. Harry Sunderland, a powerful figure in Australian rugby league, also wanted the game to develop in France.

It was not an entirely new idea: a M. Bureau had written to the RFL about it in 1912, and the touring Australians had tried to arrange a match in Paris in 1921–22, before the FFR scuppered their plans. This time, though, the troubles in French rugby union gave the idea some impetus, and events quickly gathered pace.

Articles about rugby league appeared in *L'Echo des Sports*, and an England v Australia exhibition match was staged in Paris on New Year's Eve, 1933, drawing a crowd of around 20,000. Many of them went away impressed by the speed and skill of the 'neo-rugby', described by one observer as 'lightning rugby', with rules that seemed ideally suited to the adventurous French approach to the game.

Another journalist, Maurice Blein, had advised Breyer to contact Jean Galia, a leading rugby union forward. Galia had an imposing personality, and a grudge against the FFR over allegations of receiving illicit payments from the Quillan club. He was at the game in Paris, liked what he saw, and soon asked Wilson and Sunderland when they wanted a French rugby league side to visit Britain.

A tour was arranged for the following spring, and Galia had little trouble assembling a squad. After struggling in their early games, they gained some encouragement from a 26-23 win over Hull. That April, the Ligue Française de Rugby à XIII (LFR XIII) was formed, and France made their international debut, losing 32-21 to England in Paris. English clubs visited southern and south-western France, finding that they had more in common with their hosts than expected: a mix of working-class culture, regional pride, and a sense of injustice against the rugby union establishment.

The LFR XIII was bold enough to propose a World Cup as early as 1934, but had to settle for a European Championship with England and Wales, first held the following year. It began its own league and cup competitions in 1934–35. Despite zealous opposition from the FFR, *rugby à treize* became popular with players and spectators in the south and south-west, also finding support in Paris. With its undertones of rebellion and egalitarianism, it became allied with the emerging left-wing movement, and was embraced by the Popular Front, which came to power in 1936. By then, the league had 50 clubs. Three years later, it had well over 200; while the FFR had lost around half of its clubs since 1930, many of them having switched codes.

The New Zealand squad arrived in Britain on August 29, 1939, for their first tour since the calamity of 1926–27. The day after their opening match, a win against St Helens, Britain declared war on Germany. The tourists headed for home in mid September, after just one more game.

The RFL suspended its main competitions, but, in the widespread belief that sport could help lift the nation's morale, replaced them with Lancashire and Yorkshire 'War Emergency Leagues'. The Challenge Cup was revived in 1941, and, later that year, a single league was restored. But the manpower shortage, along with the hardships of wartime life, with rationing and restrictions on travel and crowds, forced many clubs to drop out.

Eligibility rules were looser than usual, a situation that drew the attention of Dewsbury's secretary-manager, a jovial young sports journalist named Eddie Waring. Some leading players, such as Jim Sullivan, Vic Hey and Gus Risman, were based at an army camp near the town. Waring signed them up, helping the club to win the championship and Challenge Cup in 1943; but some of his signings breached even the lax wartime rules, and Dewsbury were stripped of both titles. As in the First World War, the rugby union authorities softened their stance on cross-code matters, allowing rugby league players to represent England and Wales in military matches under union rules.

Australian club competitions continued throughout the war, pretty much as normal, although there were no inter-state series between 1942 and 1944. Large crowds still turned up: around 61,000 saw the Sydney competition's 1943 Grand Final between Newtown and North Sydney. In New Zealand, though, many major leagues were suspended; most of them would never fully recover.

The game suffered an even worse fate in France. Senior FFR figures had links with politicians in the Nazi-friendly Vichy government, and encouraged them to stamp out the 'deviant form' of rugby. In December 1941, the sports ministry, led by former rugby union international Joseph Pascot, prepared an edict for prime minister Marshal Philippe Pétain to sign.

It abolished the LFR XIII, and declared that the league's assets would be confiscated, and its records destroyed. Rugby league itself was prohibited, and its former players were told to denounce it. Officially, the ban was part of a drive to rid sport of professionalism; but other professional sports were let off the hook, and the real impetus almost certainly came from the FFR's ruthless opportunism. At the stroke of a pen, an entire sport was wiped out, in a country where it had made giant strides during its brief existence.

The game was revived in 1944, after the Vichy regime had fallen, but the FFR still had some influence on those in power. The league's assets were never returned, and it was forbidden from having the word 'rugby' in its name; for decades to come, it would be the Fédération Française de Jeu à XIII (game of 13). The momentum built up in the 1930s had been lost, and rugby league has struggled to compete with its rival code in France ever since.

International rugby league sprang back into life in 1946, as England set sail for the Antipodes aboard an aircraft carrier, HMS *Indomitable*, stoking the boilers to keep themselves fit. Attendances boomed back home, with the Challenge Cup final being sold out in 1948, for the first time since its move to Wembley, as 91,465 saw Wigan beating Bradford. It was a golden period for Wigan, with four championships, two Challenge Cups and six Lancashire Cups between 1945 and 1952.

Top-class rugby league spread to Cumberland, as Workington, with many Cumbrian-born players, joined the senior league in 1945. Whitehaven joined them three years later. There was yet another burst of activity in south Wales, as an eight-team Welsh League began play in 1949, only to fold soon afterwards amid general apathy.

The 1948 Challenge Cup final was the first to be televised, but the broadcast could only be seen in the Midlands, where there was little interest. More finals appeared on TV in the early 1950s, before the RFL pulled the plug for several years, believing that attendances were being affected. In 1954, an official crowd of 102,569 crammed into Bradford's Odsal stadium for a cup final replay between Halifax and Warrington; the real figure is thought to have been closer to 120,000.

In Australia, where there would be no TV coverage until 1961, South Sydney had another spell of dominance in their city's league, reaching every Grand Final from 1949 to 1955, and losing only two of them. On the international front, 1947–48 saw New Zealand, now officially nicknamed the Kiwis rather than the All Blacks, finally completing a British tour for the first time in 21 years. Another name change came a year later, as 'England' finally adopted the name 'Great Britain' when they hosted the Kangaroos.

Anglo-Australian matches were still often testy affairs – perhaps even more than before, with relations between the two countries worsening as Australia's sense of independence grew stronger. A 1954 game between New South Wales and Great Britain was abandoned after 56 minutes, as referee Aubrey Oxford despaired of trying to control the incessant violence. Four years later, in a bruising test in Brisbane, British captain Alan Prescott played on with a broken arm sustained after just three minutes. Four other Britons suffered serious injuries, but only one (David Bolton, with a broken collarbone) left the action, and the team hung on for a 25-18 win, which went down in rugby league lore as 'Prescott's Epic'.

An international governing body, the International Board, was set up in 1948, mainly on the initiative of the French league. Only France, Great Britain and New Zealand were at the inaugural meeting; but the Australians joined a year later, after much haggling over the board's composition, and an agreement that it would control the rules of the game.

The revived French national side raised eyebrows in Australia in 1951, managing a 2-1 Test series win on their first tour of the country, and impressing spectators with their flair and innovation. Their focal point was captain Puig-Aubert (real name: Robert Aubert Puig), an eccentric full-back who often refused to tackle, and was known to drink or smoke on the pitch while play was in progress, but whose kicking skills played a big part in the team's success. France returned four years later, claiming another 2-1 series win.

The World Cup finally came to fruition in 1954, with Australia, Great Britain, New Zealand and hosts France in a round-robin contest. Britain and France finished level at the top of the table, forcing an extra game to be played, a 16-12 British win in Paris. There had been hopes of including the USA in the tournament, after some fleeting signs that the game might be stirring into life there. Mike Dimitro, an American wrestling promoter who had been in Australia during the war, had taken an 'American All-Stars' squad on an Australian tour in 1953. The players were new to the game, and performed poorly; but one of them, Al Kirkland, stayed in Australia and played 18 times for Parramatta.

Another potential growth area was Italy, where a Turin-based team was formed by disgruntled rugby union players. They toured Britain in 1950–51 and 1954–55, and played in a French league. There was more activity in the late 1950s and early 1960s, with the RFL showing an interest; but little came of it. Better progress was made in the very different setting of Papua New Guinea, which was under Australian rule from 1906 to 1975. Australian expats formed the Papuan Rugby Football League in 1949, with two teams in the capital, Port Moresby. The nearby Boroko Oval, modelled on Australian grounds, was built in 1957, and a schoolboy competition was set up five years later.

In South Africa, exhibition matches featuring Great Britain and France were staged in 1957, and two leagues, Rugby League South Africa and the National Rugby League, were formed in the 1960s. British clubs visited the country, and South African teams toured Australia and New Zealand. But the game faced fierce hostility from the rugby union authorities, while the lack of cohesion, with two rival leagues, hardly helped matters. Also, unlike the RFU, the RFL was reluctant to engage with the apartheid regime. Not surprisingly, little progress was made. However, restrictions on signing Australians led some British clubs to turn to South African rugby union players, most notably Tom van Vollenhoven, a winger who enjoyed success with St Helens.

After South Sydney's golden spell from 1949 to 1955, St George had an incredible run, winning the Sydney title 11 times in a row from 1956 to 1966. Under captain-coach Ken Kearney until 1961, and subsequently Norm Provan, the key to their superiority was in their defensive methods, influenced by Kearney's earlier spell in England with Leeds. By the mid 1960s, St George's predictable success, together with an attendance slump in Britain, was intensifying calls for more rule changes.

The latest wave of unrest had begun much earlier, with scrums once again a major issue. Many still felt that they were happening too often (along with other stoppages), making the game dull to watch, and giving an undue advantage to teams who specialised in winning possession at scrums. In an effort to remedy the problem, a rule was implemented in 1966: if a penalty was kicked into touch, the kicking team would restart play with a tap penalty, rather than a scrum.

But the main talking point now was the 'creeping barrage', where a team kept the ball for long periods while gaining little ground, by repeatedly running into tacklers and settling for a play-the-ball. Fifteen minutes from the end of a championship semi-final against Wigan in 1951, Workington were 8-5 ahead, and a man short. Captain Gus Risman ordered his teammates to stop passing and kicking, preferring them to kill the game off by keeping hold of the ball.

Three years later, Leigh chairman James Hilton suggested scrapping the play-the-ball, and reverting to the rugby union rule that required a tackled player to release the ball immediately. His idea found little support from other British clubs, or from the Australians, New Zealanders or French. But it was favoured by RFL secretary Bill Fallowfield, who often ruffled rugby league feathers with his admiration for the 15-a-side code (not to mention a habit of suing anyone who criticised him).

The suggestion was tested in experimental games over the next decade. In the 1963–64 bottom-14 play-offs (part of the RFL's latest attempt at finding the ideal format), a play-the-ball only took place after the first tackle of each possession, after which the rugby union rule was applied. The notoriously stubborn Fallowfield was determined to keep the idea alive, despite the strong opposition – many saw the play-the-ball as a crucial part of rugby league's identity.

The topic was debated at an International Board meeting in July 1966. The Australian and New Zealand delegates were reluctant to allow drastic changes, but, thanks to St George's dominance in the Sydney competition, the Australians were keen to see something happen. Fallowfield made reference to American football's downs-and-yardage system, which had been introduced in the 1880s in response to a similar problem (it is not clear whether Fallowfield was advocating it, but he did bring it up). The New Zealand camp suggested a variation on this rule, with the 'downs' but without the yardage factor: after a fourth tackle, there would be a scrum.

All the delegates liked the sound of the four-tackle rule, and agreed that it should be tested. It was first used in October 1966, in the BBC2 Floodlit Trophy, a midweek tournament that had been launched the previous year. It encouraged a more attacking, flowing form of rugby, encouraging the team in possession to make good use of the ball, before potentially losing it after a fourth tackle. The RFL had adopted it for all matches by the end of that month, and the Australian leagues followed suit in 1967.

Reactions to the new rule were reminiscent of those that had greeted the play-the-ball rule 60 years earlier. In Britain's *Rugby League Magazine*, Norman Gaulton enthused that 'the variety of tactics and spirit of adventure which have been so sadly lacking has been reintroduced again [*sic*]'. Australian Rugby League chief Bill Buckley told the RFL that the change had 'revitalised' the game in his country.

The change brought some much-needed variety to the game, especially as it was possible to bring the tackle count back to zero by recovering the ball after a forward kick. However, it soon became evident that four tackles were rarely enough for a team to build a structured attack, and a degree of panic often set in after the first couple of tackles. The limit was increased to six in 1972.

The concept of substitutions had always met strong resistance, in a sport where players were expected to withstand severe pain and to play on for as long as they physically could. Anything less would be seen as a sign of weakness, and a dereliction of duty to teammates. The legendary status of matches such as the 'Rorke's Drift' test and 'Prescott's Epic' reinforced this tradition, which was typified in a 1962 test match when Australia's Dud Beattie suffered a broken collarbone. Knowing that he could not continue, but not wanting to leave his team short-handed, Beattie picked a fight with Great Britain's Derek Turner, so that both players would be dismissed and the numbers would remain even.

Just a year later, though, the Australian leagues began allowing teams to use two substitutes each; but only for injuries, and only in the first half. A similar rule was introduced in Britain the following year. From 1971, the two substitutes could be used at any time, and for any reason.

Wakefield Trinity took centre stage in Britain in the early years under the four-tackle rule, with championships in 1966–67 and 1967–68. Among their ranks was Neil Fox, rugby league's all-time record points scorer to this day, with 6,220 at club and international levels combined. His brother and teammate Don was the unlucky man in one of the game's best-known moments, during the 1968 'Watersplash' Challenge Cup final against Leeds at a drenched Wembley. Needing to kick a straight-on, last-gasp conversion to turn an 11-10 deficit into certain victory, he missed the target and sank into the mud in despair. Eddie Waring, now a BBC TV commentator, sympathised as only he could: 'He's a poor lad.'

Waring had been BBC Television's rugby league commentator since coverage began in 1951, and would continue until 1981. Legend has it that he persuaded the corporation to adopt the game after discussing televised sport with comedian Bob Hope in the United States, en route home from covering the 1946 Ashes series as a journalist. By the mid 1970s – although TV had become a valuable source of income for rugby league – many supporters, and the RFL, were strongly critical of the BBC's presentation of the game, especially Waring's jocular, eccentric commentating style.

For better or worse, to the nation at large, Eddie Waring was the voice and face of rugby league for three decades. While his celebrity persona helped to draw attention to the sport, it also arguably reinforced its 'cloth cap and ferrets' image. Some even suggested that he was part of a BBC conspiracy to discredit rugby league[51].

Another problem for the British game in the 1970s was a continual struggle on the financial front, as its support base was eroded by the decline of manual industries in its heartlands. Additionally, many working-class boys were now attending grammar schools, where rugby league was not played, depriving the game of some potential players. As attendance figures waned, the RFL loaned money to clubs in financial trouble, while sponsorship of competitions helped to keep the game afloat. The appointment of the commercially-minded David Oxley as RFL secretary in 1974, replacing Fallowfield, also brought a more business-driven approach to the management of the game.

There were few such problems in Australia, where poker machines continued pumping money into the clubs. League regulations in New South Wales had been modernised in 1959, providing for player contracts and some freedom of movement between clubs. Along with the attractions of an Australian lifestyle, the prospect of better wages and contract terms encouraged British players to emigrate Down Under.

Great Britain's strong showing in the 1970 Ashes series led Australian clubs to take an interest in some of their players, and the likes of Mal Reilly and Mike Stephenson were soon on their way south. At the time, players could represent their countries only if they were home-based, and the mini-exodus weakened the British national side (just as Australia had been weakened in earlier times, when players had joined British clubs).

Australia's inter-state series had stagnated by the late 1970s. Most of the leading players from both states were with Sydney-area clubs, and consequently played for New South Wales. In 1980, after NSW won the first two games comfortably, the Queensland Rugby League suggested changing the format for the final game, with eligibility based on birthplace rather than players' current clubs. The Australian Rugby League, which now controlled these series, agreed to give it a try. Queensland won by 20-10, boosting interest in the event in their state. The same pattern was repeated the following year, and, from 1982 onwards, the whole series was run on an 'origin' basis. State of Origin became a highlight of

Australia's sporting calendar, renowned for intensely physical, closely-fought contests.

By this time, like their Australian Rules counterparts, some Australian coaches had turned to American football for inspiration. Jack Gibson, named 'Coach of the Century' by experts during Australian rugby league's centenary festivities in 2008, attended an NFL conference in 1969, and befriended San Francisco 49ers coach Dick Nolan. Gibson kick-started a revolution in Australian rugby league coaching, with methods involving video and statistical analysis, and with more attention being paid to fitness, motivation, discipline, and detailed game plans.

None of this was of much interest to British coaches in the 1970s and 1980s, and the difference soon became evident. The touring Kangaroos in 1982–83 won all 15 of their games in Britain, with embarrassing margins of victory in the three Tests. The Ashes series in 1984 and 1986–87 were also won comfortably by Australia, whose performances even gained some respect in rugby union circles.

After being forbidden from doing so for decades, British clubs were again allowed to sign Australian players in 1983. Leading Kangaroos such as Wally Lewis (Wakefield) and Mal Meninga (St Helens) soon wound up in Britain, helping to rejuvenate a struggling league. Australian coaches, such as John Monie at Wigan and Chris Anderson with Halifax, brought their expertise to British clubs. Despite the results, the 1984 Ashes series also gave the British game some hope, with the emergence of promising youngsters Andy Gregory, Ellery Hanley, Joe Lydon and Garry Schofield, who would help to narrow the gap between the two national sides in the years to come.

From the late 1970s to the mid 1980s, Hull FC and Hull Kingston Rovers were Britain's most successful sides, with the local rivals clinching the top two league positions in both 1982–83 and 1983–84. But it was Wigan, featuring Gregory, Hanley and Lydon, who led the pack from then until the mid 1990s. In the ten seasons from 1986–87, when they became fully professional, they finished on top of the table eight times, won four Premierships (as winners of the play-off tournament), and picked up eight Challenge Cups.

The 1980s saw renewed efforts to develop rugby league outside its heartlands, sometimes involving soccer clubs looking for new sources of revenue. Fulham's rugby league team entered the RFL's Second Division in 1980, and won promotion at the first attempt. It was the start of London's first lasting presence in the league; the team became the London Crusaders in 1991, and the London Broncos three years later (after being bought by the Brisbane Broncos), before a partnership with the Harlequins rugby union club saw another name change, to Harlequins

RL, in 2005. Clubs also sprang up in Kent, Southend, Mansfield, Sheffield and Cardiff in the 1980s, but only Sheffield made any real impact.

Wigan's domestic success meant regular appearances in the World Club Challenge, a not-quite-annual match between the champions of the British league and the Sydney competition. The first, unofficial, match was held in 1976, when Eastern Suburbs overwhelmed St Helens 25-2 in Sydney. The idea lay dormant for 11 years, until Wigan beat Manly 8-2 at home. It became official in 1989, with Widnes, Wigan's main domestic challengers, defeating Canberra in Manchester.

The Rugby League World Cup had limped along since its inception in 1954, making little impression on the world in general. The shortage of competitive teams, the irregular gaps between tournaments, and the wild variations in format hardly helped its fortunes. The 1975 tournament was arranged on a home-and-away basis, stretched out over eight months. A short format was restored in 1977, but the next competition was spread out between 1985 and 1988, with the matches integrated into regular test schedules. The same formula was used again between 1989 and 1992.

Throughout this period, the World Cup was predictably dominated by Australia and Great Britain, with New Zealand and France doing little more than making up the numbers. The French league was in the doldrums by the mid 1980s, wracked by managerial and financial crises. At least a court awarded it the right to reclaim the word 'rugby' in 1987; but this provoked a backlash by the FFR, which encouraged its clubs to offer money to rugby league players as an incentive to switch codes, despite rugby union still being supposedly amateur.

The rules of the game continued evolving, with the emphasis, as usual, on promoting positive styles of play. Drop goals were downgraded from two points to one in Australia in 1971, and in Britain three years later. From 1983, a try was worth four points, rather than three, and a sixth tackle resulted in a turnover (with a play-the-ball for the team that had been defending), instead of a scrum. The sin-bin, as a punishment for fouls that did not quite warrant a dismissal, was introduced in Australia in 1981, and in Britain in 1983.

During the 1980s, it was gradually accepted that scrums should be uncontested – that is, the team with the 'head and feed' would automatically have possession as the ball emerged. Scrums became mere formalities, with little purpose other than to create space for backs by bringing the forwards together. It was a further step away from the notion of 'contesting possession' that has always been fundamental to rugby union; as was a 1992 change to the play-the-ball rule, requiring all but two of the defending side to retreat by ten metres (or to their goal-line, if it was less than ten metres away). Additionally, the substitution rules were loosened around this time, extending to the idea of 'interchanges', with substituted players being allowed to rejoin the game.

Things were also changing off the field. In Britain, a limited free agency rule was introduced in 1987, improving the players' bargaining power. Salaries and transfer fees subsequently rocketed, leaving many clubs in serious trouble. The NSWRL tried to prevent such problems, and to keep a competitive balance in the Sydney league, by introducing a salary cap in 1990.

By this time, the so-called Sydney premiership had expanded well beyond the city, and even beyond New South Wales. With long-distance travel becoming easier, it was inevitable that commercial forces would bring Australia's larger clubs together into one league. The Canberra Raiders and the Wollongong-based Illawarra Steelers, both newly formed, joined in 1982. The Brisbane Broncos were added in 1988 (leaving their second-string team to play in the Brisbane league), along with the Gold Coast Giants and Newcastle Knights. The league's horizons spread even further in 1995, encompassing the North Queensland Cowboys, South Queensland Crushers, the Perth-based Western Reds, and even the Auckland Warriors.

A year earlier, New Zealand's first nationwide league, the National Club Premiership, had been launched, finally providing some regular semi-professional rugby league. It was hoped that the Warriors' high profile would help stimulate the game's growth in New Zealand, and help the national team to move up a gear or two.

The Sydney league had outgrown itself, and was taken over in 1995 by the Australian Rugby League, which gave its name to the competition. The league was drawing large TV audiences, attracting the attention of rival media moguls Rupert Murdoch and Kerry Packer, who were both looking to set up pay-TV channels.

Murdoch had received a proposal from Brisbane Broncos chief executive John Ribot in March 1994 for a 'Super League' scheme, which would involve restructuring the game to suit the needs of Murdoch's TV network. The plan also reached the ARL, around the time when it was taking control of the expanded Sydney league. But the ARL already had a deal with Packer, and rejected Ribot's proposal. Murdoch liked the idea, though, and his News Corporation pressed on regardless, sowing the seeds of conflict by signing contracts with clubs and players.

The ARL warned that any players involved in the Super League would be ineligible to represent Australia. Murdoch responded by hatching a plan to take control of the top level of the British game, hoping to take the sting out of the ARL's threat by depriving Australia of their main opponents. British Sky Broadcasting (BSkyB), largely under Murdoch's control, had been televising British rugby league since 1990, and was well placed to take a firm grip on it.

In April 1995, BSkyB made a staggering offer to RFL chief executive Maurice Lindsay, which he then presented to club chairmen. Lindsay, chairman at Wigan before taking up the post in 1992, had already mooted radical plans for revamping the league, as had his fellow Wigan director Jack Robinson back in 1986, when he called for a 12-team 'Super League'.

BSkyB was proposing a 'Super League Europe', with 14 teams: six existing RFL sides, six new ones to be created by merging existing clubs, and others in Paris and Toulouse. The season would be supposedly switched to the summer (in reality, from late winter to autumn), mainly to align it with the Australian season, allowing all of the teams from both Super Leagues to play in a six-round post-season tournament. As an added benefit, it would not have to compete with soccer for the entire season.

The deal was to be worth £77 million over five years – enough to overcome any misgivings the chairmen may have had. They all accepted it, but the news provoked fury among fans of the clubs that were to be merged. Warrington and Widnes, for example, were to become a single club known as Cheshire (named after a county that neither town traditionally belonged to), and, perhaps worst of all, old rivals Hull FC and Hull KR would be combined into Humberside.

Appalled at the thought of seeing their clubs lose their identities, supporters staged protest rallies. An indignant book, *Merging on the Ridiculous*, was published within a week of the announcement. There were also concerns over the degree of control that BSkyB would have over the league, perhaps affecting player transfers as well as match scheduling. Within a month, the plan was drastically modified. The merger plans were called off, and Toulouse were dropped, leaving just 12 teams; while the sum on offer was increased to £87 million.

While the plans for Super League Europe were being finalised, ARL officials were challenging the legality of the contracts that some clubs had signed with News Corporation for its Australian equivalent. A court ruled that the clubs must fulfil their ARL commitments, forcing the breakaway plan to be temporarily shelved. This also threatened Super League Europe – a clause in the RFL deal meant that Murdoch could back out if his Australian scheme fell through, which would have wrecked his plans for a combined post-season competition. A deeply acrimonious three-year battle ensued, involving Murdoch, Packer, the ARL, and hordes of lawyers.

Still, after a shortened 1995–96 season, Super League Europe kicked off in 1996, with St Helens landing the first title. From 1998, it had an

Australian-style play-off system, with a Grand Final at Old Trafford. The new ten-club Australian league finally got off the ground in 1997, as a rival to the ARL. It had its own answer to the State of Origin series: the Tri-Series, featuring New Zealand as well as New South Wales and Queensland.

The Euro-Australasian play-off tournament went ahead, with all 22 teams involved. Super League Australia, though, had been a financial disaster, and the split had been hugely damaging to just about everyone involved, lawyers excepted. The ARL and News Corporation finally came to an agreement, and a unified National Rugby League (NRL) began play in 1998.

The NRL featured a new team, the Melbourne Storm, replacing the Perth (formerly Western) Reds. It was rugby league's first major incursion into the home of Aussie Rules, and the team eventually found success, despite disappointing attendances, winning a title in 2007. The upheaval led to some mergers, with Balmain and Western Suburbs joining up to become Wests Tigers, and Manly and North Sydney combining as Northern Eagles (now Manly Sea Eagles).

The Paris team in Super League Europe lasted for only two seasons, making the league an all-British affair; but a French element was restored in 2006, when the Perpignan-based Catalans Dragons were admitted. The expansion into France's rugby heartland was more successful than the Parisian venture, with the team finding a strong level of support. Super League games were staged in Cardiff and Edinburgh in an attempt at spreading the rugby league gospel, and when the league introduced a licensing system in 2008 (replacing a problematic promotion and relegation system between it and the second-tier National League One), a place was awarded to the Bridgend-based Celtic Crusaders – yet another effort to get things going in south Wales.

This revolution in the mid 1990s, driven by television and money, had little effect on the one country where rugby league had become the national sport: Papua New Guinea. By the mid 1970s, the game had reached other towns beyond Port Moresby, and was popular with the native population as well as Australian expats. PNG was granted honorary membership of the International Board in 1974, and full membership four years later. The national team, mostly indigenous, made its bow with a 40-12 home defeat to Great Britain in 1975.

After improving somewhat over the next decade, PNG first entered the World Cup in the 1985–88 tournament. They made a promising start with a 24-22 win over New Zealand in August 1986, but were then heavily beaten by Australia and Great Britain. Although they have impressed with their speed and ball-handling, weak forward play has often let them down. Meanwhile, the game's development in PNG has been hampered by transport difficulties and a shortage of money. Further east, the Pacific Islands Rugby League Association was founded in 1991, featuring the Cook Islands, Tonga and Western Samoa. The game was also taken up in Fiji around this time.

Inevitably, rugby league chiefs have never quite given up on trying to develop their sport in the United States. The RFL started providing some support for the game there in the late 1970s. There have also been some Australian efforts, with a State of Origin match being staged in Long Beach, California, in 1987. Wigan faced Warrington in Milwaukee two years later, and US and Canadian national teams were formed in this period; but rugby league has remained largely obscure in North America, more so than rugby union. The eastern US does have a league today, though, and a small boost came in 2008 as Leeds met South Sydney in Jacksonville, Florida. The match was arranged by actor and South Sydney co-owner Russell Crowe, whose celebrity appeal helped to draw a crowd of over 12,000.

The USSR Rugby League was formed in 1990, after the RFL had identified the Soviet Union as potentially fertile ground for the game. Soon afterwards, 90 players visited the UK, to learn about rugby league, and to play against amateur and second-string teams. The league's first full season came in 1991–92, just as the USSR was breaking up, and a national Russian team was soon formed.

The game has had a troubled, stop-start history in South Africa, although the end of apartheid in the early 1990s brought some fresh hope. The new South African Rugby League won support from the National and Olympic Sports Congress, linked to the ascendant African National Congress, and North Sydney visited the country in 1993. But the sport remained in the shadow of rugby union, and the events of 1995 hardly helped: rugby union turned professional, a (marginally) multi-racial Springboks team won the World Cup on home soil, and their rugby league counterparts were hopelessly outclassed in their first World Cup appearance.

After the marathons of 1985–88 and 1989–92, a compact group format was restored for 1995's Centenary World Cup; but it did have ten teams, twice as many as before. England and Wales entered separately, and co-hosted the competition, with Fiji, Western Samoa and Tonga all entering for the first time, along with South Africa. Seven other countries played in an Emerging Nations tournament.

The World Cup was expanded even further for 2000, now with 16 teams, and was staged in the British Isles and France. The plans proved to be over-ambitious, and the tournament was blighted by atrocious weather, rail chaos, ticketing foul-ups, lopsided results, and poor turnouts in venues outside the game's heartlands. A predictable world order had emerged, with Australia and New Zealand thrashing Wales and England respectively in the semi-finals, before the Australians cruised to their sixth successive title. It was not all bad news, though: crowd figures in France were encouraging, and the much-ridiculed Lebanon team, made up of Australian-based players with Lebanese heritage, helped to get rugby league off the ground in Lebanon itself.

The tournament plunged the RFL into debt, and the next World Cup would not be held for another eight years. In 2003, though, the RFL and the French league created the Rugby League Europe Foundation, aiming to help fund the game's development in the northern hemisphere. The 2008 World Cup saw yet another overhaul, with a 'supergroup' featuring Australia, England, New Zealand and Papua New Guinea. The top three progressed straight to the semi-finals, joined by the victors of a play-off between the winners of two other three-team groups.

Meanwhile, the Tri-Nations tournament, staged first in 1999 and at various intervals afterwards, became a staple of the international game, involving Australia, New Zealand and Great Britain. With the likes of Stacey Jones and Ruben Wiki emerging as world-class players in recent years, the Kiwis have become a powerful force, overtaking the British (or English) as Australia's strongest challengers. Their shock win over Australia in the 2008 World Cup final made them only the third nation to lift the trophy. The Tri-Nations was expanded into a Four Nations in 2009, with England taking part, rather than Great Britain, and with various teams taking up the fourth slot.

Until 1995, the distinction between amateurism and professionalism was often cited as a difference between the two rugby codes. Aside from doubts over rugby union's amateur status, there was another problem with this view of things: rugby league, since its early days, has had an amateur scene of its own.

At first, amateur rugby league mainly involved 'junior' clubs in the north of England, bridging the gap between schools and the semi-professional 'senior' clubs. Junior teams often struggled with finances, organisation and a lack of suitable grounds, and complained of inadequate backing from the RFL. Leagues developed in areas such as London and south Wales, as well as northern England, but the amateur game waned in the 1950s, largely because of declining support from employers for works-based teams.

The Sports Council, formed in 1972 to provide funding for amateur sport, refused to help amateur rugby league, because of its ties with the RFL. A year later, a group of league officials in Huddersfield took matters into their own hands, forming the British Amateur Rugby League Association

(BARLA). The RFL recognised BARLA in 1974, having refused to do so at first. The amateur game was revitalised, and representative BARLA teams travelled overseas, playing against Australian university sides, and against senior clubs in weaker nations. Britain's first university team, at Leeds, was formed in 1967. Others followed, often facing hostility from university and county-level rugby union bodies; Oxford and Cambridge met in the first Varsity Match in 1981.

There was an attempt – probably the first – at establishing women's rugby league in Britain during World War I. It came to nothing, but women did play fund-raising matches during the miners' strike of 1921, and the General Strike five years later. Two women set up a five-team female league in Sydney in 1921, backed by the NSWRL. After being derided in the press for indulging in a supposedly unsuitable pastime, the women soon lost the NSWRL's support, and the competition failed to get through a season.

Things were looking up in Britain by 1980, with women's teams in Leeds, Huddersfield and St Helens. By 1994, there were 21 teams, mainly in traditional rugby league areas. The Sydney Women's Rugby League was formed in 1990, followed three years later by the Australian Women's Rugby League. The latter was affiliated to the ARL in 1998, giving birth to the New South Wales Women's Rugby League. A women's World Cup was first held in 2000, and repeated in 2005 and 2008, with New Zealand the winners each time.

Rugby league, at least in Britain, has always had something of an image problem. The RFL, clubs and fans have a long history of grumbling about the amount, and type, of coverage that the game has been given by the media. Editors, journalists, schedulers and presenters, mostly perceived to be middle class, have been accused of having a bias towards rugby union.

Back in 1927, the RFL protested to the BBC for neglecting to announce rugby league results on the radio; but the objection fell on deaf ears, as did another in 1948. Three years later, the *Rugby Leaguer* magazine followed suit with a 25,000-signature petition. A supporters' group, the 1895 Club, sent the corporation another petition in 1976, complaining bitterly about its style of presentation, particularly Eddie Waring's commentary.

Much of the UK press gives little space to rugby league, while delivering the occasional barb such as one that appeared in London's *Evening Standard* in 1993, portraying it as a game played by 'ape-like creatures watched by gloomy men in cloth caps.' After the messy World Cup in 2000 gave the game's critics fresh ammunition, the ensuing onslaught of derision prompted St Helens fan Ray Gent to start a petition aimed at the media; it attracted 30,000 signatures, was presented to the House of Commons, and was accompanied by a book. As well as the media, though, much of the criticism from supporters has been directed at the RFL, accusing it of failing to promote the game effectively.

When rugby union turned professional in 1995, the relationship between the two codes changed considerably. Until then, union authorities had often treated league as if it were a contagious disease that needed to be stamped out, particularly in the middle part of the 20th century. In 1930, when someone referred to league's popularity in Auckland to Lions tour manager James Baxter, he offered the view that 'every town must have its sewer.' Twenty years later, Rowe Harding of the Welsh union was equally blunt: 'Rugby league is only an infant, but it wants strangling.' Like its critics in the media, those in union circles typically associated league with greed and thuggery.

Whenever the 'infant' showed signs of growth in the south or Midlands, the RFU monitored its progress. Stark warnings were issued, with posters appearing in rugby union clubhouses and changing rooms, in case anyone was contemplating switching codes. Even amateur rugby league was frowned upon, and the Ministry of Defence banned the game in the armed forces.

The events of 1995 helped to thaw relations between union and league, although some union purists clung to their old attitudes: in 2001, former FFR president Albert Ferrasse wanted a France v Great Britain rugby league test in Agen to be cancelled, claiming that it would 'leave the pitch in need of decontamination.' Generally, though, union authorities became more tolerant of people with league connections, and of some cross-code co-operation, such as the Harlequins deal that was made in 2005.

Some observers predicted a merger of the codes, but usually envisaged it as, essentially, a takeover by union. Rugby league was thought to be on its last legs, as if professionalism had been the only reason for its separate existence. A merger, though, would be so difficult as to be almost unthinkable. Not only have union and league grown apart in terms of rules, tactics and skills, as shown in two cross-code games between Wigan and Bath in 1996, when each team won comfortably under its usual rules. On top of this, their entire structures – clubs, governing bodies, leagues, tournaments and international schedules – would need to be integrated. Even before any of this could happen, there would be the tricky question of who would manage the process.

Just as importantly, rugby league has its own distinct culture, rooted in working-class notions of equality and a distrust of authority. Its supporters, whose pride in the game itself is at least as strong as their club loyalties, are unlikely to embrace a hybrid rugby code. Actor and playwright Colin Welland summed up what the game means to its followers in 1979:

A Develyshe Pastime

In south-west Lancashire ... rugby league provides our cultural adrenalin. It's a physical manifestation of our rules of life, comradeship, honest endeavour, and a staunch, often ponderous allegiance to fair play.

Although league has lost a worrying number of players and coaches to union since 1995, with little traffic flowing the other way, its junior ranks have produced an ample flow of replacements; particularly in Queensland and New South Wales, where, in contrast to the north of England as a whole, it is the number-one sport.

It is hard to believe that any other sport has survived such a relentless battering – from the media, from rival sporting authorities, and even from governments – as rugby league. Although it still struggles to make an impression outside its heartlands, it enjoys enough support to keep it alive and reasonably well for the foreseeable future. Having suffered a century of attacks from paranoid rugby union officials, pompous journalists, and even Nazi collaborators, the chances are that it has been doing something right.

Chapter 12

The World's Game, Part 2

'Football is the opera of the people'
– Stafford Heginbotham, Bradford City chairman, 1985

As Britain emerged from the Second World War, life was still tough, with rationing in operation and money hard to come by. Soccer provided a cheap form of entertainment, and some light relief from austerity. When normal service was resumed (the FA Cup returned in 1945–46, the league a year later), fans poured into the grounds in bigger numbers than ever.

Attendances across the Football League's four divisions reached an all-time peak in 1948–49, averaging over 22,000. Sadly, some grounds were not ready for such a surge in numbers. At an FA Cup tie at Bolton's Burnden Park in March 1946, 15,000 fans tried to find a way in after the turnstiles had been shut; the ensuing crush left 33 dead and around 500 injured.

British football finally started shaking off its insular attitude in the post-war years, with all four UK associations rejoining FIFA. Dynamo Moscow toured Britain in 1945–46, and made quite an impression, winning two games and drawing their other two. A total of 270,000 spectators saw their matches against Chelsea, Arsenal, Cardiff and Rangers. Many were surprised by the attacking flair, technical skills and disciplined teamwork shown by the visitors, with a style based on short, quick passing. It was a sign of how far the game had progressed overseas, and of things to come.

The English, Scottish, Welsh and (Northern) Irish FAs finally showed an interest in entering the World Cup. The first post-war tournament was to be held in Brazil in 1950, and that year's Home International championship was used as a qualifying group. England won it, with Scotland in second place; although FIFA offered places in the finals for the top two teams, the Scottish FA refused to send its team, on the grounds that they had not won the British competition.

A group format was used in the World Cup for the first time since 1930, but not merely for the first stage. For the only time to date, the whole tournament was group-based, with the trophy going to the winners of a final four-team group. A knockout format would be restored for the later rounds in 1954.

The first round saw one of the cup's all-time shocks, as England, featuring such stars as Billy Wright, Tom Finney and Stan Mortensen, lost 1-0 to the United States, a cobbled-together team made up largely of college students. The result was barely noticed in the US, where soccer was now even more obscure than when the team had finished third in 1930. Even the British press paid little attention. But it alarmed the FA, who set up a technical committee to try to work out where the English game was going wrong. England had beaten Chile in their first match, but they lost their last game to Spain, and were out of the cup.

Brazil, the hosts, were gradually emerging as a major force in world football. This might have happened earlier, had it not been for arguments over team selection between the various state associations, and the exclusion of black players. Brazil had first made an impact at the 1938 World Cup, finishing in third place. Their hero that year was Leonidas da Silva, the 'Black Diamond', who was the tournament's leading scorer (with either seven or eight goals – the credit for one of their six first-round goals against Poland is disputed). Leonidas, an early exponent of the bicycle kick, had fought against racism during his days with Flamengo.

Brazil just needed a draw from their final game of the 1950 tournament to become champions. But, in front of around 200,000 at the Maracanã stadium in Rio de Janeiro, they lost 2-1 to Uruguay – world champions for the second time, in only their second attempt.

Authoritarian politicians and sport generally don't mix well, but the communist Hungarian regime's involvement in football in the late 1940s and early 1950s might have been an exception. The Ministry of Defence took over the Kispest club, near Budapest, and re-christened it as Honvéd, a name based on that of the army. The secret police adopted MTK, another club in the Budapest area.

In a scheme that was typical of Eastern Bloc countries during the Cold War, the government made sure Hungary's best players moved to these two clubs, forming the nucleus of the national side. To them, success for Hungary's football team would mean vindication for their political system. Deputy sports minister Gusztáv Sebes became their coach in 1949, and pursued his vision of team-orientated 'socialist football', in contrast to the more individualistic, supposedly 'capitalist', western style.

Whether or not these political connotations had anything to do with it, an outstanding Hungary team emerged in the early 1950s, hailed as the Magnificent (or Mighty, or Magical) Magyars; or, back home, as 'aranycsapat' – the Golden Team. Their style was built on foundations laid by pre-war coaches such as Jimmy Hogan, based on passing and fluent movement of players, but they took these ideas to a higher level.

Sebes, along with other Hungarian coaches such as Béla Guttmann and Márton Bukovi, was not satisfied with the 'WM' formation (3-2-2-3), which had become the norm by now. Instead, the new Hungarian line-up featured two strikers, two wingers, and a deep-lying 'centre-forward' who was effectively a midfielder. One of the two half-backs moved into defence, alongside the conventional centre-half. The result was, roughly, a 4-2-4 formation, but with overlapping full-backs supporting the midfielders and wingers, effectively making it a 2-4-4 when they were attacking. It was more fluid than the WM system, with players often swapping positions as the team switched between defence and attack.

Like their counterparts in other sports, all Eastern Bloc footballers were officially amateurs, with notional jobs in the army or other state organisations. This arrangement helped the communist nations to dominate Olympic football from the early 1950s until the 1980s. For a few years, the new-look Hungary played mostly against other eastern European sides, but the 1952 Olympics gave them a chance to announce themselves to the wider world.

Their captain and figurehead was Ferenc Puskás, a short, stocky striker with a powerful left foot and a knack for scoring goals. He averaged almost a goal a game in both his domestic and international careers. With him in the centre of the attack was his Honvéd teammate Sándor Kocsis, an even more prolific scorer. Nándor Hidegkuti, of MTK, was the deep-lying centre-forward, with Honvéd's József Bozsik as the other central midfielder. With left-winger Zoltán Czibor and goalkeeper Gyula Grosics (a pioneer of the 'sweeper-keeper' role, often leaving his penalty area to help the defence), these players would form the core of Hungary's team over the next four years.

Hungary won Olympic gold in 1952, and, in November 1953, inflicted the latest and most devastating blow to England's notions of football supremacy. In a friendly at Wembley, the Hungarians took their opponents apart with a dazzling display of fluent, intelligent football. Their unconventional attack left England's three-man defence bewildered. Centre-half Harry Johnston, who was used to tracking opposing centre-forwards, was lost whenever Hidegkuti dropped back into midfield – not knowing whether to follow him or to stay in his usual position at the back. The strikers, Puskás and Kocsis, were left with acres of space, and made the most of it.

England lost by six goals to three, their first home defeat to a team from outside the British Isles. In a return match in Budapest six months later, despite trying to learn lessons from the Wembley game, they lost by a shocking 7-1 scoreline. While the 1950 defeat by the USA was widely regarded as a fluke, these resounding losses made it clear that English football had been overtaken by the better tactics and techniques of some overseas teams. Geoffrey Green, *The Times* correspondent at the Wembley match, gushing over Hungary's 'new conception of football', concluded that 'English football can be proud of its past ... but it must awake to a new future.'

Unbeaten in four years, Hungary went to Switzerland in 1954 as World Cup favourites, and beat West Germany 8-3 in the opening group stage. But a surprisingly violent quarter-final against Brazil, the 'Battle of Berne', which Hungary won 4-2, left them bruised and exhausted. After overcoming Uruguay in the semi-finals, they faced the West Germans again – this time on a rain-sodden pitch, with a half-fit Puskás.

The Germans, helped by exchangeable studs on their boots (an early triumph for Adi Dassler, founder of the Adidas sportswear giant), and allegedly by performance-enhancing drugs (syringes were reportedly found in their dressing room), came back from 2-0 behind to clinch a 3-2 victory, giving a humbled, rebuilding nation something to celebrate.

Hungary bounced back with another unbeaten run, lasting nearly two years. But their heyday ended in the autumn of 1956, when Soviet tanks rolled into Budapest to quash protests against communist rule. The Honvéd players were in Spain at the time, and many of them, including Puskás, refused to return home, preferring to defect to the west. It was the end of their days in the national team, which would have to be rebuilt almost from scratch, marking the start of a seemingly terminal decline.

Meanwhile, English football's attempts at recovering some pride after those defeats to Hungary had led to the birth of a new competition. Wolves beat Spartak Moscow and Honvéd at home in friendlies in 1954–55, leading the *Daily Mail* to proclaim them 'champions of the world'. French journalist Gabriel Hanot was unconvinced, saying that Wolves would need to beat leading continental teams on foreign soil before such a claim could be justified. Hanot, a former player and manager for his country, went on to propose a Europe-wide club competition.

Floodlights were being installed at some grounds, allowing mid-week evening games to be staged. Travelling around Europe was easier, thanks to air travel. Politically, a spirit of co-operation between European nations was in the air, as the continent tried to pick itself up after the war. With arguments raging about which countries had the superior club teams, the time was right for Hanot's idea, which he had first mooted in 1934, to be put into action.

There was some disagreement over the competition's size and format, and the basis for qualification. Hanot proposed a 16-team league system, but some clubs and associations thought this would involve too many games. When the plans were finalised at a meeting in Paris in April 1955, a knockout format was chosen, but with a two-legged, home-and-away schedule, with results to be determined by aggregate scores. Matches would be played in midweek, allowing domestic schedules to continue as normal. The qualifying criteria were rather loose at first: 18 teams agreed to take part, not all of whom had yet been confirmed as national champions. At first, the competition was going to be organised by Hanot and his newspaper, *L'Équipe*.

The Union of European Football Associations (UEFA) was founded in Basel in June 1954, after various administrators had mulled over the idea of a pan-European federation for two years. French FA secretary Henri Delaunay, one of the driving forces behind the launch of the World Cup, was also a key figure in the birth of UEFA, and became its first general secretary. A month after Hanot had announced his plans for the new competition, UEFA agreed to manage it. It would be known as the European Champion Clubs' Cup, or, more commonly, the European Cup.

The competition was an instant success: it drew large crowds, was profitable, and gave leading clubs a chance to prove themselves on a bigger stage than their national leagues and cups. The first final saw Real Madrid beating Reims 4-3, in a memorable match at the Parc des Princes in Paris. Led by legendary Argentine-born forward Alfredo Di Stéfano, who would be joined by Puskás in 1958, Real won the European Cup the first five times it was staged, ending with a 7-3 win over Eintracht Frankfurt in 1960, often cited as one of the best matches in the game's history.

Around the same time, a series of friendlies between clubs from European cities that had staged trade fairs led to the Inter-Cities Fairs Cup, launched in 1955. At first, the tournament was spread over three seasons, and featured some teams that represented entire cities, rather than regular clubs. Barcelona eventually became its first winners in 1958, beating a combined London XI 8-2 on aggregate in the final. The Fairs Cup evolved into a single-season competition, with qualification based on league positions. UEFA took control of it in 1971, renaming it as the UEFA Cup, and it became established as a lesser alternative to the European Cup.

In 1954, Henri Delaunay suggested another idea to his UEFA colleagues, having already proposed it to FIFA back in 1927: a tournament for Europe's national teams. As with the European Cup, *L'Équipe* also helped to push the idea forward. Delaunay died the following year, but his idea came to fruition in 1958 as the European Nations Cup, later renamed as the European Championship. It originally featured two knockout rounds, spread over two years, followed by a four-team final tournament in France in the summer of 1960, but its format would gradually come to resemble that of the World Cup.

UEFA launched yet another European club competition in 1960 – the European Cup Winners' Cup, for winners of domestic cup competitions. By now, the lure of European football was becoming an extra incentive for clubs to achieve domestic success.

The European Cup inspired the launch of a similar competition in South America. After an unofficial, one-off South American Club Championship had been staged in 1948, the permanent Copa Libertadores was established in 1960. The champions of seven countries took part, on a knockout basis, with Uruguay's Peñarol becoming the first winners. A group format was used for the first stage in 1962; four years later, it was expanded to include other leading clubs, as well as national champions.

Béla Guttmann, one of the Hungarian pioneers of the 4-2-4 system, moved to Brazil in 1957, briefly serving as São Paulo's coach. His ideas soon caught on, and by the time Brazil appeared at the 1958 World Cup in Sweden, they were lining up Hungarian-style. Among their forwards was a 17-year-old prodigy named Pelé, known for his pace and phenomenal passing, dribbling and heading skills. With other outstanding players such as Didi, Vavá and Garrincha, Brazil attacked relentlessly and with great flair; but they were also highly trained and disciplined by coach Vicente Feola.

It was the first World Cup to be televised internationally. Soccer's premier tournament was turning from a travelling circus into a global spectacle, with the Brazilians, and particularly Pelé, the centre of attention. They beat the hosts 5-2 in the final, becoming world champions for the first time, and the first team to win the tournament outside their own continent.

In the late 1950s and early 1960s, flowing, skilful football was threatening to run riot. Brazil were not alone: like-minded club teams such as Real Madrid and Benfica (the latter coached by Guttmann from 1959 to 1962) were playing in a similar style in domestic and European competitions, and with great success. Some coaches, without such great talent at their disposal, decided to do something about this. A defensive mindset began to emerge, typified by *catenaccio* (meaning 'door-bolt'), a system that became widespread in Italy in the early 1960s.

Catenaccio's roots can be traced back to the work of Karl Rappan, a Swiss-based Austrian coach. His *verrou* (chain) system, which he employed with Servette and the Swiss national side from the early 1930s, was based on the WM formation – but with one of the half-backs often moving behind the centre-half to act as a 'security bolt', giving extra protection to the defence and goalkeeper. Italian coach Nereo Rocco adopted a similar idea at Triestina in the late 1940s and early 1950s, mostly using a 1-3-3-3 line-up, and later introduced it at Padova. Both clubs achieved remarkable results with players of moderate ability.

The man at the rear of a catenaccio system became known as the *libero*, or sweeper. His role was to collect loose balls behind the defence, and, when necessary, help them to cover the opposition's main striker. The idea was to frustrate opponents by stifling their attacking play, while looking for chances to score on the counter-attack. Fitness was crucial, as some players had to switch between defensive and attacking roles as the play dictated.

Rocco's success was noticed by AC Milan, who hired him in 1961. A year earlier, local rivals Inter had appointed Argentine-born coach Helenio Herrera, who would become more closely associated with catenaccio than anyone else (he later claimed to have invented it himself, as a player in France in the 1940s). Inter became Italian champions in 1962–63, conceding just 20 goals in their 34 games, and won two more domestic titles and two European Cups in the next three seasons.

Catenaccio could be seen as part of a wider trend that swept football, particularly in Italy, in the 1960s: a win-at-all-costs, or perhaps avoid-defeat-at-all-costs, mentality, where the game's more appealing aspects took a back seat. There was also the (alleged) practice of tactical fouling, intended to break up the flow of the opposition's attacks, and perhaps to 'take out' key players by injuring them.

AC Milan's 1964 European Cup final victory, for example, was made easier when Benfica midfielder Mario Coluna was left hobbling after a robust challenge from Gino Pivatelli. Substitutions were not yet allowed, but this was about to change: the Football League in England first allowed them in 1965–66, initially only for injuries, and only one per team. The idea gradually found acceptance worldwide over the next few years.

Systematic fouling went hand-in-hand with bribing referees, a tactic that Inter were accused of using, or trying to use, in three consecutive European Cup semi-finals. In 1963–64, Yugoslav referee Branko Tesanic turned a blind eye to a string of brutal tackles by Inter's Luis Suarez in their home leg against Borussia Dortmund; Tesanic later reportedly told a fellow holidaymaker that Inter had paid for his trip. The next year, suspicious refereeing helped them to a 6-1 aggregate win over Liverpool. Both times, Inter went on to win the trophy. A year later, Hungarian referee Gyorgy Vadas claimed that a 'fixer', working on Inter's behalf, had tried to persuade him to favour them in their encounter with Real Madrid. He refused, and Inter lost 2-1 on aggregate.

The trend towards defensive, violent football made its mark on the World Cup. The 1962 tournament was probably less memorable than any previous ones, perhaps best remembered for the infamous 'Battle of Santiago' between Italy and hosts Chile. Brazil retained the trophy, despite Pelé missing most of the competition through injury.

Four years later in England, Pelé's presence was cut short again, thanks to his being kicked relentlessly by Bulgarian and Portuguese defenders. England were criticised for their 4-4-2 formation, with a defensive midfielder in Nobby Stiles, and no orthodox wingers. But when they became champions in the final at Wembley, the accusations of dourness were largely swept aside amid the euphoria, and manager Alf Ramsey was suddenly showered with praise for his pragmatism. In the next few years, many English clubs followed the national team's lead, switching to a 4-4-2 or 4-3-3 line-up, often featuring a 'hard man' in defence or midfield.

The art of wing play was not dead just yet, though. Manchester United winger George Best dazzled English fans, while Jimmy Johnstone became a folk hero at Celtic, who beat Inter Milan in the 1967 European Cup final with an overwhelming display of attacking football, sometimes cited as a fatal blow to catenaccio. Looking back 40 years later, Inter's Sandro Mazzola told *Scotland on Sunday*:

> *No British team ever played like that against us. They*
> *were relentless and we could do nothing to stop them ...*
> *A great Celtic team had brought things to an end.*

Earlier that season, a new force in European football had announced itself on a foggy night in Amsterdam. Ajax stunned Liverpool with a 5-1 win in the first leg of a second-round European Cup tie, before drawing 2-2 in the return leg. Wingers played an important role in their system, with Piet Keizer on the left and Sjaak Swart on the right. Between them was a skinny 19-year-old who was raising eyebrows with his speed, skill and footballing instincts: Johan Cruyff.

Dutch football had only just taken its first steps into full professionalism, having been amateur until 1954, and only semi-professional until the mid 1960s. Ajax were boosted by an injection of money, mainly from local Jewish businessmen who had survived the Nazi occupation. Thanks to this financial backing, Keizer became Holland's first full professional, followed by Cruyff. Ajax also had a hard-nosed, ambitious coach in Rinus Michels, with a strong belief in the virtues of fitness, stamina and mental preparation. They were Dutch champions three times in a row from 1965–66 to 1967–68, and reached the European Cup final in 1969, losing to AC Milan.

Around this time, a term was coined to describe Ajax's style: *total football*. With the increasingly influential Cruyff as their focal point, players swapped positions continually throughout the game, passing the ball quickly and moving into open space. In his book *Brilliant Orange*,

David Winner suggests that the idea was based on a very Dutch concept of manipulating and using 'flexible space' (a useful knack when living in a small, flood-prone country): 'Total football was, among other things, a conceptual revolution based on the idea that the size of any football field was flexible and could be altered by a team playing on it.' When they had possession, Ajax moved the ball into spaces that they could exploit. When they did not, they tried to compress the space available to their opponents.

All this position-swapping, together with quick passing, was not entirely new, having been practised to some extent by Austria and Schalke 04 in the 1930s, and later by Hungary. Michels' tactical thinking was influenced by Jack Reynolds, an Englishman who coached Ajax at various times between 1915 and 1947, with Michels in the team during his last spell. But this Ajax team took the idea a stage further, with all the outfield players comfortably playing anywhere on the pitch.

Ajax were European champions three times in a row, starting in 1970–71. Their 2-0 win over Inter Milan in Rotterdam in 1972 was possibly the peak of total football, and – if it was not dead and buried already – the final nail in catenaccio's coffin. New stars such as Arie Haan, Ruud Krol and Johan Neeskens emerged during these years, while Cruyff remained as the kingpin.

However, things were already starting to fall apart. Michels had left for Barcelona in 1971. His replacement, Stefan Kovacs, had a looser management style, which is thought to have led to a breakdown in discipline. Kovacs left in 1973, and Cruyff joined Michels at Barcelona in August that year, shocked after his teammates (many of whom resented his fame and influence) had chosen Piet Keizer as captain, in an election arranged by new coach Georg Knobel. More acrimony and departures followed over the next few years, and Ajax's glory days were over. Total football, though, also appeared in the World Cup, but not before a more familiar team had reclaimed their crown in spectacular style.

After the mediocrity of 1962 and 1966, the World Cup burst back to life in Mexico in 1970, the first time it was televised in colour. Superlatives usually abound when this tournament is recalled: it arguably had international football's best-ever match (the Italy v West Germany semi-final), best save (England's Gordon Banks, from Pelé), one of the best goals (Carlos Alberto, for Brazil in the final against Italy), and its best-ever team, the Brazilians.

Pelé had announced his retirement from the World Cup after his rough treatment in 1966, but was persuaded to change his mind. With the likes of Gerson, Tostão, Jairzinho and Carlos Alberto joining him, Brazil rediscovered the attacking flair that had made such an impression in 1958, and won their third world title with a string of dazzling performances. For many, it was confirmation of Pelé's status as the best player the game had seen. Tarcisio Burgnich, who marked him in the final, said, 'I told myself before the game, he's made of skin and bones just like everyone else. But I was wrong.'

Brazil were a very different, more defensive team when they went to West Germany to defend their title four years later. Most of the attacking talent from 1970, including the retired Pelé, was missing. They finished in third place, but scored only six goals (three of them against whipping-boys Zaire) in seven games. Instead, it was the Dutch who really caught the eye, and not just because of their startlingly orange shirts. Cruyff was their captain, accompanied by former Ajax teammates such as Neeskens, Krol and Haan, and a strong Feyenoord contingent led by Wim van Hanegem.

Michels, still with Barcelona, had become the national coach a few months earlier. It was Holland's first appearance in the finals since 1938, but, with their total football in full swing, they were the tournament's main attraction. After sweeping Argentina and Brazil aside in the second group stage, the Dutch came unstuck in the final against the hosts.

West Germany had finally established a national league, the Bundesliga, just 11 years earlier. Bayern Munich had become a major force by the late 1960s, led by midfielder-turned-sweeper Franz Beckenbauer, who went on to lead the national team to the European title in 1972. Beckenbauer re-invented the *libero* position, becoming a roaming sweeper with free rein to move forward and act as a playmaker.

Against the Dutch in the 1974 final in Munich, German defender Berti Vogts followed Cruyff all over the pitch, and largely nullified him. After taking an early 1-0 lead, Holland failed to control the game, and were beaten 2-1. Holland's total football had lit up the tournament, but failed at the final hurdle. Their 1976 European Championship campaign was derailed by divisions in the squad, a recurring theme ever since. They reached the World Cup final again two years later, minus Cruyff, but lost to hosts Argentina. Dutch football was in decline, and would not recover until a new generation of talent emerged a decade later.

Hooliganism became a serious blot on football's landscape in the 1970s, particularly in England. It was not an entirely new phenomenon: Newcastle and Sunderland fans, for example, rioted on the pitch at a match in 1901 (there had even been riots at cricket matches in the 18th century). But the modern, pre-meditated violence arrived in the 1950s, with fans causing mayhem on 'football special' trains. By the early 1970s, it had developed into a form of territorial gang warfare. Soon after Manchester United supporters invaded their home pitch when their team were relegated in 1974, high fences started appearing in front of terraces around the country.

The problem was exported to the continent, with Tottenham Hotspur and Leeds United fans rioting at European finals in 1974 and 1975. England's national side attracted a violent following, which became notorious around Europe in the early 1980s. Around this time, home-grown hooligans started springing up in countries such as France, Italy, West Germany and Spain. In these countries, and in England, far-right political groups saw football crowds as a fertile recruiting ground, and the violence and chanting often had a racist or neo-Nazi element.

Safety in stadiums was another problem. Glasgow's Ibrox Park saw its second disaster in 1971, as 66 fans died in a stairway crush. Many grounds were in a poor state, having barely been improved since being built nearly a century earlier, and crowd control was sorely lacking. The twin threats of violence and unsafe stadiums led to a string of further disasters in the 1980s and early 1990s.

A wooden stand caught fire at Bradford City's ground in May 1985, killing 56 spectators. Later that month, at the European Cup final, violent surges by Liverpool fans caused a wall to collapse in the decaying Heysel Stadium in Brussels, leaving 39 dead, mostly Juventus supporters.

The Heysel disaster was the first time that violence at a football ground had resulted in a large death toll, and it sent shock waves around the game. English clubs had been dominating the European Cup, winning it seven times in the eight previous years, with Liverpool themselves as the champions on four of those occasions.

But this all came to a halt, as UEFA reacted to the events in Brussels by banning all English clubs from European competitions indefinitely (the ban was lifted after five years, or six in Liverpool's case). The country that had brought soccer to the world was becoming an outcast in the global game. In England itself, the game was now inextricably linked with fan violence in many people's minds, and prime minister Margaret Thatcher threatened to enforce an identity card scheme for supporters.

In April 1989, as English football struggled to pick itself up off the floor, tragedy struck again. At an FA Cup semi-final at Sheffield's Hillsborough stadium, 95 people were crushed to death in an overcrowded terraced area occupied by Liverpool fans. There were similar disasters on the continent during this period. In Greece, in 1981, 21 Olympiakos fans died in a crush while leaving the club's Karaiskaki Stadium. At least 66 Spartak Moscow supporters died at Moscow's Luzhniki Stadium the following year, in a crush on a stairway during a UEFA Cup tie – but the Soviet media were told to downplay the tragedy, and the actual toll may have been around 350. In May 1992, a temporary stand collapsed during a French cup tie at Bastia's stadium in Corsica, killing 17 and injuring nearly 2,000.

The responses of the British authorities to the Hillsborough disaster saw a change of tone from the previous few years. Football fans were no longer treated as a threat to society. Instead, their human face was finally noticed, as politicians and the media turned their attention to the poor state of stadiums, and began demanding better treatment for supporters. Lord Justice Taylor's inquiry into Hillsborough ended with recommendations that clubs should make their stadiums all-seater, and that the proposed identity card scheme be scrapped. With Thatcher now replaced by the more football-friendly John Major, the government even offered to help with ground improvements.

As stadiums became all-seater, the atmosphere changed. Going to a match generally became a quieter, calmer experience than it had been before. Some have said that this is why hooliganism became a rarer sight in England; in truth, it had already gone into a sharp decline after the Heysel disaster. Meanwhile, fan violence still plagues the game in some other corners of the world, often involving highly-organised *ultra* groups, some of them reportedly not only tolerated, but even encouraged, by the clubs they follow.

Hooliganism and disasters were not the only reasons why attendances generally declined in the 1980s. Although catenaccio was a thing of the past, defensive formations, and various dubious ways of getting results, were still being used. The group stage of the 1982 World Cup in Spain saw a dire mix of negativity and apparent match-fixing, as West Germany and Austria cooked up a suspiciously tame 1-0 win for the Germans, taking both teams into the next round at the expense of Algeria on goal difference. In the semi-finals, West Germany's image was hardly helped by goalkeeper Harald Schumacher's unpunished aerial assault on France's Patrick Battiston.

The European Cup finals of 1986 and 1991 were both lifeless 0-0 draws, where the eventual winners, Steaua Bucharest and Red Star Belgrade, showed little interest in scoring goals. Instead, the plan seemed to be to hold out for a penalty shoot-out (a device that had started creeping into the game in the early 1970s), which they did successfully.

Still, there were bright spots among all the gloom. Italy won the 1982 World Cup with a more appealing brand of football than they had played for some time (if ever), coached by the attack-minded Enzo Bearzot. France, led by Michel Platini, were an attractive team to watch in the early and mid 1980s, as were Brazil, reborn as an attacking force with the likes of Zico, Socrates and Falcão. Diego Maradona brilliantly led Argentina to the 1986 world title, before his career descended into chaos.

But, after a dour World Cup in Italy in 1990, FIFA decided it was time for change. The next tournament was to be held in the United States, where it would have a hard task in winning over a sceptical public. In an attempt to reduce time-wasting and speed up the flow of the game, a rule was introduced in 1992 to prevent goalkeepers handling back-passes. To encourage teams to try to win matches, rather than avoid losing, it became customary to award three points for a win instead of two – a change that had been made in England in 1981, but had taken some time to catch on around the world.

Meanwhile, the commercial side of soccer, particularly its relationship with television, was becoming ever more influential. By the late 1980s, TV companies were finding the game to be highly lucrative, and wanted to show more of it. At the same time, the governing bodies and larger clubs were demanding more money for TV rights, knowing how valuable the coverage was to the broadcasters.

A huge financial offer from Sky TV led to the creation in 1992 of England's Premier League – essentially the old First Division under new management, but separate from the Football League, and with TV revenues no longer trickling down to the lower tiers. Similar deals were struck by the Canal Plus broadcaster in France, and Premiere in Germany.

Some European clubs were owned by media tycoons, notably AC Milan's Silvio Berlusconi,, and money-spinning TV deals held an obvious attraction for them. Berlusconi and co. were far from happy with the format of the European Cup. Its knockout system put their teams at risk of early elimination; while some big clubs missed out altogether, as only one team from each country could enter.

Fears of a breakaway European league led UEFA to introduce a group stage in the European Cup in 1991. This came *after* two knockout rounds, but the format was changed over the next few years, guaranteeing more games for seeded clubs, and also gradually allowing the stronger nations to enter more teams. (By the time the competition had been opened up to non-champions, it had been renamed as the Champions League; the name was kept, even though it no longer made sense.)

The huge sums of money collected by Champions League entrants have widened the wealth gaps between them and their domestic rivals, helping to perpetuate an almost elite group of clubs in each country: a development that many observers find worrying. The G-14 group of powerful clubs (whose membership grew beyond 14, despite its name) was founded in 2000, to lobby for even more changes in the game's structure for their own benefit; but was disbanded in 2008, replaced by the more extensive, UEFA-wide, European Club Association.

For most of the 20th century, soccer was dominated by Europeans and South Americans. In recent decades, though, the rest of the world has begun to join in, particularly Africa, where the game's early progress had been sporadic.

An unofficial North African club championship was first held in 1911–12, becoming official in 1920–21, and Kenya and Uganda competed for the Gossage Trophy in 1924. The game also gained some kind of foothold in the Gold Coast (now Ghana), Nigeria, Senegal and the Ivory Coast in the 1920s and 1930s.

It also caught on in South Africa, especially in Johannesburg's black Soweto district, where the popular Orlando Pirates club was formed in 1937. Like other sports in South Africa, it was racially segregated. Club meetings were sometimes used as a cover for anti-apartheid activity. Along with Egypt, Ethiopia and Sudan, South Africa was initially set to enter the first African Nations Cup in 1957, and was a founder member of the Confederation of African Football (CAF) that year. But it had *four* football associations, each for a different racial group. After it became clear that it would not send a mixed-race team to the African Nations Cup, it was expelled from the tournament, and later from the CAF.

The all-white Football Association of South Africa (formed in 1892) joined FIFA in 1958, but was suspended four years later, and finally thrown out in 1976, after protests from other members. In the mid 1970s, though, some white players defied the system by joining black clubs in Soweto. Mixed-race football soon began to find more acceptance, long before apartheid ended.

North African countries, helped by their strong economies, had the upper hand for some time. Egypt reached the World Cup finals as early as 1934, although they only had to beat a newly-formed Palestine team over two legs to get there. When Africa first got a guaranteed berth in 1970, it went to Morocco. By this time, some African-born players had made a mark in Europe. Benfica recruited players from the Portuguese colonies of Angola and Mozambique in the 1950s and 1960s, including the great Eusebio, and many of them went on to play for Portugal.

Zaire were the first sub-Saharan African team to appear in the World Cup finals, in 1974; but were hopelessly out of their depth, scoring no goals and conceding 14 in their three games, including a 9-0 mauling by Yugoslavia. Although they showed some ability on the ball, their defensive and tactical failings reinforced a stereotyped European view of African players: that they did not have enough discipline, or understanding of the game, to make the most of their athleticism and skill.

Eight years later, though, Cameroon hit back at these criticisms with a creditable performance in Spain. They were knocked out in the first round, but without losing a game. One of their three draws came against eventual winners Italy, who qualified ahead of them on the basis of goals scored, by a single goal. Africa now had two places in the expanded 24-team format; and Algeria had a genuine grievance after their elimination following the dubious result between West Germany and Austria.

Despite Cameroon's cautious showing in Spain, black African teams were becoming renowned for attacking, entertaining football. They were also more adept at tactical aspects of the game than before. In Simon Kuper's *Football Against the Enemy*, Cameroonian professor Paul Nkwi explains that his countrymen simply learned better methods by watching European games on television.

It was Cameroon themselves, now playing a livelier brand of football, who made Africa's big World Cup breakthrough in 1990. After beating holders Argentina 1-0 in the opening match, they went on to the quarter-finals, where they lost 3-2 to a nervous England side. Nigeria performed impressively at the next two World Cups, as did Senegal in 2002.

The African Nations Cup was becoming a major attraction by now, and European clubs were scouring Africa for talent. The continent gained more recognition in 2004, as South Africa was chosen to host the 2010 World Cup. It has not all been good news, though. African football's progress has been hampered by poor administration and marketing, political interference, and a shortage of money. National teams are often entrusted to European coaches of questionable pedigree, who rarely stay in their jobs for long; while sub-Saharan clubs have no hope of retaining talented players.

Soccer reached the Far East in the late 19th century, as British traders, engineers and teachers set up clubs in such places as Hong Kong, Shanghai and Singapore. The game was also played by European migrants in Japan, and by British soldiers in India. However, it failed to catch on with indigenous people, anywhere in Asia, until the latter half of the 20th century.

The Asian Football Confederation (AFC) was founded at a meeting in Manila in 1954, with 12 countries from across the continent represented. The Asian Cup, for national teams, was first contested two years later, followed in 1967 by the Asian Club Championship. Other club competitions were set up, but were merged with the Asian Club Championship in 2002 to create the AFC Champions League.

The same year, the World Cup was staged in Asia for the first time, jointly hosted by Japan and South Korea. By this time, soccer had become well established in Japan, with the J-League having been founded in 1993, attracting well-known players and coaches from Europe and South America. The World Cup was a huge success in South Korea, with home fans creating spectacular scenes as their team progressed to the semi-finals.

As in Africa, the attention of football fans in Asia is largely focussed on their national teams, rather than clubs. The domestic game in the Far East also suffers from an annual influx of European clubs on money-spinning pre-season tours, often overshadowing the local leagues. In China, despite the huge population and booming economy, the top-level China Super League has been beset by countless problems, and faces a grim outlook.

The AFC accepted a new member in 2006: Australia, whose association left the Oceania Football Confederation (founded in 1966), largely to avoid the tricky intercontinental play-off route that faces the winners of Oceania's World Cup qualifying competition. For many years, soccer suffered from an image problem in Australia. Johnny Warren, national team captain at the 1974 World Cup, summed this up bluntly in the title of his book (brace yourself) *Sheilas, Wogs and Poofters*, reflecting the types of people that many Australians associated with the game. It was largely played and watched by minority ethnic groups, mainly from south-eastern Europe, and was an outsider in a mainstream sports scene dominated by the rugby codes, Australian Rules football, and cricket.

Changes came in the mid 2000s, helping to raise the game's profile in Australia. In 2005, the revamped governing body, Football Federation Australia, replaced the old National Soccer League with the A-League. The new league was marketed aggressively, and attendances in its first few seasons have been healthy. Another boost came from Australia's World Cup performance in 2006, reaching the second round. It could be argued that soccer is now a major sport in Australia – unlike New Zealand, where a major league seems an unlikely prospect in a rugby-mad nation of just four million (however, the A-League includes the Wellington Phoenix, who replaced the Auckland-based New Zealand Knights in 2007).

One of soccer's perennial talking points is the question of why it has never made much headway in the United States. Among the reasons sometimes suggested are the shortage of scoring, a supposed American phobia about drawn games, and even the lack of commercial breaks during each half of a match. None of these theories stand up well to scrutiny. A low-scoring baseball game is routinely hailed as an exciting 'pitching duel'. Nobody seems to have explained why Americans should be more averse to draws than anyone else, and soccer was already struggling in the US before television was invented.

The truth probably lies in events that have unfolded over the last century and a half. As explained in chapter 4, a crude version of soccer was tried, and rejected, by American students in the late 1860s and early 1870s, before they switched to rugby and adapted it into a game of their own. Baseball was already a major, serious sport by this time. Its stop-start nature, with players, managers and spectators pausing to re-assess the situation before each pitch, might well have influenced the form of football that evolved on the college playing fields; while soccer, a more continuous game, did not fit the bill[52].

Later attempts at establishing soccer in the US were plagued by poor management – notably the American League of Professional Foot Ball, created by baseball team owners in 1894, which lasted for barely two weeks. The game flickered into life in various places around the Midwest, especially St Louis, and the northeast, mainly thanks to European migrants in industrial cities. The east coast's American Soccer League, founded in 1921, enjoyed a brief heyday in the late 1920s, when the game was arguably second only to baseball among professional sports. But many team owners were hit hard by the Great Depression, and the league folded in 1933. The game would be almost invisible to Americans for decades afterwards.

The boom in televised sport in the 1960s, along with a growing awareness of overseas events (including the 1966 World Cup final, shown almost in full on the NBC network), tempted some American entrepreneurs to see soccer as a potential pot of gold. The upshot was the North American Soccer League (NASL), another shakily-organised venture, which struggled for years before getting a boost when Pelé joined the New York Cosmos in 1975.

Other stars such as George Best, Franz Beckenbauer and Johan Cruyff followed Pelé's lead. But, by the early 1980s, the NASL was in decline. The dominance of the Cosmos, along with teams starting up, closing down and relocating at a mind-boggling rate, sapped much of the public's interest, and the league fizzled out in 1984.

Still, FIFA seemed keen to exploit the USA's commercial potential. Just a few years after the NASL's demise, the nation was picked to host the 1994 World Cup. The tournament met a hostile reception from much of the American media, but confounded its critics with consistently large attendances.

As part of the negotiations over staging the World Cup, the US Soccer Federation agreed to create a 'Division 1' league, which eventually appeared in 1996 as Major League Soccer (MLS). It was set up with a host of stringent regulations, designed to prevent the instability and competitive imbalance that had plagued the NASL. In these respects, it has succeeded, with most of its original teams still intact in their original cities, and with no team becoming dominant.

MLS attendances have hovered respectably around the 15,000 mark, but the game still has not come close to rivalling American football, baseball or basketball. Even the USA's creditable World Cup performance in 2002, reaching the quarter-finals, made little difference; as has David

Beckham's on-off presence with the LA Galaxy, beyond generating a rash of media attention. Perhaps it is simply too late: other sports already occupy large parts of Americans' lives, and there is not enough 'sport space'[53] available for soccer to make an impact. It has, though, become a hugely popular recreational sport among American children and teenagers.

The story has been similar in Canada, albeit on a smaller scale. The Toronto area has a lively soccer scene, largely made up of European migrants, with teams organised along ethnic lines. MLS expanded north of the border in 2007, with the launch of the well-supported Toronto FC. However, the game still remains a minority interest in Canada as a whole.

Further south, of course, it has a much stronger following. It took some time to develop in Mexico, but that country's league could now be called the strongest in the Americas, with few of its players succumbing to the temptations of Europe. Costa Rica has become another hotbed of the game. In some Central American and Caribbean nations, though, it faces stiff competition from cricket or baseball. CONCACAF, the Confederation of North, Central American and Caribbean Association Football, was formed as the regional governing body in 1961.

Women were playing soccer in England at least as early as 1895, when a North v South match was contested in London under the auspices of the recently-formed British Ladies Football Club. The FA had little time for this kind of thing, and, in 1902, banned member clubs from playing against 'lady teams'. But the women's game had a revival during World War I, when many teams were formed by female factory workers, to raise money for war charities.

The best-known were the Dick Kerr's Ladies, from a Preston munitions factory. Formed in 1917, they drew huge crowds, and their fame continued growing after the war. In 1920, they represented England in the first women's international, against a Paris-based France side. On Boxing Day of that year, a game against St Helens Ladies drew 53,000 to Everton's Goodison Park.

By now, FA officials were even more nervous about women's football. A year later, they forbade female teams from playing on member clubs' grounds. Officially, this was because of allegations that some of the money they had raised had been misused; but the FA also believed the sport was unsuitable for women.

The women's game was badly affected by the ban, and went into decline in England for half a century, with little progress being made elsewhere. It came back to life in the late 1960s and early 1970s, when sex equality became a major issue in social and political life. In England, the

Women's FA was formed in 1969, and launched a knockout tournament (evolving into today's Women's FA Cup) in 1970–71. The FA lifted its ban on women using member clubs' grounds in 1971. Women's leagues, cup competitions and national teams sprang up around the world over the next two decades, with semi-professional players first emerging in Italy in the early 1970s.

In the USA, the seeds for the growth of women's soccer were sown in 1972 with the advent of the Title IX law (as explained in chapter 10, this mandated that schools and colleges should spend money equally on sport for both male and female students). As a result, girls and women found more opportunities to take part in sport, and more resources were dedicated to their training. Even in these enlightened times, American football was generally thought unsuitable for women; instead, many ended up playing soccer. By the 1990s, Title IX had helped to nurture a generation of outstanding female players, who first made their mark by winning the inaugural Women's World Cup in China in 1991.

The women's game had made important strides in other countries by now, such as Norway (world champions in 1995), Sweden, Brazil and China. But its peak to date came in 1999, when the World Cup in the US drew massive crowds – building on the success of the first women's Olympic tournament in Atlanta three years earlier, which had attracted large attendances and TV audiences. More than 90,000 attended the final at the Rose Bowl in Pasadena, near Los Angeles, with the hosts beating China on penalties. For a brief spell, women's soccer was a major talking point in American sport, with players such as Mia Hamm, Julie Foudy and Brandi Chastain becoming household names, while the men's game still struggled for recognition.

It was not to last. After the World Cup euphoria had died down, there was little to sustain the public's interest: no major league, or meaningful internationals. In an attempt to capitalise on the national team's popularity, the world's first all-professional women's league, the Women's United Soccer Association, was created. But when it was launched in the spring of 2001 – surely a year too late – attendances and TV viewing figures were disappointing. The league made crippling financial losses, and was scrapped after its third season. The league was relaunched in 2009, under the banner of Women's Professional Soccer.

A little-known Belgian player, Jean-Marc Bosman, became a household name in the mid 1990s – and not because of anything he achieved on the field. After Bosman's club, RFC Liège, refused to let him leave when his contract ran out, he and his lawyers challenged football's transfer system at the European Court of Justice. In 1995, the court forced UEFA to concede that players were free to move on when their contracts expired. At first, the ruling only applied to cross-border moves within the European Union, but it was soon adopted globally, for both domestic and international transfers. UEFA also had to scrap its limit of three foreign players per team in its club competitions.

The Bosman rule made life difficult for many clubs outside the small European elite, making it harder for them to keep their better players. Clubs now had little incentive to spend money on youth development: Ajax, for example, bred an outstanding crop of young players in the early 1990s, only to see most of them move to richer clubs on free 'Bosman' transfers in the latter half of the decade. A highly-valued player, in the last year or two of his contract, could now demand a new, more lucrative deal, while the club faced the threat of losing him on a free transfer soon afterwards if his demands were not met. As a result, players and their agents had more power in contract talks than ever before.

Another effect of the Bosman decision has been an increasing globalisation of the player market, with players flooding into the major European leagues from the Americas, Africa and Europe's weaker footballing countries. Even some middle-ranking leagues, in regions such as eastern Europe and Scandinavia, became far more cosmopolitan than they were in the mid 1990s.

In earlier times, each domestic league reflected a national or regional football culture. Teams were dominated by native players, were usually run by native coaches, and played in styles similar to those of their respective national teams. But this pattern was diluted by the increasing movement of players and coaches around the globe.

What evolved was a mix-and-match world of tactics, formations and styles, as players and coaches from different footballing cultures tried to work together. All this was exacerbated by the impatience of many club owners and executives, with a revolving-door approach to hiring and firing coaches, along with the prevalence of loan deals and short-term player contracts.

However, the 2007 Copa America suggested that there is still a South American way of playing the game, based on skill, creativity and attacking flair; and that many European-based South American players revert to it when freed from the constraints imposed by their club coaches. The most glaring exceptions (and, perhaps significantly, the tournament winners) were the Brazilians, who relied largely on size, physical power and negating the attacking moves of their opponents. Three years earlier, Greece had also shown that negative tactics could bring success, becoming surprise European champions while showing little talent for anything other than defending and fouling.

Soccer became plagued by a vast range of problems. Fan violence continued to flare up in many countries, sometimes with horrific results. Racism, fascism and sectarianism often arose. Some clubs in the former Yugoslavia, for example, became almost synonymous with ethnic identities, and matches became used as vehicles for displays of hatred. It could be argued that the Celtic–Rangers rivalry does not merely reflect Glasgow's sectarian divide, but also helps to sustain it.

Corruption became another recurring theme, highlighted by match-fixing scandals in Germany, Italy, Poland, the Czech Republic and Brazil in the 2000s. Managers of leading English clubs have been accused of accepting illegal payments in transfer deals, and even FIFA has been the subject of various allegations of wrongdoing. There are also concerns about the ownership of clubs, with many being taken over by billionaire business moguls with dubious or unclear motives. Along with the global marketing strategies adopted by many clubs, this trend is detaching clubs from their roots and traditions.

On the field, there are continual problems with diving, play-acting and weak refereeing. The game is also handicapped by its antiquated timekeeping system, which encourages time-wasting, and leads to arguments about the amount of added time.

Despite all of this, none of soccer's negative aspects have undermined its popularity. Fans' loyalties run deep, and are not easily broken. With sensationalist media coverage so prevalent in many countries, perhaps each controversy or scandal has bolstered the game's profile even further, by giving fans a new talking point. After all, this is a sport that has become a huge part of many people's lives. It has helped to put many countries on the map, especially former European colonies in Latin America and Africa. Mention the name 'Brazil' to anyone on the planet, and football might well be the first thing that springs to mind.

It has even been accused of starting wars, such as the so-called 'Football War' of 1969 involving Honduras and El Salvador, supposedly sparked by a riot at a World Cup qualifier between the two countries. Some have claimed that Yugoslavia's civil war began with the mayhem at a Dynamo Zagreb v Red Star Belgrade game in May 1990 – particularly the moment where Dynamo's Zvonimir Boban kicked a policeman, as the police tried to stop his club's hooligans charging at Red Star fans.

In both cases, the significance of the riots has almost certainly been exaggerated; but these stories illustrate how important the game has become in many people's minds. Football definitely did *stop* a war (temporarily) in 1967, when a two-day truce was called in the Biafran War in Nigeria, to let the troops watch Pelé and his visiting Santos side in action.

The game also thrives at grass-roots level around the world, with vast numbers of children, and amateur adults, playing regularly. Regardless of its trials and tribulations, soccer seems untouchable in its status as the world's game. Nothing else comes close to rivalling it for global popularity, either as a spectator sport or as a recreational one; and this seems unlikely to change.

Chapter 13

Radically Canadian?

'Every six months or so, we are obliged, as a service to our readers, to announce the imminent demise of the Canadian Football League.'
– Ken Fidlin, *Toronto Sun*, January 1996

Mention Canadian football to almost anyone outside North America, and the chances are they will ask: 'What is Canadian football?' It is a good question. Whether it is a sport in its own right, or merely a version of what could be called North American football, is debatable. But it does have its own story, a complex one with many twists, turns and questions of national identity – a little like the history of Canada itself.

As in Australia, British migrants to Canada in the 18th and 19th centuries took their sports and pastimes with them, helping them feel at home in a strange land. Hunting, cockfighting and horse racing were especially popular, particularly in festival celebrations. Early in the 19th century, people began forming organised clubs for winter activities, such as snow-shoe racing and the Scottish game of curling. Around the middle of the century, the indigenous sport of lacrosse thrived in Montreal, while wealthy Englishmen played cricket, and the working classes of southern Ontario took up baseball.

The British elite and military had much to do with the growth of organised sport, nowhere more so than in the booming city of Montreal, where the locally-based army garrison played an important role. Contemporary British notions of amateurism and gentlemanliness helped to shape the city's sporting scene.

Loosely-structured football games are thought to have been played in various parts of Canada before 1861, but it was then that the first recorded match took place, at the University of Toronto. Rugby rules, of a sort, were the order of the day. Little more seems to have happened until the middle of that decade, when British officers from the Montreal garrison began playing against civilian sides, which included students from McGill University. Canada's first rugby football clubs, Montreal and their neighbours Britannia, were formed in 1868.

Rugby made a tentative entry into school life in Ontario, as Dr Egerton Ryerson, the province's superintendent of education – a fan of muscular Christianity and Dr Thomas Arnold's methods at Rugby School – began advocating sport as a way of developing 'physical health and vigour'. It had caught on at secondary and private schools by the late 1860s, although only as an extracurricular activity.

Hamilton, at the western tip of Lake Ontario, joined the action in 1869, with the founding of Hamilton Foot Ball Club. Three years later, clubs sprang up at the University of Toronto and in Quebec City. Toronto's Argonaut Rowing Club formed a rugby team in 1873, wearing dark and light blue, in homage to the university rowers at Oxford and Cambridge. The club lives on, still sporting the same colours, in the shape of the Canadian Football League's Toronto Argonauts, North America's oldest non-collegiate football club. Ottawa Football Club was set up three years later.

As outlined earlier, it was the McGill University team who introduced rugby to their Harvard counterparts in 1874, sowing the seeds for the evolution of American football. Other collegiate teams were formed around this time at Queen's University and the Royal Military College, both in Kingston, Ontario. The University of Toronto went south of the border to take on the University of Michigan in 1879.

The British troops left Montreal in 1872, without having adopted the rules that the RFU had drawn up a year earlier. The football scene in Canada was left to make its own way forward, with little direction or cohesion – a problem that would plague it for decades, as different rules and playing styles evolved in different cities. An early attempt at ending the confusion came in 1873, when a proposal from Montreal led to the birth of the Canadian Football Association. Seven difficult years later, though, it was no more, having failed to unify the game.

Inevitably, with towns such as Toronto and Hamilton lying near the border, American features were starting to rub off on Canadian rugby, although there seems to have been little appetite for a wholesale adoption of the US rules.

In particular, the *open scrimmage*, with the forwards aligned in a single row, replaced the closed scrum. A typical Canadian offensive line-up at the time – still with 15 players, rather than 11 as in the US – had nine forwards in a lateral formation, along with a quarterback, three halfbacks, a fullback, and a 'flying wing' behind one end of the forward line.

Although Ontario and Quebec had their differences, each province had enough internal uniformity for a governing body to be set up. Both the Ontario Rugby Football Union (ORFU) and its namesake in Quebec (the QRFU) were founded in January 1883. Both unions arranged club competitions.

The ORFU devised a points-based scoring system in its first season. Six points were awarded for a drop-kicked field goal; four for a try (as it was still known) or a conversion, penalty kick[54] or free kick; two for a *safety touch* (where a player carried the ball behind his own goal-line and touched it down); and one for a *kick-to-deadline* (kicking the ball through the end zone) or a *touch-in-goal* (a failure to run the ball out of the end zone). The Canadian free kick, now defunct, involved a place kick following a 'fair catch' or 'mark'. The Quebec union stuck with a goals-based system at first, but copied Ontario's points scheme in 1884.

Early that year, in another attempt at unification, delegates from both unions met to form the Canadian Rugby Football Union (CRFU). At a meeting in July, the new union tried to come up with a standard set of rules, based on a mix of the Ontario rules (which the ORFU had declared a success at its first annual meeting, also getting a thumbs-up from McGill University) and the latest RFU laws from England.

They considered the American practice of heeling the ball backwards from the scrimmage, rather than kicking it forwards in the traditional rugby manner, but felt that this would be too radical a departure from British rugby (although heeling the ball out of a scrum was finding some acceptance in Britain around this time). A set of compromise rules was agreed, including Ontario's points system.

Some of the more conservative delegates complained that the provincial championships had led players to follow the letter, rather than the spirit, of the law. Still, a national championship, of sorts, was launched that year, with the Ontario and Quebec champions facing each other. Montreal FC were the first winners, trouncing the Toronto Argonauts by 30 points to nil.

Soon, though, there were more arguments about the rules. The ORFU preferred to allow the centre (who lined up in the middle of the forward line, and restarted play after each tackle) to restart play by heeling the ball backwards, while being held in place by two or more teammates known as *scrim-supports*, helping him to fend off onrushing opponents. Some Quebec clubs, though, insisted on the ball being kicked forwards. The CRFU refused to allow heeling, a decision that prompted the ORFU to withdraw from it in 1887. The CRFU had lost its reason to exist, and was soon dissolved.

The subsequent years saw a flurry of minor rule changes in both Ontario and Quebec, often involving their scoring systems. A full account of these tweakings would be a little excessive for these pages; suffice it to say that the overall trend, as in rugby and American football, was for tries or touchdowns to be worth more points than before, and for kicked goals to be worth fewer.

Harmony prevailed yet again in December 1891, as representatives of both unions formed the Canadian Rugby Union (CRU). It drew up a set of rules, mainly based on those used in Ontario, including heeling the ball back from the scrimmage. The scoring system included another long-lost Canadian oddity, the *flying kick*, where the quarterback threw the ball back towards the feet of a teammate, who would kick for goal as it bounced. The CRU held its first championship game the following year, with Osgoode College of Toronto beating Montreal FC at Rosedale Field, Toronto.

The creeping Americanisation continued in 1897, when the CRU adopted a downs-and-yardage system. A team could only keep possession if it advanced the ball at least five yards, or was forced back at least 20 yards, in three downs. However, the game in Canada was still relatively simple, compared with that south of the border, with no coaches, no play signals and little in the way of practice.

It was also pretty rough, as highlighted by an 1897 clash between Ottawa City (aka Ottawa AAA) and Ottawa College. In a game littered with flying fists and boots, an Ottawa City wingman by the name of Walters was sent off the field for kicking an opponent as he lay on the ground after a fight. He duly punched the referee, and asked another official to reinstate him; when he refused, Walters punched and kicked the official and ran away, never to be seen again. It was one of many violent scenes involving Ottawa City, who were soon suspended from the QRFU.

Although most of Canadian football's main action in the late 19th century took place in Ontario and Quebec, things also began to stir in the interior west, thanks largely to players migrating westwards and taking the game with them. Winnipeg Football Club was formed in 1879; nine years later, it was a founding member of the Manitoba Rugby League, which gained honorary membership of the CRU in 1892, by which time it had been renamed as the Manitoba Rugby Union.

The first known match in Alberta was played in 1890, between Edmonton and Clover Bar. Its first championship was decided a year later, with Edmonton beating Calgary 6-5 on aggregate over two games. Clubs in Alberta and Manitoba, though, had little contact with those in Ontario and Quebec, and often played against sides from neighbouring US states. As a result, American football had more influence in the interior western provinces than in the east. Further west, though, rugby union would be British Columbia's main football code for decades to come.

By the late 1890s, although there was finally some consistency in the playing rules, trouble was brewing over questions of amateurism and ethics. 'City' clubs were often accused of paying players in the form of gifts or bogus jobs, and of being overly competitive. On the other side of the fence were the university teams, where the Victorian British ideals of amateurism and muscular Christianity were still much in evidence.

Then again, not all of the collegiate teams appear to have been spotless. Some allegedly fielded 'ringers', including Queen's University, whose senate ruled in 1897 that only genuine students could play in the varsity team. The issue led to the birth of the Canadian Intercollegiate Rugby Football Union (CIRFU) that year, with Queen's, McGill and the University of Toronto as its senior members. The previous year, the CRU had declared that all players – in both city and collegiate teams – must be amateur, a stance that the ORFU backed up in 1901 by insisting on all its players signing amateur 'cards'.

The CIRFU launched its own competition in 1898, with teams contesting the Yates Cup, named after Dr H.B. Yates of McGill. It was a sign that the city and university teams were growing apart, as the former began drawing large crowds and became more business-oriented. It would, however, be decades before they stopped playing against each other. A governing body for university sport, the Canadian Intercollegiate Athletic Union, was born in 1906 (its name would later be prefixed with the word 'Central'). A year later, another multi-sport institution, the Canadian Amateur Athletic Union, expelled the Toronto Argonauts and Montreal AAA for breaching its amateur code.

After a brief period of calm, the playing rules once again became a contentious topic around the turn of the century. At the centre of the storm were the *Burnside Rules*, drawn up in 1898 by University of Toronto captain J.T.M. 'Thrift' Burnside. Under his American-influenced scheme, designed to make for a more open game, teams would be reduced from 15 men to 12, with six at the line of scrimmage at the start of each down. The ball would be snapped, rather than heeled, into play (in other words, the centre would throw it backwards between his legs). The five-yards, three-downs rule would be kept, and the line-out would be replaced by a restart from scrimmage.

Burnside's proposed rules were largely ignored until 1903, when they were adopted by the ORFU, with one alteration: to keep possession, a team would need to gain ten yards, not five, in three downs[55]. Two years later, the QRFU, CRU and CIRFU considered the Burnside Rules, but declined to accept them in full; although they did introduce some, or variations of them, around this time. The QRFU and CRU reduced teams to 12 players. The CIRFU adopted a ten-yards, three-downs rule; but the CRU came up with a slightly different idea: a team could keep the ball by carrying it five yards past the line of scrimmage, or by kicking it forwards, on the *third down*.

Points systems were frequently altered during these uncertain years, with all of the unions increasing the value of a try from four points to five. In 1905, with relations between the unions looking fragile, half of the CRU's championship game was played under QRFU rules, and the other half under those of the CIRFU.

As the major city clubs became ever more popular, they lost their appetite for facing lowlier opponents, preferring to play against each other in front of large crowds. The Toronto Argonauts and Montreal AAA were also stung by their expulsion from the Canadian Amateur Athletic Union. In 1907, along with the Hamilton Tigers and Ottawa Rough Riders (a reincarnation of the banned Ottawa City), they withdrew from their provincial unions and formed the Interprovincial Rugby Football Union (IRFU), often known as the Big Four, while staying under the CRU's umbrella. The QRFU, shorn of its leading teams, dropped out of top-level football.

The CRU adopted the CIRFU's ten-yards, three-downs rule in 1907, as did the IRFU and ORFU soon afterwards, finally bringing some lasting cohesion to the game across Quebec and Ontario. Other than some minor variations used by the CIRFU, the rules followed by the various unions were now fairly consistent. Tactics and strategies were evolving quickly: signals had first been used in 1898, and an American, Tom 'King' Clancy, pioneered the role of a coach in Canadian football, after taking the reins at Ottawa College in 1902.

In 1909, Lord Earl Grey, Canada's Governor General, offered to donate a trophy to the CRU, to be awarded to the nation's champion 'amateur' rugby[56] team – following an example set by a predecessor, Lord Stanley of Preston, donor of ice hockey's hallowed Stanley Cup[57].

At first, the route to the Grey Cup game was a simple knockout tournament. The University of Toronto were the first winners, defeating Parkdale Canoe Club in front of a modest 3,807 attendance at Toronto's Rosedale field in December that year. Adding to the sense that the Grey Cup[58] was not a major event just yet, the trophy was not actually made until the following spring.

A year later in Hamilton, though, an official crowd of 12,000 – plus many others who forced their way in – saw the holders retain the Cup against the Hamilton Tigers. The national press took a keen interest this time, and the Grey Cup was on its way to becoming Canada's biggest annual sporting occasion. By now, although ice hockey was the nation's best-loved sport, Canadian football had a strong following in Toronto, Montreal, Hamilton and Winnipeg; while it had made little impact on the west coast, in the eastern Maritime region, or among French speakers in Quebec.

The Grey Cup was claimed by the University of Toronto yet again in 1911. Much of the credit for their success went to 'honorary coach' Harry Griffiths, and to the powerful running of Smirle Lawson, nicknamed the 'Big Train'. Like some of his rugby league contemporaries, Lawson was known to hurdle over tacklers while carrying the ball.

In contrast with American colleges, though, those in Canada saw football as secondary to academic studies. McGill University, who had improved strongly after hiring another American coach, Frank 'Shag' Shaughnessy, in 1912, pulled out of the Grey Cup that year because of exam commitments. They did so again a year later, in protest at alleged professionalism among the Big Four clubs.

The 1914 Grey Cup was the last before the First World War, although non-collegiate football continued play in 1915 before shutting down. Some football was resumed in 1919, but with a general air of apathy that kept the Grey Cup on hold until the following year. Still, the first post-war Grey Cup drew a respectable crowd of over 10,000 in Toronto, for an all-local clash between the university side and the Argonauts, as interest in the game started to build up again.

The Cup had been exclusive to Ontario and Quebec teams so far, but that was all about to change. The game had been developing steadily in the western prairie lands: not only in Manitoba and Alberta, but now also in Saskatchewan, where clubs in Moose Jaw, Regina and Saskatoon formed a union in 1910. The Alberta Football Union was founded a year later, as was the Western Canada Rugby Football Union (WCRFU), an alliance of the Alberta, Manitoba and Saskatchewan unions, which soon became an associate member of the CRU.

The Hamilton Tigers toured the west in 1913, helping to whip up enthusiasm for the game. Western universities began fielding teams: Alberta in 1910, Saskatchewan in 1914, and Manitoba in 1920. British Columbia eventually followed suit in 1924. After being rebuffed several times, the WCRFU was granted full membership of the CRU in 1921, and its teams became eligible to compete for the Grey Cup.

That year also saw yet another spate of rule changes. The CRU embraced the Burnside rules, almost in their entirety, 23 years after they were devised. Teams still consisted of 12 players, with free substitution allowed – although, with a maximum of 18 players per squad, the 'two-platoon' system that would emerge in the US in the 1940s was not yet possible. The ball had to be snapped back from the scrimmage by hand, rather than heeled, and at least five players had to be positioned at the line of scrimmage.

Hamilton went on another western tour that year, as roving ambassadors of the CRU's new brand of football. The western teams, though, having played often against opponents from across the border, already preferred a more American style of play than the one seen in the major cities of Ontario and Quebec (although, in some Ontario towns near the US border, such as Windsor and Sault Ste. Marie, full-blown American rules were the norm).

The 1921 Grey Cup, the first east-v-west encounter, saw a clash of styles. The Edmonton Eskimos, whose coach Deacon White had introduced a US-influenced 'T' formation, had a strategy based around short gains, with the quarterback usually handing the ball off to a running back, who would then try to find a way through the scrimmage. The Toronto Argonauts, on the other hand, used a lop-sided *single-wing* offence, and would often string passes together, rugby-style. The Argonauts were helped to victory by the efforts of the latest 'Big Train', Lionel Conacher, scorer of 15 of their 23 unanswered points that day. Conacher also starred at baseball, ice hockey and lacrosse, earning comparisons with Jim Thorpe.

The 1920s saw some rapid progress in coaching. Bill Hughes, at Queen's University, was the first coach to use film in his research, while McGill's Frank Shaughnessy imported American concepts such as the huddle and the 'training table' (laying on food for players after practice). With the help of professional coaches and dubious recruitment methods, university teams enjoyed great success either side of World War I, culminating in Queen's winning three Grey Cups in a row from 1922 to 1924. But, as the game became increasingly professionalised, it outgrew the university sides, and the city clubs began to get the upper hand.

Meanwhile, western teams struggled in the Grey Cup for many years after entering the picture in 1921, and sometimes did not make it to the big game at all – either because of the costs and loss of wages that it would entail (the venue was always in Ontario or Quebec) or even, in the case of the Winnipeg Victorias in 1924, thanks to a quarrel over which train service to use.

The 1921 rule changes brought the game closer to American football, distancing it further from rugby union. It still lacked two major American features: blocking and forward passing. Shaughnessy advocated the latter as early as 1921, arguing that it would open up the game; but the CRU was not quite ready for such a radical change.

By the autumn of 1929, though, the economic depression was forcing the CRU to contemplate ways of revitalising the game, in the hope of drawing larger crowds. It tentatively introduced forward passing that year, initially just at collegiate, junior and school levels, but then took the bolder step of allowing it in the Grey Cup game. Western unions (including the Western Intercollegiate Rugby Football Union, formed in 1927), always more open to Americanisms than those to the east, welcomed the forward pass. The following year, though, the CRU forbade it in the Grey Cup, on the grounds that it had not been used in the east that year.

The CIRFU approved forward passing in 1931, and the CRU soon permitted it in all leagues under its umbrella. As in the US, it came with tight restrictions, which would later be loosened. A forward pass could only be thrown from at least five yards behind the line of scrimmage, and not from within 25 yards of the opponents' goal-line. It was prohibited on the third down; and players in certain positions were ineligible to receive passes. The size and shape of the ball were soon altered to make passing easier; as a result, drop-kicking became trickier, and fell out of favour.

Montreal AAA won the 1931 Grey Cup, anchored by quarterback Warren Stevens, an American whom Frank Shaughnessy had recently hired to coach his McGill University players in the use of the forward pass. It was a sign of things to come, as American players began flocking north of the border, joining clubs that coveted their skills and expertise in forward passing and the various manoeuvres that came with it.

While some Canadians welcomed the forward pass as a way of making football more varied and exciting, it dismayed many traditionalists, especially as Montreal AAA used it extensively – rather than as a surprise tactic or a last resort – in their successful 1931 season. Some equated forward passing with professionalism, believing that it made the game too complex for genuine amateurs; there was also resentment over the American influx. A writer in the *Herald* of Hamilton seemed particularly bitter:

> *When the Canadian Rugby Football Union turned Yankee and accepted the forward pass into the Canadian game, it was the intention of that governing body that the pass be learned by Canadians and developed in this country without the aid of exponents of it from across the border.*

Two years later, an ominous note was sounded in the *Toronto Globe*: 'Before long, there may be no more Canadian football ... it is high time for a showdown.' The American invasion was the final straw for the university teams. The CIRFU withdrew from the CRU (and, consequently, from Grey Cup contention) in 1934, citing objections to the hiring of US professionals by city clubs, and the pressure of exams.

Western clubs were quick to make good use of American players. The Winnipeg 'Pegs (formed in 1930 as an amalgamation of the city's clubs, with the uninspired name of the Winnipeg Winnipegs) were the first western Grey Cup winners, in 1935, with nine Americans in the squad that beat Hamilton. A year later, as the Winnipeg Blue Bombers, they were founder members of the Western Interprovincial Football Union (WIFU) – superseding the WCRFU – along with the Calgary Bronks and Regina Roughriders.

Winnipeg's success fuelled anger over the marginalisation of Canadian players. The CRU responded in 1936, limiting 'imports' to five per team. Americans could only play in the Grey Cup if they had lived in Canada for at least a year. This was just one of many issues that drove a wedge between east and west, a divide that was not limited to football.

Western Canadians often resented the dominance of Ontario and Quebec in running the nation's affairs, a feeling strengthened by the hardships of the Great Depression. Particularly in Saskatchewan, there was a rebellious 'pioneer' spirit, and a distrust of the ruling classes in Toronto, Montreal and Ottawa. Winnipeg's 1935 Grey Cup win was celebrated across western Canada as a victory for the whole region. In 1940, though, they were excluded from the showpiece game, because of differences in the rules between east and west.

By this time, the outbreak of war had already led the CIRFU to suspend university football after the 1939 season. The major non-collegiate unions, the IRFU and WIFU, played on for two more years, and shut down before the 1942 season, starting up again in 1945 and 1946 respectively. From 1942 to 1944, the Grey Cup was contested by military teams.

The IRFU welcomed an important addition in 1946, with the launch of the Montreal Alouettes, filling the gap left by Montreal AAA's demise in the 1930s. The Toronto Argonauts won the first three post-war Grey Cups with all-Canadian squads, becoming the last club to win the trophy without American help.

The Calgary Stampeders, with a host of US veterans, took it from them in 1948. Their colourful supporters caused a stir when visiting Toronto for the big game, wearing wild west clothing, drinking copiously, and even riding a horse through the lobby of the Royal York Hotel. The (then) normally staid city had never seen anything quite like it, and the Calgary fans' show of fervour that weekend has gone down in Canadian sporting legend. Another famous Grey Cup occasion came two years later, as hosts Toronto beat Winnipeg in swamp-like conditions, in a game remembered as the 'Mud Bowl'.

By this time, the CRU had abandoned all pretences of its game being amateur at its higher levels, as a big-business ethos had undeniably taken over. Even in 1937, journalist Lewis Brown had urged the union to admit that the battle had been lost, citing numerous cases of 'shamateurism', including players with works-based teams who only turned up at their supposed workplaces to collect their pay cheques.

The word 'rugby' was still being used, at least in the names of some governing bodies – creating confusion both for American 'imports' and for newly-arrived British migrants who tried to form rugby union clubs. Meanwhile, rugby union had survived as the main football code in the eastern Maritimes until World War II, when servicemen from other regions introduced Canadian football to the locals.

Halifax, Nova Scotia, had 12 rugby union teams in 1930, but none at all in 1955. A Canadian football league was formed there in 1947, a sign that Nova Scotia was loosening its British ties and becoming more integrated with the rest of Canada. The University of New Brunswick formed a Canadian football team in 1948, and a league was set up in the province a year later. The Maritime Intercollegiate Football League was founded in 1958, with teams in Nova Scotia, New Brunswick and Prince Edward Island.

Canadian football also found its feet on the west coast after the war, finally becoming a truly national game in what many now regard as its golden age. A stadium was being built in Vancouver for the 1954 British Empire and Commonwealth Games, providing an ideal opportunity for a big-league football team to be launched. The result was the birth of the BC (British Columbia) Lions, formed in 1953 and starting play in the WIFU the following year. Their home, the Empire Stadium, was the first western venue to stage the Grey Cup, in 1955.

The Grey Cup was first televised in 1952, after the CRU had struck a deal with the state broadcaster, CBC. However, the game could only be seen in Toronto; the first nationwide broadcast came in 1957. By that time, IRFU games had appeared on American screens, thanks to a contract agreed with NBC in 1954. It was a sign of Canadians' confidence in their own brand of football, and prompted talk of a possible 'World Series' between the NFL champions and Grey Cup winners.

The demise of the All-American Football Conference left many American players looking for work. Canadian clubs, flush with money from the NBC deal, snapped them up in great numbers. While Canadian players entering the professional ranks could only be signed via a draft, the clubs could sign Americans on a free-for-all basis.

Canadian scouts attended the 1954 East-West Shrine Game, US college football's 'all-star' event, something that their NFL counterparts were prohibited from doing. More than 40 NFL players and draft picks were recruited by Canadian clubs that year, provoking an angry reaction from the NFL. Although Toronto and Ottawa had threatened to boycott the Montreal Alouettes when the latter considered signing a black player in 1946, many black American players felt they would face less prejudice north of the border than in their homeland (including Drake University star Johnny Bright, as mentioned in chapter 10).

The Canadian leagues seemed poised to overshadow the NFL, but it was not to be. After a promising start, NBC's viewing figures waned, as Americans struggled to get used to what they saw as a strange brand of football. The contract was not renewed for a second year. The NFL tightened up its player contracts, making it harder for Americans to join Canadian clubs, who soon found themselves being outbid by NFL teams as salaries escalated out of their reach. Cross-border pacts were agreed, and the normal order of things was swiftly resumed.

Despite being put in its place by the NFL, Canadian football was in rude health in the mid 1950s, and the 39,417 attendance at the 1955 Grey Cup in Vancouver demonstrated its nationwide appeal. The ORFU and QRFU clubs had been overshadowed by those in the IRFU and, increasingly, the WIFU. By 1956, they had been excluded from the Grey Cup, making it a contest between the champions of the latter two unions.

The IRFU and WIFU formed a loose alliance, the Canadian Football Council, in January 1956 – hoping to secure a lasting peace with the NFL, and to improve the running of the game at the top level. Two years later it broke away from the CRU, and was renamed as the Canadian Football League (CFL), in line with the American model of autonomous 'major leagues'. Soon the IRFU and WIFU were also renamed, as the Eastern Football Conference and Western Football Conference respectively. Air travel had made cross-country fixtures more viable, and inter-conference games started appearing in the regular season schedule.

In 1966, the CFL took control of the Grey Cup from the CRU, which became the Canadian Amateur Football Association a year later (eventually adopting its current name, Football Canada, in 1986). The former CIRFU had become the Senior Intercollegiate Football League in the 1940s, the first in a long series of name changes and mergers. That troublesome word 'rugby', scorned by American players and coaches, had finally been excised from the upper tiers of Canadian football[59].

The large American presence in the CFL remained a contentious issue. By 1965, league rules limited each 32-man squad to 14 Americans, plus three 'naturalised Canadians'. After a string of controversies, the rules were rewritten that year to introduce the concept of *imports* (players trained outside Canada) and *non-imports*. They also allowed one *designated import*, via a convoluted arrangement whose effect was to encourage clubs to employ American quarterbacks, who would not count towards the import quota.

Since then, no Canadian has found a regular starting role as a CFL quarterback. The last was the great Russ Jackson, who joined Ottawa primarily as a defensive back in 1958, eventually getting his chance at quarterback when other players were injured, and leading the Rough Riders to three Grey Cups. Another leading quarterback of the era was

Ron Lancaster, an American who initially shared the Ottawa role with Jackson. Lancaster went on to break a host of records with Saskatchewan, before using his tactical expertise to coach Edmonton and Hamilton to Grey Cup success.

The rules of the game gradually became even more Americanised, with a touchdown (no longer a 'try') being upgraded from five points to six in 1956. Ten years later, unlimited blocking was allowed whenever the ball was being carried. Player positions were renamed along American lines in 1957: the snap was now a centre, while inside, middle, outside and flying wings became guards, tackles, ends and wingbacks respectively. Around this time, unlimited substitution was introduced, allowing players to specialise in offensive, defensive and special-team roles. Players in Canada had also been gradually adopting American-style protective gear for some time, with helmets becoming mandatory in 1949.

Despite this, the game still had some distinctive features, which have survived. A punt or missed field goal attempt could earn a point, if the defending team failed to run it out of the end zone. Offensive backs could move freely before the snap, there were only three downs, and teams were 12-a-side, with the extra man (in comparison with American football) used as a flanker on offence, or a safety on defence.

Helped by a booming economy, and the positive impact of television, the CFL enjoyed another fruitful spell in the early 1970s. Trouble was brewing, though, as plans for the World Football League (WFL) – mainly US-based, but also with a team to be known as the Toronto Northmen – were announced in 1973. As well as worrying about fans deserting the Toronto Argonauts, the CFL feared that a bidding war with the WFL might lead to a talent drain.

Even the Canadian parliament, concerned about the game's future, found time to debate bill C-22: 'The Canadian Football Act: An Act Representing Canadian Professional Football.' The bill was not passed, but the general commotion was enough to persuade the Northmen's ownership to switch their plans to Tennessee, predictably renaming their proposed team as the Memphis Southmen.

An air of paranoia surrounded the CFL, with a belief that many Canadians felt an inferiority complex towards the US, and took it for granted that the NFL was of a higher standard than the CFL (which, in the North American scheme of things, was therefore seen as 'minor league'). This was reflected in player recruitment and team selection: the most prominent positions were almost always occupied by American players, who were assumed to be superior to Canadians, and were perceived to be bigger crowd-pullers.

As a result, Canadians were mostly consigned to the less glamorous, lower-paid roles, such as linemen and kickers. Jamie Bone, a Canadian quarterback with Hamilton in the late 1970s, was so frustrated by the lack of opportunities afforded to him – allegedly because of his nationality – that he took his grievance to the Ontario Human Rights Commission. Bone was awarded $10,000, a decision which further discouraged clubs from acquiring Canadian quarterbacks in the first place.

The late 1970s and 1980s were a more trying era. Costs were rocketing, and attendances slumped as the public found new ways of spending their time and money. Among them was major-league baseball: the Toronto Blue Jays started up in 1977, joining the Montreal Expos, who had made their debut eight years earlier. Some CFL clubs fell into financial difficulties, including the Montreal Alouettes, who folded in June 1987. The league could scarcely afford to lose its presence in one of Canada's two major cities, and, not for the first or last time, some media observers claimed that it was on its last legs.

In an effort to stop the bleeding, the CFL imposed an expenditure cap, covering all forms of spending by clubs, in 1988. Things improved somewhat the following year. The Toronto Argonauts (along with the Blue Jays) moved into the spectacular new SkyDome – the first North American stadium with a retractable roof, and a boost for the city's profile. The 1989 Grey Cup was arguably the best ever, with Saskatchewan edging out Hamilton thanks to a last-gasp field goal.

Fresh investment helped the league in the early 1990s, notably when a group including actor/comedian John Candy and ice hockey icon Wayne Gretzky bought the Argonauts in 1991. The cash injection helped the club to stage a shocking coup that year, signing wide receiver and kick-off returner Raghib 'Rocket' Ismail, widely expected to be the first pick in the NFL draft, on a lucrative contract involving an unprecedented 'personal services' deal. Calgary quarterback Doug Flutie, with a track record of heroics in US college football, was another marquee name helping to draw attention to the league.

All was not well, though. Ismail left for the NFL after just two of the four years for which he had signed. Bruce McNall, the third member of the Toronto ownership group, soon proved to be in serious financial trouble (later ending in jail for bank fraud and conspiracy). Ottawa and Calgary were also sinking deep into debt and needed bail-outs by the CFL to stay afloat.

The league badly needed new sources of income. John Candy suggested expanding into the US, targeting medium-sized cities without NFL teams, and met various groups of potential American team owners in 1991. Despite tricky issues such as field dimensions and how to apply the 'import' rule, new CFL commissioner Larry Smith backed the idea and made it into a reality, announcing it as a 'strategic move' at a press conference in November 1992.

The following season, the Sacramento Gold Miners became the league's first US-based team. Their home games drew decent-sized crowds, attracted by the fast-flowing Canadian brand of football. They were exempt from the import rule, and expectations were high; but they struggled none the less, hampered by poor preparation and a lack of CFL experience among the coaching staff.

Three more US teams joined the fray in 1994. The Las Vegas Posse had trouble attracting spectators in the stifling summer heat in the early part of the season[60], also a problem in Sacramento. In Louisiana, the Shreveport Pirates lost their first 14 games, eventually winning just three out of 18. Baltimore fared better, on the back of anti-NFL sentiment after the Colts had moved to Indianapolis. The team, originally to be called the Colts before a court prevented it, and known unofficially as the Baltimore Football Club or Baltimore CFLers, performed well, and even reached the Grey Cup.

The CFL's American adventure had hardly been a roaring success, and in its third year, 1995, it went horribly wrong. A relocation of the Las Vegas Posse to Jackson, Mississippi, fell through, and the team folded. The Sacramento Gold Miners became the San Antonio Texans, and two new dubiously-named teams, the Birmingham Barracudas and Memphis Mad Dogs, joined the league.

For one season only, the league was split into Northern and Southern (in other words, Canadian and US) divisions, rather than Western and Eastern. Meanwhile, some Canadian-based clubs were still in deep trouble. All this chaos drew ridicule from the media, typified by this barb from *Calgary Herald* columnist Allan Maki:

> *There are only two things in this world more disorganised than the Canadian Football League. One is a train wreck. The other is a prison riot. You could add a grade-school fire drill, but there are eight-year-olds with a better sense of direction and crisis management than CFL commissioner Larry Smith.*

Birmingham's summer home games were well attended; but, being in the University of Alabama's backyard, they faded into obscurity when the college football season began. In Memphis, as well as the weather factor, there were problems in fitting a CFL-sized playing field into an American football stadium. Both teams failed to attract the corporate support they needed. Memphis president Pepper Rodgers suggested a further Americanisation of the rules, including four downs; and sparked fury in Canada by mocking the province of Saskatchewan.

The CFL's marketing slogan, 'Longer, Wider, Faster', was doing little to win Americans over.

Still, the Baltimore Stallions, as they now were, had another good season in 1995 – this time going one better and winning the Grey Cup. By this time, though, the NFL's Cleveland Browns had announced plans to move to Baltimore (where they became the Ravens), instantly putting the Stallions in the shade. After landing the cup in front of a 52,564 crowd in Regina, they returned to find just 200 fans at a victory rally. The Memphis Mad Dogs were also thwarted by an NFL relocation, as the Houston Oilers moved to their city. On top of all this, Calgary owner Larry Ryckman became embroiled in a stock fraud scandal. The Stallions moved to Montreal, eventually adopting the name of the defunct Alouettes. All of the other US teams folded.

Why had the CFL failed in the United States? While the Canadian style of play did have its attractions, the game appeared peculiar to many Americans. There is, of course, nothing inherently bizarre about having 12 players, three downs, or a 110-yard field. American sports fans, though, being well versed in the finer points of their game, do tend to find Canadian football a little odd-looking, preferring NFL or high-grade college football whenever it is available.

As well as the oppressive summer weather, and NFL teams popping up in Cleveland and Memphis, other factors that have been cited include the name of the league itself (with the word 'Canadian' suggesting that it did not belong in the US) and the weak Canadian dollar. The CFL management was also blamed, for being too hasty in accepting franchise bids and getting teams up and running, without doing enough research.

The CFL limped into the 1996 season in distinctly unhealthy shape. The American experiment was practically dead, although there was some talk, in the next few years, of expanding into northern US cities. In a vain attempt to revive flagging interest in Toronto, the league engineered a move for Doug Flutie from Calgary to the Argonauts, allowing the latter to breach the salary cap. Montreal, Ottawa and BC were in serious financial peril (BC went into receivership in August), as were Saskatchewan and Winnipeg by the autumn. In October, CFL chairman John Tory admitted that the league itself might not survive until the end of the season.

The league launched a marketing campaign with patriotic overtones, hinging on the game's supposedly Canadian character, under the slogan 'Radically Canadian' – trying to put a positive spin on the failure of the American venture, which itself had been an act born of desperation[61]. Other slogans included 'The Definition of the CFL – It's Not American!', and – raising eyebrows when it appeared on T-shirts – 'Our Balls are Bigger' (the ball used in the CFL is slightly larger than that used in the NFL).

Canadians were not used to such aggressive advertising, and the campaign did little to improve attendance figures. Again, though, an exciting Grey Cup game – with Toronto beating Edmonton 43-37 on a snow-covered field in Hamilton – helped to keep interest alive.

The Ottawa Rough Riders folded after that season, and there was unease over a mystery group of investors who bought the BC Lions. The CFL began discussions with the NFL, looking for help in its fight for survival. It was thought that the CFL might become a 'farm' system for the NFL, effectively a developmental league for budding NFL players. The idea provoked an outburst from Jim Hunt in the *Toronto Sun*, harking back to the Harvard–McGill encounters in 1874: 'Americans took over Canadian football as if they invented it.'[62]

As it turned out, the deal announced in April 1997 just involved a $3 million (US) loan from the NFL to the CFL, help from the NFL in securing corporate sponsorship for the Canadian league, and some rules governing player movement between the leagues. It may have seemed like an act of largesse on the part of the NFL, but some suspected that it was an attempt to avoid legal action under anti-trust (monopoly) laws.

Things began to look up in the late 1990s and early 2000s. CFL attendances and TV viewing figures increased each year, and regular Friday-night TV coverage was launched on cable channel TSN. The Montreal Alouettes thrived after moving from the unloved Olympic Stadium to the more intimate Molson Stadium, on the McGill campus.

The game was gaining popularity in other parts of Quebec, helped by Laval University's Vanier Cup victory in 1999 (as Canada's intercollegiate champions), and there were rumours of a CFL team being launched in Quebec City. Bilingual Montreal players got involved in marketing campaigns that helped to popularise the game among the province's Francophone community, and RDS, TSN's French-language sister channel, began drawing a large audience among young adults.

Doug Flutie's NFL success with the Buffalo Bills reflected well on the CFL, and was felt with pride north of the border. Although some team owners considered an outlandish plan to merge the CFL into the XFL (the ill-fated, supposedly 'tougher' league concocted by wrestling mogul Vince McMahon), the league was in a healthy enough state to reject it. A new Ottawa team, the Renegades, was unveiled in 2001.

The CFL, though, had a prolific record of shooting itself in the foot, and faced extinction again in 2003 as ex-commissioner Michael Lysko filed a lawsuit for $5.2 million (Canadian). Lysko had been deposed the previous year, after a blazing public row with Toronto Argonauts officials over a range of issues, including their plans to stage a wet T-shirt contest as pre-game entertainment. The Ottawa Renegades made heavy losses, and were mothballed in 2006, supposedly for a year (at the time of writing, plans for a revival were underway, but with 2011 as the earliest realistic date).

Another setback came in 2008, when an exclusive deal with TSN meant that the Grey Cup would not be shown on terrestrial TV. Although the league showed that it could still draw the occasional big-name American in 2006, when star running back Ricky Williams joined Toronto, even this raised questions over the league's ethics: Williams was only available because he was under suspension from the NFL after a string of drug violations. One more cloud appearing on the horizon in 2008 was the growing rumour that the Buffalo Bills would move to Toronto.

While college football in the US has long been a huge attraction, and a major part of campus life, this has never been the case in Canada. Full athletic scholarships are not generally allowed, there are no full-time professional coaches, and sport takes a back seat to academic study. As a result, football players tend to leave university with weaker skills, and a poorer tactical education, than their counterparts south of the border, making it difficult for them to compete with 'imports' for places in CFL squads. Recently, though, some budding Canadian players have attended US colleges with mid-ranking football programmes.

After the universities withdrew from Grey Cup contention in 1934, they gradually developed their own football framework. Until 1961, however, there was neither a nationwide governing body for college football, nor a national championship. The Canadian Interuniversity Athletic Union (now known as Canadian Interuniversity Sport) was formed that year, and the first national championship game, of sorts, was staged in 1965, with the winners of five conferences eligible to be invited. Three years later, with only four conferences now involved, a mini-tournament was launched, with semi-finals and a final. The final became known as the Canadian College Bowl, with the winners receiving the Vanier Cup.

Canadian football also has a junior circuit, with teams vying for places in the Canadian Bowl, first established in 1908 as the Leader-Post Championship. Perhaps unsurprisingly, given the sport's precarious existence, there is little to report on the subject of women's Canadian football. Football Canada runs a 'Women in Football' programme, to promote female involvement as players, coaches and administrators. The New Brunswick Women's Football League was set up in 2004; now under the guise of the Maritime Women's Football League, it features four teams, and has a championship decider known endearingly as the SupHer Bowl.

Somehow, having apparently teetered on the brink of extinction at times, Canadian football is still with us. The CFL's survival has long been threatened by public apathy, mismanagement, and intense competition for the 'entertainment dollar' from ice hockey, baseball, basketball and (mainly via television) American football, heightened by the widespread feeling that American sports and sportsmen are innately superior to Canadian ones.

With only eight or nine teams, the league faces real danger whenever just two or three of them are in danger of folding. Without the CFL, Canadian football as a whole might well disappear; but, each time the league has found itself in danger, Canadians have found a way to rescue it.

The game still has something of a distinct flavour. With only three downs rather than four, punting and field goal attempts are more common than in American football, and the 'rouge' or 'single' makes them a bigger offensive threat. The number of downs, along with the 20-yard deep end zones (twice as deep as in the US), also encourages a passing game. With timekeeping rules that generally force the offence to restart play more quickly, it is a more fast-moving, expansive game than the American version. Perhaps the main factor that keeps it in American football's shadow is the lesser quality of its players: essentially a mixture of NFL cast-offs and Canadians who might well be replaced by other NFL cast-offs were it not for the 'imports' rule.

Sociologist Robert Stebbins once described the evolution of Canadian football as 'an historical compromise between British and American influences, one that today is uncertain of its loyalties to the former but stubbornly wary of becoming too much like the latter'. Because of this, Stebbins suggested, the game 'can be seen as a master-symbol of Canadian culture'.

Its history also reflects the power struggles and antipathy between the 'establishment' cities of Toronto, Montreal and Ottawa, and the mutinous spirit of the west. Sports historian Wray Vamplew has drawn parallels between Canadian and Australian Rules football, arguing that both young nations have tried to forge their own 'cultural symbols', including football codes.

Despite its many tribulations, and a stream of attacks from the media, Canadian football – especially the Grey Cup – still holds an important place in many Canadians' hearts and minds; even while many CFL players can walk the streets unnoticed. Anyone who expects the league to crumble in the foreseeable future should take a look at its history, and think again. As legendary player and coach Annis Stukus put it in the 1970s, 'The CFL's been dying for 30 years – it'll be dying 30 years from now.'

Chapter 14

Oddballs

'It's just not football. What do they think they are doing?'
– Marcus George, bemused observer at a rollersoccer
game in London, 2005.

Just as today's major football codes evolved from earlier forms of football, they, in turn, have spawned all manner of adaptations, bastardisations and hybrids. Among the earliest was indoor soccer, which first sprang up in the north-eastern USA as an alternative to playing on frozen fields. There is evidence of 11-a-side indoor games in the Boston area, and five-a-side ones in Newark, New Jersey, from as early as the 1880s. There was also an 11-a-side indoor league in Boston in 1923.

Around 1930, Juan Carlos Ceriani, an Argentine exiled in Uruguay, grew tired of rain-soaked pitches ruining the football schedule at the Montevideo YMCA where he worked, and organised an indoor five-a-side competition. The format soon became popular with children and youth groups around the city. Meanwhile, up in Brazil, small-sided soccer was evolving on the streets of São Paulo, and a set of rules was published in 1936.

Gradually, the Brazilian version moved indoors, and the two scenes coalesced into a single sport, known as *fútbol de salón* in Spanish, and *futebol de salão* in Portuguese ('football in a room'), which spread across South America. Paraguay won the first international tournament, the South American Cup, in 1965. Some budding stars of the outdoor game, including Pelé, first honed their skills indoors. The game reached Europe, and a worldwide governing body, FIFUSA (Federación Internacional de Fútbol de Salón) was born in 1971. Brazil became the first world champions in São Paulo in 1982, helped by some familiar faces from outdoor soccer.

FIFA grabbed control of a large slice of the indoor game in 1989, branding it as *futsal*. FIFUSA, though, kept going, and both organisations have continued staging their own World Cups. In recent years, professional leagues have been created in many countries around South America, Europe and Asia. Following in Pelé's footsteps, some of the current big names in outdoor soccer, such as Ronaldinho and Cristiano Ronaldo, learnt much of their trade in futsal.

The playing area has boundary lines, and the ball is smaller, with less bounce, than the one used outdoors. Along with a basketball-style accumulated fouls system, these aspects of the game are designed to encourage skilful, attractive play; Andy Roxburgh, UEFA's Technical Director, once described futsal as 'a paradise for the technical player'.

While futsal was spreading its wings, the version of indoor soccer favoured in the US evolved in its own way – the crucial difference being that its playing area was bounded by boards rather than lines, with play continuing if the ball hit them. It developed sporadically in the post-war years, after a violent seven-a-side tournament at New York's Madison Square Garden in 1941. The National Soccer League (actually confined to the Chicago area) staged a season of indoor games, some of them televised, in 1950.

Things began to pick up in the 1970s, as the briefly successful North American Soccer League put on some indoor games. It faced stiff competition from the Major Indoor Soccer League (MISL), launched in 1978. The MISL allowed on-the-fly substitutions, and players could charge opponents into the boards. The set-up of the playing court encouraged frequent shooting, in the hope of scoring from rebounds. It was a far cry from the technical sophistication of futsal, but it produced the high-octane excitement that American sports promoters thought was missing in outdoor soccer.

For some years – particularly after the NASL's demise in 1984, which left the US without professional outdoor soccer – the indoor game thrived, giving arena owners a useful revenue stream outside the basketball and ice hockey seasons. The good times did not last, though, and the former MISL (renamed as MSL by this time, with the word 'indoor' having become redundant) folded in 1992. Perhaps its strongest legacy comes from the way it was presented, with flashing lights and bursts of loud music – ideas that would be adopted in other, more popular sports in the US.

A similar form of indoor soccer has become popular at recreational level in the UK, and had a brief heyday in the 1980s, with top-flight Football League clubs fielding first-team players in six-a-side competitions. In recent years, it has appeared on television in the form of the Masters tournaments, backed by Sky TV, with veterans of the outdoor game representing their former clubs. A more extreme miniaturisation is *jorkyball*, a two-a-side game played in a cage, invented by Frenchman Gilles Paniez in 1987.

In February 1981, when NFL marketing man Jim Foster was at an MISL game, an idea popped into his head. If the alien sport of soccer could draw large crowds in indoor arenas, why not American football? Foster drew sketches and jotted ideas on an envelope, and, although it would take several years, his concept would come to life.

Not that it was an entirely new one. The 1932 NFL championship game was moved indoors and some other indoor games were played that decade. A contest at the Boston Garden, billed as Collegiate All-Stars v Notre Dame Alumni, degenerated into chaos: the crowd turned angry on realising that some of the players were not the big names who had been announced; while the players complained that the surface, made from dirt left behind after a rodeo show, was becoming unplayable and reeked of horse manure.

Jim Foster and co. had no such mishaps, staging a trial game in 1986, and a 'showcase' game in Chicago the following February, before launching the four-team Arena Football League (AFL) in 1987. Attendances were encouraging, averaging over 11,000 in that first season. The title decider, Arena Bowl I, was televised nationally on ESPN, with the Denver Dynamite beating the Pittsburgh Gladiators. Exhibition games were even staged in London and Paris in 1989.

The AFL grew in the 1990s, finding a niche in medium-sized 'markets' that were too small to attract NFL franchises. It appealed to a family audience, encouraged by low ticket prices. Arena football is played eight-a-side, with no punting and plenty of passing and scoring. The goals are just nine feet wide, with large taut nets on either side. Kick-offs rebound from these nets, and back into play. There are no sidelines: play continues all the way out to the padded fences, giving many spectators a close-up view of the action.

As is usually the case in professional American sport, a host of rival leagues sprang up during the AFL's lifetime, but it remained the market leader. A co-operation agreement was signed with the NFL in 1999, and some NFL team owners became involved with AFL teams. The league's profile got a boost when former Denver Broncos quarterback John Elway and rock star Jon Bon Jovi bought the Colorado Crush and Philadelphia Soul respectively; both played a large role in the AFL's promotional material.

It also gained some credibility in the 1999 NFL season, when Kurt Warner quarterbacked the St Louis Rams to Super Bowl success, just two years after leaving the AFL's Iowa Barnstormers. The league gained a foot-hold in major cities such as New York, Los Angeles and Chicago, and there were plans to expand it into Europe. However, the harsh economic conditions led the league to suspend its 2009 season, and to fold soon afterwards; leaving a clutch of lesser-known leagues to keep the sport alive.

Rugby, on the other hand, has never caught on as an indoor sport. Perhaps the prospect of unpadded bodies crashing onto artificial turf has never held much appeal, at least for players. It has been tried, though, by World Arena Rugby, the American brainchild of sports promoter Buckeye Epstein. The game was played seven-a-side, and was based on rugby union. But, as suggested by its acronym, WAR, its main selling points were furious action and unhinged violence (described as a 'kill-the-man-with-the-ball' attitude), hardly the kind of thing that rugby union purists like to draw attention to. After a trial game in Dallas in 1998, the plans stalled, and – despite its promoters hailing indoor rugby as 'the sport for the new millennium' – it seems unlikely that their league will ever get off the ground.

Australian Rules football has also found its way indoors, courtesy of Perth entrepreneur Graham Rickman, who recently devised *Indoor Rules*, which has been adopted at some leisure centres in the Melbourne area. It is played on artificial turf, with netting around the boundaries. Indoor Rules is a non-contact game, designed to be safer and cleaner than the outdoor version; more of a social activity than a competitive sport.

As well as indoor arenas and sports halls, football has found itself in other new settings. The twin Brazilian loves of beaches and soccer led to impromptu kickabouts on Rio de Janeiro's Copacabana Beach in the 1970s and 1980s, gradually evolving into the distinct sport of beach soccer. The first official club, VTF, was formed in 1987, and the game spread north to California and Florida around this time. In 1992, Giancarlo Signorini, an Italian based in the US, drew up the first standard rules, and a trial event was held in Los Angeles.

The first professional tournament took place the following year, at Miami Beach. Brazil won the first official World Championship, in Rio, in 1995, after an unofficial one had been staged there the previous year. As interest grew, the Pro Beach Soccer Tour was launched, with 60 games in Europe, Asia, South America and the US. The European Pro Beach Soccer League (sometimes, unfortunately, known as the Euro BS League) was founded in 1998, attracting attention from broadcasters and sponsors. As with futsal, FIFA got in on the act, arranging its own World Cup in 2005, by which time such well-known 'field soccer' veterans as Eric Cantona and Romario were beginning to appear.

Beach soccer is usually played by teams of five, with substitutions on the fly and no offside – much like futsal on sand. The soft surface is conducive to aerial skills such as flying kicks and diving headers, while the lack of bounce encourages flicks, volleys and ball-juggling. Meanwhile, as well as soccer, Gaelic football and various forms of rugby have also been organised on beaches.

Soccer on ice is a very different proposition, and faces its share of difficulties. Kicking a ball hardly helps a skater to stay balanced, and early experimenters found that the ball moved too quickly for their liking. Early in the 21st century, though, Michigan resident Doug Taylor found an answer to the latter problem, when trying to think up a game to play with friends on a nearby frozen lake at a get-together.

Instead of a ball, they used a stuffed, elongated bag. Taylor set up a company, Taylor Sports, which patented his version of *ice soccer*, and branded the bag as the *Foot'r*. Players wear winter boots rather than skates, along with helmets and padding. The company has staged games in ice hockey arenas, and has ambitions to launch professional leagues by 2015.

Some better-known Americans, the Kennedy family, took football to the ski slopes in the 1970s during their winter retreats in Aspen, Colorado. In *ski football*, players throw a ball to each other as they ski downhill; a player can only hold it for ten seconds at a time. Scoring is usually achieved by placing the ball between two posts positioned along the slope. In another version of the game, touchdowns are scored by having possession of the ball at the bottom of the slope. Ski football hit the headlines in shocking fashion on New Year's Eve, 1998, claiming Michael Kennedy's life as he slammed into a tree while playing.

One day in December 1995, Zack Phillips was roller-skating in San Francisco when a soccer ball crossed his path. He kicked it, instantly giving himself an idea. Soon, yet another American-born football game – *rollersoccer* – was a regular sight in the city's Golden Gate Park, after Phillips persuaded some friends to join him. The Rollersoccer International Federation was formed in 1996. Sometimes known as *inline football*, the game caught on in New York, Hong Kong and Taipei, and its first world championship was staged in London in 2003. It is generally played five-a-side, on indoor roller-skating rinks, with scoring only allowed from at least five yards out.

Other forms of football on wheels include *bikeball*, a soccer-like game played on bicycles, with no apparent international structure; and *motorcycle ball* (sometimes known as *motoball*, *motorcycle polo* or *motopolo*), invented in 1928, in which players can kick the ball or hit it with their wheels. A motorcycle ball European Cup was launched in 1970.

In 1977, some quadriplegic athletes in Winnipeg were looking for an alternative to wheelchair basketball. The game they conjured up, initially known as *murderball*, but later as *wheelchair rugby*, has elements of both basketball and rugby. It is played by teams of four, on a basketball court. A player may hold on to the volleyball-style ball for up to ten seconds without bouncing or passing it, and can score by carrying it over the opponents' goal-line. A Canadian championship was held in 1979. The game reached other countries in the 1980s, and the International

Wheelchair Rugby Federation was founded in 1993. After finding a place in the World Wheelchair Games, it joined the Paralympics schedule in 1996 as a demonstration sport, and gained official status in 2000.

That year, a rather different game, *wheelchair rugby league* (or *wheelchair tag rugby league*) was invented by Frenchmen Robert Fassolette and Wally Salvan, based on the 13-man code. It was demonstrated in Australia in 2000, and reached Britain in 2005. Players are tackled by removing flags or tags attached to their sleeves. Play is then restarted with an adaptation of rugby league's 'play-the-ball': the tackled player puts the ball down, before throwing it backwards to a teammate. After five consecutive tackles on the same team, the ball is turned over to the opposition.

Wheelchair rugby league is played five-a-side, using a rugby ball, on a handball court with miniature rugby-style goalposts. The scoring system is identical to that of regular rugby league. To score a try, the ball must be touched down; while penalties, conversions and drop-goals involve punching the ball, rather than kicking it. The game is open to able-bodied players, as well as the wheelchair-bound. Its first World Cup was held in Australia in 2008, won by England.

Some have claimed that *underwater rugby* was invented in 1961 by Ludwig von Bersuda at the Cologne-based German Underwater Club. Another theory involves French marine infantrymen in Kenya, in the same year, using a coconut as a ball. Either way, the game caught on at various underwater clubs in Germany, and a tournament was staged in Müllheim in 1965.

It was played eight-a-side at first, later changing to six-a-side. The ball is the same size as a water polo ball, filled with a saltwater solution to prevent it floating to the surface. Goals are scored by putting it into a bucket at the opponents' end. Underwater rugby was adopted in other central and eastern European countries, and a European Championship was first contested in 1978, followed two years later by a World Championship.

A Canadian variation, known as *underwater football*, was devised in the late 1960s by a scuba diving instructor in Manitoba. It is played using either a rubber-coated brick or a ball similar to those used in Canadian and American football, filled with corn syrup, which must be touched down in a goal area for a score to be registered.

The hard-hitting nature of American football has often caused serious injuries, and, in earlier times, even deaths. Naturally, people have tried to devise safer forms of the game, suitable for children, or for adults looking for exercise or a spot of harmless fun. The concept of *touch football*, where a tackle is completed by merely touching the ball-carrier, emerged in the 1930s.

In some cases, though, the touching was more forceful than was strictly necessary. An alternative known as *flag football* was devised, in which players had flags tucked into their belts, which had to be snatched away in order for tackles to be made. The idea was widely adopted in the US military during World War II, in the hope of reducing injuries. Flag football soon became popular with the wider American population and recreational leagues began to spring up around the country in the late 1940s.

Both touch and flag football have continued spreading and evolving over the years, with a multitude of organisations, leagues and tournaments being set up, covering various age groups, levels and localities. The Title IX act, which increased the funding of girls' and women's sport in US schools and colleges, helped to encourage female involvement in the 1970s. More recently, the International Women's Flag Football Association has arranged tours and 'clinics' in Europe. Flag football has progressed to semi-professional and even professional levels: the Professional Flag Football League was launched in 1997, with teams aiming to reach the Pro Flag Bowl.

The rules of both games vary widely. Some organisations allow contact between offensive and defensive linemen only, some allow downfield blocking on running plays, while others prohibit all contact other than tackling. In some competitions, offensive linemen are ineligible to catch forward passes (as in 'full-tackle' American football); others allow anyone to do so.

The touch-tackling idea also caught on in Australia in the 1950s, initially as a training exercise for rugby teams (both league and union). *Touch rugby*, often known in Australasia as *touch football*, or just *touch*, became popular as a safe, recreational game. Associations and competitions were set up in eastern Australia and New Zealand in the 1960s and 1970s, and many schools adopted the game. The Federation of International Touch was formed in 1985, and first staged a World Cup three years later.

Touch rugby's rules are mainly based on those of rugby league. The play-the-ball is replaced with a *rollball*, in which the tackled player rolls the ball back to a teammate, with all opponents standing at least five metres back. A sixth tackle results in a turnover. No kicking is allowed, other than tap-kick restarts. As a result, goalposts aren't needed, and tries are the only method of scoring. There is also a lesser-known version based more on rugby union, mostly played in the southern hemisphere.

In a similar game, *tag rugby*, each player has a strip of cloth stuck to a Velcro patch on his or her shorts, which has to be removed for a tackle to be made. As with rugby league and touch rugby, possession changes hands after six tackles. Kicking is allowed, but only below shoulder height. Australian expats in London have also devised *Touch Aussie Rules*, a self-explanatory, mixed-gender, recreational game.

Yet another version of rugby can be traced back to 1883, when the Scottish Border club Melrose was arranging a day of fund-raising events. A local butcher, Adam 'Ned' Haig, suggested staging a rugby tournament. Although it was agreed that it would be impractical to cram a normal rugby competition into one day, Haig's boss, David Sanderson, came up with the idea of reducing teams to seven players and shortening the matches, and *rugby sevens* was born. Other clubs in the region started arranging tournaments, and the idea gradually spread to other rugby-playing centres. The Middlesex Sevens, at Twickenham, were first held in 1926, as were the Evening Mail Sevens in Ireland.

It took a while for Australasians to pick up on the sevens format: it first appeared in New Zealand in 1949, and finally reached Australia in 1971. A World Sevens tournament was held in Scotland in 1973, followed three years later by the high-profile Hong Kong Sevens, which would become a showcase for budding rugby union stars such as David Campese and Jonah Lomu. The International Rugby Board staged the first World Cup Sevens in Edinburgh in 1993, and later launched the annual IRB World Sevens Series.

With cross-code relations thawing somewhat after rugby union turned professional, the Wigan rugby league side competed in, and won, the Middlesex Sevens in 1996. Rugby sevens was added to the Commonwealth Games in 1998, and there are hopes that it could become an Olympic sport.

Its rules are similar to those of rugby union, other than the difference in team size. Scrums are three-a-side; another difference is that tries can only be converted via drop-kicks, rather than place-kicks. The extra space allows a faster, more free-flowing game, suited to quick runners with strong ball-handling skills. Matches are often played in a festive atmosphere, less serious than at a typical 15-a-side game.

Rugby league also has a sevens format, which is thought to have debuted in Australia in 1961. A Sydney-based tournament, first organised in 1988, went international four years later and became the Sydney World Sevens, featuring overseas national sides as well as local clubs. Rugby league *nines* is also played, and has made progress in such non-traditional rugby league outposts as Italy and Spain. An annual international nines tournament is staged in York, and the sport is featured in the South Pacific Games.

By the time Australia emerged as a nation in the early 20th century, the cricketing rivalry between New South Wales and Victoria had captured the public's imagination. The same might well have happened on the football field, but for one problem: the footballers of the two states played by different rules. Late in the 19th century, the New South Wales Rugby Union had considered copying elements of what was then known as Victorian Rules football – abolishing scrums and allowing punted goals – but the then all-powerful Rugby Football Union had refused to allow such changes.

In 1908, though, when rugby league was established in New South Wales, the state's new league was free to do as it liked. James Giltinan, a key figure in the birth of the New South Wales Rugby League (NSWRL), proposed a set of compromise rules to the Victorian Football League, also hoping the Northern Union would adopt them in England. But Giltinan's finances and credibility took a battering when he led Australia's shambolic rugby league tour of Britain in 1908–09, and his plans came to nothing.

The subject came up again in 1914, with a series of meetings between the NSWRL and the Australasian Football Council. They devised a hybrid game, to be played on an oval field with rugby goalposts. The ball could be thrown backwards, but not punched. There would be no scrums, and players could claim marks, as in Australian Rules. Scoring would come in the form of tries (two points) and kicked goals (one point). But the two bodies couldn't agree on an offside rule, and the outbreak of war brought the talks to an end.

Until 1933, that is, when rugby league officials met their Australian Rules counterparts in Melbourne, en route to Britain for a Kangaroos tour. Hopes were higher this time, and a conference was arranged, with officials talking excitedly of what would be grandly called *Universal Football*. An Australian Rules delegate from Queensland claimed the new code would be 'a game with which to storm the world', whereas a Mr More of the Victorian Football League scoffed at worries about a split with English rugby league, urging his fellow plotters to 'search for a game for Australia, and forget about England.'

A trial match was played, drawing mixed reactions. Confused players reportedly kept pulling notes out of their pockets to remind themselves of the rules. In any case, all this enthusiasm came to nought, as NSWRL president Harry 'Jersey' Flegg dismissed the scheme, accusing its backers of being disloyal to rugby league. 'If they want a new game,' he stormed, they should 'get out of our game and form their own.' The idea was scrapped at the next NSWRL meeting, never to come up again.

A decade later, Aussie Rules devotees came across another football code. American troops had arrived in Melbourne, after the US and Australia had entered World War II. Tensions were running high between Australian and American military men, often boiling over into violence, and the authorities hoped that some sort of sporting activity would help bring them closer together. Some US servicemen played American football in front of locals, who were largely unimpressed. They also had a stab at Australian Rules, but struggled with the kicking game.

Former Carlton player Ern Cowley, by now a baseball reporter for a Melbourne newspaper, offered a solution. Under a set of compromise rules, players could throw the ball forwards, American-style, and could also make a mark from a forward pass or a kick. The new game, somewhat clumsily named *Austus* (*Aust*ralia + *US*), came to fruition, and drew large crowds in 1943, raising money for war charities. The Americans and Australians were effectively playing different games on the same field, with the former tending to throw the ball, and the latter preferring to punt it. It was hoped that Austus could continue after the war had ended; but, not surprisingly, it vanished once the American troops had gone home.

Still, even this would not be the last attempt at blending Australian Rules with another code. One day in the mid 1960s, Melbourne businessman and former Aussie Rules umpire Harry Beitzel chanced upon a game of Gaelic football on TV. He was struck by its similarities to the game he knew, and saw a rare chance for the latter to engage with the outside world.

After failing to arouse much interest from the Victorian Football League, Beitzel arranged a trip to Ireland in 1967 for a squad of leading Aussie Rules players, led by Carlton captain-coach Ron Barassi, raising the necessary funds himself. The Galahs, as they were known, agreed to play, under mostly Gaelic rules with only minor concessions to the Australian game, against Meath and Mayo at Dublin's Croke Park. An Irish expat in Melbourne gave them a crash course in Gaelic football. The Irish players, media and public hardly expected their visitors to put up a strong challenge, but were shocked by the size, strength, fitness and ball skills they exhibited as they won both games. Meath exacted revenge the following year, visiting Australia and winning all five of their matches against state teams.

After another Australian trip to Ireland in 1968, the idea faded somewhat, with only sporadic activity in the 1970s. In the early 1980s, though, tours of Ireland by Australian schoolboy teams, and a return visit by a combined Dublin Colleges squad, helped to revive it, and soon there was talk of arranging matches at full international level. The Gaelic Athletic Association and VFL got involved this time, and the first *Compromise Rules* series was staged in Ireland in 1984.

Gaelic-style goalposts were used, but with additional 'behind' posts outside them, as in Australian Rules. The pitch was rectangular, the ball was round, and each team had 15 players (the same as in Gaelic football, but three fewer than in Australian Rules). A *goal*, where the ball passed under the crossbar, was worth six points; an *over* (between the two central posts, but over the crossbar) would score three; and a single point would be gained for a *behind*, where the ball went between the central goal and an outer post. Players could carry the ball for up to six steps, and could pick it up off the ground. An Australian-style mark could be achieved by catching the ball on the full after a kick.

Unfortunately, the rules were unclear about how a ball-carrier could be tackled. This was one reason why the first two series (the second took place in Australia in 1986) both featured massed brawls, putting the future of Compromise Rules into some doubt. There was also disquiet in Irish circles over the Australians' perceived win-at-all-costs attitude, perhaps an inevitable clash of ideals when amateurs face professionals. There were other problems, too: paltry attendances in Australia, a lack of interest from Irish broadcasters, and the VFL's preoccupation with expanding into a nationwide league (it became the *Australian* Football League in 1989).

The idea was shelved after the 1990 series, but bounced back strongly in 1998. By now, the game had been given the more appealing name of *International Rules*, and the laws were clearer on tackling. The Ireland v Australia series became an annual event, and a women's series was added to the schedule in 2006. There was even some low-key activity in other countries, notably South Africa.

There was still squabbling over the rules, though, and more ugly incidents in the (men's) Ireland–Australia matches. High tackling was largely to blame, with punch-ups often sparked by Australian arms crashing into Irish faces. The wild tackles and brawls in 2006 prompted the GAA to put International Rules on hold, and the following year's series was scrapped. But an agreement between the GAA and AFL on disciplinary rules led to a revival in 2008, when a more peaceful series helped to get the hybrid game back on track.

There is *some* optimism for the future of International Rules, not least because it gives Gaelic and Australian Rules players their only conceivable chance of representing their countries. But it only generates a modest amount of interest, hardly surprising for a sport that is only played, at a high level, twice a year. Meanwhile, its 'international' aspect is of limited value, given that it only involves two countries, with relatively small populations, on opposite sides of the world. As Australia coach Leigh Matthews said of the 1998 matches:

> *The International Rules series was a bit like the*
> *Vietnam War. Nobody at home cared about it,*
> *but everyone involved sure did.*

Another hybrid football-related game, *speedball*, was invented in 1921 by Elmer Mitchell at the University of Michigan, as part of its physical education programme. It could be regarded as a mixture of soccer, rugby and flag football, and is still played, mainly outdoors, at some American colleges. Each side has 11 players. One of them is a goalkeeper, the only player allowed in a marked area in front of the goal. The goalposts are similar to those used in rugby or American football.

When the ball is rolling or bouncing (a *ground ball*), players can only kick it. However, an *air ball* (as with a mark in Australian Rules) can be caught, after which the player may carry it, throw it in any direction, or drop-kick it. A ball-carrier can be tackled by pulling off his 'flag belt', and must then put the ball down and kick it, although not at the goal. Speedball has a variety of scoring systems, with points awarded for a field goal (kicking the ball between the posts and under the crossbar), a drop-kick over the crossbar, a touchdown or a penalty kick.

A broadly similar game, *volata*, was devised in Italy in the late 1920s by National Fascist Party chairman Augusto Turati. He presented it as a classically Italian, amateur alternative to soccer, which (much like some of today's more bombastic British newspaper columnists) he saw as a morally corrupt game, 'full of verminous mercenaries'.

Volata was played eight-a-side, with goalkeepers. The ball could be played with the hands or legs, and could only be held for up to three seconds. A player could be tackled by grabbing him above waist level. As in handball, the object of the game was to throw the ball into a goal, from outside a marked area.

Under some fascist-style coercion from the authorities, hundreds of teams were formed. A national championship was organised, with dictator Benito Mussolini reportedly attending the finals. But the rise of soccer's popularity with Italians was unstoppable, and there was little genuine interest in the new sport, particularly after the national team's Mussolini-approved 1934 World Cup victory. Volata, once lauded by Turati as 'a superfascist sport for the Italians of tomorrow', quietly disappeared, and all references to it were wiped from the party's records.

Lurking on the outer fringes of the 'football' world are a number of sports closely related to tennis and volleyball. Their only link with football is that they involve kicking a ball, which, as explained earlier, might not be how the word 'football' came about in the first place.

The very English game of *lawn football* was conceived in Winchester in the 1880s, by A. Tebbutt and G.A. Du Soulay. It was played at Winchester College, and the English Lawn Football Association was formed in 1895. It can be played in either a singles or doubles format, on a court divided into two halves with a crossbar between them. Each half has a circle, five feet in diameter, and the object is to make the ball land in the opposition's circle.

A related game known as *footballtennis* was invented in the 1920s. Accounts differ as to whether this happened in Czechoslovakia or Switzerland, but a Swiss man, Josef Rothenfluh, published a brochure about it, describing it as 'a sport for the gentleman football player'.

Footballtennis can be played with one, two or three players on each side. As with tennis, the court is divided into two halves by a net. The rules are close to those of tennis, but the ball is struck using the feet and other body parts (anything but the arms and hands), and a player may touch the ball twice in succession. In doubles and triples, a team can make as many as three touches, but no more than two consecutive touches by the same player. The first official footballtennis tournament was held near Prague in 1940, and the International Footballtennis Association (now the Federation International Footballtennis Association, whatever that may mean) was formed in 1987.

The south-east Asian sport of *sepak takraw* is the modern form of a game that has existed in various forms, in different countries, perhaps dating back to the 15th century. It is essentially volleyball played with the feet, by teams of three, and is known for its spectacular high kicking. 'Sepak takraw' (from the Malaysian word for 'strike' or 'kick', and the Thai for 'rattan ball') was chosen as the name of the standardised version in 1965, when it became part of the South-East Asian Peninsular Games (now the South-East Asian Games), which still feature the sport today, as do the Asian Games.

A much newer and quirkier soccer-volleyball hybrid, *bossaball*, also has a touch of gymnastics about it. It is played on an inflatable court, with a trampoline in each half. Each team has between three and five players, one of whom can use the trampoline to gain extra height for his flying kicks. Bossaball is often played on Brazilian beaches, and is thought to have been influenced by the Brazilian 'fight-dance' art of *capoeira*, which perhaps makes it a surprise to learn that it was invented in Belgium.

One day in 1972, an Oregon man, Mike Marshall, casually started kicking a bean-bag around in the air. A friend, John Stalberger, had undergone knee surgery, and saw this as a useful exercise to help his recovery. The pair labelled their new hobby as 'hacking the sack'. It caught on quickly, and they developed a tailor-made bag which they trademarked as the *Hacky Sack*, a name that would later be used to refer to various games played with it. A widely-used, more generic name for these games, and for the sack itself, is *footbag*.

Today, *competitive footbag* is similar to sepak takraw, while other variations include *freestyle footbag* and even *footbag golf*. Footbag became a popular activity worldwide in the 1980s, and a world championship event was first held, in the Denver suburb of Golden, in 1986.

The story doesn't quite end there. Various codes of football have also influenced the invention of other sports, which few people, if any, would regard as having anything to do with football. American football was almost certainly on James Naismith's mind when he devised basketball, now one of the world's most popular sports, in 1891. Basketball, in turn, gave rise to netball. The development of handball, in central Europe and Scandinavia in the late 19th and early 20th centuries, was partly inspired by soccer and rugby. Water polo was conceived in 19th-century England as an aquatic version of rugby, although it now has more in common with handball.

Leaving aside such tenuously-related sports as basketball, perhaps what distinguishes these 'minor' football codes from the 'major' ones covered in other chapters is that they have never entered the public's consciousness in such a deep and lasting way.

Some of them, of course, do attract large crowds. Others have been designed primarily for the benefit of players, rather than a mass audience. But none have attracted fanatical devotion, of the sort that drives people to travel vast distances to follow their teams, and fuels endless arguments in offices and bars. The difference could be summed up by saying that these sports attract *spectators*, rather than *fans*. Most of them also have short histories, and, therefore, little in the way of tradition. The world's bookstore shelves are hardly groaning under the weight of historical books on the likes of arena football and touch rugby.

Despite this, it is a safe bet that more football-related concoctions will spring up in the future. Sport is, of course, a highly lucrative business, when it finds the right audience and is managed effectively. There will always be a wide-eyed entrepreneur, somewhere, convinced that he or she has stumbled upon the next big thing in the sports world, and some form of football might well be its inspiration.

Epilogue

The Ghosts of Football Past

> *'If this is what Englishmen call playing, it would be impossible
> to imagine what they would call fighting.'*
> – A French observer at a Shrove Tuesday folk
> football match in Derby, early 19th century

These, so I am told, are perfect conditions for Harrow football. It is strangely mild for January, with rain falling intermittently, but the last few days have seen an almost constant downpour. On the Hemstall Fields, a long downhill trudge away from the school buildings, the ground is as boggy as anything I can remember. The fields are part of the school's own farm, and they have the cow-pats to prove it.

Harrow football recently lost its 'major' status among the school's sporting activities, displaced by soccer. Perhaps it was inevitable that the opportunities for inter-school play provided by soccer and rugby would push the old game aside, even if it did take nearly a century and a half (the Harrow football school XI can play only against old-boy teams, such as an Oxford University side who visited recently). But, whatever its official status, Harrow football is thriving. There is huge enthusiasm for the game, and around 350 pupils – nearly half of the school – are taking to the mud on this Sunday afternoon, to play in three competitions.

Top of the bill is the inter-house tournament, now at the end of its initial round-robin stage. This is the same competition in which Charles Alcock played, back in the 1850s, and which was almost certainly an influence when he dreamed up the FA Cup in 1871. I watch the first half of a match between the strong Moretons House team and the less-fancied West Acre, before wandering off to see some action in another set of playing fields (stupidly clambering over a mud-caked stile to get there), and returning later to see Moretons complete a convincing win.

For the first few minutes of play, to these untrained eyes, it is difficult to work out what on earth is going on, even after studying the rules and hearing so much about the game. It seems as if nobody knows what they are doing, as the ball bobbles back and forth repeatedly between opposing players. Soon, though, it starts to make sense.

I had been under the impression that nobody kicks the ball forwards, simply because they can't – it is too big, heavy and unwieldy, and the ground is too swampy. In fact, the players *do* kick the ball forwards, and very often – but not very far. When it comes my way, and I kick it towards a player looking to take a throw-in, it becomes clear just how difficult it is to get any purchase on it (albeit with a wellington-clad foot), as it trundles a few short yards before grinding to a halt.

The rugby-style offside rule precludes forward passing, while backward and lateral passing are rarely tried – perhaps because the ball is so difficult to control, making it risky to attempt to gather a pass. The concept of possession has little meaning in this game. Instead, much of the play consists of short forward kicks. Each kick usually ends up at the feet of an opponent, but the kicker, 'followed up' by teammates in a diamond formation, chases after the ball in order to close down the space available to the opponent, hoping to block the anticipated kick. In other words, it is largely a territorial game, with each side generally trying to make small gains, and to prevent their opponents from doing so. Players do sometimes dribble the ball over short distances, but, with this ball on this surface, it is a difficult skill to master.

Things change a little when the ball goes near a *base* (goal), as the attackers try to create a chance to score. This is often done via a short, lofted, backward kick into the hands of a teammate, who calls for 'yards' (similar to a mark, or fair catch, in other codes), before kicking the ball over the heads of opposing defenders, aiming for the base. Wisely, nobody tries to head the ball, but high kicks and throw-ins are often blocked using the shoulder, a technique known confusingly as *fouling*.

Harrow football is a physical game, with shoulder-charging a regular feature, and players often sending each other sprawling into the sludge (although it is an offence to charge players in front of a teammate who has the ball at his feet, known as *minesweeping*). Other than the occasional skirmish, though, there is a friendly, playful spirit. Some matches are clearly more serious than others. One of this afternoon's games, on a pitch so boggy that the ball barely moves at all, quickly dissolves into little more than a lark around in the mud.

Looming on the horizon a couple of miles to the south-east, barely visible in the gloom, is the arch hanging over the new Wembley stadium.

Earlier in the afternoon, providing another neat link between football's past and present, I had met former Premier League soccer referee David Elleray – Master of Druries House and a familiar figure in Harrow football.

Although the Harrow game is far from being soccer's only ancestor, it is arguably its closest, most direct predecessor, other than the Cambridge University game of the 1850s and early 1860s, which itself was partly based on Harrow football. Seeing the old game first-hand, it is easy to see how it evolved into soccer, helped along by changes in the rules and playing conditions.

As Old Harrovians (along with others) began playing on firmer surfaces, using smaller, lighter and rounder balls, they developed the arts of dribbling and long-distance shooting. Later, the FA's offside rule change of 1867 paved the way for a more expansive passing game, which gradually came to fruition – largely thanks to the Scots – in the 1870s, and was taken to further levels of skill and sophistication as it spread overseas.

One final point about the relationships between Harrow football, soccer and the other codes is worth considering. Had it not been for the swamp-like conditions at Harrow, the football game that developed here in the 19th century would most likely have featured scrummaging of some sort, as was the case at Eton, Rugby, Shrewsbury and Winchester. (Anyone caught at the bottom of a collapsed scrum at Harrow might never have been seen again.) If this had happened, scrummaging might well have carried on into Cambridge Rules football, and subsequently into soccer, doubtless making it a very different game from the one we know.

Yards away from the Hemstall fields lies a firm, pristine soccer pitch. This, in turn, is next to an artificial field surrounded by an athletics track – all part of a multi-million pound revamp of the school's sports facilities, which left the Harrow football fields untouched. Not that anybody is complaining – as far as the boys who play the old game are concerned, these neglected, muddy old fields are exactly the way they should be.

Of course, this was not quite where it *all* began. A little over two weeks later, it is Shrove Tuesday, and I am in the Derbyshire market town of Ashbourne. And that can only mean one thing: Royal Shrovetide Football, the best-known living symbol of Britain's folk football tradition.

Just before noon, two hours before the start of the game, a crowd is gathering in the courtyard of the Green Man pub in the town centre. Some of them will be at the pre-match luncheon, where the ball – a lavishly-decorated work of art – will be unveiled. Meanwhile, in the nearby streets, the pubs are overflowing, traffic is being diverted out of harm's way, and there is a sense of anticipation in the air. It is easy to see which people are planning to get into the thick of the action: they're generally large, male, and clad in sturdy work-boots, robust sweatshirts or rugby jerseys, and jeans or combat trousers.

Nobody knows exactly when this tradition was born, but it is believed that a poem written by Derbyshire writer Charles Cotton in 1683, describing a football contest between two towns, was about Ashbourne and Compton (the latter is now a part of Ashbourne).

The game's future was in doubt for much of the 19th century, when the local authorities threatened to force it out of the town, and many participants were prosecuted. But the early 1890s saw a campaign to keep the game alive, and players added to its sense of respectability by forming a committee. It even gained royal approval in 1922, hence its present title. Six years later, the future King Edward VIII 'turned up' the ball to get the game underway. In 2003, another Prince of Wales, Charles, followed in his footsteps. Other eminent 'turner-uppers' have included such soccer legends as Stanley Matthews and Brian Clough.

The game is largely defined by the River Henmore (shallow enough to be sometimes referred to as a brook), which flows across the town centre. It is contested by the *Up'ards*, from north of the river, and the *Down'ards* from the area to the south, formerly the separate town of Compton. The goals are specially-made stone plinths overlooking the river, on the sites of former mills in Clifton (the Down'ards' target), a mile and a half south-west of central Ashbourne, and in Sturston, a similar distance to the east.

Play starts at 2pm, and can continue until 10pm. The ball is 'goaled' by tapping it against the target three times. If this happens before 6pm, another ball is turned up; otherwise, it ends the game. The next day, Ash Wednesday, they do it all over again. The starting point is Shaw Croft – once a patch of grassland, but now a car park behind a Somerfield supermarket. The ball is turned up from a platform adorned with commemorative plaques and Union flags.

This year's turner-upper for Shrove Tuesday is David Wheatcroft, the district council's chief executive. After the traditional procession from the Green Man to Shaw Croft, a brief speech, and the singing of *Auld Lang Syne* and *God Save the Queen*, he tosses the ball into the throng in front of him, and battle commences.

Within seconds, there's a rush towards the south side of the car park, where I am standing. Adding to the mild sense of panic, the heavens suddenly open, and the public address system emits some eerie squawking noises (either that, or some cats have wandered into the wrong place at the wrong time).

Ashbourne football is dominated by the *hug*, a pack of dozens of players crowding around the rarely-seen ball. The best clue to the ball's whereabouts is usually a cloud of steam, rising from the mass of bodies swarming around it. Occasionally it pops up into the air, prompting gasps and cheers from those a little further away from the action. Anyone who is simply there to watch – your not-so-intrepid author, for instance – needs to look out for sudden surges coming their way. Sometimes, though, the ball is prised out of the hug, and someone makes a 'break', carrying it into open space.

The rain soon eases off for a while, and the hug makes its way back across the car park, before squeezing through an alley and emerging onto the town's main street, near the Green Man. Soon it swarms into Market Place, the main square. Players climb onto window ledges, and anything else they can get onto, where they shout, point and gesticulate. There is some method to this madness: some players have pre-arranged roles, either in the hug or lurking outside it – much like forwards and backs in rugby.

After a long hiatus in front of Smith's Tavern, the play returns to the car park where it began, but soon finds itself among a neighbouring complex of three-storey blocks of flats. Residents on the upper floors have the best view in town, while the rest of us get thoroughly drenched in a violent downpour. The sight of that immense, steaming throng, surging through a gap in one of these buildings in these hellish conditions, is something I will not forget in a hurry.

The Down'ards make some progress to the south-west, out of the housing complex and past the Somerfield store, before a long period of stalemate ensues alongside Ashbourne Health Centre. The rain has stopped, and the mood lightens. The shops and cafés are boarded up for the afternoon; but the pubs stay open all day, probably doing more than enough business to cover any minor damage they might suffer. Beer is everywhere, but then this is no everyday occurrence in Ashbourne – it is a festival, a celebration of the town and its traditions.

One striking feature of the game, compared with the more familiar brands of football, is that the players and spectators are largely interchangeable. Although some of the people here are clearly committed to playing a serious part in the action, while some others (those in prams, for example) will obviously keep well away, many people hover around the fringes of the game, sometimes joining in, sometimes not. When friends bump into each other, they often ask, 'Have you been in?' (meaning 'in the hug'), a typical answer being, 'Nah, I'm not that daft'. This is, perhaps, the essence of folk football – the ultimate 'people's game', where the players and spectators are virtually one and the same.

Despite the relentless pushing, the determination, and the inevitable minor injuries, the game is played in a good spirit, with no sense of malice. Police and yellow-bibbed 'Shrovetide Marshals' are on duty, but rarely need to get involved, other than ushering players and spectators off private property. Ambulances are also on hand, and, sadly, the danger is real: the 2007 Tuesday game claimed the life of 51-year-old David Johnson, who suffered a heart attack, the first fatality since William Tunnicliffe died from hypothermia 101 years earlier.

After the lull in the action by the health centre, the Down'ards force the ball across Compton Street and past the bus station, before the action spills over into some grassland near Station Road, and descends to the edge of the river. Some players wade into the water, thigh-deep, in case the ball (filled with cork, to keep it afloat) falls in.

There will be much more of this to come – the game is not yet two hours old – but this is where I leave, not being sufficiently hardcore to stay the distance for a possible six more hours. For the record, Stuart Leeman goaled the ball for the Up'ards at 8pm. His colleague Matt Burtonshaw repeated the feat the next day with just four minutes to spare, after a 15-minute run.

How this wonderful mayhem is allowed to go ahead, on a day when some local councils have even banned pancake races on health and safety grounds, is quite mind-boggling. Perhaps – despite the occasional tragedy – we should be grateful that some authorities still recognise the value of local traditions, particularly those, such as Ashbourne's Shrovetide football games, which bring the people of a town together for a day or two. This old ritual is very much alive in the modern world, not seeming antiquated in any way.

Ashbourne is not alone: Hugh Hornby's *Uppies and Downies* documents 14 other British towns where various festival days are celebrated with a wide variety of football games. Five of them are clustered together in the Borders region of Scotland; the popularity of these *ba' games* might well have been a factor in the early growth of rugby in these towns.

We have seen how football has grown enormously, from these localised games into today's world of big-money leagues, tournaments and events. It could be argued that the catalyst behind all this was a coming together, mainly in 19th-century Britain, of middle-class sporting culture (with its emphasis on authority, organisation and gentlemanly 'honour') and the energy, fervour and will-to-win of the urbanised working classes, as the latter finally had reasonable amounts of time and money to spend on leisure pursuits.

Middle-class values prevailed at first, as associations and membership-based clubs led the way, establishing frameworks for football and insisting on pure amateurism. As working-class players, supporters and administrators grew in influence, the clash of cultures tore rugby apart, while soccer managed to find a unified way forward.

Meanwhile, as the British diaspora took the football codes overseas through colonialism, commerce and industry, more conflicts were triggered – not only between social classes, but also between British attitudes and other cultural influences. As a result, football evolved in different ways in various parts of the world. In some cases, the outcome was a range of playing styles under a common set of rules; in others, distinct sports began to emerge. The amateur–professional schism that hit Britain in the late 19th century soon repeated itself, with varying results, in Australia, New Zealand, the US and Canada, and later caused unrest in other parts of the world.

The one glaring exception to this pattern is Gaelic football, which evolved by itself, with little outside influence, and remained amateur. Although its folk roots are related to the British precursors of soccer and rugby, it is the only modern football code whose ancestry does not involve the British public school old-boy scene of the mid 19th century.

Clearly, the history of football – particularly in Britain and its former colonies – is inextricably linked with the social and cultural, and, in some cases, political, histories of the countries concerned. Nowhere is this more obvious than in the way that rugby diverged into two different sports, mainly on the basis of class.

It would be naïve to regard football as a single sport (or to downplay soccer's global dominance). But, as we have seen, the football codes have much in common in terms of their roots and traditions, despite their many differences. No other family of sports has come close to exerting such a hold on the world's consciousness, and the story of how this came about is a remarkably eventful one, with a vast range of factors coming into play.

Perhaps the last word should go to soccer manager Alan Latchley, a comic creation of the late, very great Peter Cook. I'd like to believe that he was thinking of *all* forms of football when he uttered these words. Then again, he clearly was not, and this is just a feeble excuse to end the story with this pearl of wisdom.

Because football is about nothing, unless it's about something.
And what it is about, is football.

Endnotes

1   This might be the origin of the use of the word 'derby' to mean a game between two neighbouring teams, although it has also been claimed that the term was coined in the Middle Ages.

2   The term *rouge* has found its way into Canadian football, where a point is conceded if a team fails to return a kicked ball out of its end zone.

3   It is interesting to note that the conversion method used in the North American codes, where the ball is 'snapped' back to a player who catches it and holds it in place for the kicker, is more faithful to the original Rugby School procedure than the one used today in rugby.

4   The word 'soccer' is usually credited to Charles Wreford-Brown, an Oxford student in the 1880s who went on to captain England's national team. When asked one day whether he wanted to play 'rugger' – slang for 'rugby' (an example of the *Oxford '-er'*, a habit of nicknaming things by abbreviating them and adding '-er' or '-ers', such as 'brekkers' for breakfast), he supposedly replied that he would rather play 'soccer', meaning association football. Other accounts suggest that it evolved from other nicknames such as 'a-soc' and 'socca'.

5   Many claims have been made as to which was the first soccer club, the first rugby club, and so on, but most of them are open to dispute. Such was the informality of football in the mid 19th century, that a 'club' might have been little more than a loosely-formed group of men who sometimes gathered in a park to play around with a ball, perhaps never going so far as to adopt a set of rules or organise games against other clubs.

6   A valuable and meticulously researched book, blighted by some astounding outbursts of snobbery and self-righteous elitism.

7   *Bandy* was a variant of hockey, sometimes played on grass, sometimes on ice. The ice version soon caught on in Canada, and evolved into ice hockey.

8   Another Sheffield tournament, a year later, was organised by another theatre manager with the striking name of Oliver Cromwell.

9   Not to be confused with Hely Hutchinson Almond, headmaster and rugby zealot at Loretto School near Edinburgh.

10 For convenience, the word *soccer* includes the codes of both the London-based FA and the Sheffield FA, and other local variants.

11 There should have been 22, but the Wasps delegate rolled up at the wrong venue (and, according to at least one account, on the wrong day and at the wrong time), got drunk, and missed the meeting altogether.

12 The College of New Jersey moved from Elizabeth to Princeton in 1756, and became generally known as Princeton University, but would not be officially named as such until 1896.

13 The Harvard squad had obtained a copy of the RFU rules. Unsurprisingly, not having seen the game being played in the English style, they struggled to understand its intricacies.

14 This theory is a little dubious, as it is debatable whether soccer or rugby was the major football code at Oxford and Cambridge at this time.

15 Since the beginning of intercollegiate play, the team with the best record at the end of each season had been declared as champions; but this was a loose arrangement, as the schedules were uneven, with some teams playing more games than others.

16 Although historians tend to imply that Camp conjured up the 'scrimmage' idea out of thin air, there is evidence suggesting that the Harvard players had started the trend as early as October 1875 in a game against an 'All Canada' team. One

of their opponents later recalled that Harvard put only two men into each scrum, helping the ball to emerge sooner; they would also heel the ball backwards to teammates, rather than forcing it forwards, a tactic that came into use in British rugby around this time. While the 1880 decision marked a major change in the written rules, it may have been little more than a formalisation of the way that the game was already being played in the US (including confirmation that a teammate of a tackled player could heel the ball back into play, uncontested).

17 A field goal 'from placement' is one where another player holds the ball on the ground for the kicker; as opposed to a drop-kicked field goal, which is still permitted, but went out of common use decades ago.

18 Not to be confused with FA founding father Ebenezer Cobb Morley.

19 There are echoes here of the controversy over the proposed breakaway 'Super League' a century later (paving the way for the Premier League), when the Football League was portrayed as an egalitarian institution that was under threat from the money men. Before it began, the Football League itself was being derided as 'a mere money-making scheme' for a self-appointed elite band of clubs.

20 Despite his support for broken-time payments in this period, Newsome would go on to serve as RFU president from 1902 to 1904.

21 This was just two years after Everton had left their Anfield ground for Goodison Park, following a rent dispute with Anfield's landlord. Some rebel directors formed Liverpool FC at the old ground, prompting a protest from the rugby club of the same name.

22 Although soccer had made no major impact in North America, it was finding a foothold in some areas, mainly sustained by European immigrants.

23 Race was a hot issue in South American football at this time. At the first continental championship in 1916, Chile protested after a 4-0 defeat to Uruguay, claiming that their opponents had included two 'Africans' – the Uruguayan-born Isabelino Gradín and Juan Delgado. Five years later, Brazilian president Epitácio Pessoa insisted that his country's team must be all-white.

24 This term can be used without ambiguity until we reach 1922, when Ireland was partitioned. The Belfast-based (and largely unionist) Irish FA insisted on keeping its name, its jurisdiction over the whole island, and the right to field a team known as Ireland, featuring players from both sides of the border. But a new, mainly nationalist, association sprang up in Dublin (now known as the FA of Ireland), claiming similar rights. The stand-off would not be fully resolved until 1950, when the Belfast association's team was renamed as Northern Ireland, and FIFA restricted each association to picking players from its own side of the border.

25 In at least one case, the influence worked in the opposite direction. A young Bill Nicholson spent much of the war as a trainer and instructor, ending up in the Army Physical Training Corps – an experience that helped him become a hugely successful manager at Tottenham.

26 It has been suggested that the father of William Webb Ellis, the supposedly pivotal figure in rugby history, may have seen caid being played while he was stationed in Ireland with the Dragoons, and told his son about it. However, there seems to be no substantial evidence to back this up.

27 Strangely, J.K. Bracken's son Brendan went on to become Viscount Bracken, a member of the British cabinet during World War II.

28 From here onwards, scores would be shown in a 'goals-points' format. For example, '2-5' would mean two goals and five points, giving a total of 11, calculated as $(2 \times 3) + 5$.

29 Later in his life, O'Hehir also found fame in Britain as a horse racing commentator.

30 Soccer writers tend to cite Sheffield FC as the world's first soccer club (or first 'football' club, with 'football' meaning soccer); but it seems unlikely that they would regard Melbourne FC as a club that played the same game, even though its rules were very similar to Sheffield's – an illustration of how historical views

of football are often shaped by writers' biases towards particular codes and countries.

31 Today, the action of kicking a loose ball is known as 'soccering'.

32 In *The Cultural Bond: Sport, Empire, Society*, G.M. Hibbins suggests that the roles played by Hammersley, Thompson and Smith in forming the rules have been overlooked by Australian sports historians, in favour of born-and-bred Australians, particularly Wills.

33 The Collingwood and Richmond clubs mentioned here were not the current clubs of the same names.

34 This is one of a number of examples of how the game was influenced by cricket. It was also conventional for each team to appoint an umpire, and for certain types of decisions to depend on players appealing for them.

35 Just as the soldiers who played in these games were renowned for their aggression, some of their colleagues who watched them were pretty boisterous. It has been claimed that the verb to 'barrack' originates from their rowdiness at these matches, based on the word 'barracks'.

36 The Australian pound was the national currency until February 1966, when it adopted the dollar, converting at a rate of two dollars to the pound.

37 The word 'Western' refers to the western suburbs of Melbourne, rather than the west of Australia, perhaps reflecting a certain degree of parochialism that has not quite gone away.

38 It would be some time before anyone started referring to the two codes as 'rugby union' and 'rugby league'. In fact, for the first two years after the split, the playing rules were almost identical. However, to keep things simple, the term 'rugby union' (or just 'rugby' where no qualification is needed) will be used from here onwards to mean the game as played under the RFU, its counterparts in other countries and regions, and the International Board.

39 Until 1910, the British Isles teams that toured overseas were unofficial, with no involvement from the national unions or the IRB. The 1910 tour of South Africa was the first to be organised by the RFU; the Irish, Scottish and Welsh unions would not play a part until 1950. In the early days, the squad was not intended to feature the very best players from the 'home nations'; this only became a factor when South Africa and New Zealand started presenting a serious challenge, early in the 20th century. The team first became known as the British Lions in 1924, although the term was already politically dubious by that time, two years after Ireland was partitioned. The more accurate (but unwieldy) 'British and Irish Lions' was eventually coined in 2001.

40 Another memorable quote came at an international meeting in 1924, in a discussion of the rule proposed by the New Zealand and New South Wales unions to limit kicking into touch. It was hoped that this would improve the flow of the game by reducing the number of scrums, but a sceptical Scottish delegate was concerned about its potential effect on schoolboy rugby: 'The squeezing of these little boys in the scrum is of very great value to their health.'

41 At this stage, it was common for other backs, apart from the quarterback, to throw forward passes.

42 In most major team sports in most countries, the idea of rival leagues is almost unthinkable. This is not the case in the United States, where the main sports have no governing bodies comparable to the likes of the FA and RFU. Each league is an independent business, answerable to nobody except the law enforcement agencies; the US is one of the few countries without a ministry of sport.

43 In 1948, the L.A. Rams also became the first team to wear painted helmets, thanks to the artistic skills of halfback Fred Gehrke.

44 In the fall-out after a play-off defeat in early 2003, Indianapolis Colts quarterback Peyton Manning dismissed public criticism from kicker Mike Vanderjagt as the rantings of an 'idiot kicker'. This expression spoke volumes about the low regard in

which kickers are held in this sport, where players, writers and fans often refuse to accept them as 'real football players'.

45 *Monday Night Football* spawned a host of anecdotes. At a game in Denver in 1973, co-commentator Don Meredith did little to halt rumours of a marijuana habit by telling viewers, 'Welcome to the Mile High City, and I sure am.' At an L.A. Rams home game the following year, California governor and renowned hippie-hater Ronald Reagan was found (off-air) with his arm around fellow guest John Lennon, explaining the rules of the game to him. Six years later, many Americans learned of Lennon's murder from Cosell, as the news broke during a Monday Night Football broadcast.

46 New York Times, Nov 22, 1925

47 As in chapter 9, the terms 'rugby union' and 'rugby league' are used for convenience here, even though they were not widely used until around 1920.

48 This was the last time a combined Australasian squad would tour overseas.

49 Both Lancashire and Yorkshire had league and cup competitions. With the league title and Challenge Cup also up for grabs, each team had four potential titles each season. The Lancashire and Yorkshire league tables were based on results of intra-county matches in the Division One schedule.

50 Liverpool Stanley became Liverpool City (no relation to the club of the same name that had performed so miserably in 1906–07) in 1951, and later played under the guises of Huyton, Runcorn Highfield, Highfield, and Prescot Panthers; finally giving up the ghost in 1997 after failing to find a modicum of success anywhere.

51 In Waring's defence, his deep love and knowledge of the game have been acknowledged; and his increasingly idiosyncratic commentating style in his later years has been attributed to Alzheimer's disease.

52 It could be argued that ice hockey has also suffered in the US from the near-continuous nature of its play; and that basketball was only saved from the same fate by the introduction of the shot clock, which forces a team to shoot within 24 seconds of starting an attack, making the game more orientated towards 'set-piece' play.

53 A term used by Andrei S. Markovits and Steven L. Hellerman in *Offside: Soccer and American Exceptionalism.*

54 As explained in chapter 3, the RFU had introduced penalty kicks in 1882, but would not allow goals to be scored from them until 1888. The idea was never espoused in American football, where fouls have only ever been punished by loss of yardage and/or downs.

55 As mentioned in chapter 10, Walter Camp saw this rule in action, and persuaded his fellow Americans to adopt it – a rare, perhaps unique, case of American football being influenced by the Canadian game.

56 The terms 'rugby' and 'rugby football' were still widely used, even though the game in Canada had moved much closer to American football, and was radically different from rugby union and rugby league.

57 Back home, Lord Stanley's son became the 17th Earl of Derby, honorary president of the Rugby Football League from 1911.

58 In contrast with, say, the FA Cup, the term 'Grey Cup' generally refers only to the annual game, not to the games leading up to it.

59 The Rugby Union of Canada, a governing body for rugby union, had existed from 1929 to 1939, and had been reformed in 1965, as the precursor to the present-day Rugby Canada.

60 By now, the CFL season lasted from early July until November.

61 The sudden about-turn highlights a dilemma for Canadian football. It could hope to widen its appeal by becoming more Americanised, catering to the expectations of American sports fans (as well as American players, coaches and team owners). On the other hand, the further it goes in this direction, the more it will lose its

sense of being unique, and, consequently, its reason to exist.

62 Hunt's claim was a slightly hysterical, seemingly anti-American distortion of events. Robert Sproule, Toronto Argonauts statistician and author of many articles on Canadian football history, had offered a more balanced view in 1982: 'In short, football came to Canada from England in the form of rugby. We taught the Americans that game and they refined it to modern-day football. We liked what they did so well we adapted it to our style of play and have been as happy as pigs in mud ever since.'

Bibliography

Pre-industrial ball games and 19th-century public school football

Cadiou, Georges, *Les Origines des Sports en Bretagne et dans les Pays Celtiques* (Skol Vreizh, 1995).

Charlesworth, Michael, et al, *Shrewsbury School Football* (Greenbank, 1995).

Harris, H.A., *Sport in Greece and Rome* (Thames & Hudson, 1972).

Harvey, Adrian, *Football: The First Hundred Years – The Untold Story* (Routledge, 2005).

Hornby, Hugh, *Uppies and Downies: The Extraordinary Football Games of Britain* (English Heritage, 2008).

Lyttelton, R.H., Page, Arthur and Noel, Evan B. (eds), *Fifty Years of Sport at Oxford, Cambridge and the Great Public Schools* (Walter Southwood & Co., 1922).

Miller, Stephen G., *Arete: Greek Sports from Ancient Sources* (University of California Press, 2004).

American and Canadian football

Bernstein, Mark F., *Football: The Ivy League Origins of an American Obsession* (University of Pennsylvania Press, 2001).

Bissinger, H.G., *Friday Night Lights: A Town, a Team, and a Dream* (Yellow Jersey Press, 2005).

Coenen, Craig R., *From Sandlots to the Super Bowl: The National Football League, 1927-1967* (University of Tennessee Press, 2005).

Crowley, Joseph N., *In the Arena: The NCAA's First Century* (online edition on www.ncaa.org) (National Collegiate Athletic Association, 2005).

Finoli, David and Aikens, Tom, *The Birthplace of Professional Football: Southwestern Pennsylvania* (Arcadia, 2004).

Metcalfe, Alan, *Canada Learns to Play: The Emergence of Organised Sport, 1807-1914* (McClelland & Stewart, 1987).

Morrow, Don, et al, *A Concise History of Sport in Canada* (Oxford University Press Canada, 1989).

Nelson, David M., *The Anatomy of a Game: Football, the Rules and the Men who Made the Game* (University of Delaware Press, 1994).

O'Brien, Steve, *The Canadian Football League: The Phoenix of Professional Sports Leagues* (self-published, 2004).

Peterson, Robert, *Pigskin: The Early Years of Pro Football* (Oxford University Press US, 1997).

Smith, Ronald A., *Play by Play: Radio, Television, and Big-Time College Sport* (Johns Hopkins University Press, 2001).

Watterson, John Sayle, *College Football: History, Spectacle, Controversy* (Johns Hopkins University Press, 2000).

Australian Rules football

Blainey, Geoffrey, *A Game of Our Own: The Origins of Australian Football* (Black Inc., 2003).

De Moore, Greg, *Tom Wills: His Spectacular Rise and Tragic Fall* (Allen & Unwin, 2008).

Hess, Rob and Stewart, Bob (eds), *More Than a Game: The Real Story of Australian Rules Football* (Melbourne University Press, 1998).

Gaelic football

Corry, Eoghan, *The GAA Book of Lists: Outstanding Facts and Figures From the GAA*

(Hodder Headline Ireland, 2005).

De Búrca, Marcus, *The GAA: A History* (Gill & Macmillan, 1999).

Keane, Colm, *Gaelic Football's Top 20* (Mainstream, 2004).

Lennon, Joe (compiler), *The Playing Rules of Football and Hurling, 1884-1995* (Northern Recreation Consultants, 1997).

Mahon, Jack, *A History of Gaelic Football* (Gill & Macmillan, 2001).

Rugby

Collins, Tony, *Rugby League in Twentieth Century Britain* (Routledge, 2006).

Collins, Tony, *Rugby's Great Split: Class, Culture and the Origins of Rugby League Football* (Frank Cass, 1998).

Dunning, Eric and Sheard, Kenneth, *Barbarians, Gentlemen and Players: A Sociological Study of the Development of Rugby Football* (Routledge, 2005).

Gent, Ray, *The Petition: Rugby League Fans Say 'Enough is Enough'* (Parrs Wood Press, 2002).

Hadfield, Dave, *Up and Over: A Trek Through Rugby League Land* (Mainstream, 2004).

Marshall, Rev. Frank, *Football: The Rugby Union Game* (Cassell & Company, 1892).

Moorhouse, Geoffrey, *A People's Game: The Official History of Rugby League* (Hodder & Stoughton, 1995).

Richards, Huw, *A Game For Hooligans: The History of Rugby Union* (Mainstream, 2006).

Sommerville, Donald, *The Encyclopaedia of Rugby Union* (Aurum Press, 1997).

Titley, U.A. and McWhirter, Ross, *Centenary History of the Rugby Football Union* (Redwood Press, 1970).

Soccer

Ball, Phil, *Morbo: The Story of Spanish Football* (WSC Books, 2003).

Butler, Bryon, *The Official History of the Football Association* (Queen Anne Press, 1991).

Connolly, Kevin and MacWilliam, Rab, *Fields of Glory, Paths of Gold: The History of European Football* (Mainstream, 2006).

Galeano, Eduardo, *Soccer in Sun and Shadow* (Verso, 2003).

Heatley, Michael, *A History of Football* (Green Umbrella, 2004).

Hesse-Lichtenberger, Ulrich, *Tor! The Story of German Football* (WSC Books, 2003).

Kuper, Simon, *Ajax: The Dutch, the War – Football in Europe During the Second World War* (Orion, 2003).

Kuper, Simon, *Football Against The Enemy* (Orion, 1994).

Murphy, Brendan, *From Sheffield With Love: Celebrating 150 Years of Sheffield FC, The World's Oldest Football Club* (SportsBooks, 2007).

Walvin, James, *The People's Game: The History of Football Revisited* (Mainstream, 2000).

Wangerin, David, *Soccer in a Football World: The Story of America's Forgotten Game* (WSC Books, 2006).

Winner, David, *Brilliant Orange: The Neurotic Genius of Dutch Football* (Bloomsbury, 2000).

Miscellaneous / general

Baker, William Joseph, *Sports in the Western World* (University of Illinois Press, 1988).

Balmer, Randall Herbert, *Encyclopaedia of Evangelicalism* (Baylor University Press, 2004).

Birley, Derek, *A Social History of English Cricket* (Aurum Press, 1999).

Birley, Derek, *Sport and the Making of Britain* (Manchester University Press, 1993).

Booth, Keith, *The Father of Modern Sport: The Life and Times of Charles W. Alcock* (Parrs Wood Press, 2002).

Findling, John E. and Pelle, Kimberley D., *Encyclopaedia of the Modern Olympic Movement* (Greenwood Publishing Group, 2004).

Harris, H.A., *Sport in Britain* (Stanley Paul 1975).

James, Simon (compiler), *Chambers Sporting Quotations* (W. & R. Chambers, 1990).

Lipoński, Wojciech, *The World Sports Encyclopaedia* (Motorbooks International, 2003).

Mangan, J.A. (ed.), *The Cultural Bond: Sport, Empire and Society* (Routledge, 1992).

Markovits, Andrei S. and Hellerman, Steven L., *Offside: Soccer and American Exceptionalism* (Princeton University Press, 2001).

Melville, Tom, *The Tented Field: A History of Cricket in America* (Bowling Green State University Popular Press, 1998).

Naismith, James and Baker, William J., *Basketball: Its Origin and Development* (University of Nebraska Press, 1996).

Nauright, John, *Sport, Cultures and Identities in South Africa* (Continuum International Publishing Group, 1997).

Szymanski, Stefan and Zimbalist, Andrew S., *National Pastime: How Americans Play Baseball and the Rest of the World Plays Soccer* (Brookings Institution Press, 2005).

Williams, Graham, *The Code War: English Football Under the Historical Spotlight* (Yore, 1994).

Newspapers, magazines and journals (including online versions)

Pre-industrial ball games and 19th-century public school football
Al-Ahram Weekly – www.weekly.ahram.org.eg
Cheshire Sheaf Volume 1 (reprinted from the Chester Courant by the Courant Steam Printing Works, 1880)
The Harrovian

American and Canadian football
American Chronicle – www.americanchronicle.com
American Heritage – www.americanheritage.com
The Boston Globe – www.boston.com
College Football Historical Society Newsletter bulletins
The Globe and Mail (Canada) – www.theglobeandmail.com
Japan Today – archive.japantoday.com
The Toronto Star – www.thestar.com

Gaelic football
The Belfast Telegraph – www.belfasttelegraph.co.uk
The Carlow Nationalist – www.carlow-nationalist.ie
The Irish Examiner (via TCH Archives) – www.archives.tcm.ie
The Irish Times – www.irishtimes.com

Rugby
The Dominion Post (Wellington, New Zealand) – www.stuff.co.nz
Florida Times-Union – www.jacksonville.com
Rugby League Review – www.rugbyleaguereview.com
The Scotsman – sport.scotsman.com

Soccer
The International Herald Tribune – www.iht.com
When Saturday Comes – www.wsc.co.uk
World Soccer

Miscellaneous / general
The Age (Melbourne) – www.theage.com.au
Australian Society for Sports History bulletins
Christianity Today – www.christianitytoday.com
The Daily Telegraph – www.telegraph.co.uk
Football Studies bulletins
The Guardian – www.guardian.co.uk
The Independent – www.independent.co.uk
International Sports Studies bulletins
Journal of Sport History bulletins
The New Statesman – www.newstatesman.co.uk
The New York Times – www.nytimes.com
Newsweek – www.newsweek.com
The Observer – observer.guardian.co.uk
Scotland on Sunday – www.scotlandonsunday.scotsman.com
Sporting Traditions bulletins
Sports Illustrated – www.sportsillustrated.cnn.com
The Sunday Herald (Glasgow) – www.sundayherald.com
The Sydney Morning Herald – www.smh.com.au
Time – www.time.com
The Times – www.timesonline.co.uk

Web resources

Pre-industrial ball games and 19th-century public school football
Authentic Maya – www.authenticmaya.com/ball_game.htm
Do or Die: The Radical History of Football – www.eco-action.org/dod/no9/football.
   htm
El Museo del Barrio – www.elmuseo.org/taino/ballgame.html
Eton College – www.etoncollege.com
Expert Football – www.expertfootball.com
Football Network – www.FootballNetwork.org
Harrow School – www.harrowschool.org.uk
Hood Museum of Art – www.hoodmuseum.dartmouth.edu
International School Sport Federation – www.isfsports.org/sports/default.
   asp?id=385
Life in Italy – www.lifeinitaly.com/sport
Mesoamerican Ball Game – www.ulama.freehomepage.com
Minnesota State University Emuseum – www.mnsu.edu/emuseum
Nihon Zatsuroku: kemari article – www.sengokudaimyo.com/miscellany/kemari.
   html
Rugby School – www.rugbyschool.net
Sports Fact Book – www.sportsfactbook.com/history
Staffordshire University – www.staffs.ac.uk
Westminster School – homepages.westminster.org.uk
Winchester College – www.winchestercollege.co.uk

American and Canadian football
Bleacher Report – www.bleacherreport.com
Bowl Championship Series – www.bcsfootball.org
Canada Sports Hall of Fame – www.cshof.ca
Canadian Football Hall of Fame – www.cfhof.ca
Canadian Football League – www.cfl.ca
Canadian Interuniversity Sport – www.universitysport.ca
CBC – www.cbc.ca

Celebrate Boston – www.celebrateboston.com/firsts/footballclub.htm
College Football Data Warehouse – www.cfbdatawarehouse.com
College Football Encyclopedia – www.footballencyclopedia.com
College Football Hall of Fame – www.collegefootball.org
College Football Poll – www.collegefootballpoll.com
College Football Rankings – www.collegefootballrankings.net
Credenda Agenda – www.credenda.org/issues/14-6historia.php
Dartmouth College – www.dartmo.com/football
Football Canada – www.footballcanada.com/history.asp
Grey Cup – greycup.cfl.ca
Harvard Crimson – www.thecrimson.com/fmarchives
Historica – www.histori.ca
Humbersport.org – www.humbersport.org
International Federation of American Football – www.ifaf.info
Mansfield University (Pennsylvania) – pr.mansfield.edu/1890s/19centftbl.htm
National Collegiate Athletic Association – www.ncaa.org
Pop Warner – www.popwarner.com
Pro Football Hall of Fame – www.profootballhof.com/history
Pro Football Reference – www.pro-football-reference.com
Professional Football Researchers' Association – www.footballresearch.com
Rose Bowl – www.sports-venue.info/NCAAF/Bowls/T_Rose_Bowl_Timeline.html
Sacramento Sirens: women's American football history – www.sacramentosirens.
  com
Semi-Pro Football Headquarters – www.semiprofootball.org
The Canadian Encyclopedia – www.thecanadianencyclopedia.com
The Game (Harvard–Yale) – www.the-game.org
Tournament of Roses (Rose Bowl) – www.tournamentofroses.com/history
TSN – www.tsn.ca
University of North Carolina Press – www.ibiblio.org/uncpress/newsbytes/
  octnov98/oriexcpt.html
University of Pennsylvania archives – www.archives.upenn.edu
Walter Camp Football Foundation – www.waltercamp.org

Australian Rules football

Aussie Rules International – www.aussierulesinternational.com
Australian Football League – www.afl.com.au
Australian Sports Commission – www.ausport.gov.au
City of Melbourne – www.melbourne.vic.gov.au
Coleman Medal – www.colemanmedal.com
Convict Creations – www.convictcreations.com
Documenting Democracy – www.foundingdocs.gov.au
Full Points Footy – www.fullpointsfooty.net
Only Melbourne – www.onlymelbourne.com.au/melbourne_details.php?id=1543
World Footy News – www.worldfootynews.com

Gaelic football
An Fear Rua – www.anfearrua.com
Athenry GAA: Gaelic football history – www.athenrygaa.ie/site/index.
  php?option=com_content&task=view&id=25&Itemid=94
Ballintubber GAA: Gaelic football history – www.ballintubbergaa.com/History
Ballykelly Ladies: women's Gaelic football history – www.kildare.ie/ballykellyladies/
  history.html
Croke Park – www.crokepark.ie
Cúchulainns GAA: All-Ireland history – www.cuchulainnsgaa.com/
  allirelandgaelicfootball.html
Gaelic Athletic Association – www.gaa.ie

Bibliography

Hogan Stand – www.hoganstand.com
Michael Cusack Centre – www.michaelcusack.ie
National Library of Ireland – www.nli.ie
Princess Grace Irish Library – www.pgil-eirdata.org/html/pgil_datasets

Rugby

All Blacks – www.allblacks.com
Australian Rugby Union – www.rugby.com.au
Bishops Diocesan College (South Africa) – www.bishops.org.za/info/museum/sport.
     asp
Blackheath FC – www.blackheathrugby.co.uk/history1.asp
British & Irish Lions tour history – www.lions-tour.com/history
British Amateur Rugby League Association – www.barla.org.uk/About/History.asp
Colonial Rugby – www.colonialrugby.com.au
Darlington Mowden Park Sharks: women's rugby union history – www.
     mowdensharks.co.uk/history.aspx
Dictionary of New Zealand Biography – www.dnzb.govt.nz
eRugbyNews – www.erugbynews.com
European Cup Rugby – www.ercrugby.com/eng
International Rugby Hall of Fame – www.rugbyhalloffame.com
Le Monde du Rugby XIII – lemondedurugby.chez-alice.fr/histfranc.html
Lions Rugby – www.lionsrugby.com
Magners League – www.magnersleague.com/120_32.php
Napit.co.uk Sports Database – www.napit.co.uk
New Zealand History Online – www.nzhistory.net.nz/culture/nativestour-
     introduction
New Zealand Rugby League – www.nzrl.co.nz
New Zealand Rugby Museum – www.rugbymuseum.co.nz
NRL: Century of Rugby League – www.centenaryofrugbyleague.com.au
Planet Rugby – www.planet-rugby.com
Queensland Rugby League – www.qrl.com.au
Queensland Rugby Union – www.qru.com.au/qru/qru.rugby/page/62650
RL1895 – www.rl1895.com
RL1908 – www.rl1908.com
Rleague.com – www.rleague.com
Rugby 365 – www.rugby365.com
Rugby Football History – www.rugbyfootballhistory.com
Rugby Football League – www.therfl.co.uk
Rugby Football Union – www.rfu.com
Rugby League Central – www.rugbyleaguecentral.com
Rugby League Hall of Fame – www.rlhalloffame.org.uk/history.htm
Rugby League Heritage Centre – www.rlheritage.co.uk/history.html
Rugby league statistics – www.stats.rleague.com
RugbyRugby – www.rugbyrugby.com
Rugby World Cup – www.therugbyworldcup.co.uk
RugbyData – www.rugbydata.com
Six Nations Rugby – www.6nationsrugby.net
South African Rugby League – www.sarugbyleague.co.za/history.htm
Sporting Pulse – www.sportingpulse.com
State of Origin – www.stateoforigin.com.au
Stellenbosch Rugby Club – student.sun.ac.za/rugby/club/rugbymuseum.asp
The Vault (rugby league records) – www.users.hunterlink.net.au/~maajjs
Wes Clark: Rugby Readers' Review – www.wesclark.com/rrr

Soccer
American Soccer History Archives – www.sover.net/~spectrum/index.html
Association of Football Statisticians – www.11v11.co.uk
Cambridge University AFC – www.cuafc.org
Confederation of African Football – www.cafonline.com
CONMEBOL – www.conmebol.com
Corinthian-Casuals – www.corinthian-casuals.com
English Football Archive (no longer available)
European Cup History – www.europeancuphistory.com
FA Cup Final Results – www.fa-cupfinals.co.uk/results.html
FIFA – www.fifa.com
Football Association – www.thefa.com
Football Club History Database – www.fchd.info
Football Federation Australia – www.footballaustralia.com.au
Football Historical – www.footballhistorical.co.uk
National Soccer Coaches' Association of America – www.nscaa.com/
    subpages/2006033115392999.php
Planet World Cup – www.planetworldcup.com
Rec.Sport.Soccer Statistics Foundation – www.rsssf.com
Sheffield FC – www.sheffieldfc.com
Sir Norman Chester Centre for Football Research, University of Leicester – www.
    le.ac.uk/footballresearch
UEFA – www.uefa.com

Miscellaneous/general
American Beach Soccer – www.americanbeachsoccer.com
Arena Fan – www.arenafan.com
Arena Football League – www.arenafootball.com
Asociacion Mundial de Futbol de Salon – www.amfutsal.com.py
Australian Dictionary of Biography – www.adb.online.anu.edu.au/biogs
BBC – www.bbc.co.uk
BeachSoccer-Online – www.beachsoccer-online.com
Bossaball – www.bossaball.com/english.html
Britannica – www.Britannica.com
British Council – www.britishcouncil.org
British Wheelchair Tag Rugby League Association – www.bwtrla.btik.com
Encarta – www.encarta.msn.com
Encyclopedia Britannica 1911 (from the *Love to Know Classic Encyclopedia* project) –
    www.1911encyclopedia.org
Encyclopedia of New Zealand, 1966 – www.teara.govt.nz/1966
Federation International Footballtennis Association – www.fifta.com
Federation of International Touch – www.international-touch.org
FlagFootball.org – www.flagfootball.org
Footbag.org – www.footbag.org
FreakSports – www.freaksports.net
History Home – www.historyhome.co.uk
Ice Soccer – www.icesoccer.com
Indoor Rules – www.innovated.gov.au/Innovated%5Ccase_studies%5CIndoor_
    Aussie_Rules.pdf
Informaworld – www.informaworld.com
International Wheelchair and Amputee Sports Federation – www.iwasf.com
International Wheelchair Rugby Federation – www.iwrf.com
International Women's Flag Football Association – www.iwffa.com
Jorkyball – www.jorkyball.org
Know Britain – www.know-britain.com
LA84 Foundation – www.la84foundation.org

Bibliography

Manitoba Underwater Council – www.manunderwater.com
McGill University Athletics – www.athletics.mcgill.ca
Paralympics – www.paralympic.org
Parasport – www.parasport.org.uk
Rollersoccer – www.rollersoccer.com
Sevens Rugby – www.sevensrugby.co.za
Spartacus Educational – www.spartacus.schoolnet.co.uk/Fhistory.htm
Sporting Chronicle – www.sportingchronicle.com
Sports Business Daily – www.sportsbusinessdaily.com
Stadiums and Attendances – www.stadium-attendances.com
Touch Aussie Rules – www.touchaussierules.com
Touch Football Australia – www.austouch.com.au
Touch New Zealand – www.touchnz.co.nz
Underwater Rugby – ec05.sukeltaja.fi/nayta_teksti.php?lang=en&aihe=90
Underwater Sport – www.uwsport.de/2_3_2.php
United States Flag Football Association – www.usffa.org
United States Indoor Soccer Association – www.usindoor.com
US Futsal – www.futsal.org
Victoria University – www.staff.vu.edu.au
Virtual Library of Sport – www.sportsvl.com
Wales Touch – www.walestouch.co.uk
Wellington School (Columbus, Ohio): speedball article – www.wellington.org/
    miller/speedball.htm
World Cup Web – www.worldcupweb.com

Snippets of information were also obtained from the websites of countless clubs and associations, and many other sites, too numerous to list here. The wonderful but flawed *Wikipedia* was used mainly as a tool for finding other sources on the web; any apparent 'facts' gleaned from the site itself were only used if they could be verified elsewhere.

Index

Index